BASIC
Grammar in Context

Teacher's Annotated Edition

SANDRA N. ELBAUM

JUDI PEMÁN

HILARY GRANT

THOMSON
HEINLE

United States • Australia • Canada • Mexico • Singapore • Spain • United Kingdom

THOMSON

HEINLE

Grammar in Context, Basic
Teacher's Annotated Edition
SANDRA N. ELBAUM
JUDI PEMÁN
HILARY GRANT

Publisher, Academic ESL: *James W. Brown*
Executive Editor, Adult ESL: *Sherrise Roehr*
Director of Content Development:
  Anita Raducanu
Director of Marketing: *Amy Mabley*
Marketing Manager: *Laura Needham*
Senior Print Buyer: *Mary Beth Hennebury*

Editors: *Susan Johnson, Maria Hetu*
Compositor: *Parkwood Composition Service, Inc.*
Project Manager: *Debbie Mealey*
Photo Researcher: *Connie Gardner*
Illustrators: *James Edwards, Gershom Griffith,*
  Keith Lesko, Meredith Morgan, and Len Shalansky
Interior Designer: *Jerilyn Bockorick*
Cover Designer: *Joseph Sherman*
Printer: *West Group*

Cover Image: © Jerry Emmons

Copyright © 2006 by Thomson Heinle, a part of The Thomson Corporation. Thomson, Heinle and the Thomson logo are trademarks used herein under license.

All rights reserved. No part of this work covered by the copyright hereon may be reproduced or used in any form or by any means—graphic, electronic, or mechanical, including photocopying, recording, taping, Web distribution or information storage and retrieval systems—without the written permission of the publisher.

Printed in the United States of America.
1 2 3 4 5 6 7 8 9 10   10 09 08 07 06

For more information contact Thomson Heinle, 25 Thomson Place, Boston, Massachusetts 02210 USA, or you can visit our Internet site at elt.thomson.com

Photo Credits:

1, left James Leynse/CORBIS, *right* Adrian Peacock/Picturequest; *7,* Catherine Karnow/CORBIS; *12, quarter* David Young Wolff/PhotoEdit, *dime* Jonathan Nourock/PhotoEdit, *dollar bill* Joseph Sohm/The Image Works, *penny* Bill Aron/PhotoEdit; *14,* Susan Van Etten/PhotoEdit; *17,* Tim Boyle/Getty Images; *23, top* Howard Dracht/The Image Works, *center* Martin Gerten/Getty Images, *bottom* Bob Daemmrich/The ImageWorks; *33,* Royalty Free/CORBIS; *38,* David M. Grossman/The Image Works; *40,* Michael Newman/PhotoEdit; *43, left* Andrew Holbrooke/The Image Works, *right* John Griffin/The Image Works; *44, card* David Young Wolf/PhotoEdit, *license* Clayton Sharrard/PhotoEdit, *passport* Index Open, *marriage certificate* Clayton Sharrard/PhotoEdit, *college ID* David Barber/PhotoEdit; *48,* Jeff Greenberg/PhotoEdit; *54,* MAK/The Image Works; *57, left* Paul Barton/CORBIS, Michael Newman/PhotoEdit, *right* Royalty Free/CORBIS; *67,* Ted Horowitz/CORBIS; *73,* Lindsey Hebbard/CORBIS; *74,* Cathrine Wessel/CORBIS; *86,* Rudi von Briel/PhotoEdit; *89 left* Ryan McVay/Getty Images, *right* Rob and SAS/CORBIS; *111, left* Bob Daemmrich/PhotoEdit; *right* Will and Deni McIntyre/CORBIS; *117,* Charles Gupton/CORBIS; *124,* RNT Productions/CORBIS; *131,* Dave Nagel/Getty Images; *135, left* Jeff Zaruka/CORBIS, *right* James Leynse/CORBIS; *142,* Amy Etra/PhotoEdit; *143,* Ronnie Kaufman/CORBIS; *152,* Jeff Greenberg/PhotoEdit; *155,* Tim Boyle/Getty Images; *159,* Dennis MacDonald/PhotoEdit; *163, left* Rudi von Briel/PhotoEdit, *right* Ryan McVay/Getty Images; *164,* David Young Wolff/PhotoEdit; *166,* Tony Freeman/PhotoEdit; *172,* Jeff Greenberg/PhotoEdit; *182,* Jim West/Alamy; *185, left* Network Production/The Image Works, *right* Larry Kolvoco/The Image Works; *198,* Tom and Dee Ann McCarthy/CORBIS; *201,* Michael Newman/PhotoEdit; *203,* David Young Wolff/PhotoEdit; *206,* Myrleen Cate Ferguson/PhotoEdit; *209, left* Don Mason/CORBIS, *right* Colin Young Wolff/PhotoEdit; *212,* Bob Mahoney/The Image Works; *215,* Christina Kennedy/PhotoEdit; *217,* Bob Daemmrich/The Image Works; *219,* Mark Gamba/CORBIS; *222,* Mark Richard/PhotoEdit; *231, left* Left Lane Productions/CORBIS, *right* Michael Newman/PhotoEdit; *232, left* FRISHLING STEVEN E/CORBIS SYGMA, *right* Ed Bock/CORBIS; *246,* David Young Wolff/PhotoEdit; *256, left* Reuters/CORBIS, *right* FogStock LLC/IndexStock Imagery RF; *257, child* Ellen Senisi/The Image Works, *building house* Jim West/The Image Works, *helping with groceries* Tony Freeman/PhotoEdit; *273,* Bob Daemmrich/The Image Works; *280* Ed Bock/CORBIS; *276,* A. Ramey/PhotoEdit

For permission to use material from this text or product, submit a request online at http://www.thomsonrights.com

Any additional questions about permissions can be submitted by email to thomsonrights@thomson.com

ISBN: 1-4130-0827-5

Contents

Unit 1

GRAMMAR Subject Pronouns; *Be*; Contractions; Singular and Plural; *This/That/These/Those*; Adjectives; Expressions with *It*

CONTEXT Welcome to the U.S.

Lesson 1 — 2

READING We Are Here to Help — 3

1.1 Subject Pronouns — 4
1.2 Forms of *Be* — 5

Lesson 2 — 8

READING Help at the Laundromat — 9

1.3 Contractions (Short Forms) — 10
1.4 Singular and Plural — 12
1.5 *This, That, These, Those* — 12

Lesson 3 — 14

READING Help at the Supermarket — 15

1.6 Negative Forms of the Verb *Be* — 16
1.7 Adjectives — 18
1.8 Expressions with *It* — 19
1.9 Singular and Plural — 20

Editing Advice and Quiz — 21
Learner's Log — 22
Expansion Activities — 22

Unit 2

GRAMMAR Possessive Nouns; Possessive Adjectives; Irregular Plural Forms; *Be*—*Yes/No* Questions and Short Answers; *Be*—Information Questions; Articles *A/An*

CONTEXT Time and Money

Lesson 1 — 24

READING My Clock Is Fast — 25

   2.1 Possessive Nouns — 26
   2.2 Possessive Adjectives — 27

Lesson 2 — 28

READING Time Is Money — 29

   2.3 *Yes/No* Questions and Short Answers — 30
   2.4 Singular and Plural—Irregular Forms — 33

Lesson 3 — 34

READING At the ATM — 35

   2.5 Information Questions — 36
   2.6 Articles *A/An* — 38

   Editing Advice and Quiz — 41
   Learner's Log — 42
   Expansion Activities — 42

Unit 3

GRAMMAR Imperatives; *Let's*; Object Pronouns
CONTEXT Filling Out Forms

Lesson 1 — 44

READING Getting a Social Security Card — 45

   3.1 Imperative Forms—Affirmative — 46
   3.2 Imperative Forms—Negative — 47

Lesson 2 — 50

READING Financial Aid Application — 51

   3.3 *Let's* — 52
   3.4 Compare Subject and Object Pronouns — 53

   Editing Advice and Quiz — 55
   Learner's Log — 56
   Expansion Activities — 56

Unit 4

GRAMMAR The Simple Present Tense; Frequency Words
CONTEXT American Lifestyles

Lesson 1 58

READING Having Fun 59

   4.1 The Simple Present Tense—Affirmative Statements 60
   4.2 Spelling of the -s Form 61
   4.3 Uses of the Simple Present Tense 62
   4.4 Frequency Words 63

Lesson 2 66

READING Working in the U.S. 67

   4.5 Simple Present Tense—Negative Forms 68
   4.6 Expressions of Time with the Simple Present Tense 70
   4.7 Infinitives with Simple Present Verbs 71

Lesson 3 74

READING Eating Customs 75

   4.8 *Yes/No* Questions in the Simple Present Tense 76

Lesson 4 80

READING Exercise 81

   4.9 Information Questions in the Simple Present Tense 82
  4.10 Question Words as Subjects 85

      Editing Advice and Quiz 87
      Learner's Log 88
      Expansion Activities 88

Unit 5

GRAMMAR Modal Verbs: *Can, Should, Have To*
CONTEXT Driving

Lesson 1 90

READING Getting a Driver's License 91

5.1	*Can*	92
5.2	*Should*	93
5.3	*Have To*	94

Lesson 2 — 100

READING	Car Safety for Children	101
5.4	*Yes/No* Questions with *Can*, *Should*, and *Have To*	102
5.5	Information Questions with Modal Verbs	105
5.6	Question Words as Subjects	107
	Editing Advice and Quiz	109
	Learner's Log	110
	Expansion Activities	110

Unit 6

GRAMMAR *Must* and *Have To*; Noncount Nouns; Quantity Expressions

CONTEXT School

Lesson 1 — 112

READING	School Lunch Programs	113
6.1	*Must*	114
6.2	*Must* and *Have To*	116
6.3	*Must Not* and *Don't Have To*	117

Lesson 2 — 118

READING	Maya's School Lunch	119
6.4	Count and Noncount Nouns	120
6.5	Quantity Expressions with Noncount Nouns	122
6.6	*Much/A Lot Of/A Little* with Nouncount Nouns	124
6.7	*Some/Any* with Nouncount Nouns	125

Lesson 3 — 126

READING	School Supplies	127
6.8	Count and Noncount Nouns with *Some/Any*	128
6.9	Count vs. Noncount Nouns: *A Lot Of/Much/Many*	129
6.10	Count vs. Noncount Nouns: *A Few/A Little*	130
6.11	Count vs. Noncount Nouns: *How Much/How Many*	130
	Editing Advice and Quiz	133
	Learner's Log	134
	Expansion Activities	134

Unit 7

GRAMMAR	Prepositions; *There Is/There Are*	
CONTEXT	Shopping	

Lesson 1 — 136

READING	Twenty-Four/Seven	137
7.1	Prepositions of Time	138
7.2	Time Expressions Without Prepositions	139
7.3	Prepositions of Place	140
7.4	Prepositions in Common Expressions	141

Lesson 2 — 144

READING	Good Prices or Good Service	145
7.5	*There Is* and *There Are*	146
7.6	Negative Forms with *There Is/There Are*	148
7.7	Quantity Words	149

Lesson 3 — 152

READING	Choices	153
7.8	*Yes/No* Questions with *There Is/There Are*	154
7.9	Information Questions with *There Is/There Are*	156
	Editing Advice	160
	Editing Quiz	161
	Learner's Log	162
	Expansion Activities	162

Unit 8

GRAMMAR	The Present Continuous Tense; Time Expressions	
CONTEXT	Errands	

Lesson 1 — 164

READING	At the Post Office	165
8.1	Present Continuous Tense—Affirmative Statements	166
8.2	Spelling of the *-ing* Form of the Verb	167
8.3	Uses of the Present Continuous Tense	168
8.4	Present Continuous Tense—Negative Forms	170
8.5	Expressions of Time with the Present Continuous Tense	171

Contents   vii

		Lesson 2	174
READING		The Drive-Through	175
	8.6	*Yes/No* Questions with the Present Continuous Tense	176
	8.7	Information Questions with the Present Continuous Tense	178
	8.8	Question Words as Subjects	180
		Editing Advice and Quiz	183
		Learner's Log	184
		Expansion Activities	184

Unit 9

GRAMMAR	The Future Tense with *Be Going To*; Expressions of Time in the Future
CONTEXT	Making Changes

		Lesson 1	186
READING		Getting Ready for a New Baby	187
	9.1	Affirmative Statements with *Be Going To*	188
	9.2	Negative Statements with *Be Going To*	189
	9.3	Uses of the Future Tense with *Be Going To*	190
	9.4	Expressions of Time with *Be Going To*	191

		Lesson 2	196
READING		Moving to a New Apartment	197
	9.5	*Yes/No* Questions with *Be Going To*	198
	9.6	Information Questions with *Be Going To*	200
	9.7	Questions with *How Long* and *Be Going To*	202
	9.8	Subject Questions with *Be Going To*	204
		Editing Advice and Quiz	207
		Learner's Log	208
		Expansion Activities	208

Unit 10

GRAMMAR	Comparatives; Superlatives
CONTEXT	Choices

Lesson 1 — 210

READING Community Colleges — 211

- 10.1 Comparative Forms of Adjectives — 213
- 10.2 Spelling of the *-er* Form — 213
- 10.3 Comparisons with Nouns and Verbs — 217

Lesson 2 — 220

READING Choosing a Used Car — 221

- 10.4 Superlative Forms of Adjectives — 223
- 10.5 Spelling of *-est* Forms — 224
- 10.6 Superlatives with Nouns and Verbs — 226

Editing Advice and Quiz — 229
Learner's Log — 230
Expansion Activities — 230

Unit 11

GRAMMAR The Past Tense of *Be*; Regular Verbs in the Simple Past Tense; Irregular Verbs in the Past Tense; Time Expressions with the Past Tense

CONTEXT Getting a Job

Lesson 1 — 232

READING Applying for a Job in a Store — 233

- 11.1 Affirmative and Negative Statements with *Be* — 234
- 11.2 Expressions of Time in the Past — 235
- 11.3 *Yes/No* Questions with *Be* — 236
- 11.4 Information Questions with *Be* — 237
- 11.5 Subject Questions with *Be* — 238

Lesson 2 — 240

READING Applying for a Job in an Office — 241

- 11.6 Affirmative Forms of Regular Past Tense Verbs — 242
- 11.7 Spelling of the Regular *-ed* Form — 243
- 11.8 Irregular Forms of the Simple Past Tense — 244
- 11.9 Negative Forms of Regular and Irregular Past Tense Verbs — 245

Lesson 3 — 248

READING Jobs of the Future — 249

- 11.10 *Yes/No* Questions in the Past—Regular and Irregular Verbs — 250

11.11	More Irregular Verbs in the Past Tense	251
11.12	Information Questions in the Past	252
11.13	Subject Questions	253
11.14	More Irregular Verbs in the Past Tense	253
	Editing Advice and Quiz	255
	Learner's Log	256
	Expansion Activities	256

Unit 12

GRAMMAR Verb Review: Simple Present Tense; Present Continuous Tense; Future Tense; Simple Past Tense; Modal Verbs: *Can, Should, Must, Have To*

CONTEXT Giving Back

Lesson 1 — 258

READING Helping Others — 259

12.1	Review of Verb Tenses—Affirmative and Negative	260
12.2	Review of Infinitives	263
12.3	Review of Modal Verbs	264
12.4	Review of Time Expressions	266

Lesson 2 — 268

READING Volunteer Activities — 269

12.5	*Yes/No* Questions	270
12.6	Review of Information Questions	272
	Editing Advice and Quiz	279
	Learner's Log	280
	Expansion Activities	280

Appendices

A.	The Calendar and Numbers	AP1
B.	Spelling Rules for Verbs and Nouns	AP3
C.	Spelling of Comparative and Superlative Forms of Adjectives	AP6
D.	Alphabetical List of Irregular Past Forms	AP6
E.	Capitalization Rules	AP8
F.	Glossary of Grammatical Terms	AP9
G.	The United States of America: Major Cities	AP13

Index — I1

For

Cassia, Gentille, Chimene, Joseph and Joy

Acknowledgments

Many thanks to Dennis Hogan, Jim Brown, Sherrise Roehr, and Sally Giangrande from Thomson Heinle for their ongoing support of the *Grammar in Context* series. We would especially like to thank our editor, Charlotte Sturdy, for her keen eye to detail and invaluable suggestions.

And many thanks to our students at Truman College, who have increased our understanding of our own language and taught us to see life from another point of view. By sharing their observations, questions, and life stories, they have enriched our lives enormously.

Heinle would like to thank the following reviewers:

Lisa DiPaolo
Sierra College
Rocklin, CA

Maha Edlbi
Sierra College
Rocklin, CA

Kathy Krokar
City College of Chicago/Harry Truman
Chicago, IL

Robert Wachman
Yuba College
Yuba City, CA

Joan Amore
Triton College
River Grove, IL

Herbert Pierson
St. John's University
Queens, NY

The *Grammar in Context* Series

Students learn more, remember more, and use language more effectively when they learn grammar in context.

Learning a language through meaningful themes and practicing it in a contextualized setting promote both linguistic and cognitive development. In **Grammar in Context**, grammar is presented in interesting and culturally informative readings, and the language and context are subsequently practiced throughout the chapter.

New to this edition:

- **New and updated readings** on current American topics such as Instant Messaging and eBay.
- **Updated grammar charts** that now include essential language notes.
- **Updated exercises and activities** that provide contextualized practice using a variety of exercise types, as well as additional practice for more difficult structures.
- **New lower-level *Grammar in Context Basic*** for beginning level students.
- **New wrap-around Teacher's Annotated Edition** with page-by-page, point-of-use teaching suggestions.
- **Expanded Assessment CD-ROM** with ExamView® Pro Test Generator now contains more questions types and assessment options to easily allow teachers to create tests and quizzes.

Distinctive Features of the *Grammar in Context* Series:

Students are prepared for academic assignments and everyday language tasks.

Discussions, readings, compositions, and exercises involving higher-level critical thinking skills develop overall language and communication skills.

Students expand their knowledge of American topics and culture.

The readings in **Grammar in Context** help students gain insight into and enrich their knowledge of American culture and history. Students have ample exposure to the practicalities of American life, such as getting a driver's license, applying for a Social Security card, writing a resume, dealing with telemarketers, and getting student internships. Their new knowledge helps them adapt to everyday life in the U.S.

Students learn to use their new skills to communicate.

The exercises and Expansion Activities in **Grammar in Context** help students learn English while practicing their reading, writing, listening, and speaking skills. Students work together in pairs or groups to find more information about topics and about each other, to make presentations, to play games, and to role-play. Their confidence in using English increases, as does their ability to communicate effectively.

Welcome to Grammar in Context Basic

Students learn more, remember more and use language more effectively when they learn grammar in context.

Grammar in Context Basic connects grammar with rich, American cultural content, providing learners of English with a useful and meaningful knowledge base.

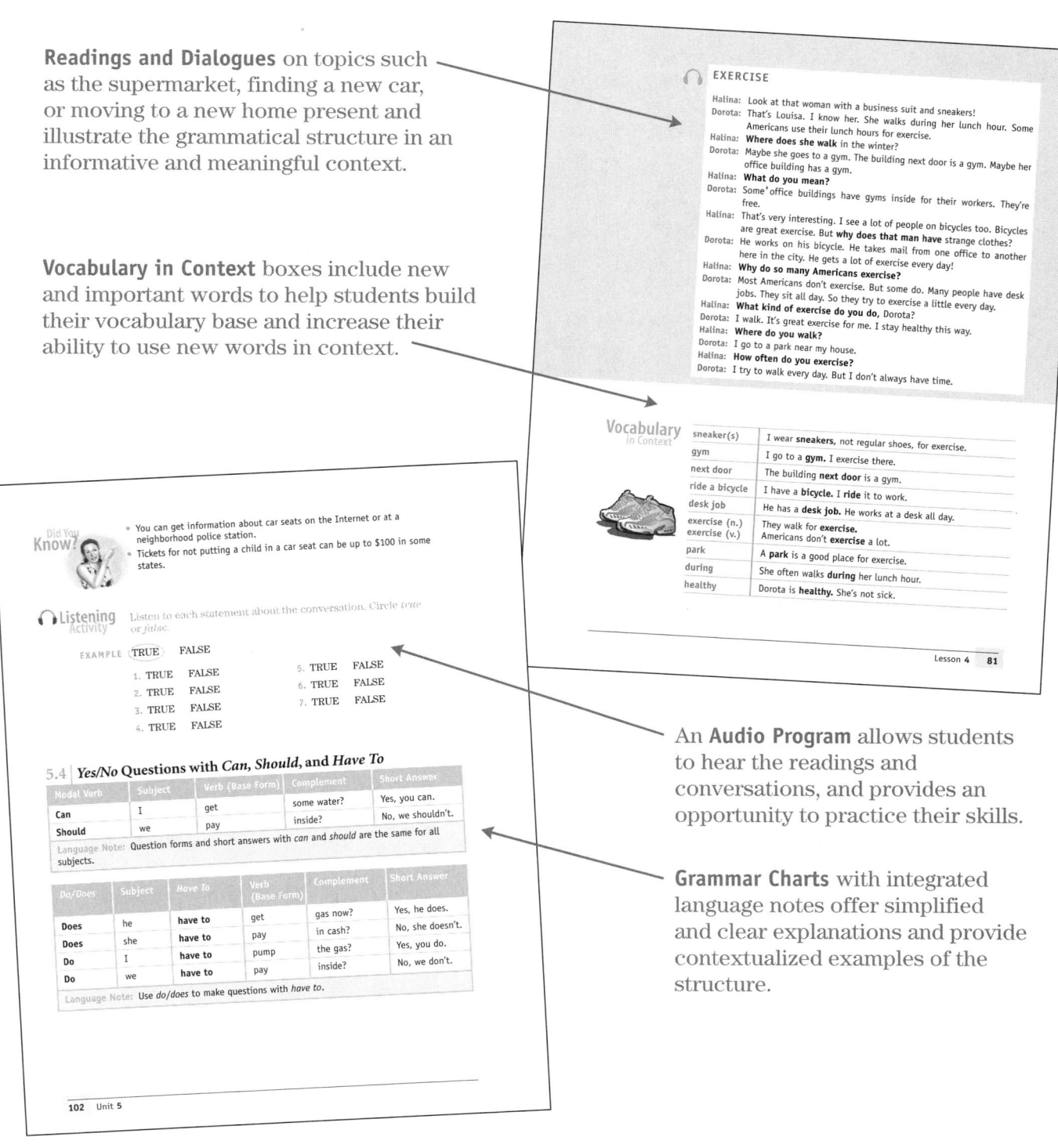

Readings and Dialogues on topics such as the supermarket, finding a new car, or moving to a new home present and illustrate the grammatical structure in an informative and meaningful context.

Vocabulary in Context boxes include new and important words to help students build their vocabulary base and increase their ability to use new words in context.

EXERCISE

Halina: Look at that woman with a business suit and sneakers!
Dorota: That's Louisa. I know her. She walks during her lunch hour. Some Americans use their lunch hours for exercise.
Halina: **Where does she walk** in the winter?
Dorota: Maybe she goes to a gym. The building next door is a gym. Maybe her office building has a gym.
Halina: **What do you mean?**
Dorota: Some office buildings have gyms inside for their workers. They're free.
Halina: That's very interesting. I see a lot of people on bicycles too. Bicycles are great exercise. But **why does that man have** strange clothes?
Dorota: He works on his bicycle. He takes mail from one office to another here in the city. He gets a lot of exercise every day!
Halina: **Why do so many Americans exercise?**
Dorota: Most Americans don't exercise. But some do. Many people have desk jobs. They sit all day. So they try to exercise a little every day.
Halina: **What kind of exercise do you do**, Dorota?
Dorota: I walk. It's great exercise for me. I stay healthy this way.
Halina: **Where do you walk?**
Dorota: I go to a park near my house.
Halina: **How often do you exercise?**
Dorota: I try to walk every day. But I don't always have time.

Vocabulary in Context

sneaker(s)	I wear **sneakers**, not regular shoes, for exercise.
gym	I go to a **gym**. I exercise there.
next door	The building **next door** is a gym.
ride a bicycle	I have a **bicycle**. I **ride** it to work.
desk job	He has a **desk job**. He works at a desk all day.
exercise (n.)	They walk for **exercise**.
exercise (v.)	Americans don't **exercise** a lot.
park	A **park** is a good place for exercise.
during	She often walks **during** her lunch hour.
healthy	Dorota is **healthy**. She's not sick.

Lesson 4   81

Did You Know?
- You can get information about car seats on the Internet or at a neighborhood police station.
- Tickets for not putting a child in a car seat can be up to $100 in some states.

Listening Activity Listen to each statement about the conversation. Circle *true* or *false*.

EXAMPLE (TRUE)   FALSE

1. TRUE FALSE   5. TRUE FALSE
2. TRUE FALSE   6. TRUE FALSE
3. TRUE FALSE   7. TRUE FALSE
4. TRUE FALSE

5.4 Yes/No Questions with *Can, Should,* and *Have To*

Modal Verb	Subject	Verb (Base Form)	Complement	Short Answer
Can	I	get	some water?	Yes, you can.
Should	we	pay	inside?	No, we shouldn't.

Language Note: Question forms and short answers with *can* and *should* are the same for all subjects.

Do/Does	Subject	Have To	Verb (Base Form)	Complement	Short Answer
Does	he	have to	get	gas now?	Yes, he does.
Does	she	have to	pay	in cash?	No, she doesn't.
Do	I	have to	pump	the gas?	Yes, you do.
Do	we	have to	pay	inside?	No, we don't.

Language Note: Use *do/does* to make questions with *have to*.

102   Unit 5

An **Audio Program** allows students to hear the readings and conversations, and provides an opportunity to practice their skills.

Grammar Charts with integrated language notes offer simplified and clear explanations and provide contextualized examples of the structure.

Welcome to Grammar in Context Basic   **xiii**

EXERCISE 3 Match the statements on the left with a possible question on the right. The first one is done as an example.

1. The baby is only six months old. — Can you go with me?
2. She's on the way to another city. — Should she wash them?
   Can I hold her in the car?
3. She's 10 years old. — Does she have to stop for gas?
4. She needs a new car seat. — Should we try another gas station?
5. The car windows are dirty. — Does she have to sit in a car seat?
6. I want to take a trip. — Can she put it in the front seat?
7. Gas here is expensive.

EXERCISE 4 ABOUT YOU Ask your partner about people and customs in his/her native country. Use the words given. Your partner can give a short answer.

EXAMPLE: <u>Can people buy</u> food and drinks at gas stations? *Yes, they can.*
          (people/can/buy)

1. _____ their own gas at gas stations?
   (people/have to/pump)
2. _____ in special car seats?
   (children/have to/sit)
3. _____ a small child in a car?
   (a mother/can/hold)
4. _____ in the front?
   (children/can/sit)
5. _____ a seatbelt?
   (a driver/have to/use)
6. _____ for their gas at the pump?
   (people/can/pay)
7. _____ for gas with cash?
   (people/have to/pay)

104 Unit 5

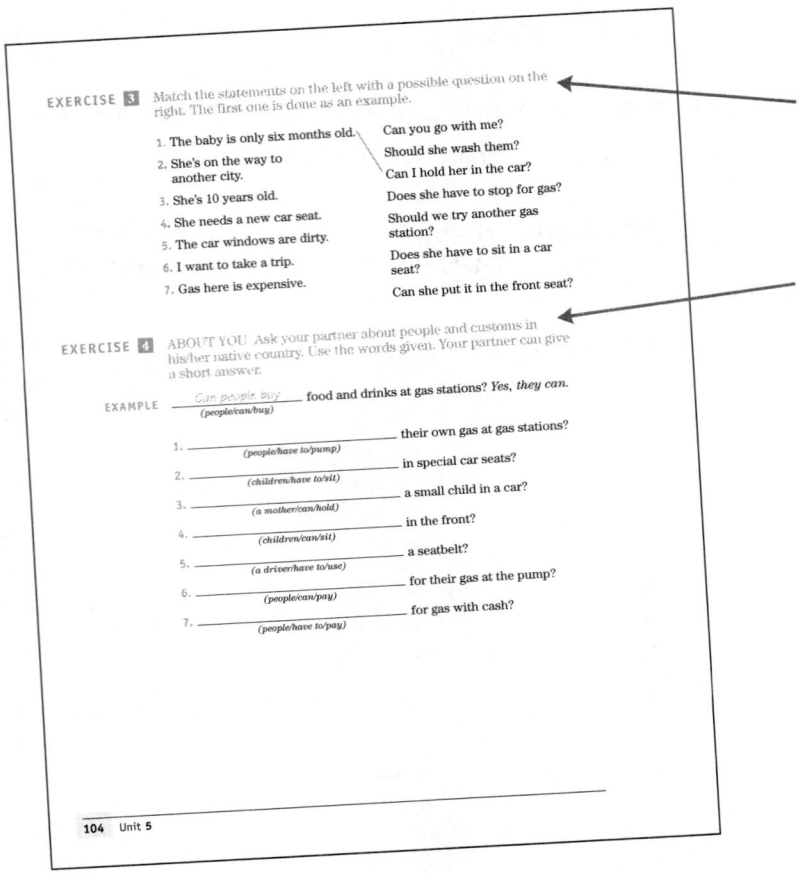

A variety of contextualized activities keeps the classroom lively and targets different learning styles.

About You activities provide for language personalization and communication opportunities.

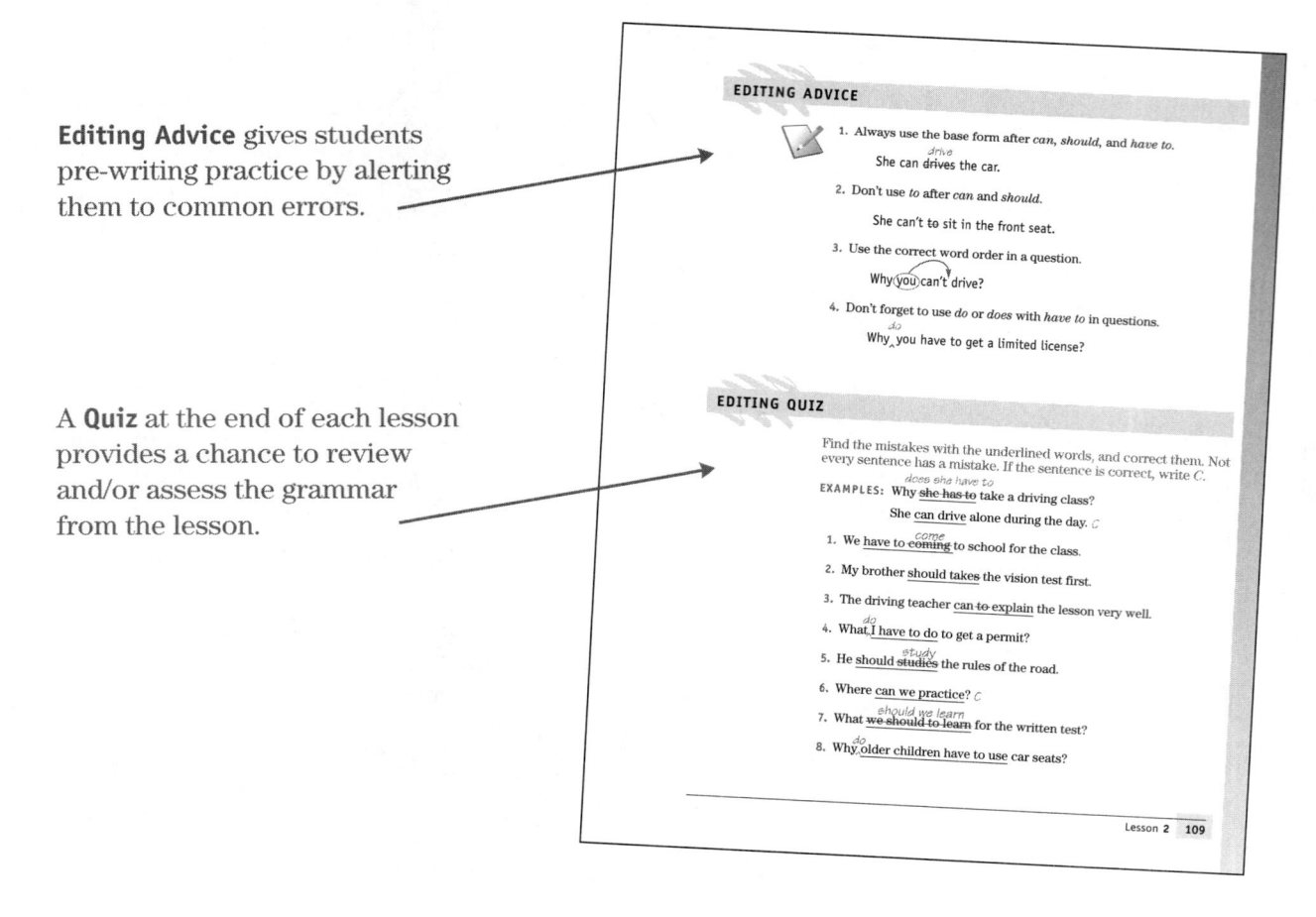

Editing Advice gives students pre-writing practice by alerting them to common errors.

A **Quiz** at the end of each lesson provides a chance to review and/or assess the grammar from the lesson.

EDITING ADVICE

1. Always use the base form after *can*, *should*, and *have to*.
   drive
   She can ~~drives~~ the car.

2. Don't use *to* after *can* and *should*.
   She can't ~~to~~ sit in the front seat.

3. Use the correct word order in a question.
   Why (you) can't drive?

4. Don't forget to use *do* or *does* with *have to* in questions.
   do
   Why ∧ you have to get a limited license?

EDITING QUIZ

Find the mistakes with the underlined words, and correct them. Not every sentence has a mistake. If the sentence is correct, write *C*.
                does she have to
EXAMPLES: Why <u>~~she has to~~</u> take a driving class?
          She <u>can drive</u> alone during the day. *C*

1. We <u>have to ~~coming~~</u> to school for the class.
              come
2. My brother <u>should ~~takes~~</u> the vision test first.
3. The driving teacher <u>~~can to~~ explain</u> the lesson very well.
                do
4. What ∧ <u>I have to do</u> to get a permit?
5. He <u>should ~~studies~~</u> the rules of the road.
              study
6. Where <u>can we practice</u>? *C*
             should we learn
7. What <u>~~we should to learn~~</u> for the written test?
           do
8. Why ∧ <u>older children have to use</u> car seats?

Lesson 2 109

---

xiv Welcome to Grammar in Context Basic

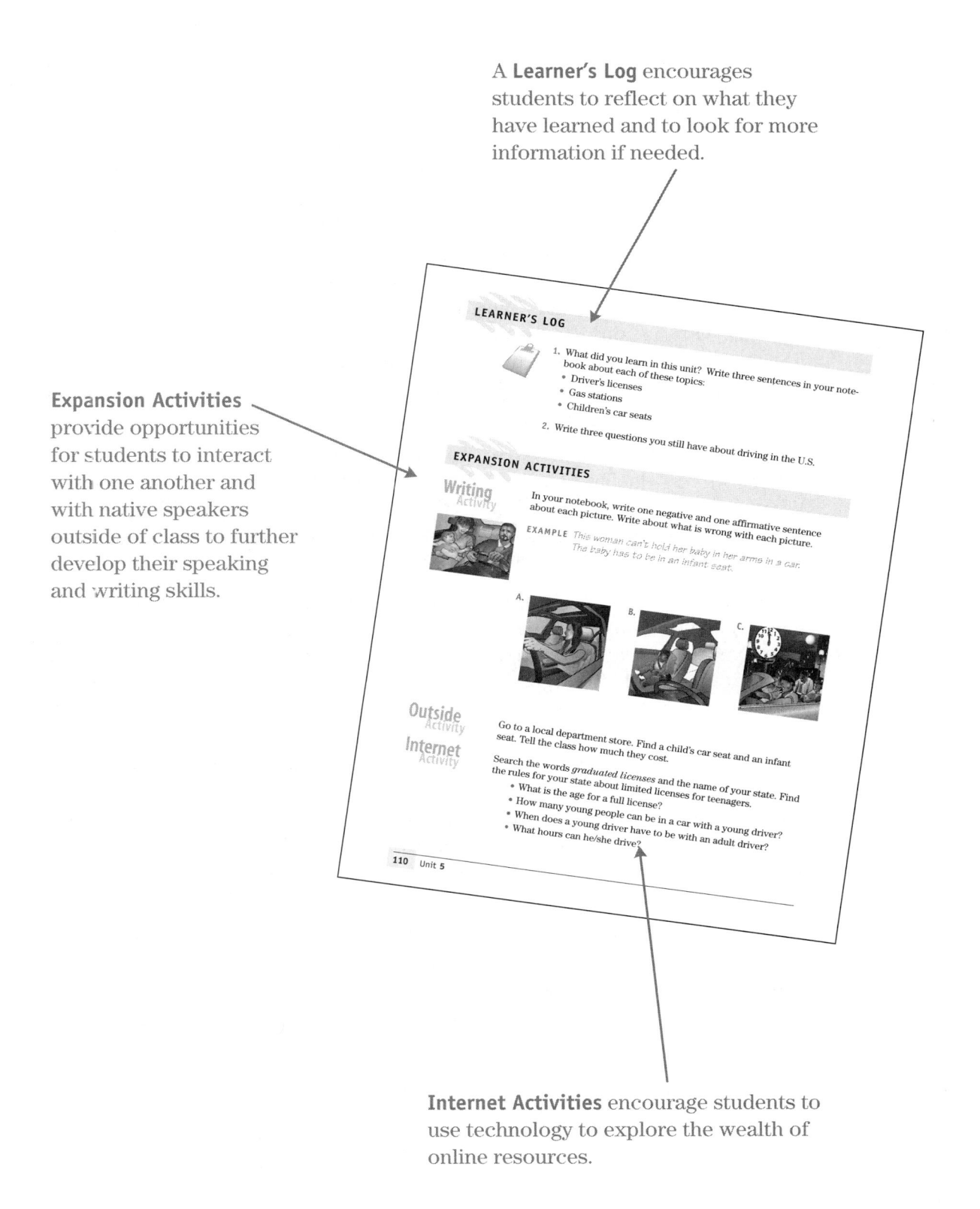

A **Learner's Log** encourages students to reflect on what they have learned and to look for more information if needed.

Expansion Activities provide opportunities for students to interact with one another and with native speakers outside of class to further develop their speaking and writing skills.

LEARNER'S LOG

1. What did you learn in this unit? Write three sentences in your notebook about each of these topics:
   - Driver's licenses
   - Gas stations
   - Children's car seats

2. Write three questions you still have about driving in the U.S.

EXPANSION ACTIVITIES

Writing Activity

In your notebook, write one negative and one affirmative sentence about each picture. Write about what is wrong with each picture.

EXAMPLE: *This woman can't hold her baby in her arms in a car. The baby has to be in an infant seat.*

A. B. C.

Outside Activity

Go to a local department store. Find a child's car seat and an infant seat. Tell the class how much they cost.

Internet Activity

Search the words *graduated licenses* and the name of your state. Find the rules for your state about limited licenses for teenagers.
- What is the age for a full license?
- How many young people can be in a car with a young driver?
- When does a young driver have to be with an adult driver?
- What hours can he/she drive?

110　Unit 5

Internet Activities encourage students to use technology to explore the wealth of online resources.

Welcome to Grammar in Context Basic　　**xv**

About this book:

Grammar in Context Basic, an all-new addition to the *Grammar in Context* series, is a beginning level text book for low level ESL students who have had some exposure to English. Each unit continues the American culture theme that is the focus of the *Grammar in Context* series, but does so in a more personal way through the use of recurring characters. *Grammar in Context Basic* introduces Simon and Dorota, two immigrant Americans who help other immigrants adjust to life in the U.S. Throughout the book, Simon and Dorota take their new friends to the places that are part of everyday American life and help them learn to do things that will make their new lives easier: buy a used car, interview for a job, go shopping, fill out applications, and more.

The charts and exercises are similar to those found in the rest of the series but are designed with the beginning learner in mind. New to this level are Vocabulary in Context boxes, Listening Activities, and a Learner's Log, all features that are created to help beginning learners increase their overall language skills.

There are 12 Units (topically and structurally thematic), and each Unit has from two to four Lessons within. Each Lesson starts with a picture to introduce a reading (a narrative or a conversation), a Vocabulary in Context box that highlights unfamiliar or useful words in the reading, and a Listening Activity to practice comprehension. Clear and concise grammar charts highlight target structures using sentences from the Lesson theme. The exercises that follow also refer to the theme of the Lesson. Each Unit ends with Editing Advice reviewing the grammar in the Lesson, a Quiz, a Learner's Log, Expansion Activities, and Internet Activities. Each Unit should take approximately three to four classroom hours, depending on the complexity of the structure and the needs of your students.

At the end of *Grammar in Context Basic*, students should have a good introduction to the most common grammatical structures of the English language. Students will then be ready for more in-depth study and practice of each structure as found in *Grammar in Context* Books 1, 2, and 3.

Enjoy using *Grammar in Context Basic*!

    Sandy and Judi

Grammar in Context Student Book Supplements

Audio Program
- Audio CDs and Audio Tapes allow students to listen to every reading in the book and hear Listening Activity questions.

More Grammar Practice Workbooks
- Workbooks can be used with *Grammar in Context* or any skills text to learn and review the essential grammar.
- Great for in-class practice or homework.
- Includes practice on all grammar points in *Grammar in Context*.

Teacher's Annotated Edition
- New component offers page-by-page answers and teaching suggestions.

Assessment CD-ROM with ExamView® Pro Test Generator
- Test Generator allows teachers to create tests and quizzes quickly and easily.

Interactive CD-ROM
- CD-ROM allows for supplemental interactive practice on grammar points from *Grammar in Context*.

Split Editions
- Split Editions for Books 1, 2, 3 provide options for short courses.

Instructional Video/DVD
- Video offers teaching suggestions and advice on how to use *Grammar in Context*.

Web Site
- Web site gives access to additional activities and promotes the use of the Internet.

It is nice to meet you!

Dorota Marta Simon Amy Ed Tina Peter with Anna Halina

Lisa   Maya Victor   Shafia & her husband   Sue   Rick   Val   Rhonda   Matt   Elsa

UNIT 1

GRAMMAR
Subject Pronouns
Be
Contractions
Singular and Plural
This/That/These/Those
Adjectives
Expressions with *It*

CONTEXT
Welcome to the U.S.

Expansion

Theme The topic for this unit can be enhanced with the following ideas:
1. A large map or atlas to locate students' countries
2. An American passport, and if possible, passports from other countries
3. Pictures of urban, small town, and rural scenes in the U.S.

Unit | 1
Unit Overview

GRAMMAR

1. Say: *This is English grammar class. Welcome to class! What grammar will we study in Unit 1?* Point out the objectives for Unit 1 in the Student Book. (subject pronouns, *be*, contractions, singular and plural, *this/that/these/those*, adjectives, expressions with *It*) Check that students are looking at page 1. Say the objectives. Give examples of each objective and write them on the board.
2. Point to yourself and say: *I am [name]. I'm from [country]. What's your name? Where are you from?* Elicit students' names and countries. Have some students introduce a classmate. (He is John. He is from Venezuela.)

CONTEXT

1. Point out and say the unit context title. *(Welcome to the U.S.)* Activate students' prior knowledge. Say: *In this unit, we will talk about a new life in the U.S. How is your life different in the U.S.? Are stores different? Are prices different? What else is different?* Have students share their personal experiences. Write students' answers on the board.
2. Direct students' attention to the photos. Say: *This is a supermarket. That's a Laundromat. What are the people doing?* (buying food, washing clothes) Ask: *Do you like American supermarkets? American Laundromats?* Encourage students to share their knowledge and personal experiences.

Unit 1   1

Lesson 1 | Overview

GRAMMAR

1. Point out the objectives on page 2 of the Student Book. Write on the board: *Subject Pronouns* and *Be*. Have a male and female student stand in front of the class. Introduce them using *he* and *she* (e.g., *He is Paulo. She is Ma Li.*) Write the sentences on the board. Underline the pronouns. Say: He *and* she *are subject pronouns.* Point to the male student and say: *he.* Point to the female student and say: *she.*
2. List subject pronouns and forms of be on the board (*I am; you are; he/she/it is; we are; you are; they are*). Have students repeat the items after you.

CONTEXT

1. Say: *We will read about two people who help. I am a teacher. I help you learn English. My friend is John. He helps me with the computer. Who helps you?* Elicit responses from students. Prompt students to name persons and use pronoun references in sentences. *(Mi San. She helps me.)*
2. Direct students' attention to the picture. Say: *This is Dorota and Simon. They help people. Who do they help?* (immigrants in the U.S.) *Are they helping now?* (yes)

BEFORE YOU READ

1. Go over each statement as a class. Have a volunteer read the statements or read them to the class yourself. Ask students to circle *yes* or *no*.
2. Ask for a few volunteers to share their answers with the class.

🕐 To save class time, skip "Before You Read" or have students prepare answers for homework ahead of time.

LESSON **1**

GRAMMAR
Subject Pronouns
Forms of *Be*

CONTEXT
We Are Here to Help

Before You Read

Circle *yes* or *no*.

1. Many things are new for me in this country.   YES   NO
2. People help me with new things.   YES   NO

2   Unit **1**

Culture Note
Many immigrants in the U.S. come from ten countries: Mexico, India, the Philippines, China, El Salvador, the Dominican Republic, Vietnam, Colombia, Guatemala, and Russia.

WE ARE HERE TO HELP

Dorota: Welcome! My name **is** Dorota. I **am** from Poland, but I **am** a citizen of the U.S. now. My first language **is** Polish. This **is** Simon. He **is** from Mexico. We **are** here to help you.

Simon: Hi. My name **is** Simon. I **am** from Mexico, but I **am** a citizen now. Spanish **is** my first language. We **are** both here to help you.

Dorota: You **are** new in this country. You **are** immigrants. Life **is** different here. Many things **are** different for you—the supermarket **is** different, the Laundromat **is** different, the doctor's office **is** different, and the bank **is** different. Everything **is** new for you. Maybe you **are** confused.

They **are** helpful.

Simon: We **are** here to help you in new places. The Laundromat and supermarket **are** the first places to go.

Vocabulary in Context

citizen	Dorota is a **citizen** of the United States.
both	Dorota and Simon are **both** here to help.
immigrant	I am from Colombia. I am new to the U.S. I am an **immigrant**.
life	**Life** in the U.S. is new for me.
supermarket	We buy food in a **supermarket**.
Laundromat	The **Laundromat** is a place to wash clothes.
different	The supermarket in the U.S. is **different**.
bank	He needs money. He is at the **bank**.
everything	**Everything** is new—the bank, the supermarket, and the Laundromat.
helpful	Dorota and Simon are **helpful**.
confused	I am new here. Everything is different. I'm **confused**.

Lesson 1   3

Reading Variation

To practice listening skills, have students listen to the audio before opening their books. Ask a few comprehension questions: *Who is talking?* (Dorota and Simon) *Who are they talking to?* (new immigrants) Repeat the audio if necessary. Then have students open their books and read along as they listen to the audio.

Vocabulary Teaching Ideas

Use the following ideas to teach these terms:

immigrant: Show pictures of immigrant neighborhoods in large U.S. cities. Say: *Immigrants in the U.S. come from many countries.*
different: Display two items, one a variation of the other. (e.g., a jar of peanut butter and a jar of jelly)
confused: Bring in a strange-looking gadget and mime confusion.

Expansion

Reading Have students practice the conversation in pairs. Ask volunteers to roleplay the conversation in front of the class.
Vocabulary in Context To check comprehension, have volunteers in pairs or groups act out selected vocabulary, such as *both, Laundromat, supermarket, bank, helpful,* and *confused.*

We Are Here to Help (Reading) CD 1, Track 1

1. Have students look at the picture. Point to the man and woman. Ask: *Are these people new?* (yes) *Who helps them?* (Dorota and Simon)
2. Have students look at the title of the reading. Ask: *What is the reading about? Is this about Simon and Dorota?* Have students use the title and picture to make predictions about the reading.
3. Have students read the dialogue silently. Tell them to pay special attention to the verb *be*. Then play the audio and have students read along silently.
4. Check students' basic comprehension. Ask questions, such as: *Is Simon from the United States?* (no) *Where is Dorota from?* (Poland) *Where is Simon from?* (Mexico). *Is life different here?* (yes) *What is different?* (supermarket, Laundromat, bank, doctor's office)

To save class time, have students do the reading for homework ahead of time.

VOCABULARY IN CONTEXT

1. Model the pronunciation of each new vocabulary word and have students repeat.
2. Make sure students understand the meaning of each vocabulary word. Review the examples in the book and create additional example sentences. For example, say: *citizen. Dorota is a citizen of the United States.* Then say: *I am a citizen of the United States.* Show an American passport. *Is Simon a citizen of the U.S.?* (yes) To elicit a negative response, ask a student you know is not a U.S. citizen if he or she is a U.S. citizen. Go over each vocabulary word similarly, using visuals and realia when appropriate. When possible, point to pictures in the book that illustrate the new vocabulary items, such as *Laundromat* and *supermarket* on page 1, *bank* on page 23.
3. Have students underline an example of each new vocabulary item in the reading. Point out that the word *helpful* is not in the reading, but that it is a useful word to describe Dorota and Simon.

Unit **1**   3

DID YOU KNOW?

Tell students that many agencies in the U.S. help immigrants. Say: *These offices can help new people:*

find a home
shop for food
go to the bank
get a job

Explain that not only government agencies help immigrants, but that many religious and private agencies help also.

LISTENING ACTIVITY

🎧 **CD 1, Track 2**

1. Make sure students understand the meaning of *true* and *false*. Demonstrate with students in the class. Say: *True or false? [Name of student] is from [student's native country].* (true) *True or False? [Name of student] is from New York.* (false)
2. Say: *Listen to the sentences about Dorota and Simon. Circle* true *or* false. Play the listening selection one time without pausing. Then play it through again, pausing and replaying as necessary.
3. Go over the answers as a class. Ask students to volunteer answers.

1.1 | Subject Pronouns

Have students look at the pictures in grammar chart **1.1** on page 4. Give students time to read the dialogue bubbles in the chart. Ask: *Who does he mean?* (Simon) Have them turn to the reading on page 3 if they have trouble remembering Simon's name. Repeat with *I, you,* and *we*. Use the photos of the supermarket and Laundromat on page 1 to demonstrate *it*. If students have difficulty with *I*, have them find *I* in the reading and match it to the speaker's name in the text.

Did You Know? Many agencies and volunteers help immigrants.

Listening Activity Listen to the sentences about the story and picture. Circle *true* or *false*.

EXAMPLE TRUE (FALSE)

1. (TRUE) FALSE
2. TRUE (FALSE)
3. TRUE (FALSE)
4. (TRUE) FALSE
5. (TRUE) FALSE
6. TRUE (FALSE)

1.1 | Subject Pronouns

- I am Dorota.
- I am Simon.
- We are here to help.
- She is from Poland.
- He is from Mexico.
- It is a supermarket.
- They are banks.
- You are new.
- They are new here.

4 Unit 1

Expansion

Listening Activity Create true or false statements about the class: *Simon is a U.S. citizen.* (true) Say the sentences out loud and have students write *true* or *false* on a piece of paper. Go over the answers as a class.

Grammar Chart Have students work in pairs to create similar dialogues using students from the class. Students write new sentences. (e.g., *I am Juliana.*)

---

4   *Grammar in Context Basic* Teacher's Edition

EXERCISE 1 Fill in the blanks with the correct subject pronoun.

EXAMPLE ___You___ are immigrants.

1. Dorota is from Poland. ___She___ is here to help.
2. ___I___ am new to this country.
3. Simon is from Mexico. ___He___ is from Mexico City.
4. You and I are new. ___We___ are confused.
5. The bank is near my house. ___It___ is big.
6. Simon and Dorota are citizens now. ___They___ are helpful.
7. Halina: Thank you for your help.
   Simon: ___You___ are welcome.

1.2 | Forms of *Be*

Subject	Form of *Be*	Complement
I	am	a citizen.
The supermarket It Dorota She Simon He	is	different. big. from Poland. helpful. from Mexico. an American citizen.
We You Dorota and Simon They	are	here to help. new here. American citizens. helpful.

EXERCISE 2 Fill in the missing words: *am*, *is*, or *are*.

EXAMPLE The Laundromat ___is___ different.

1. You ___are___ new here.
2. We ___are___ here to help you.
3. He ___is___ confused.
4. Some things ___are___ new.
5. I ___am___ a citizen now.
6. They ___are___ helpful.
7. She ___is___ from Poland.

Lesson 1   5

Expansion

Exercise 2 Have students work in pairs to create four sentences telling the national origin of students in the class. Tell students to use different forms of the verb *be*.

EXERCISE 1

1. Have students read the direction line. Ask: *What words do we use here?* (I, you, he, she, it, we, they) Go over the example in the book. Then do #1 with the class.
2. Have students complete the rest of Exercise 1 individually. Check the answers as a class. If necessary, review grammar chart **1.1** on page 4.

1.2 | Forms of *Be*

1. Have students look at grammar chart **1.2** on page 5. Say: *There are three forms of* be: am, is, *and* are. *For* I, *use* am. *For a subject that is one person or thing, use* is. *For a subject that is more than one person or thing, use* are. Ask volunteers to read the examples.
2. Have students close their books. List some subjects on the board, such as *Dorota, I, it, the bank, Simon, you, Halina and Dorota, we,* and *My name.* Activate students' prior knowledge. Point to each subject and ask: *Is [subject] one subject or more than one? What form of be goes with [subject]?* Say each subject and pause for students to call out the verb form.
3. Have students refer back to grammar chart **1.1** on page 4. Ask students to underline the verb *be* in the dialogues and match each form to its subject.

EXERCISE 2

1. Have students read the direction line. Go over the example in the book. Have a volunteer do #1.
2. Have students complete the rest of Exercise 2 individually. Then have students check their answers in pairs. Circulate to observe pair work. Give help as needed.
3. If necessary, review grammar chart **1.2** on page 5.

Unit 1   5

EXERCISE 3

1. Have students read the direction line. Ask: *What are the forms of* be? *(am, is, are)* Have a volunteer complete the first sentence.
2. Have students complete the rest of Exercise 3 individually. Then have students compare answers with a partner. Circulate to observe pair work. Give help as needed.
3. If necessary, review grammar chart **1.2** on page 5.

EXERCISE 4

1. Say: *This exercise is about you.* Have students read the direction line. Go over the examples in the book. Have volunteers model the first three items.
2. Have students complete Exercise 4 individually. Then have students compare answers with a partner. Say: *Read the sentences you checked to your partner. Use the map on page 7 to show your partner where you're from.* Circulate to observe pair work. Give help as needed.
3. If necessary, review grammar chart **1.2** on page 5.

EXERCISE 3 *Conversation*: Dorota and Halina are talking. Fill in the blanks with the correct form of *be*.

Dorota: You __are__ (1) new.
Halina: Yes. I __am__ (2) from Poland.
Dorota: I __am__ (3) from Poland too. I __am__ (4) an American citizen now. I __am__ (5) here to help you. Simon __is__ (6) here to help you too. He __is__ (7) from Mexico.
Halina: Many things __are__ (8) new for me.
Dorota: Yes. Life __is__ (9) different here. But we __are__ (10) both here to help you.
Halina: Thank you.

EXERCISE 4 ABOUT YOU Check the items that are true for you.

EXAMPLE ___✓___ I am new to the U.S.
            _____ I am a citizen of the U.S.

Answers will vary.

1. _____ I am new to the U.S.
2. _____ I am new at this school.
3. _____ Life is different in a new country.
4. _____ I am confused about life in the U.S.
5. _____ I am a citizen of the U.S.
6. _____ I am an immigrant.
7. _____ Americans are helpful.
8. _____ I am from Mexico.
9. _____ Spanish is my native language.
10. _____ My family is in the U.S.

6 Unit 1

Expansion

Exercise 3 Have students practice the dialogue in pairs. Circulate to help students with pronunciation.

Exercise 4 Have students compare answers with a different partner. Say: *Now read the sentences you checked to your new partner. Use the map on page 7 to show your partner where you're from.* Circulate to observe pair work. Give help as needed.

EXERCISE 5 ABOUT YOU Fill in the blanks.

EXAMPLE I am a citizen of _____Peru_____.

1. My name is _____.   *Answers will vary.*
2. I am from _____.
3. My country is _____.
4. I am confused about _____.
5. _____ is helpful in my life here.
6. _____ is different for me.

Lesson 1   7

EXERCISE 5

1. Say: *This exercise is about you.* Have students read the direction line. Say: *Fill in the blanks with information that is true about you.* Go over the example in the book. Model the example and then have a volunteer model the example.
2. Have students complete Exercise 5 individually. Then have students compare answers with a partner. Circulate to observe pair work. Give help as needed.
3. If necessary, review grammar chart **1.2** on page 5.

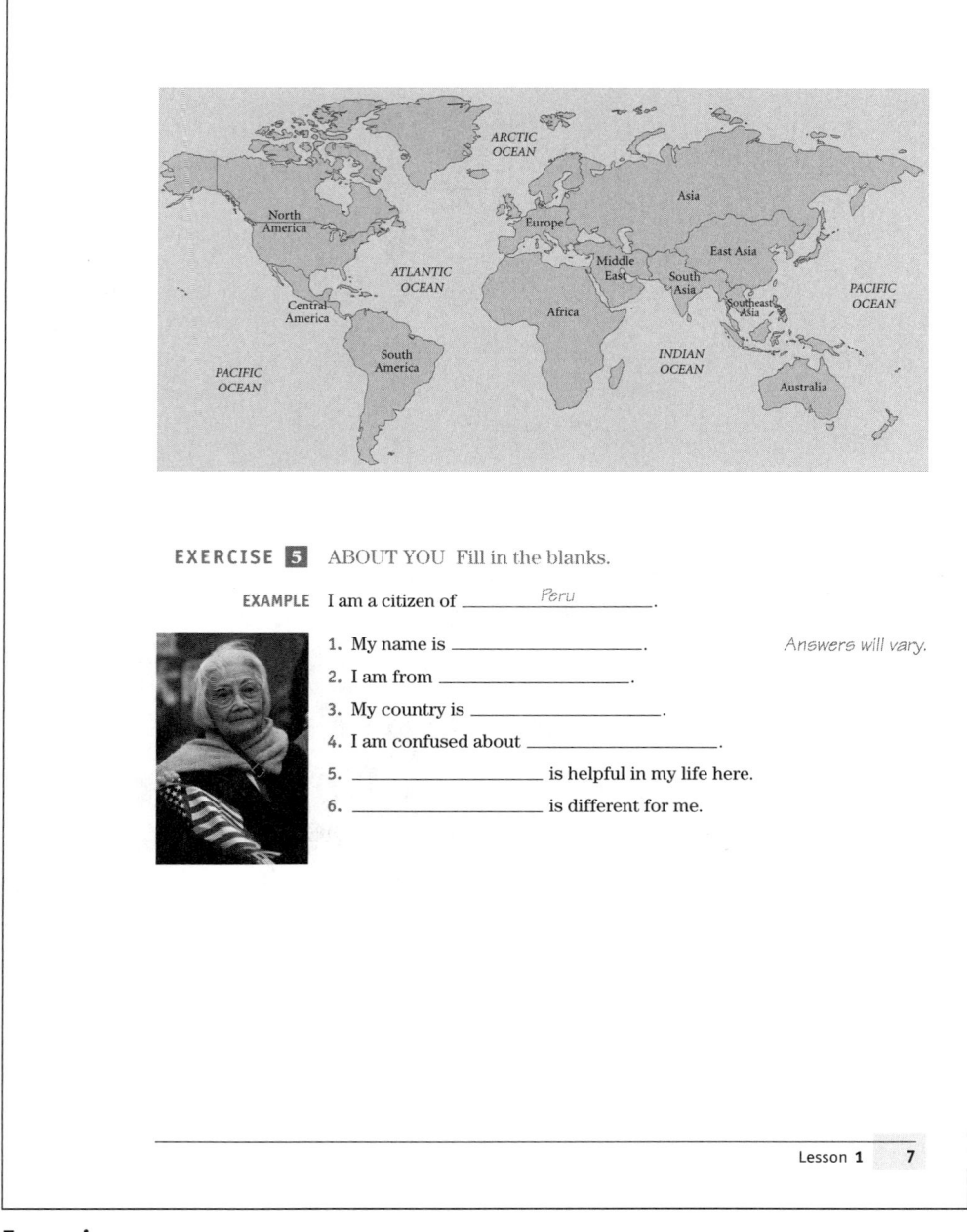

Expansion

Exercise 5 Have students share their answers to #4, #5, and #6. Ask: *What are you confused about? Who is helpful in your life? What is different for you?* Write students' ideas on the board.

Unit **1**   7

Lesson 2 | Overview

GRAMMAR

Ask: *What did we study in Lesson 1?* (subject pronouns and *be*). *What will we study in Lesson 2?* Point to each objective in the Student Book, read it out loud, and give an example, such as: *I am = I'm* (contractions); *one bank, twp banks* (singular and plural). For the demonstrative adjectives, point to objects in the room and make phrases, such as: *This is a book. That is a clock. These are pens.* Ask volunteers for more examples and write them on the board.

CONTEXT

1. Say: *We're going to talk about the Laundromat. Laundromats are helpful. Washing machines are helpful. You don't have to wash clothes by hand. Do you have Laundromats like this in your country?* Have volunteers share their answers and personal experience with the class.
2. Direct students' attention to the picture. Ask volunteers to read the labeled items.

BEFORE YOU READ

1. Go over each statement as a class. Have a volunteer read the statements or read them to the class yourself. Ask students to circle *yes* or *no*.
2. Ask for a few volunteers to share their answers with the class.

⏱ To save class time, skip "Before You Read" or have students prepare answers for homework ahead of time.

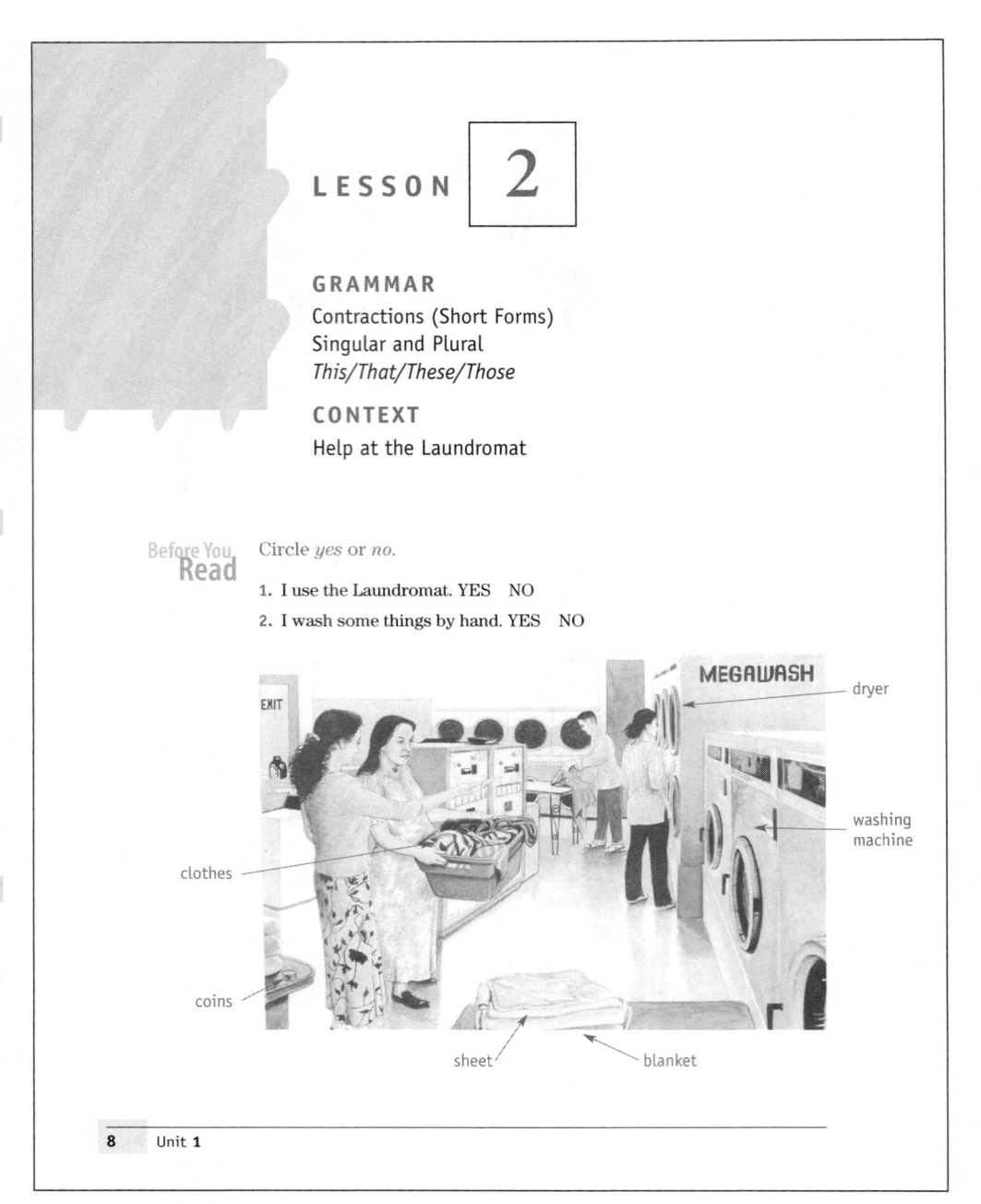

LESSON 2

GRAMMAR
Contractions (Short Forms)
Singular and Plural
This/That/These/Those

CONTEXT
Help at the Laundromat

Before You Read

Circle *yes* or *no*.

1. I use the Laundromat. YES   NO
2. I wash some things by hand. YES   NO

8   Unit 1

Expansion

Theme The topic for this lesson can be enhanced with the following ideas:
1. Items found at a Laundromat (e.g., tokens, packets of laundry detergent and softeners)
2. Different types of clothing labels with washing instructions and symbols

Culture Note

In some parts of the U.S. Laundromats are called *washettes* or *washaterias*.

HELP AT THE LAUNDROMAT

Dorota and a new immigrant, Shafia, are at the Laundromat.

Dorota: **We're** at the Laundromat.
Shafia: The **Laundromat's** new for me. **I'm** confused.
Dorota: **Don't worry**. **We're together**. **I'm** here to help you.
Shafia: Thanks. My clothes are dirty.
Dorota: These are the washing machines. The small machines are for small items—clothes, towels, and sheets. Those big machines are for big items, like blankets. Coins are necessary for the machines.
Shafia: Those machines are different.
Dorota: Yes. **They're** dryers.
Shafia: **It's** hot inside the Laundromat.
Dorota: **You're** right.
Shafia: **It's** easy to wash clothes in a Laundromat.
Dorota: Yes, it is.
Shafia: These two washers are empty. **I'm** ready to wash my clothes.

Vocabulary in Context

don't worry	**Don't worry**. I'm here to help you.
together	We're **together**.
right	A: It's hot here.
	B: Yes, you're **right**.
item(s)	These machines are for small **items**.
clothes	These are my **clothes**.
towel(s)	The **towels** are clean.
sheet(s)	The **sheets** are clean.
blanket(s)	The **blankets** are big.
coin(s)	**Coins** are necessary for the machines.
washing machine(s)	Those are the **washing machines**.
dryer(s)	Those are the **dryers**.
empty	The dryer is **empty**.
clean	My clothes are **clean** now.
dirty	Your clothes are **dirty**.

Lesson 2   9

Help at the Laundromat (Reading) CD 1, Track 3

1. Have students look at the picture of the Laundromat on page 8. Say: *Dorota and Shafia are at the Laundromat now.*
2. Have students look at the title of the reading. Ask: *Who needs help—Dorota or Shafia?* (Shafia) *What does Shafia want to do?* (wash her clothes) Have students use the title and picture to make predictions about the reading.
3. First, have students read the dialogue silently. Then play the audio and have students read along.
4. Check students' basic comprehension. Ask true or false questions, such as: *Dorota is confused. True or false?* (false) *Shafia helps Dorota.* (false)

To save class time, have students do the reading for homework ahead of time.

VOCABULARY IN CONTEXT

1. Model the pronunciation of each new vocabulary word and have students repeat.
2. Make sure students understand the meaning of each vocabulary word. Review the examples in the book and create additional example sentences. For example, say: *don't worry. Teacher, I don't speak English. Don't worry. I'm here to help you.* Go over each new vocabulary word similarly, using visuals and realia when appropriate. When possible, point to pictures that illustrate the new vocabulary items, such as *clothes, towels, sheets, blankets, coins, washing machines,* and *dryers* on page 8.
3. Have students underline an example of each vocabulary item in the reading. Point out that the word *clean* is not in the reading, but that it is useful to describe clothes.

Reading Variation

To practice listening skills, have students listen to the audio before opening their books. Ask a few comprehension questions: *Where are Dorota and Shafia?* (at the Laundromat) Repeat the audio if necessary. Then have students open their books and read along as they listen to the audio.

Vocabulary Teaching Ideas

Use the following ideas to teach these terms:

together: Ask a volunteer to stand next to you at the front of the classroom. Stand close to the student and then far away from the student.
right: Hold up two objects, such as pens. Ask: *How many [pens] do I have?* (two) Then say: *You're right!* Repeat with another quantity.
empty: Display a container with pencils and pens in it and another that is empty.

Expansion

Reading Have students practice the conversation in pairs. Ask volunteers to roleplay the conversation in front of the class.
Vocabulary in Context To check comprehension, have volunteers in pairs or groups act out selected vocabulary, such as *don't worry, together,* and *(you're) right.*

Unit 1   9

DID YOU KNOW?

Say: *Clothes can tell you how to wash them.* Bring in some of your own articles of clothing and show students their washing labels. Point out the written instructions and symbols. Draw a rectangle with a circle in it. Say: *This means you can put the clothing in the dryer.* Draw many dots in the circle. Say: *Dots in the circle tell how hot the dryer can be. Many dots mean that it is safe to put the clothing in a very hot dryer.*

LISTENING ACTIVITY

🎧 **CD 1, Track 4**

1. Say: *Listen to the sentences about the Laundromat. Circle* true *or* false. Play the listening selection one time without pausing. Then play it through again, pausing and replaying as necessary.
2. Go over the answers as a class. Ask students to volunteer answers.

1.3 | Contractions (Short Forms)

1. Have students look at grammar chart **1.3** on page 10. Use an overhead projector to review the chart with the class. Discuss the rule for each contraction: *For* I'm, *take out the* a *and add an apostrophe*).
2. Have students close their books. Say: *Here is a subject and verb.* Life/is. *What is the contraction?* (Life's). Continue with more examples, such as *Everything/is, Simon/is, they/are.* Then reverse the procedure. Give students a contraction and ask for the separate subject and verb. If this task is difficult for students, allow them to keep their books open.
3. Point out the Language Note. Go over the rule and the example. Write these sentences on the board: *The towels 're big. The blankets are dirty.* Ask: *Which is right? Why?*

Did You Know? Clothes have washing instructions on the label.

hand wash only, cold water

🎧 **Listening Activity** Listen to the sentences about the story. Circle *true* or *false*.

EXAMPLE (TRUE)   FALSE

1. (TRUE)   FALSE   4. (TRUE)   FALSE
2. TRUE   (FALSE)   5. TRUE   (FALSE)
3. (TRUE)   FALSE

1.3 | Contractions (Short Forms)

Long Form	Contraction (Short Form)	Examples
I am	→ I'm	**I'm** here to help.
She is	→ She's	**She's** from Poland.
He is	→ He's	**He's** from Mexico.
It is	→ It's	**It's** hot in here.
Life is	→ Life's	**Life's** different.
Everything is	→ Everything's	**Everything's** new.
Dorota is	→ Dorota's	**Dorota's** from Poland.
The Laundromat is	→ The Laundromat's	The **Laundromat's** hot.
You are	→ You're	**You're** very helpful.
We are	→ We're	**We're** together.
They are	→ They're	**They're** dryers.

Language Note: Do not use a contraction (short form) with a plural noun + **are**. The **dryers are** empty.

10   Unit 1

Expansion

Grammar Chart Have students work in pairs to create a similar grammar chart using people and things in the class. Students write new sentences with contractions for the chart. (e.g., I'm new. You're a student.)

10   *Grammar in Context Basic* Teacher's Edition

EXERCISE 1 Write the contraction.

EXAMPLE (I am) __I'm__ new here.
1. (Simon is) __Simon's__ from Mexico.
2. (He is) __He's__ a citizen of the U.S. now.
3. (Dorota is) __Dorota's__ from Poland.
4. (She is) __She's__ a citizen too.
5. (They are) __They're__ both very helpful.
6. (The Laundromat is) __The Laundromat's__ big.
7. (It is) __It's__ hot in the Laundromat.
8. (You are) __You're__ confused.
9. (I am) __I'm__ confused too.
10. (We are) __We're__ both confused.

EXERCISE 2 Maria and Sara are new immigrants. This is their conversation. Fill in the blanks to complete the contraction.

Maria: I'__m__ (example) from Mexico. __You__ (example) 're from Mexico too, right?

Sara: No. __I__ (1) 'm from Peru. It'__s__ (2) in South America. I'__m__ (3) in the U.S. with my parents. They'__re__ (4) old.

Maria: __I__ (5) 'm here alone. I'__m__ (6) confused.

Sara: We'__re__ (7) both confused. Many things are new here.

Maria: Life'__s__ (8) different here. The bank'__s__ (9) new for me. The school'__s__ (10) new for me.

Sara: Simon and Dorota are citizens now. Simon'__s__ (11) from Mexico. __He__ (12) 's helpful. Dorota'__s__ (13) from Poland. __She__ (14) 's helpful too.

Maria: __We__ (15) 're both very helpful to new immigrants.

Sara: You'__re__ (16) right.

Lesson 2   11

EXERCISE 1
1. Have students read the direction line. Go over the example in the book.
2. Have students complete Exercise 1 individually. Go over the answers as a class.
3. If necessary, review grammar chart **1.3** on page 10.

EXERCISE 2
1. Have students read the direction line. Say: *You are going to complete the contractions.* Go over the example.
2. Have students complete the rest of Exercise 2 individually. Then have students compare answers with a partner. Circulate to observe pair work. Give help as needed.
3. If necessary, review grammar chart **1.3** on page 10.

Expansion

Exercise 2 Have students practice the dialogue in pairs. Circulate to help students with pronunciation.

Create a short conversation, based on Exercise 2, with a volunteer. Substitute your information for the book's information: *I'm from the United States. You're from the United States too, right?* Then have students work in pairs to create their own conversation with information that is true for them.

Unit 1   11

1.4 | Singular and Plural

1. Have students close their books. Write the nouns from grammar chart **1.4** on the board. Write some as singular nouns and others as plural, such as *machines, coin, towel,* and *blankets.*
2. Ask students if the nouns are singular or plural. Then have students look at grammar chart **1.4** on page 12. Say: *Check your work.* Ask: What do we add to make a noun plural? (-s)

EXERCISE 3

1. Have students read the direction line. Go over the example in the book.
2. Have students complete Exercise 3 individually. Go over the answers as a class.
3. If necessary, review grammar chart **1.4** on page 12.

1.5 | *This, That, These, Those*

1. Have students close their books. Use simple objects such as books to demonstrate *this, that, these,* and *those.* For example, hold a book in your hand and say: *This book.* Place a second book on a student's desk, step away and point to it. Say: *That book.* Repeat the procedure for *these* and *those.*
2. Have students look at grammar chart **1.5** on page 12. Say: *This and these are for objects that are close to you. That and those are for objects not close to you. This and that are singular. These and those are plural.*
3. Go over the Language Note. Review the rule and the example sentence. Review the Pronunciation Note and pronounce the sentences in the chart. Then say: *Listen to these words. Raise your hand when you hear the word this: this machine/these machines; this sister/these sisters; these seats/this seat; these sheets/these towels.*

1.4 | Singular and Plural

Singular means one. *Plural* means more than one. A plural noun usually ends in -s.

Singular	Plural
one machine	five machine**s**
one coin	six coin**s**
one towel	three towel**s**
one blanket	two blanket**s**

EXERCISE 3 Write the plural form of the words.

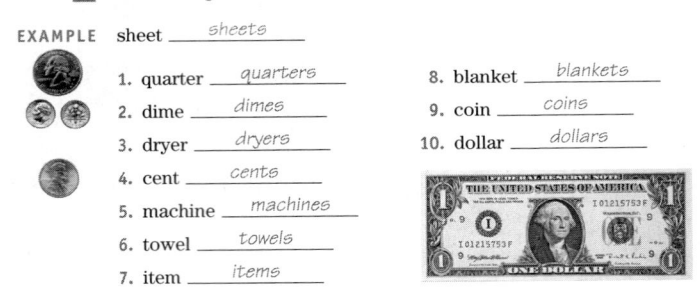

EXAMPLE sheet ___sheets___

1. quarter ___quarters___
2. dime ___dimes___
3. dryer ___dryers___
4. cent ___cents___
5. machine ___machines___
6. towel ___towels___
7. item ___items___
8. blanket ___blankets___
9. coin ___coins___
10. dollar ___dollars___

1.5 | *This, That, These, Those*

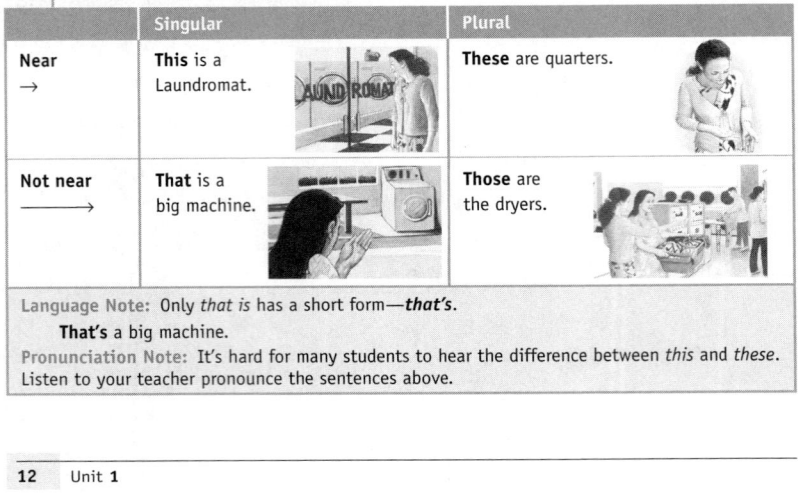

	Singular	Plural
Near →	**This** is a Laundromat.	**These** are quarters.
Not near →	**That** is a big machine.	**Those** are the dryers.

Language Note: Only *that is* has a short form—*that's.*
  That's a big machine.
Pronunciation Note: It's hard for many students to hear the difference between *this* and *these.* Listen to your teacher pronounce the sentences above.

12 Unit 1

Expansion

Grammar Chart Have students practice the sentences in grammar chart **1.5** in groups. Have groups make a circle. Ask students to take objects out of their bags and to place some objects close to them and some far away. Have students take turns making sentences with the objects and the demonstrative adjectives. (e.g., This is a cell phone. Those are pencils.) Circulate to help students with vocabulary and to check comprehension of demonstrative adjectives.

---

12 *Grammar in Context Basic* Teacher's Edition

EXERCISE 4   Fill in the blanks with *this is, that's, these are,* or *those are.*

EXAMPLE   __That's__ the coin machine.

1. __This is__ a dollar.
2. __These are__ coins.
3. __Those are__ quarters.
4. __These are__ the big washing machines.
5. __This is__ a hot Laundromat.
6. __Those are__ dryers.

EXERCISE 5   Circle the correct word.

EXAMPLE   The (sheet/**sheets**) are white.

1. The blankets (is/**are**) big.
2. (**These**/This) are the dryers.
3. (**They're**/They) hot.
4. (Quarter/**Quarters**) are necessary for the machine.
5. (That/**Those**) machines are empty.

Lesson 2   13

EXERCISE 4

1. Have students read the direction line. Remind students that only *that is* can be contracted *(that's)*. Go over the example in the Student Book.
2. Have students complete Exercise 4 individually. Go over the answers as a class.
3. If necessary, review grammar chart **1.5** on page 12.

EXERCISE 5

1. Have students read the direction line. Go over the example in the Student Book.
2. Have students complete Exercise 5 individually. Have students compare answers with a partner. Circulate to observe pair work. Give help as needed.
3. If necessary, review grammar charts **1.4** and **1.5** on page 12.

To save class time, have students complete the exercise for homework.

Unit **1**   **13**

Lesson 3 | Overview

GRAMMAR

1. Ask: *What did we study in Lesson 2?* (contractions, singular and plural, *this/that/these/those*). *What will we study in this lesson?* Read the objectives out loud (negative forms of the verb *be*, adjectives, expressions with *It*, and singular and plural).
2. Activate students' prior knowledge. Write *blanket* on the board. Ask: *What is the plural of* blanket? (blankets) *What is the singular of* blankets? (blanket) Give examples of adjectives and expressions with *It* that students have learned, such as *big* and *empty*, and *It's hot*. Ask volunteers for additional examples and write them on the board.

CONTEXT

1. Say: *We're going to learn about supermarkets in the U.S. Most American supermarkets are big. They sell many things: food, kitchen things, medicine, and toys. Are American supermarkets different from supermarkets in your country?* Have students share their knowledge and personal experiences.
2. Direct students' attention to the picture. Ask: *Where are they?* (supermarket)

BEFORE YOU READ

1. Go over each statement as a class. Have a volunteer read the statements or read them to the class yourself. Ask students to circle *yes* or *no*.
2. Ask for a few volunteers to share their answers with the class.

 To save class time, skip "Before You Read" or have students prepare answers for homework ahead of time.

LESSON 3

GRAMMAR
Negative Forms of the Verb *Be*
Adjectives
Expressions with *It*
Singular and Plural

CONTEXT
Help at the Supermarket

Before You Read Circle *yes* or *no*.

1. American supermarkets are confusing. YES NO
2. Prices are the same in every supermarket. YES NO

14   Unit 1

Expansion

Theme The topic for this unit can be enhanced with the following ideas:
1. Circulars from nearby supermarkets
2. U.S. coins and bills, a checkbook, a debit card, and a credit card
3. Supermarket coupons

Culture Note

Supermarkets are big stores that sell groceries, meat, and produce. Many have a deli and a bakery. Generally, supermarkets carry around 15,000 different items.

HELP AT THE SUPERMARKET

Dorota: We're at the supermarket now. It's early. The supermarket **isn't** crowded. The parking lot**'s not** crowded.
Halina: This is my first time in an American supermarket. **I'm not** sure what to do.
Dorota: I'm here to help you.
Halina: Thanks. The prices **aren't** on the products.
Dorota: The prices are on the shelves, under the products. A code is on each package.
Dorota: Prices **aren't** the same every week. Some things are on sale each week. Look—bananas are on sale this week. They're usually 69¢ a pound. This week they**'re not** 69¢ a pound. They're 29¢ a pound.
Halina: Look! These cookies are free.
Dorota: The samples are free, but the bags of cookies **aren't**.
Dorota: We're finished. This line is empty.
Halina: The cashier**'s not** here.
Dorota: It's an automatic checkout.

Vocabulary in Context

early	It's 8 a.m. It's **early**.
crowded	The store is empty. It isn't **crowded**.
sure	I'm not **sure** what to do.
price	The **price** is 29¢ a pound.
product(s)	The supermarket has many **products**.
shelf/shelves	The prices are on the **shelves**.
code	A **code** is on each product.
package(s)	The cookies are in **packages**.
the same	Prices aren't **the same** every week.
on sale	Bananas are **on sale** this week.
pound(s)	Americans use **pounds**, not kilograms.
free	The bags of cookies are not **free**.
sample(s)	The **samples** are free.
cashier(s)	The **cashiers** are in the front of the store.
automatic checkout	You can use the **automatic checkout**.

Lesson 3   15

Reading Variation

To practice listening skills, have students listen to the audio before opening their books. Ask a few comprehension questions: *Where are they?* (at the supermarket) *What's on sale?* (the bananas) Repeat the audio if necessary. Then have students open their books and read along as they listen to the audio.

Vocabulary Teaching Ideas

Use the following ideas to teach these terms:

free: Hold up two books and say: *This book cost $30*. Write $30 on the board. Say: *This book was free*. Write on the board: *free = $0*.

the same: Hold up two identical books. Hold up a different book and say: *This book is not the same*.

Expansion

Reading Have students practice the conversation in pairs. Ask volunteers to roleplay the conversation in front of the class.

Vocabulary in Context To check comprehension, have volunteers in pairs or groups act out selected vocabulary, such as *sure* and *cashier*.

Help at the Supermarket (Reading) 🎧 CD 1, Track 5

1. Have students look at the picture of the supermarket on page 14. Say: *Dorota and Halina are at the supermarket now.*
2. Have students look at the title of the reading. Ask: *What is the reading about? Who needs help— Dorota or Halina?* (Halina) *Why does she need help?* (She's new. This is her first time in an American supermarket.) Have students use the title and photo to make predictions about the reading.
3. Have students read the dialogue silently. Then play the audio and have students read along.
4. Check students' basic comprehension. Ask true or false questions such as: *The parking lot is empty. True or false?* (true) *Halina is confused.* (true) *Prices change.* (true)

   ⏱ To save class time, have students do the reading for homework ahead of time.

VOCABULARY IN CONTEXT

1. Model the pronunciation of each new vocabulary word and have students repeat.
2. Make sure students understand the meaning of each vocabulary word. Review the examples in the book and create additional example sentences. For example, point to objects in the room and identify them: *This is a clock*. Then say: *I know. I'm sure [this is a clock]*. Go over each new vocabulary word similarly, using visuals and realia when appropriate. Point to items in the picture on page 14 that illustrate some of the vocabulary items, such as *shelves, cashier,* and *automatic checkout*.
3. Have students underline an example of each vocabulary item in the reading.

Unit 1   15

DID YOU KNOW?

Show students examples of each item below and explain the terms as follows:

circular: a "newspaper" that shows items on sale

cash: money in coins and bills

check: a written order telling a bank to pay money

debit card: a card used to get money from a checking account

credit card: a bank card used to buy items and pay later

coupon: a piece of paper that lets you buy items at sale prices or for free

LISTENING ACTIVITY

🎧 *CD 1, Track 6*

1. Say: *Listen to the sentences about the supermarket. Circle true or false.* Play the listening selection one time without pausing. Then play it through again, pausing and replaying as necessary.
2. Go over the answers as a class. Ask students to volunteer answers.

1.6 | Negative Forms of the Verb *Be*

1. Have students look at grammar chart **1.6** on page 16. Demonstrate the rule for making negative contractions with *be*. Write on the board: *You are not serious.* Cross out *a* and write *You're not.* Rewrite the sentence. Cross out *o* and write *You aren't.* Stress the use of the apostrophe. Write on the board: *I am not. = I'm not.* Say: *There is only one way to do the negative contraction for* I am not. Review each example in the chart.
2. Point out the Language Note. Review the rule and the example. Elicit plural nouns from students and write them on the board. Ask students to use a noun in a sentence with a negative contraction. (e.g., Coins. The coins aren't big.).
3. Have students look at the comparison chart. Review the examples in the chart.

Did You Know?
- You can use cash, a check, a debit card, or a credit card to shop at the supermarket.
- Supermarkets produce papers that show all the sale items for the week.

Listening Activity Listen to the sentences about the story and pictures. Circle *true* or *false*.

EXAMPLE   TRUE   (FALSE)

1. (TRUE) FALSE   4. (TRUE) FALSE
2. TRUE   (FALSE)   5. TRUE   (FALSE)
3. TRUE   (FALSE)   6. (TRUE) FALSE

1.6 | Negative Forms of the Verb *Be*

Negative Long Form	Negative Short Form	Negative Short Form
I **am not** sure.	I**'m not** sure.	
You **are not** serious.	You**'re not** serious.	You **aren't** serious.
She **is not** sure.	She**'s not** sure.	She **isn't** sure.
He **is not** at home.	He**'s not** at home.	He **isn't** at home.
The store **is not** small.	The store**'s not** small.	The store **isn't** small.
It **is not** crowded.	It**'s not** crowded.	It **isn't** crowded.
We **are not** in the Laundromat.	We**'re not** in the Laundromat.	We **aren't** in the Laundromat.
They **are not** on sale.	They**'re not** on sale.	They **aren't** on sale.

Language Note: There is only one negative short form for a plural noun + **are**.
   The cookies **aren't** free.

Compare affirmative and negative.	
Affirmative	**Negative**
We **are** at the supermarket.	We **aren't** at home.
The cheese **is** fresh.	It **isn't** old.
I **am** new here.	I**'m not** sure about many things.
The samples **are** free.	The cookies **aren't** free.
You **are** from the U.S.	You**'re not** confused.
Halina **is** a new immigrant.	Dorota **isn't** a new immigrant.

16   Unit 1

Expansion

Listening Activity Create false affirmative statements about the class, such as: *[Maria] is a U.S. citizen.* Say the sentences out loud and have volunteers give you the true negative statement. ([Maria] isn't a U.S. citizen.)

Grammar Chart Have students create negative statements from the affirmative statements in the comparison chart. (e.g. We aren't in the supermarket.)

EXERCISE 1 Fill in the blanks with a negative form of the underlined verbs. Use short forms.

EXAMPLE   The supermarket is big. It __isn't__ small.

1. The date is on packages. The date __isn't__ or __'s not__ on fruit.
2. We're at the supermarket. We __aren't__ or __'re not__ at the Laundromat.
3. Bananas are 29¢ this week. They __aren't__ or __'re not__ 29¢ every week.
4. I'm in the supermarket. I __'m not__ in the Laundromat.
5. The store is empty. It __isn't__ or __'s not__ crowded.
6. You're helpful. You __aren't__ or __'re not__ confused.
7. Prices are on the shelves. They __aren't__ or __'re not__ on the products.
8. The sample cookies are free. The bags of cookies __aren't__ free.

EXERCISE 2 Check the true statements. Change the other statements to the negative. Answers may vary.

EXAMPLE   ____✓____ Supermarkets are big.
          _____ I'm a new immigrant. *I'm not a new immigrant.*

Answers will vary.
1. _____ I'm confused about supermarkets.
2. _____ Life in the U.S. is easy.
3. _____ Supermarkets are clean.
4. _____ Americans are helpful.
5. _____ Supermarkets are crowded in the morning.
6. _____ Bags are free.
7. _____ Supermarkets are noisy.
8. _____ Prices are the same every week.

Lesson 3   17

EXERCISE 1

1. Have students read the direction line. Ask: *What do you fill in the blanks with?* (The negative of the underlined verb.) Go over the example in the book. Do #1 with the class.
2. Have students complete the rest of Exercise 1 individually. Go over answers as a class.
3. If necessary, review grammar chart **1.6** on page 16.

EXERCISE 2

1. Have students read the direction line. Go over the examples in the book. Point out the photo of the supermarket on page 17. Use the picture to help answer questions about vocabulary.
2. Have students complete Exercise 2 individually. Then have students compare answers in pairs.
3. If necessary, review grammar chart **1.6** on page 16.

Exercise 1 Variation

Have students negate each beginning statement with a contraction. (e.g., The supermarket isn't big.) Remind students that *I am not* can only be contracted one way—*I'm not*. Also, reiterate that there is only one negative short form for a plural noun + *are*.

Unit **1**   17

1.7 | Adjectives

1. Say: *Adjectives describe nouns. For example, they tell if a thing or person is big or small, hot or cold.* Write on the board: *The parking lot is empty.* Ask: *What word is the noun?* (parking lot) *What word describes the noun?* (empty) *Empty is an adjective. It describes the parking lot.*
2. Have students look at grammar chart **1.7** on page 18. Go over the examples. Point out that adjectives come after the verb *be* and that they can also come before a noun. Ask: *What are the adjectives in these sentences?* (empty, crowded, free, big) *Are the adjectives before or after the verb* be? (after) *Are the adjectives before or after the nouns?* (before)
3. Point out the Language Note. Review the rule and the examples. Write these sentences on the board:
    1. *Those are bigs washing machines.*
    2. *Those are big washing machines.*
   Ask: *Which sentence is correct?* (Sentence 2 is correct.) *Why?* (You can't make adjectives plural.) Stress to students that adjectives in English do not show number (plural or singular) or gender (feminine, masculine, neutral).

EXERCISE 3

1. Tell students they are going to read two conversations about supermarkets and Laundromats. Have students read the direction line. Go over the example in the book.
2. Have students complete Exercise 3 individually. Then have students compare answers in pairs.
3. If necessary, review grammar chart **1.7** on page 18.

1.7 | Adjectives

An **adjective** gives a description of a noun.

Examples	Explanation
Subject / Be / Adjective The parking lot / is / **empty.** The store / isn't / **crowded.** The samples / are / **free.**	An adjective can follow the verb *be*. subject + *be* + (*not*) + adjective
Those are **free** samples. These are **big** packages.	An adjective can come before a noun. adjective + noun
Language Note: Descriptive adjectives are always singular. Only the noun is plural. one **free** sample two **free** samples	

EXERCISE 3 In each of the conversations below, fill in the blanks with an adjective from the box.

Vocabulary for Conversation A

| new ✓ | early | helpful | different |
| crowded | easy | big | |

Conversation A: Halina and Dorota are at the supermarket.

Halina: I'm ___new___ to this country. Everything is
   (example)
___different___ for me.
   (1)
Dorota: Don't worry. I'm here with you.
Halina: You're very ___helpful___.
   (2)
Dorota: This is the supermarket. It's ___easy___ to shop in a
   (3)
supermarket.
Halina: This supermarket is ___big___. In my country, stores are
   (4)
small.
Dorota: Bananas are on sale this week; only 29¢ a pound.
Halina: The supermarket and the parking lot aren't ___crowded___. Why
   (5)
not?
Dorota: It's only 10 a.m. It's ___early___.
   (6)

Expansion

Exercise 3 Have students practice the conversations in pairs. Ask volunteers to roleplay the conversations in front of the class.

Vocabulary for Conversation B

small	open	different
hot	big	

Conversation B: Simon is showing a new immigrant, Victor, the Laundromat.

Simon: This is the Laundromat.
Victor: It's ___hot___ in here.
              (7)
Simon: Yes, it is. But the door is ___open___.
                                    (8)
Victor: Some machines are ___small___ and some are ___big___.
                           (9)   (10)
Simon: The big machines are for big items, like blankets.
Victor: All of these machines are the same, but those are ___different___.
                                                          (11)
Simon: These are washing machines. Those machines are dryers.
Victor: In my country, sometimes my wife is the washer and the air is the dryer!

1.8 | Expressions with *It*

Examples	Explanation
It's hot in the Laundromat. **It's** cold outside.	Use *it* with weather or temperature.
It's 10 a.m. **It's** early. **It** isn't late.	Use *it* with time.
It's easy **to wash** clothes at the Laundromat. **It** isn't hard. **It's** early. **It's** a good time **to shop**.	Use *it* with impersonal expressions: *it's easy, it's hard, it's good*. A *to*-phrase often follows.

EXERCISE 4 Fill in the blanks with one of the words from the list below. Answers may vary.

early	important	necessary	easy ✓
hard	good	hot	

Lesson 3   19

1.8 | Expressions with *It*

1. Have students look at grammar chart **1.8** on page 19. Go over the examples and explanations in the chart. Demonstrate the meaning of *temperature:* Draw a thermometer on the board. Draw an arrow going up, say *hot*, and mime sweating. Draw an arrow going down, shiver, and say *cold*.
2. Stress that a *to* phrase often follows an impersonal expression with *it*. Define *easy* and *hard* and give more examples: *It's hard to learn English. It's easy to speak [student's language]*. Say: Easy *means no problem*. Hard *means not easy*. Ask: *What is easy? It's easy to _____*. Write students' ideas on the board. Repeat for *hard*.

EXERCISE 4

1. Have students read the direction line. Check that students know the meanings of the adjectives in the box. Elicit things that are *necessary* or *important*, or look at your watch and ask if the time is *early* or late. Use the pictures to remind students the meanings of the words on page 20. Go over the example.
2. Have students complete Exercise 4 individually. Go over the answers with the class.
3. If necessary, review grammar chart **1.7** on page 18 and grammar chart **1.8** on page 19.

Expansion

Exercise 4 Take a class survey. Find out if students agree with the statements in the exercise. Ask: *Is it hard or easy to live in a new country?* Write students' responses on the board.

Unit 1   19

1.9 | Singular and Plural

1. Have students look at grammar chart **1.9** on page 20.
2. Go over the examples and explanations. Pronounce the singular and plural forms. Remind students that the *–es* on nouns that end in *–sh* and *–ch* is pronounced as an extra syllable.
3. Write additional examples on the board: *glass, desk, way,* and *knife.* Ask volunteers to form the plural. (glasses, desks, ways, knives)
4. Point out the Pronunciation Note. Review the rule. Say: *With some noun endings we need to pronounce an extra syllable when we add –s. Nouns that end in /s/ and /z/ sounds have an extra syllable in the plural.* Pronounce the example words. Write these additional pairs of singular/plural nouns on the board: *rose > roses, hose > hoses, ace > aces, race > races.* Pronounce the pairs and have students repeat.

EXERCISE 5

1. Have students read the direction line. Go over the example.
2. Have students complete Exercise 5 individually. Then go over the answers with the class.
3. If necessary, review grammar chart **1.9** on page 20.

EXAMPLE It's ____easy____ to fill in the blanks.

1. It's ____hot____ today.
2. It's ____early____. It's only 9:45. My class is at 10:00.
3. It isn't ____hard____ to live in a new country.
4. It's ____important____ to learn English in the U.S.
5. It's ____good____ to learn a new language.
6. It isn't ____necessary____ to work and go to school.

1.9 | Singular and Plural

Singular	Plural	Rule
coin dime dollar	coin**s** dime**s** dollar**s**	Add *-s* to form the plural of most nouns.
dish watch	dish**es** watch**es**	Add *-es* to make the plural of nouns that end in *-sh* and *-ch*. Pronounce an extra syllable.
family baby	famil**ies** bab**ies**	Change final *y* to *i* and add *-es* when a word ends in a consonant + *y*.
day toy	day**s** toy**s**	Add only *-s* when a word ends in a vowel + *y*.
shelf life	shel**ves** li**ves**	Change final *f* or *fe* to *–ves*.

Pronunciation Note: Sometimes we need to pronounce an extra syllable. Listen to your teacher pronounce these words.
price—prices   noise—noises

EXERCISE 5 Fill in the blanks with the plural form of the noun in parentheses ( ).

EXAMPLE The ____cars____ are in the parking lot.
(car)

1. The ____prices____ are under the ____shelves____.
(price)   (shelf)
2. The ____matches____ are on the shelf.
(match)
3. Some ____babies____ are in the supermarket today.
(baby)
4. It's Saturday and many ____families____ are at the supermarket.
(family)
5. The soap for washing ____dishes____ costs $1.89.
(dish)
6. The ____bananas____ are on sale this week.
(banana)

20   Unit 1

Expansion

Grammar Chart Have students practice the pronunciation of the nouns in pairs. Circulate to observe pair work and to help with pronunciation.

EDITING ADVICE

1. Use the correct form of *be*.
   You ~~is~~ *are* at the Laundromat.
2. Every sentence has a subject.
   ~~Is~~ *It's* 10:15 a.m.
   ~~Is~~ *It's* important to know English.
   ~~Is~~ *It's* hot in the Laundromat.
3. Don't confuse *this* and *these*.
   ~~This~~ *These* are big machines.
4. In a short form (contraction), put the apostrophe in place of the missing letter.
   Your'e → *You're* late.
5. Use an apostrophe, not a comma, in a short form (contraction).
   I,m → *I'm* at the supermarket.
6. Don't make adjectives plural.
   These are ~~bigs~~ machines.

EDITING QUIZ

Find the mistakes with the underlined words, and correct them. Not every sentence has a mistake. If the sentence is correct, write *C*.

EXAMPLES We <u>is</u> late. *are*
The <u>supermarket</u> <u>is</u> big. *C*

1. <u>Is</u> easy to use <u>this</u> dryers. *It's / these*
2. You <u>are'n't</u> late.
3. <u>She's not</u> in the bank. *C*
4. <u>This</u> machines are empty. *These*
5. <u>We</u> are <u>new</u> immigrants. *C*
6. <u>Is</u> hot inside the Laundromat. *It's*
7. The machines are <u>hots</u>.
8. <u>I,m</u> late.
9. <u>You'r'e</u> helpful.

Lesson 3   21

Editing Advice

1. Have students close their books. Write the example sentences without editing marks or corrections on the board. For example:
   1. You is at the Laundromat.
   2. Is 10:15 a.m.
   Ask students to correct each sentence. This activity can be done individually, in pairs, or as a class. After students have corrected each sentence, tell them to turn to page 21. Say: *Now compare your work with Editing Advice in the book.*
2. Go over answers with the class. For troublespots, review the appropriate grammar chart.

Editing Quiz

1. The Editing Quiz may be used as an in-class quiz, a take-home quiz, or as a review. Have students read the direction line. Ask: *Does every sentence have a mistake?* (no) Go over the examples with the class.
2. Have students complete the quiz individually. Collect the completed quizzes for assessment or have students check each other's work. Review the answers with the class. Elicit the relevant grammar point for each correction. For example, for #1 (Answer: *It's* ~~Is~~ *easy to use* ~~this~~*these dryers.*), ask: *Why do we use It's?* (Use *it* with impersonal expressions.) Then ask: *Why do we change this to these?* (*Dryers* is plural.)

Learner's Log

1. Have students close their books. Ask: *What did you learn about American Laundromats and supermarkets in this unit? What else do you want to know about them?* Prompt students with questions, such as: *How much does it cost to wash clothes? Do vegetables go on sale?* Write ideas on the board. Discuss ways in which students can find out more about Laundromats and supermarkets.
2. Have students open their books to complete the Learner's Log.

Expansion Activities

These expansion activities provide opportunities for students to interact with one another and further develop their speaking and writing skills. Encourage students to use grammar from this unit whenever possible.

To save class time, assign parts of the activities as homework. Then use class time for interaction and communication. If students do not need additional speaking practice, some of the activities may be assigned as writing activities for homework, or skipped altogether.

WRITING ACTIVITY

1. Point out the picture of the display of apples in a supermarket. Say: *The paragraph in this activity is about different kinds of apples.* Have students read the direction line. Go over the example.
2. Have students complete the activity individually at home or in class.
3. Collect for assessment.

OUTSIDE ACTIVITIES

Have the class share their experiences of going to a supermarket and Laundromat.

INTERNET ACTIVITY

Have students get into groups to tell each other what prices and common items they found at online supermarkets or other stores.

LEARNER'S LOG

1. What did you learn in this unit? Write three sentences in your notebook about each topic.
   - An American Laundromat
   - An American supermarket
   - Items in an American supermarket
2. Write three questions you still have about the Laundromat or supermarket.

EXPANSION ACTIVITIES

Writing Activity

Rewrite the following paragraph in your notebook. Change the singular nouns and pronouns to plurals. Change other necessary words, too.

This is a yellow apple. It's on sale. It's very big. It's only 75¢ a pound. That is a red apple. It isn't on sale. It's not very big. It's 75¢ a pound too. This is a free sample of the yellow apple. It's not very fresh. That's a free sample of the red apple. It is fresh. The red apple is good. The yellow apple isn't good today.

EXAMPLE *These are yellow apples.*

Outside Activities

1. Go to a supermarket in your neighborhood. Find an item on sale. Tell the class the usual price and the sale price. Find an item with samples. Tell the class the name of the item and the price.
2. Go to a Laundromat in your neighborhood. Tell the class the name and location. Find the price to wash and dry clothes.

Internet Activity

Search the words *online grocery store* or *online supermarket*. Find a common item. Find the price in two different online stores. Tell the class about the item and the prices.

Expansion

Learner's Log Have students compare logs in pairs.

Writing Activity Variation

Have students exchange papers with a partner for proofreading.

Internet Activity Variation

Tell students that if they don't have Internet access, they can use Internet facilities at a public library. Alternatively, students who have no access to the Internet can look for prices in store and supermarket circulars.

UNIT 2

GRAMMAR
Possessive Nouns
Possessive Adjectives
Irregular Plural Forms
Be—*Yes/No* Questions and Short Answers
Be—Information Questions
Articles *A/An*

CONTEXT
Time and Money

Expansion

Theme The topic for this unit can be enhanced with the following ideas:

1. A watch, a digital clock, and a clock whose hands can be moved easily
2. A large calendar with holidays circled
3. A list of popular banks in the area
4. A list of services banks provide

Unit | 2
Unit Overview

GRAMMAR

1. Ask: *What did we study in Unit 1?* (subject pronouns, *be*; contractions, singular and plural, *this/that/these/those*, adjectives, and expressions with *it*) *What will we study in Unit 2?* Point out the objectives in the Student Book. Give examples of each objective and write them on the board.
2. Activate students' prior knowledge. Ask: *What are some subject pronouns and possessive adjectives?* Write examples on the board, such as: *I > my*. Write *Information Questions* and *Yes/No Questions* on the board. Then write the following: *Where is my class? Who is my teacher? Is this English class? Are you a student?* Say the questions. Ask volunteers to answer them. Say: *Yes/No questions get short answers. Information questions get long answers.*

CONTEXT

1. Say: *This unit is about time and money.* Point to your wrist. *I [do/don't] wear a watch. I [always/never] know what time it is. What about you? Is time important?*
2. Direct students' attention to the photos. Ask: *Where is this? There are many clocks.* (a park) *Who has a watch?* (a man) *What's he doing?* (checking the time) *Where are the woman and man?* (in a bank) *What do you get at a bank?* (money) *What are some American banks?* Write names of popular banks on the board. Circle the one you use. Say: *This is my bank.*

Unit 2   23

Lesson 1 | Overview

GRAMMAR

1. Write on the board: *Possessive Nouns*. Touch a student's chair and say: *[Juan]'s chair*. Write the words on the board. Underline the possessive noun. Say: *This is a possessive noun.*
2. Go around the room touching different students' chairs and using the possessive noun.
3. Touch your chair and say: *My chair*. Write the words on the board. Underline the possessive adjective. Say: *This is a possessive adjective.*

CONTEXT

1. Direct students' attention to the picture. Say: *There is a clock in the car, and Victor has a watch.*
2. Point to your watch or to a clock in the classroom. Say: *It's [time]*. Ask: *Who has a watch?* Walk around looking at the students' watches and say the time followed by: *Your watch is slow/fast.* Emphasize the time difference between the clock on the wall and each student's watch.

BEFORE YOU READ

1. Go over each statement as a class. Have a volunteer read the statements or read them to the class yourself. Ask students to circle *yes* or *no*.
2. Ask for a few volunteers to share their answers with the class.

 To save class time, skip "Before You Read" or have students prepare answers for homework ahead of time.

LESSON 1

GRAMMAR
Possessive Nouns
Possessive Adjectives

CONTEXT
My Clock Is Fast

Before You Read

Circle *yes* or *no*.

1. I use a watch every day.   YES   NO
2. I have a clock in every room of my house.   YES   NO

24   Unit 2

Culture Note
Daylight savings time is the expression used for the practice in the U.S. of turning the clock back in the fall or forward in the spring to "save daylight."

---

24   *Grammar in Context Basic* Teacher's Edition

MY CLOCK IS FAST

It's **Simon's** turn to help Victor today. But Simon is home. **His** wife, Marta, is at the hospital. **Marta's** father is sick. **Simon's** kids are home because today is a school holiday. So Dorota is here to help Victor at the bank.

Dorota: Hi, Victor. I'm here.
Victor: And Simon?
Dorota: He's busy. He's with **his** kids today. **Their** school is closed for a holiday. **His** wife is at the hospital with **her** father.
Victor: It's late. Look at **your** clock. It's 4:30. The bank is closed.
Dorota: No, it isn't. **My** clock is fast. It's only 4:15.
Victor: So **your** clock is broken.
Dorota: No, it isn't. **My** clock is always fast. And **my** watch is always fast. That way I'm always on time.
Victor: I'm confused. **Your** clock is fast, and that's OK with you?
Dorota: Yes. I'm never late. Time is important for Americans. **Their** ideas about time are different from **our** ideas about time.
Dorota: We're here now. Oh, no. The bank is closed. Today is a holiday. It's Columbus Day. Come again tomorrow with Simon.

Vocabulary in Context

turn	It's Simon's **turn** to help.
wife	Simon has a **wife**. Her name is Marta.
kid(s)	**Kids** are children.
holiday	It's a **holiday**. The school is closed.
clock	Look at the **clock**. It's 4:30.
fast	Your clock is **fast**.
on time	You're **on time**. You're not late.
broken	My clock isn't **broken**.
watch	My **watch** is fast. It's 4:15.

Lesson 1   25

My Clock is Fast (Reading) CD 1, Track 7

1. Have students look at the picture. Ask: *What's his name?* (Simon) *Who are these people?* (His family) Have students look at the title of the reading. Ask: *Where is Victor? Who is he with? What is the reading about?* Have students use the title and picture to make predictions about the reading.
2. Have students read the text silently. Then play the audio and have students read along.
3. Check students' basic comprehension. Ask questions, such as: *Is Simon helping Victor today?* (No, Dorota is.) *Is the bank open?* (no)

To save class time, have students do the reading for homework ahead of time.

VOCABULARY IN CONTEXT

1. Model the pronunciation of each new vocabulary word and have students repeat.
2. Make sure students understand the meaning of each vocabulary word. Review the examples in the book and create additional example sentences. For example, say: *kids. These are my kids.* (Show a picture if possible.) Then ask: *Do you have kids?* Have volunteers share information. Go over each new vocabulary word similarly, using visuals and realia when appropriate. When possible, point to pictures in the book that illustrate new vocabulary items, such as *wife* on page 25 and *watch* on page 24.
3. Have students underline an example of each word in the reading.

Reading Variation

1. To practice listening skills, have students listen to the audio before opening their books. Ask a few comprehension questions: *Where is Simon?* (at home) *Where is Marta?* (at the hospital) Repeat the audio if necessary. Then have students open their books and read along as they listen to the audio.
2. Alternatively, have students begin by listening to the audio as they read along.

Vocabulary Teaching Ideas

Use the following ideas to teach these terms:

turn: Ask students one at a time to do a task, such as go to the board and write his/her name. Point to another student and say: *OK, your turn. Please write your name.*
broken: Bring in a broken clock or use a pen without a spring or ink cartridge. Mime trying to use the object, but failing, several times.

Expansion

Reading Have students practice the conversation in pairs. Ask volunteers to roleplay the conversation in front of the class.
Vocabulary in Context To check comprehension, have volunteers use vocabulary in sentences. (e.g., Sports cars are fast.) Write students' examples on the board.

Unit **2**   25

DID YOU KNOW?

Tell students about some customs of popular holidays, such as these:

New Year's Eve: celebrations with toasting and kissing at midnight
Thanksgiving: family gatherings with turkey and pumpkin pie
Christmas: exchanging gifts, singing carols, and decorating homes with lights

LISTENING ACTIVITY

🎧 **CD 1, Track 8**

1. Say: *Listen to the sentences about Dorota and Victor at the bank. Circle* true *or* false. Play the listening selection one time without pausing. Then play it through again, pausing and replaying as necessary.
2. Go over the answers as a class. Ask students to volunteer answers.

2.1 | Possessive Nouns

Have students look at grammar chart 2.1. Review the rule and examples. Stress that an apostrophe + *s* means ownership. Say: *Whose wife?* (Simon's) *Whose father?* (Marta's). Go around the room and point to students' objects. Say: *[Maria's] desk. Whose desk?* (Maria's) Write the examples on the board.

EXERCISE 1

1. Have students read the direction line. Go over the example in the Student Book. Direct students to the picture of the clock in Dorota's car on page 24.
2. Have students complete Exercise 1 individually. Check the answers as a class. Note that for #5, two answers are possible (Simon's, Marta's). If necessary, review grammar chart 2.1 on page 26.

EXERCISE 2

1. Have students read the direction line. Go over the example in the Student Book. Direct students to the picture of Simon's family on page 25.
2. Have students complete Exercise 2 individually. Have them compare answers in pairs when they have finished. Circulate to observe pair work. If necessary, review grammar chart 2.1 on page 26.

Did You Know?
- On national holidays, the post office and most schools and banks are closed. Some businesses are open.
- Some American holidays are: New Year's Day, President's Day, Memorial Day, Independence Day, Labor Day, Thanksgiving, and Christmas.

🎧 **Listening Activity** Listen to the sentences about the conversation. Circle *true* or *false*.

EXAMPLE (TRUE) FALSE

1. TRUE (FALSE)   4. (TRUE) FALSE
2. TRUE (FALSE)   5. TRUE   (FALSE)
3. TRUE (FALSE)   6. (TRUE) FALSE

2.1 | Possessive Nouns

Examples	Explanation
Simon's wife is at the hospital. **Marta's** father is sick. **Dorota's** clock isn't broken.	Use noun + *'s* to show ownership or relationship.

EXERCISE 1 Fill in the blanks with the correct form: *Marta's, Simon's,* or *Dorota's*.

EXAMPLE   __Dorota's__ clock is fast.

1. __Simon's__ wife is Marta.
2. __Marta's__ father is sick.
3. Today it's __Simon's__ turn to help, but he's at home with the kids.
4. __Dorota's__ language is Polish.
5. __Simon's__ language is Spanish.

EXERCISE 2 Fill in the blanks. Put the words in the correct order. Add an apostrophe (').

EXAMPLE   (kids/Simon) __Simon's kids__ aren't in school today.

1. (son/Victor) __Victor's son__ isn't with him.
2. (children/Simon) __Simon's children__ are at home.
3. (father/Marta) __Marta's father__ is sick.
4. That's (car/Dorota) __Dorota's car__.

Expansion

Listening Activity Create statements about the class: *[Ahmed] is usually late.* Say the sentences out loud and have students write *true* or *false* on a piece of paper. Go over the answers as a class.

Exercises 1 and 2 Have students work in pairs to create sentences about the class using possessive nouns. (e.g., Jean-Pierre's children are at home.)

2.2 | Possessive Adjectives

Compare subject pronouns and possessive adjectives.

Examples	Explanation
I am late. **My** watch is slow.	I → **My**
You are late. **Your** watch is slow.	You → **Your**
He is late. **His** watch is slow.	He → **His**
She is late. **Her** watch is slow.	She → **Her**
We are late. **Our** clock is slow.	We → **Our**
They are late. **Their** clock is slow.	They → **Their**

EXERCISE 3 Fill in the blanks with *my, your, his, her, our,* or *their.*

EXAMPLE You are with __your__ kids.

1. She is with __her__ kids.
2. They are with __their__ kids.
3. I am with __my__ kids.
4. He is with __his__ kids.
5. We are with __our__ kids.

EXERCISE 4 ABOUT YOU Circle *true* or *false.*

Answers will vary.
1. My watch is correct.   TRUE   FALSE
2. Time is important to me.   TRUE   FALSE
3. Money is important to me.   TRUE   FALSE
4. I am with my classmates. Their language is different from my language.   TRUE   FALSE
5. My teacher's name is hard for me.   TRUE   FALSE

EXERCISE 5 Simon and Dorota are on the telephone. Fill in the blanks with *my, your, his, her, their,* or *our.*

Simon: Hi, Dorota. This is Simon. I'm busy today. Marta's busy too. __Her__ (1) father is sick. __Our__ (2) kids are at home today. __Their__ (3) school is closed. It's __my__ (4) turn to help Victor today, but I'm busy.

Dorota: That's OK. __Your__ (5) kids need you. I'm not busy today.

Lesson 1   27

Expansion

Exercise 4 Do a class survey. How did students respond to each question? Write the results on the board.

Exercise 5 Have students practice the conversation in pairs. Ask volunteers to roleplay the conversation in front of the class.

Have students work in pairs to create a similar conversation. Ask volunteers to roleplay their new conversations in front of the class.

2.2 | Possessive Adjectives

1. Have students close their books. Elicit subject pronouns. Begin by saying *I, you.* Write the pronouns on the board. Then write *my* next to *I.* Point to your chair and say: *My chair.* Touch a student's chair and say: *Your chair.* Write *your* on the board next to *you.*
2. Have students look at grammar chart **2.2** on page 27. Say: *Now let's study possessive adjectives.* Review the examples and explanations. Elicit and write on the board the remaining possessive adjectives next to the appropriate subject pronouns.

EXERCISE 3

1. Have students read the direction line. Go over the example in the Student Book. Have a volunteer do #1.
2. Have students complete the rest of Exercise 3 individually. Go over the answers as a class.
3. If necessary, review grammar chart **2.2** on page 27.

EXERCISE 4

1. Say: *This exercise is about you.* Have students read the direction line. Have a volunteer do #1.
2. Have students complete the rest of Exercise 4 individually. Then have students compare answers with a partner. Circulate to observe pair work. Give help as needed.
3. If necessary, review grammar chart **2.2** on page 27.

EXERCISE 5

1. Have students read the direction line. Direct students to the picture on page 27. Say: *Simon and Dorota are talking on the phone.*
2. Have students complete Exercise 5 individually. Have students compare answers in pairs. Circulate to observe pair work. Give help as needed.
3. If necessary, review grammar chart **2.2** on page 27.

To save class time, have students complete the exercise for homework.

Lesson 2 | Overview

GRAMMAR

1. Elicit a *yes/no* response by asking a student: *Are you [name]?* Say: *That's a yes/no question.* Go around the room asking the same question.
2. Say: *In this lesson we're going to learn about yes/no questions and short answers. We're also going to learn more about the singular and plural forms of nouns.*

CONTEXT

1. Say: *In this lesson we're going to talk about time and money. Americans say, "Time is money." What does this mean?* (Time is important; being late makes people lose money.)
2. Say: *Sometimes I'm fifteen minutes late for class. Is it OK to be late for appointments? Is it important to be on time in your country?* Have students share their ideas and experiences. If students say it is OK to be late, encourage them to say by how long (e.g., Twenty minutes is OK. One hour is not OK.)
3. Direct students' attention to the picture. Ask: *What's wrong with Simon?* (He's worried because he's late.)

BEFORE YOU READ

1. Go over each statement as a class. Have a volunteer read the statements or read them to the class yourself. Ask students to circle *yes* or *no*.
2. Ask for a few volunteers to share their answers with the class.

   To save class time, skip "Before You Read" or have students prepare their answers for homework ahead of time.

LESSON 2

GRAMMAR
Yes/No Questions and Short Answers
Singular and Plural—Irregular Forms

CONTEXT
Time Is Money

Before You Read

Circle *yes* or *no*.

1. I'm usually on time. YES   NO
2. My doctor is usually on time. YES   NO

28 Unit 2

Culture Note

Being on time is very important in the U.S. If you are late for business and social occasions, it's considered rude and disrespectful. If you know you're going to be late by more than a few minutes, you should call and let the person know.

TIME IS MONEY

Simon: **Am I late?** I'm sorry. Traffic is bad today.
Victor: You're not late. It's only 10:15.
Simon: Oh, I'm 15 minutes late, then. I'm sorry.
Victor: Fifteen minutes is nothing.
Simon: In the U.S., people are usually on time.
Victor: Really? **Are you serious?**
Simon: Yes, I am.
Victor: **Are people on time for everything?**
Simon: For most things. They're on time for appointments.
Victor: **Is this an appointment?**
Simon: Yes, it is. I'm here to help you with the bank.
Victor: My doctor is never on time. She's always late.
Simon: That's different. Doctors are always behind schedule.
Victor: **Is it necessary to be on time with friends?**
Simon: It's not necessary, but it's polite.
Victor: Look. The time and temperature are outside the bank. **Is time always on your mind?**
Simon: Yes, it is. "Time is money." Time is always on our minds.

Vocabulary in Context

traffic	I'm late. **Traffic** is bad today.
serious	Are you **serious**? Is it true?
appointment	She has an **appointment** with her doctor.
behind schedule	The doctor is **behind schedule.**
polite	It's **polite** to say "please" and "thank you."
temperature	The **temperature** is 75 degrees today.
on (my, your) mind	Time is always **on my mind.** I think about it a lot.
usually	Students are **usually** on time for class.
never	Some people are **never** on time.
always	Some people are **always** late.

Lesson 2 29

Time is Money (Reading)
🎧 *CD 1, Track 9*

1. Say: *Do you remember the conversation in Lesson 1? Dorota and Victor go to the bank. Was the bank open?* (no) *Why?* (It was Columbus Day, a holiday.) *What's happening now? Is the bank open?* (yes) *Is Simon on time?* (no) Have students look at the title of the reading. Ask: *What is the reading about? What do you think Simon says to Victor? What does Victor say?* Have students use the title and picture to make predictions about the reading.
2. First, have students read the dialogue silently. Then play the audio and have students read along.
3. Check students' basic comprehension. Ask true or false questions, such as: *Simon is late. True or false?* (true) *People in the U.S. are always late. True or false?* (false)

🕐 To save class time, have students do the reading for homework ahead of time.

VOCABULARY IN CONTEXT

1. Model the pronunciation of each new vocabulary word and have students repeat.
2. Make sure students understand the meaning of each vocabulary word. Review the examples in the book and create additional example sentences. For example, say: *on my mind. I think about my students every day. You're always on my mind.* On the board, draw a teacher with a thought bubble. In the thought bubbles, draw students. Go over each new vocabulary word similarly, using visuals and realia when appropriate. When possible, point to pictures in the book that illustrate the new vocabulary items, such as *traffic* and *temperature* on page 28.
3. Have students underline an example of each new vocabulary item in the reading.

Reading Variation

1. To practice listening skills, have students listen to the audio before opening their books. Ask a few comprehension questions: *Is Simon late?* (yes) *Are doctors ever on time?* (no) Repeat the audio if necessary. Then have students open their books and read along as they listen to the audio.
2. Alternatively, have students begin by listening to the audio as they read along.

Vocabulary Teaching Ideas

Use the following ideas to teach this term:

appointment: Draw a page from a desk calendar that includes specific times on the board. Write in: "Appointment with Dr. Garcia" in one of the time slots.

Say: *Use appointment for business and medical meetings.*

Expansion

Reading Have students practice the conversation in pairs. Ask volunteers to roleplay the conversation in front of the class.
Vocabulary in Context To check comprehension, have volunteers in pairs or groups act out selected vocabulary, such as *serious*, *polite*, and *on my mind*.

Unit 2 29

DID YOU KNOW?

Explain to students why the U.S. continues to use Fahrenheit to measure temperature. Say: *Fahrenheit was invented in 1714. Celsius was invented in 1742 and many countries began to use Celsius. Today, English-speaking countries say it is too expensive to change. Also, the U.S. and Great Britain like the old Fahrenheit system and do not want to change it.*

LISTENING ACTIVITY

🎧 **CD 1, Track 10**

1. Say: *Listen to the questions about Simon and Victor at the bank. Circle the correct short answer.* Play the listening selection one time without pausing. Then play it through again, pausing and replaying as necessary.
2. Go over the answers as a class. Ask students to volunteer answers.

2.3 | *Yes/No* Questions and Short Answers

1. Have students look at grammar chart **2.3** on page 30. Review the questions and answers in the chart. Explain that in a question, the verb comes before the subject. Point out that only the subject and the verb are included in a short answer.
2. Compare statements and questions with *be*. Ask volunteers to point out the differences between the statements and the questions (the position of subjects and verbs is reversed).
3. Point out the Pronunciation Note. Explain that *yes/no* questions have rising intonation. Demonstrate with the example sentences in both charts.
4. Point out the Punctuation Note. Ask: *What punctuation goes at the end of a question?* (question mark)

Did You Know?
- Americans use Fahrenheit (F) for temperature. Other countries use Celsius (C).
- American banks often show time and temperature.

🎧 **Listening Activity** — Listen to the following questions about the conversation. Circle the correct answer.

EXAMPLE (Yes, it is.)   No, it isn't.

1. Yes, he is.   (No, he isn't.)
2. (Yes, they are.)   No, they aren't.
3. Yes, they are.   (No, they aren't.)
4. Yes, it is.   (No, it isn't.)
5. Yes, they are.   (No, they aren't.)

2.3 | *Yes/No* Questions and Short Answers

Put the form of *be* before the subject to ask a question.

Be	Subject	Complement	Short Answer
Am	I	late?	No, you aren't.
Is	traffic	bad?	Yes, it is.
Is	Simon	on time?	No, he isn't.
Are	you	serious?	Yes, I am.
Are	they	at the bank?	Yes, they are.

Compare statements and questions with *be*.

Statements	Questions
I am late.	**Am I** very late?
Time is important.	**Is time** always on your mind?
People are on time.	**Are people** always on time?
It is necessary to be on time.	**Is it** necessary to be on time with friends?

Pronunciation Note: A *yes/no* question has rising intonation. Listen to your teacher pronounce the statements and the questions above.
Punctuation Note: Put a question mark (?) at the end of a question.

30   Unit 2

Expansion

Grammar Chart Have students turn to Vocabulary in Context on page 3. Say: *Make the statements into questions.* (e.g., Is Dorota a citizen of the United States?) Then ask students to write short answers for the questions. (Yes, she is.)

Review how to tell time with students. Use a clock with movable hands or draw a clock on the board. Elicit times from students. Write the times out on the board (e.g., It's three o'clock. It's 1:45. It's 12:30. It's twenty minutes til two.) Then ask *yes/no* questions about the times (e.g., *Is it six o'clock? Is it 1:40?*).

EXERCISE 1 Fill in the form of *be* and a noun or pronoun to make a question.

EXAMPLES <u>Are Simon and Victor</u> at the supermarket? No, they aren't.
<u>Are they</u> at the bank? Yes, they are.

1. <u>Is it</u> open? Yes, it is.
2. <u>Am I</u> late? No, you're not.
3. <u>Is it</u> necessary to be on time? No, it isn't.
4. <u>Are they</u> inside the bank? No, they aren't.
5. <u>Are we</u> on time? Yes, we are.
6. <u>Is he</u> polite? Yes, he is.

EXERCISE 2 Answer with a short answer.

EXAMPLE Is the bank open? <u>Yes, it is</u>.

1. Is Simon on time? <u>No, he isn't</u>.
2. Are Simon and Victor at the bank? <u>Yes, they are.</u>
3. Is Simon with Dorota? <u>No, he isn't</u>.
4. Are doctors usually on time? <u>No, they aren't</u>.
5. Is it necessary to be on time with friends? <u>No, it's not</u> or <u>No, it isn't</u>.
6. Are Americans usually late for appointments? <u>No, they aren't</u>.

EXERCISE 3 ABOUT YOU Answer with a short answer. You may work with a partner.

EXAMPLE Are you usually on time?
Yes, I am.

Answers will vary.
1. Are you confused about some things in this country?
2. Is your apartment big?
3. Are you a serious student?
4. Are you an immigrant?
5. Are you an American citizen?
6. Is this class easy for you?
7. Is English hard for you?
8. Are your classmates from your native country?
9. Is this your first English class?
10. Is your dictionary new?

Lesson 2   31

Expansion

Exercise 3 Take a class survey. How did students answer the questions? Write the results of the survey on the board.

EXERCISE 1

1. Have students read the direction line. Ask: *What do we write on the blanks?* (a noun or pronoun and a verb) Go over the examples in the book. Tell students that they must look at the answer to decide what the subject is.
2. Have students complete Exercise 1 individually. Go over the answers as a class.
3. If necessary, review grammar chart 2.3 on page 30.

EXERCISE 2

1. Tell students that this exercise is based on the reading. Have students read the direction line. Direct students to the picture of the bank on page 31. Ask: *Is the bank open or closed?* (open) Go over the example in the Student Book.
2. Have students complete Exercise 2 individually. Then have students check answers in pairs. Say: *Take turns asking and answering questions.* Circulate to observe pair work. Give help as needed.
3. If necessary, review grammar chart 2.3 on page 30.

To save class time, have students do the exercise for homework ahead of time.

EXERCISE 3

1. Say: *This exercise is about you.* Have students read the direction line. Go over the example in the Student Book. Model the example with a student volunteer. Then have a pair of volunteers model the example again.
2. Have students complete Exercise 3 orally in pairs. Say: *Take turns asking and answering questions.* Circulate to observe pair work. Give help as needed.
3. If necessary, review grammar chart 2.3 on page 30.

To save class time, have students do the exercise on a piece of paper for homework ahead of time.

Unit 2   31

EXERCISE 4

1. Tell students this exercise has two conversations: Conversation A and Conversation B. Explain that they will complete questions and answers. Point to the picture of Dorota and Victor in the car. Ask: *Where are Dorota and Victor?* (at the bank) Go over #1 and #2. Point out the question and answer blanks. Say: *Victor is asking a question. How do you know?* (question mark punctuation). Continue by saying: *In #1 Victor asks, Am I on time? How do you know?* (because he says "on time" and Dorota answers, "Yes, you are.") Tell students to use short *yes/no* answers to questions.
2. Have students complete the rest of Conversation A individually. Then point to the picture of Simon and Marta talking on the phone. Ask: *Are Simon and Marta together, in the same place?* (no) Have students complete Conversation B individually. Then have students compare answers in pairs.
3. If necessary, review grammar chart **2.3** on page 30.

EXERCISE 4 Fill in the blanks.

Conversation A: Dorota and Victor

Victor: __Am I__ (1) on time?
Dorota: Yes, you __are__ (2).
Victor: __Are we__ (3) at the bank?
Dorota: Yes, we __are__ (4). We're here to learn about the bank.
Victor: __Is it__ (5) open?
Dorota: No, it __isn't__ (6). It's only 8:48. We're a few minutes early.

Conversation B: Simon and Marta

Simon: Hello?
Marta: Hi, Simon.
Simon: __Are you__ (7) in the car?
Marta: No, I'm __not__ (8). I'm at the supermarket now.
Simon: It's 9 p.m. __Is it__ (9) open now?
Marta: Yes, it __is__ (10). This store is open 24 hours a day.
Simon: __Are you__ (11) serious?
Marta: Yes, I am.
Simon: We need bananas. __Are they__ (12) on sale?
Marta: Yes, they __are__ (13). They're only 29¢ a pound this week.
Simon: Buy bread too. __Is it__ (14) fresh?
Marta: Yes, it is. It's still warm.

32 Unit 2

Expansion

Exercise 4 Have students practice the conversations in pairs. Have volunteers roleplay the conversations in front of the class.

---

32 *Grammar in Context Basic* Teacher's Edition

2.4 | Singular and Plural—Irregular Forms

Singular	Plural	Explanation
child person	children people	Sometimes the plural form is a different word.
man woman	men women	Sometimes the plural form has a vowel change.

Pronunciation Note: You hear the difference between *woman* and *women* in the first syllable. Listen to your teacher pronounce the singular and plural forms.

EXERCISE 5 Fill in the blanks with the plural form of the noun in parentheses ( ).

EXAMPLE The __men__ are late.
(man)

1. Two __people__ are in front of the bank.
(person)
2. __Children__ are in the supermarket.
(child)
3. Two __women__ are in front of me.
(woman)
4. The __men__ are in line.
(man)

EXERCISE 6 Fill in the blanks with *is* or *are*.

EXAMPLE The people __are__ helpful.

1. The child __is__ with her mother.
2. The woman __is__ busy.
3. A person __is__ alone.
4. The people __are__ on time.
5. The children __are__ with their parents.
6. The man __is__ late.

Lesson 2   33

2.4 | Singular and Plural—Irregular Forms

1. Write the following examples on the board:

   person/people
   man/men

   Say: *Some plural forms are different words.* Point to #1. Say: *Some plural forms only have a vowel change.* Circle *a* in *man* in #2 and draw an arrow to *e* in *men*. Write *vowel* on the board.

2. Have students look at grammar chart **2.4** on page 33. Go over the singular and plural forms and the explanations.

3. Go over the Pronunciation Note. Model the pronunciation of *woman* and *women*. Then say: *I am going to say some words. For singular, hold up one hand. For plural, hold up two hands.* Say: *people/person, child/children, book/books, woman/women.*

EXERCISE 5

1. Have students read the direction line. Go over the example in the Student Book. Point out the picture of the men waiting in line. Explain the meaning of *ATM* if necessary.
2. Have students complete Exercise 5 individually. Go over the answers as a class.
3. If necessary, review grammar chart **2.4** on page 33.

EXERCISE 6

1. Have students read the direction line. Go over the example in the Student Book. Point out the picture of the man looking at his watch. Ask: *Is he early or late?*
2. Have students complete Exercise 6 individually. Then have students compare answers with a partner. Circulate to observe pair work. Give help as needed.
3. If necessary, review grammar charts **2.4** on page 33 and **1.2** on page 5.
   To save class time, have students do the exercise for homework ahead of time.

Unit 2   33

Lesson 3 | Overview

GRAMMAR

1. Say: *Listen to these questions: "Are you at the bank?" "Why are you at the bank?" Can you answer yes or no to both questions?* (no) *Which question wants information?* (the second) Activate prior knowledge. Ask: *What are some information question words?* (who, what, when, where, why) *What are some information questions?* Have volunteers work together to make a question. Write the question on the board.
2. Say: *We're also going to study the articles* a *and* an. Say: *This is a book. This is an envelope.* Ask: *Can you hear the difference between* a *and* an?

CONTEXT

1. Say: *We're going to talk about banks and money again. In the U.S. people often get money from an ATM. What is an ATM?* (a machine that gives money when you put in a special card) *Do people in your country use ATMs? How often?* Have volunteers share their knowledge and experiences with the class.
2. Direct students' attention to the picture. Ask: *What is happening in the picture? Where are they? Is it early or late? Why do people use ATMs?*

BEFORE YOU READ

1. Go over each statement as a class. Have a volunteer read the statements or read them to the class yourself. Ask students to circle *yes* or *no*.
2. Ask for a few volunteers to share their answers with the class.
   ⏱ To save class time, skip "Before You Read" or have students prepare answers for homework ahead of time.

LESSON 3

GRAMMAR
Information Questions
Articles *A/An*

CONTEXT
At the ATM

Before You Read

Circle *yes* or *no*.

1. I have a bank account.   YES   NO
2. I have an ATM card.   YES   NO

34   Unit 2

Expansion

Theme The topic for this unit can be enhanced with the following ideas:
1. An ATM card
2. Maps of the location of bank branches and/or ATM machines in the area.

---

34   *Grammar in Context Basic* Teacher's Edition

AT THE ATM

Dorota: Hi, Victor. **How are you?**
Victor: Fine, thanks. **Where are we?**
Dorota: We're at the First Community Bank.
Victor: **What time is it?**
Dorota: It's 7:30 p.m. The bank is closed now.
Victor: **When is the bank open?**
Dorota: This bank is open from 9 to 4, Monday through Thursday. It's open from 9 to 7 on Friday and 9 to 1 on Saturday.
Victor: **Who's that woman inside?**
Dorota: She's a security guard.
Victor: **Why are we here?**
Dorota: I need cash. I need to go to the supermarket. The ATM is always open.
Victor: **What's an ATM?**
Dorota: ATM means Automatic Teller Machine. It's a machine for cash.
Victor: **What's that?**
Dorota: This is my bank card. It's the key to open the door and get cash.
Victor: Is it easy to get cash?
Dorota: Yes, it is. But a PIN is necessary. And cash in your account, of course!
Victor: **What's a PIN?**
Dorota: It's a personal identification number.
Victor: **What's your PIN?**
Dorota: That's a secret!

Vocabulary in Context

security guard	The **security guard** is in the bank.
ATM	The **ATM** is always open.
cash	We are at the bank. We need **cash**.
PIN	A **PIN** is a personal identification number.
account	I have a bank **account**.
secret	No one knows the number. It's a **secret**.
of course	A: Is the ATM always open?
	B: Yes, **of course**.
through	The bank is open Monday **through** Friday.

Lesson 3   35

Reading Variation

To practice listening skills, have students listen to the audio before opening their books. Ask a few comprehension questions: *Why does Dorota need cash?* (She needs to go to the supermarket.) Repeat the audio if necessary. Then have students open their books and read along as they listen to the audio.

Vocabulary Teaching Ideas

Use the following ideas to teach these terms:

account: Write the name of a bank on the board. Say: *I put my money in this bank. I put it in my account. Do you have a bank account? Where do you put your money?* Elicit answers to check comprehension.

secret: Whisper something simple into a student's ear, such as *I like apples.* Then say out loud: *It's a secret. Don't tell!*

Expansion

Reading Have students practice the conversation in pairs. Ask volunteers to roleplay the conversation in front of the class.

Vocabulary in Context Have volunteers act out selected vocabulary, such as *security guard*, *cash*, and *PIN*.

At the ATM (Reading)
CD 1, Track 11

1. Have students look at the title of the reading. Ask: *Where are Dorota and Victor? What is the reading about?* Have students look at the picture on page 34. Ask: *What is Dorota doing?* (getting money from an ATM). *Why doesn't Dorota go inside the bank?* (It's closed.) Have students use the title and picture to make predictions about the reading.
2. Have students read the dialogue silently. Then play the audio and have students read along.
3. Check students' basic comprehension. Ask true or false questions such as: *The bank is closed. True or false?* (true) *Victor needs cash.* (false) *A PIN is not necessary.* (false)

To save class time, have students do the reading for homework ahead of time.

VOCABULARY IN CONTEXT

1. Model the pronunciation of each new vocabulary word and have students repeat.
2. Make sure students understand the meaning of each vocabulary word. Review the examples in the book and create additional example sentences. For example, to illustrate the word *cash*, take out both a credit card and cash from your wallet. Hold up the cash and say: *I have only [amount] in cash.* Go over each new vocabulary word similarly, using visuals and realia when appropriate. When possible, point to pictures in the book that illustrate the new vocabulary items, such as *security guard* and *ATM* on page 34.
3. Have students underline an example of each vocabulary item in the reading.

Unit 2   35

DID YOU KNOW?

Explain to students that online banking is also called PC banking, home banking, electronic banking, and Internet banking.

LISTENING ACTIVITY

🎧 **CD 1, Track 12**

1. Say: *Listen to the questions about the conversation we just read between Dorota and Victor. Circle the correct answer.* Play the listening selection one time without pausing. Then play it through again, pausing and replaying as necessary.
2. Go over the answers as a class. Ask students to volunteer answers.

2.5 | Information Questions

1. Have students look at grammar chart **2.5** on page 36. Stress that information questions begin with a question word. Go over the list of question words (*where, what, what time, why, when, who, how*). Review the word order of questions. Go over the examples and answers.
2. Have students cover their charts. Write on the board: *Where is the ATM? It is outside.* Ask students to identify the word order in each sentence.
3. Point out the Language Note. Review the meanings of question words. Read each question in the chart. Ask: *What kind of information is wanted?* (e.g., Where = place. We want to know the place). Explain that question words can be contracted with *is*. Go over the examples.

Did You Know? You can do your banking online too.
- Pay bills
- Transfer money
- Invest

🎧 **Listening Activity** Listen to the following questions about the conversation. Circle the answer.

EXAMPLE (At the bank.)   At the supermarket.

1. Yes, it's late.   (It's 7:30 p.m.)
2. 24 hours a day   (Monday through Saturday)
3. from 9 to 4   (24 hours a day)
4. (It's a machine for cash.)   It's at the bank.
5. at 10:15   (To get cash.)
6. 924   (It's a secret.)

2.5 | Information Questions

Information questions begin with *where, when, why, who, what,* and *how*. Observe the word order in an information question.

Question Word	Be	Subject + . . .	Answer
Where	are	we?	We're at the ATM.
What	is	that?	It's a machine.
What time	is	it?	It's 10:15.
Why	are	we here?	We're here to get cash.
When	is	the bank open?	It's open from Monday through Saturday.
Who	is	that woman?	She's a security guard.
How	are	you?	I'm fine, thanks.

Language Notes:
1. Study the meaning of the information question words:

   where = place   why = reason   when = time   how = health
   what = thing   who = person   what time = exact time   how old = age

2. You can make a short form (contraction) with information words and *is*.

   What's that?   **When's** the bank open?
   Who's she?   **Why's** he here?

36   Unit 2

Culture Note

Today most banks offer online banking and regular banking. Some small banks do not offer online services. Other banks are only online. These banks are called "virtual" banks.

Expansion

Grammar Chart Have students work in pairs. Tell partners to ask each other the questions in grammar chart **2.5** on page 36. Have students give answers that are true for the class or true for themselves. Model an example: *Who is that woman? She's my English teacher.*

Compare statements and information questions.

Statements	Questions
The bank **is** open.	When **is the bank** open?
We **are** at the ATM.	Why **are we** at the ATM?
You **are** a student.	How old **are you**?
I **am** at a bank.	Where **am I**?
She **is** inside the bank.	Why **is she** inside the bank?
Dorota **is** from Poland.	Who **is Dorota**?

Pronunciation Note: Information questions have a falling intonation. Listen to your teacher pronounce the statements on the left and the questions on the right.

EXERCISE 1 Write a question word.

Dorota: _____How_____ are you?
       (example)

Victor: I'm fine. _____Where_____ are we?
                      (1)

Dorota: We're at the Laundromat.

Victor: _____What_____'s that?
            (2)

Dorota: It's a dryer.

Victor: _____Why_____ are we here?
            (3)

Dorota: To learn about the Laundromat.

Victor: _____Who_____'s that woman?
            (4)

Dorota: She's the manager.

Victor: _____When_____ is the Laundromat open?
            (5)

Dorota: Every day from 7 a.m. to 9 p.m.

Victor: _____What time_____ is it?
            (6)

Dorota: 8:45. We're late!

Lesson 3 37

2.5 | Information Questions (cont.)

4. Have students compare statements and information questions in the second part of the chart on page 37. Ask students to identify the subject and the verb in both the statements and questions. Have students underline the subject once and the verb twice (e.g., The bank *is* open.)
5. Direct students to the Pronunciation Note. Explain that information questions have a falling intonation. Have students close their books. Pronounce the statements and questions in the chart in random order. Have students raise their hands when they hear a question.

EXERCISE 1

1. Have students read the direction line. Ask: *What do we write on the blanks?* (question words) Go over the example in the Student Book.
2. Have students complete Exercise 1 individually. Go over answers as a class.
3. If necessary, review grammar chart **2.5** on pages 36 and 37.

Expansion

Grammar Chart Have students work in pairs to practice the falling intonation of information questions found in **2.5** on page 37. Circulate to observe pair work.

Exercise 1 Have students practice the conversation in pairs. Ask volunteers to perform the conversation in front of the class.

Unit 2 37

EXERCISE 2

1. Have students read the direction line. Say: *In this exercise, you will be comppleting questions.* Go over the example in the Student Book.
2. Have students complete Exercise 2 individually. Then have students compare answers in pairs.
3. If necessary, review grammar chart **2.5** on pages 36 and 37.

EXERCISE 3

1. Say: *This exercise is about you.* Have students read the direction line. Say: *The answers to the questions should be true for you.* Have a volunteer model #1.
2. Have students complete Exercise 2 individually. Then have students take turns asking and answering questions in pairs. Circulate to observe pair work. Give help as needed.
3. If necessary, review grammar chart **2.5** on pages 36 and 37.

2.6 | Articles *A/An*

1. Have students close their books. Ask: *How do we use the articles* a *and* an? *It depends on sounds and singular and plural nouns.*
2. Write this matching exercise on the board to do with the class:
   1. It's a bank.
   2. It's an ATM.
   3. They're ATMs.
   4. The bank is big. / It's a big bank.

   Do not use a *or* an *before a plural noun.*
   Use an *before a vowel sound.*
   Use a *or* an *before an adjective only if a noun follows the adjective.*
   Use a *before a consonant sound.*
3. Say: *Let's match the examples with the rules.* Read each rule and ask students to name the example. Ask students to explain their choices.
4. Have students look at grammar chart **2.6** on page 38. Go over the examples and explanations together as a class.

EXERCISE 2 Complete the question.

EXAMPLE It's late. What time ___is it___?

1. They're at the bank. Why ___are they at the bank___?
2. I'm fine. How ___are you___?
3. The bank is open today. What time ___is it___?
4. We're late. Why ___are we late___?
5. The ATM is near here. Where ___is it___?
6. That woman is in the bank. Who ___is she___?

EXERCISE 3 ABOUT YOU Answer the questions. Write a sentence.

1. Where are you from? ___Answers will vary.___
2. What's your name? _____
3. Who's your English teacher? _____
4. Where's your English teacher from? _____
5. Where's your school? _____
6. When is the school open? _____
7. When are you at home? _____
8. Why are you here? _____

2.6 | Articles *A/An*

\multicolumn{2}{l}{Use *a/an* before a singular noun to identify the subject.}
Examples	**Explanation**
What's this? It's **a** bank. Who's that woman? She's **a** security guard.	Use *a* before a consonant sound.
What's that? It's **an** ATM. I'm **an** immigrant.	Use *an* before a vowel sound. The vowels are *a, e, i, o,* and *u*.
What are those? They're ATMs. Quarters and dimes are coins.	Do not use *a/an* before a plural noun. *Wrong:* They're **an** ATMs. *Wrong:* Quarters and dimes are *a* coins.
The bank is big. It's **a** big bank.	Use *a* or *an* before an adjective only if a noun follows the adjective. *Wrong:* The bank is *a* big.

38 Unit 2

Expansion

Exercise 3 Write five information questions on the board. Then create two rings of students. Have half of the students stand in an outer ring around the classroom. Have the other half stand in an inner ring, facing the outer ring. Instruct students to ask and answer the questions on the board. Call out *turn* every minute or so. Students in the inner ring should move one space clockwise. Students now ask and answer the questions with their new partner. Have students ask questions in random order. Make sure students look at each other when they're speaking.

EXERCISE 4 Fill in the blanks with *a* or *an*.

EXAMPLES This is __a__ bank.
That's __an__ ATM.

1. I'm __an__ immigrant.
2. I'm __a__ new immigrant.
3. This is __a__ PIN.
4. This is __an__ easy PIN.
5. A quarter is __a__ coin.
6. Simon isn't __an__ old man.
7. Dorota is from Poland. Poland is __an__ eastern European country.
8. I'm __a__ busy person.

EXERCISE 5 Fill in the blanks with the correct form of *be* and *a* or *an*. Do not use *a* or *an* with plural nouns.

Victor: What's that?
Dorota: It __'s an__ ATM.
           (example)
Victor: What's an ATM?
Dorota: It __'s a__ machine for cash.
           (1)
Victor: What are these?
Dorota: These __are__ envelopes.
              (2)
Victor: What are they for?
Dorota: Depositing checks.
Victor: What __'s a__ check?
              (3)
Dorota: Look. This __is a__ check. It __'s a__ paycheck.
                    (4)   (5)
Victor: What __are__ those?
              (6)
Dorota: Those __are__ drive-up ATMs.
              (7)
Victor: Americans __are__ busy people. They __'re__ always in their cars.
                   (8)   (9)
Dorota: It __'s an__ easy way to use the bank.
           (10)

Lesson 3   39

Expansion

Exercise 5 Have students practice the conversation in pairs. Ask volunteers to perform the dialogue in front of the class.

EXERCISE 4

1. Have students read the direction line. Go over the examples in the Student Book. Elicit from students the rules for using *a* and *an* in the examples (*a* before a consonant: *bank*; *an* before a vowel: *ATM*)
2. Have students complete Exercise 4 individually. Then have students compare answers in pairs.
3. If necessary, review grammar chart **2.6** on page 38.

EXERCISE 5

1. Have students read the direction line. Remind students that *a* and *an* are not used with plural nouns. Go over the example in the Student Book.
2. Have students complete Exercise 5 individually. Then have students compare answers in pairs.
3. If necessary, review grammar chart **2.6** on page 38.

To save class time, have students do the exercise for homework ahead of time.

EXERCISE 6

1. Have students read the direction line. Ask: *When do we use* a *with an adjective?* (in front of an adjective that begins with a consonant sound) *When do we use* an? (in front of an adjective that begins with a vowel sound) Go over the example in the Student Book.
2. Have students complete Exercise 6 individually. Then have students compare answers in pairs. Circulate to observe pair work. Give help as needed.
3. If necessary, review grammar chart **2.6** on page 38.

⏱ To save class time, have students do the exercise for homework ahead of time.

EXERCISE 6 Add the adjective in parentheses ( ) to the sentence. Change *a* to *an* or *an* to *a* if needed.

EXAMPLE It's a bank. (old).
It's an old bank.

1. You are an immigrant. (new)
   You are a new immigrant.
2. You're a person. (busy)
   You're a busy person.
3. I'm an American. (new)
   I'm a new American.
4. This is a way to get cash. (easy)
   This is an easy way to get cash.
5. That's a machine. (empty)
   That's an empty machine.
6. He's a man. (helpful)
   He's a helpful man.

40 Unit 2

Expansion

Exercise 6 Have students work in pairs to create new sentences with the adjectives from Exercise 6. Write an example on the board (e.g., *That's an empty dryer.*).

EDITING ADVICE

1. *People* is a plural word. Use a plural verb.
   The new people ~~is~~ late. [are]

2. Use the correct possessive adjective.
   She is with ~~his~~ father. [her]   They are with ~~they~~ mother. [their]

3. Don't confuse *you're* and *your*.
   What's ~~you're~~ name? [your]   ~~Your~~ never late. [You're]

4. Use the correct word order in a question.
   Why ~~you are~~ late? [are you]   Is ~~big the supermarket~~? [the supermarket big]

5. Use *a* or *an* before a singular noun.
   E is [a] vowel. This is [an] easy lesson.

6. Don't use *a* or *an* with plural nouns.
   Victor and Dorota are ~~an~~ immigrants.

EDITING QUIZ

Find the mistakes with the underlined words, and correct them. Not every sentence has a mistake. If the sentence is correct, write *C*.

EXAMPLES   You <u>are</u> nice person. [a]
Simon and Dorota <u>are nice people</u>. *C*

1. Why <u>~~we are~~</u> here? [are we]
2. <u>Is it 10:15 now</u>? *C*
3. When <u>~~the bank is~~</u> open? [is the bank]
4. Where <u>is the bank</u>? *C*
5. She's <u>a</u> kind woman. *C*
6. Dorota is at the hospital. <u>~~His~~ father</u> is sick. [Her]
7. He is <u>~~a~~</u> old man. [an]
8. Where's <u>~~you're~~</u> book? [your]
9. Ten people <u>~~is~~</u> in the bank. [are]
10. Who are those people? What are <u>~~they~~</u> names? [their]
11. *U* is <u>vowel</u>. [a]
12. *A E I O U* are <u>~~a~~ vowels</u>.

Lesson 3   41

Editing Advice

1. Have students close their books. Write the example sentences without editing marks or corrections on the board. For example:
   1. The new people is late.
   2. She is with his father. They are with they mother.

   Ask students to correct each sentence. This activity can be done individually, in pairs, or as a class. After students have corrected each sentence, tell them to turn to page 41. Say: *Now compare your work with Editing Advice in the book.*

2. Go over answers with the class. For troublespots, review the appropriate grammar chart.

Editing Quiz

1. The Editing Quiz may be used as an in-class quiz, a take-home quiz, or as a review. Have students read the direction line. Ask: *Does every sentence have a mistake?* (no) Go over the examples with the class.

2. Have students complete the quiz individually. Collect their completed quizzes for assessment or have students check each other's work. Review the answers with the class. Elicit the relevant grammar point for each correction. For example, for #1 (Answer: *Why ~~we are~~ are we here?*), ask: *What's the rule for questions?* (The verb comes before the subject.)

Unit 2   41

Learner's Log

1. Have students close their books. Ask: *What did you learn about time and money in the U.S.? What else do you want to know?* Prompt students with questions, such as *How do you use an ATM? Are banks open every day? When are they open?* Write ideas on the board. Discuss ways in which students can find out more about time, ATMs, and holidays in the U.S.
2. Have students open their books to complete the Learner's Log.

Expansion Activities

These expansion activities provide opportunities for students to interact with one another and further develop their speaking and writing skills. Encourage students to use grammar from this unit whenever possible.

To save class time, assign parts of the activities as homework. Then use class time for interaction and communication. If students do not need additional speaking practice, some of the activities may be assigned as writing activities for homework, or skipped altogether.

WRITING ACTIVITIES

1. Have students read the direction line. Go over the example. Have students complete the activity individually at home or in class. Collect for assessment.
2. Have students read the direction line. Go over the example sentence and write it and the second sentence on the board: *Simon and Marta are at the bank early today It's a bank near their work place.* Underline the changes in the sentences.

OUTSIDE ACTIVITY

Have students get into groups to share their experiences of visiting banks.

INTERNET ACTIVITY

Have students tell if their watch had the correct time or was fast or slow.

LEARNER'S LOG

1. What did you learn in this unit? Write three sentences in your notebook about each topic.
   • Time in the United States
   • ATM machines
2. Write three questions you still have about ATM machines or time in the U.S.

EXPANSION ACTIVITIES

Writing Activity

1. In your notebook, write a short paragraph of five to six sentences about Marta and her daughter, Amy, in the picture.

   EXAMPLE   *Marta is with her daughter, Amy.*

2. In your notebook, rewrite the following paragraph. Change *I* to *Simon and Marta*. Make all the necessary changes in verbs and possessive pronouns.

   I'm at the bank early today. It's a bank near my work place. It's not open. But I'm not worried. The ATM machine is always open. This bank is not my bank. It's $1.50 to get my cash here. But it's easy to get cash with my ATM card.

   EXAMPLE   *Simon and Marta are at the bank early today.*

Outside Activities

Find a bank in your neighborhood. Tell the class the name and address of the bank. When is the bank open? Where is the ATM machine?

Internet Activities

Search the words *exact time* or *official clock*. Find the time in your part of the country. Then look at your watch. What time is it on your watch?

Expansion

Learner's Log Have students compare logs in pairs.

Writing Activities Variation

Have students exchange papers with a partner for proofreading.

Internet Activity Variation

Tell students that if they don't have Internet access, they can use Internet facilities at a public library. Alternatively, students may check banks and mail facilities for international clocks. They can record the times and share the information with classmates. For example, *It's 1:00 in New York. It's 6:00 in London.*

UNIT
3

GRAMMAR
Imperatives
Let's
Object Pronouns

CONTEXT
Filling Out Forms

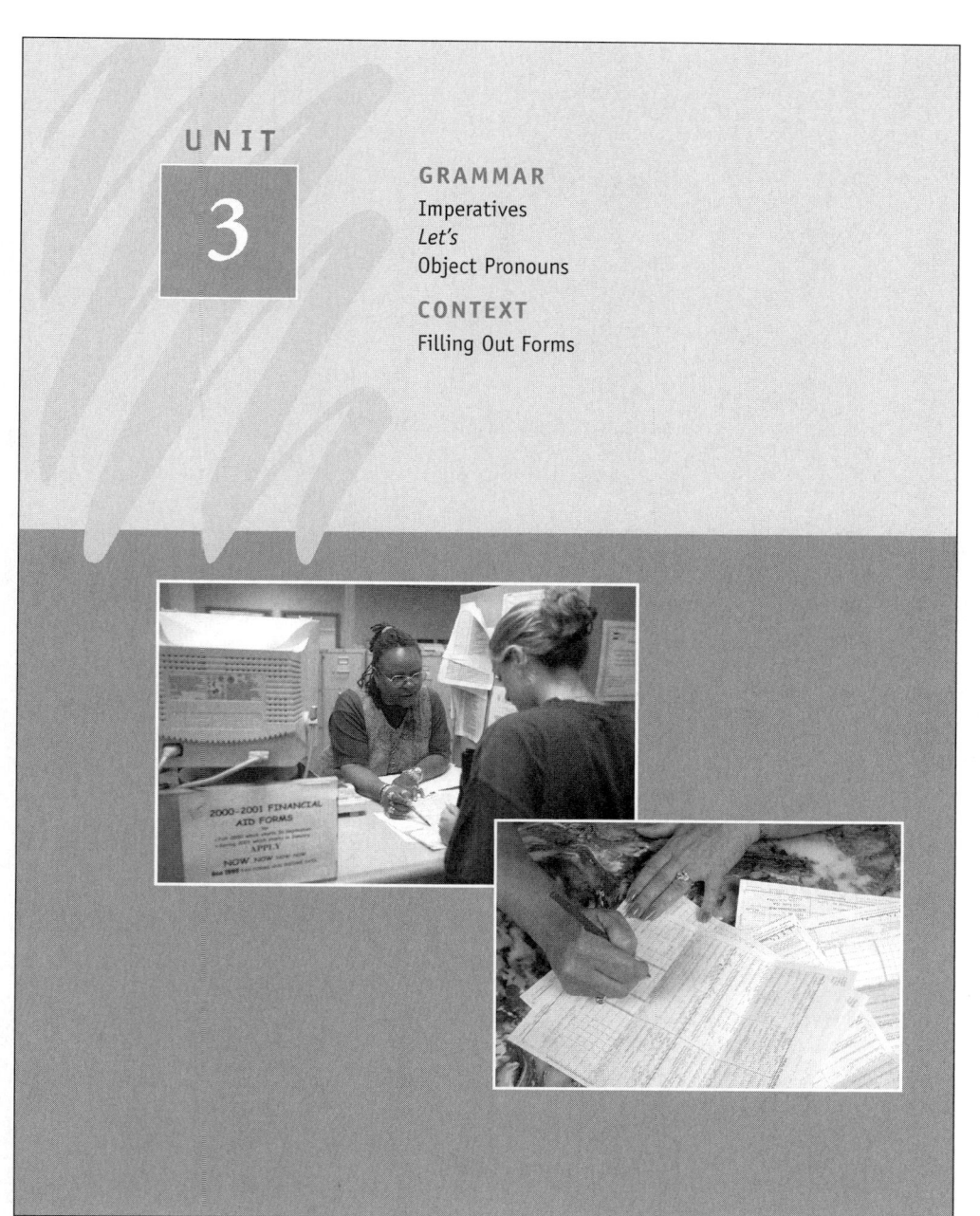

Expansion

Theme The topic for this unit can be enhanced with the following ideas:
1. Forms for school admissions and financial aid, for bank cards and supermarket cards
2. Enlarged examples of hand-printed information and written information

Unit | 3
Unit Overview

GRAMMAR

1. Briefly review Unit 2 objectives. Say: *We studied possessive nouns and adjectives. We studied two kinds of questions (yes/no questions and information questions) and two articles (a and an). We also studied irregular plural forms. Let's name examples.* List examples on the board.
2. Say and write on the board: *Imperatives, Let's, Object Pronouns.* Say: *In Unit 3 we will study ways to tell or suggest what to do. Listen: Go! Let's go. Eat! Let's eat. Are they the same?* (no) Elicit more examples. Write them on the board. Say: *What else will we study?* (object pronouns) Say and write examples on the board (e.g., *me, him, her,* and *them*).

CONTEXT

1. Say: *In the U.S. we use many forms!* Hold up forms that students will recognize (e.g., a school application, a financial aid form). Say: *These are* forms. *Schools give you forms. What will we talk about in this lesson?* (filling out forms)
2. Direct students' attention to the bottom photo. Ask: *What's she doing?* (filling out a form) Point to the office photo. Ask: *Where's this?* (financial aid office) *Does the student know what to do?* (no) *How do you know?* (The woman is helping the student.)
3. Ask: *Where do you fill out forms: at the bank? at the supermarket?* Hold up a supermarket card. *Is it easy or hard?* Have students share their personal experiences.

Unit 3   43

Lesson 1 | Overview

GRAMMAR

Ask: *What's an imperative?* Demonstrate by performing the actions as you say the commands: *Stand! Sit!* Write: *Imperatives* and the verbs on the board. Turn to the class, gesture, and say: *Sit!* After students are seated, say: *Imperatives are commands. Commands are Do!* and *Don't! They can be affirmative and negative.*

CONTEXT

1. Say: *This lesson is about Social Security cards. You need this card to work. Who gets it?* (U.S. citizens) *In this country, workers pay money to Social Security. Social Security pays money to you when you are old, sick, or cannot work. How do you get a card?* (fill out a form)
2. Direct students' attention to the pictures. Ask: *What are these?* (a form and a Social Security card). Point to the boxes on the form. Ask: *How many boxes of information do you fill out?* (17; many) *What information is on the card?* (a number; your name).
3. Ask: *Did you fill out this form? Who helped you? Was it hard? Do you write or print the information?* Write your own name on the board both in script and print to show the difference. Have students share their experiences.

BEFORE YOU READ

1. Go over each statement as a class. Have a volunteer read the statements or read them to the class yourself. Ask students to circle *yes* or *no*.
2. Ask for a few volunteers to share their answers with the class.

To save class time, skip "Before You Read" or have students prepare answers for homework ahead of time.

LESSON 1

GRAMMAR
Imperative Forms—Affirmative
Imperative Forms—Negative

CONTEXT
Getting a Social Security Card

Before You Read

Circle *yes* or *no*.

1. I have a Social Security card.   YES   NO
2. I write the day before the month (November 6 = 11/6).   YES   NO

Culture Note

The official Web site of the Social Security Administration gives information in 15 different languages.

GETTING A SOCIAL SECURITY CARD

This is a conversation between Dorota and Halina.

Dorota: I have something for you. **Look.**
Halina: What is it?
Dorota: It's an **application**. It's for a Social Security card.
Halina: I'm not sure what to do.
Dorota: **Don't worry.** It's easy. **Let** me help.
Halina: OK. I have a pencil.
Dorota: No, no. **Don't use** a pencil. **Use** a blue or black pen.
Halina: OK.
Dorota: Here's a pen. **Fill** out all the information. **Print,** but **sign** in Box 16.

Halina: I'm finished.
Dorota: What's your date of birth?
Halina: 11-6-70.
Dorota: Is your birthday in November?
Halina: No. It's in June.
Dorota: **Don't write** 11-6. **Write** the month, then the day. That's the American way.
Halina: OK. 6-11-70.
Dorota: **Don't write** 70. **Write** 1970.

Halina: I'm finished. What's next?
Dorota: **Don't forget. Sign** your name. **Make** a copy of your birth certificate. Then **go** to the Social Security office. **Take** your birth certificate and another identity document with you.

Vocabulary in Context

application	This is an **application** for a Social Security card.
let	**Let** me help you.
fill out	**Fill out** the application with a pen.
print	**Print** the information. Don't write it.
sign	**Sign** your name.
date of birth	My **date of birth** is June 11.
birthday	My **birthday** is June 11.
forget	Don't **forget** your Social Security number.
birth certificate	A new baby has a **birth certificate.**
identity document	Here's my driver's license. It's my **identity document.** It shows who I am.

Lesson 1   45

Getting a Social Security Card (Reading)
CD 1, Track 13

1. Have students look at the title of the reading. Say: *Dorota and Halina are talking. Dorota has something for Halina. What is it? Will Halina know what to do?* Have students use the title to make predictions about the reading.
2. Have students read the dialogue silently. Then play the audio and have students read along silently.
3. Check students' basic comprehension. Ask true or false questions, such as: *Use a pencil to fill out a social security application.* True *or* false? (false) *Halina's birthday is in June.* True *or* false? (true) *Halina was born in 1907.* True *or* false? (false) *Take two identity documents to the Social Security office.* True *or* false? (true)

🕐 To save class time, have students do the reading for homework ahead of time.

VOCABULARY IN CONTEXT

1. Model the pronunciation of each new vocabulary word and have students repeat.
2. Make sure students understand the meaning of each vocabulary word. Review the examples in the book and create additional example sentences. For example, say: *print.* Then tell a student volunteer: *Print your name on the board.* Go over each new vocabulary word similarly, using visuals and realia when appropriate. When possible, point to pictures in the book that illustrate the vocabulary items, such as *application* on page 44 and *birth certificate* on page 45.
3. Have students underline an example of each word in the reading.

Reading Variation

1. To practice listening skills, have students listen to the audio before opening their books. Ask a few comprehension questions: *What is the application for?* (a Social Security card) *When is Halina's birthday?* (June 11) Repeat the audio if necessary. Then have students open their books and read along as they listen to the audio.
2. Alternatively, have students begin by listening to the audio as they read along.

Vocabulary Teaching Ideas

Use the following ideas to teach these terms:

forget: Write a long number on the board. (e.g., 670789321) Say: *Everyone look at this number. Memorize it. Don't forget it.* Then erase the number. Ask: *What's the number? Did you forget?* Ask volunteers to try and remember the number.

Expansion

Reading Have students practice the conversation in pairs. Ask volunteers to roleplay the conversation in front of the class.

Vocabulary in Context Have volunteers act out selected vocabulary, such as *fill out* and *sign your name.*

Unit 3   45

DID YOU KNOW?

Explain to students that the U.S. does not have a national identity card. Say: *Most people use a driver's license as their identity card. States also offer non-drivers an identity card.*

LISTENING ACTIVITY

🎧 **CD 1, Track 14**

1. Say: *This listening activity is based on Dorota and Halina's conversation about Social Security Card applications. Listen to the instructions. Circle true or false.*
2. Play the listening selection one time without pausing. Then play it through again, pausing and replaying as necessary.
3. Go over the answers as a class. Ask students to volunteer answers.

3.1 | Imperative Forms—Affirmative

1. Have students look at grammar chart **3.1** on page 46. Say: *We use imperatives when we explain or suggest what to do. We also use them to get someone's attention.*
2. Go over the examples and explanations in the chart. Say: *Tell me the imperative: to use a pen/Using a pen/Use a pen.* (Use a pen.) How do you know? (form of verb) Stress that the base form is used for the imperative. Stress that adding the word *please* to an imperative makes the command polite.
3. List examples for each use of imperatives. Write on the board and say: *Instructions: Print your name. Suggestions: Use this pen. It's black. Get someone's attention: Look over there.* Have students give examples. Write their examples on the board.

Did You Know?
- On an application, DOB means *date of birth*.
- Identity documents include:
  Driver's license   Marriage certificate
  Passport   School ID (identification) card

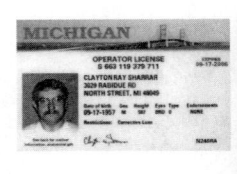

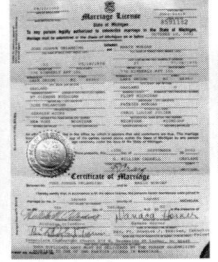

🎧 **Listening Activity**

Listen to these instructions. If the instruction is correct for the Social Security application, circle *true*. If the instruction is not correct, circle *false*.

EXAMPLE (TRUE)   FALSE

1. (TRUE) FALSE   4. TRUE (FALSE)
2. (TRUE) FALSE   5. (TRUE) FALSE
3. TRUE   (FALSE)   6. TRUE (FALSE)

3.1 | Imperative Forms—Affirmative

Use the imperative:
- to give instructions or directions
- to give suggestions
- to get someone's attention

Examples	Explanation
Look at this. **Use** a pen. **Write** your date of birth.	Use the base form of the verb for the imperative.
Help me, **please**. **Please** help me.	Add *please* to be more polite.

46   Unit 3

Expansion

Grammar Chart Play a game. Divide the class into two or more teams. Create a list of imperatives. Don't show them to students. Have a member of each team go to the front of the class. Say the imperative (e.g., *Print your name on the board.*) The first student who correctly performs the command earns a point for his or her team.

EXERCISE 1 Fill in the blanks with one of the verbs from the box below.

| Fill | Use | Take | Sign |
| Go | Write | Make ✓ | Help |

EXAMPLE __Make__ a copy of your birth certificate.

1. I'm confused. __Help__ me, please.
2. __Fill__ out the application today.
3. __Use__ a pen.
4. __Write__ the month before the day.
5. __Go__ to the Social Security office today.
6. __Take__ your birth certificate with you.
7. __Sign__ your name in Box 16.

3.2 | Imperative Forms—Negative

Examples	Explanation
Don't worry. Don't write 11-6 for June 11. Don't forget.	Use *do not* + base form for the negative. The short form (contraction) is *don't*.

EXERCISE 2 Fill in the blanks with the negative imperative of a verb from the box below.

| put | print | be | forget |
| worry ✓ | write | drive | |

EXAMPLE It's not hard. __Don't worry__. I can help you.

1. Take your papers with you. __Don't forget__.
2. Stay here. __Don't drive__ your car to the Social Security office now.
3. Print. __Don't write__ your information.
4. Be on time. __Don't be__ late.
5. Stop. __Don't put__ one more word on the application.
6. Sign your name in Box 16. __Don't print__ it.

EXERCISE 1

1. Have students read the direction line. Go over the example in the Student Book. Say: *Make a copy means to make a photocopy on a machine.*
2. Have students complete Exercise 1 individually. Check the answers as a class. If necessary, review grammar chart **3.1** on page 46.

3.2 | Imperative Forms—Negative

1. Have students look at grammar chart **3.2** on page 47. Ask volunteers to read the examples. Explain that the negative is formed with *do not* or the contraction *don't*. Ask volunteers to write the long form of *don't worry, don't write,* and *don't forget* on the board.

EXERCISE 2

1. Have students read the direction line. Go over the example in the Student Book. Point out the picture of a person's hand signing his name. Say: *Don't forget to sign your name. Did he forget?* (no)
2. Have students complete Exercise 2 individually. Go over the answers as a class.
3. If necessary, review grammar chart **3.2** on page 47.

Expansion

Grammar Chart Have students go back to Exercise 1 on page 47. Say: *Write a negative imperative for every verb in the box.*

EXERCISE 3

1. Have students read the direction line. Point out the photo on page 48. Say: *Some people are filling out an application and waiting.* Go over the example.
2. Have students complete Exercise 3 individually. Then have students compare answers with a partner. Circulate to observe pair work. Give help as needed.
3. If necessary, review grammar chart **3.2** on page 47.

EXERCISE 3 Fill in the blanks with an affirmative or negative imperative. Use the verbs from the box below.

use	put	worry ✓
forget	write	bring

EXAMPLE __Don't worry__ about the application. I am here to help.

1. __Don't use__ a pencil to fill out your application.
2. __Don't forget__ to sign your application at the end.
3. __Bring__ two forms of ID with you to the Social Security office.
4. __Write__ all four numbers for the year (*1970*, not *70*).
5. __Don't put__ the day first in your date of birth.

48 Unit 3

Expansion

Exercise 3 Have students work in pairs to create sentences with affirmative and negative imperatives. Brainstorm a list of verbs and nouns that students have learned and used so far (e.g., forget/go/eat/ and vegetables/clothes/appointment). Write them on the board.

EXERCISE 4 This is a conversation between Amy and her mother, Marta. Fill in the blanks with one of the verbs from the box below. Use two verbs twice.

don't ask	make ✓	wash	say
don't touch	let	be	give

Amy: **Make** *(example)* me a jelly sandwich, Mommy.

Marta: I'm busy now. Later.

Amy: What's that, Mommy?

Marta: It's my application. Your hands are dirty. **Don't touch** (1) the application.

Amy: What's an application, Mommy? And what's that?

Marta: It's my birth certificate. Please **don't ask** (2) so many questions. Mommy's busy now.

Amy: I'm thirsty. **Give** (3) me a glass of milk, Mommy.

Marta: Later. **Be** (4) quiet now, please, and **let** (5) me finish. This is very important.

Marta: OK. I'm finished now.

Amy: **Make** (6) me a jelly sandwich.

Marta: **Say** (7), "Please."

Amy: Please.

Marta: And **wash** (8) your hands.

Marta: Here is your sandwich and milk. **Say** (9) "Thank you."

Amy: Thank you, Mommy.

Lesson 1 49

EXERCISE 4

1. Have students read the direction line. Point out the picture on page 49 of Amy and her mother. Ask: *What's Amy doing? What is her mother doing?* Encourage students to make predictions. Go over the example in the Student Book.
2. Have students complete Exercise 4 individually. Then have students compare answers with a partner. Circulate to observe pair work. Give help as needed.
3. If necessary, review grammar chart **3.2** on page 47.

Expansion

Exercise 4 Have students practice the conversation between Amy and her mother in pairs. Ask volunteers to roleplay the conversation in front of the class.

Unit 3 49

Lesson 2 | Overview

GRAMMAR

1. Say: *Let's begin Lesson 2. Let's learn about subject and object pronouns. Is this a command?* (no) Say: *Let's is a strong suggestion. Let's take a break. Let's sing a song.* Write a few verbs on the board (e.g., *go, eat, walk*). Ask volunteers to make suggestions with the verbs using *Let's*.
2. Say: *Let's look at subject and object pronouns.* Write on the board: *John: I gave the book to Mary. I gave it to her. Mary: John gave me the book. He gave it to me.* Underline the pronouns. Ask students to identify the subject and object pronouns in the sentences and name the referents.

CONTEXT

1. Ask: *Let's talk about applications for financial aid. You can fill out many applications online. How do you do it? Is it fast? Do you use a password?* Have students share their knowledge and experiences.
2. Direct students' attention to the picture. Say: *What are they doing?* (filling out a financial aid application) *Where are they?* (at home) *Are they working online?* (yes) *How do you know?* (They're at a computer.)

BEFORE YOU READ

1. Go over each statement as a class. Have a volunteer read the statements or read them to the class yourself. Ask students to circle *yes* or *no*.
2. Ask for a few volunteers to share their answers with the class.

🕐 To save class time, skip "Before You Read" or have students prepare their answers for homework ahead of time.

LESSON 2

GRAMMAR
Let's
Compare Subject and Object Pronouns

CONTEXT
Financial Aid Application

Before You Read

Circle *yes* or *no*.

1. I have financial aid.
   YES   NO
2. Online forms are easy.
   YES   NO

50   Unit 3

Expansion

Theme The topic for this unit can be enhanced with the following ideas:
1. A financial aid application
2. A copy of instructions for completing an online application

---

Culture Note

Students in the U.S. pay for their college education. More than 73 percent of full-time undergraduate students receive some financial aid. The average amount is about $8,000.

50   *Grammar in Context Basic* Teacher's Edition

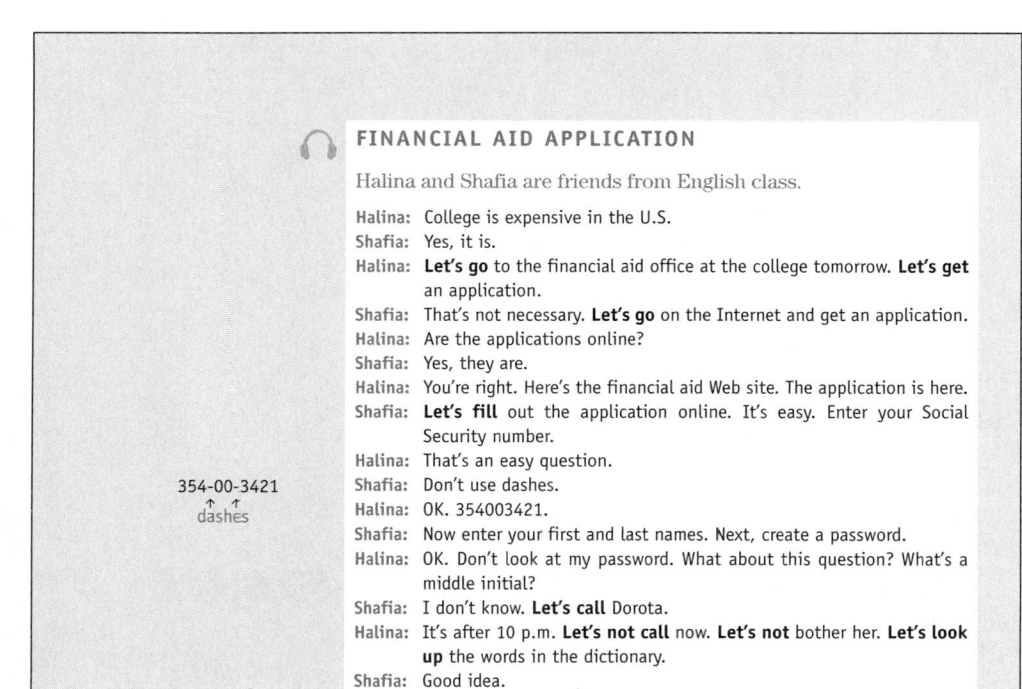

FINANCIAL AID APPLICATION

Halina and Shafia are friends from English class.

Halina: College is expensive in the U.S.
Shafia: Yes, it is.
Halina: Let's go to the financial aid office at the college tomorrow. **Let's get** an application.
Shafia: That's not necessary. **Let's go** on the Internet and get an application.
Halina: Are the applications online?
Shafia: Yes, they are.
Halina: You're right. Here's the financial aid Web site. The application is here.
Shafia: Let's fill out the application online. It's easy. Enter your Social Security number.
Halina: That's an easy question.
Shafia: Don't use dashes.
Halina: OK. 354003421.
Shafia: Now enter your first and last names. Next, create a password.
Halina: OK. Don't look at my password. What about this question? What's a middle initial?
Shafia: I don't know. **Let's call** Dorota.
Halina: It's after 10 p.m. **Let's not call** now. **Let's not** bother her. **Let's look up** the words in the dictionary.
Shafia: Good idea.

354-00-3421
↑ ↑
dashes

Vocabulary in Context

expensive	College is **expensive** in the U.S.
financial aid	**Financial aid** is money to help pay for college.
available	Financial aid is **available** for some students.
online	The application is available **online**. It's on the Internet.
dash(es)	Write your Social Security number. Don't use **dashes**.
create a password	**Create a password.** It's a secret number or word.
enter	**Enter** your name on line 3 on the computer application.
what about	**What about** this question? What is it?
middle initial	My name is Dorota R. Nowak. My **middle initial** is R.
bother	Let's not **bother** her. She's busy.
look up	**Look up** the word in the dictionary.

Lesson 2   51

Reading Variation

1. To practice listening skills, have students listen to the audio before opening their books. Ask a few comprehension questions: *Is college in the U.S. expensive?* (yes) *Does Halina use dashes?* (no) Repeat the audio if necessary. Then have students open their books and read along as they listen to the audio.
2. Alternatively, have students begin by listening to the audio as they read along.

Vocabulary Teaching Ideas

Use the following ideas to teach these terms:

look up: Have students look up a few words in the dictionary, such as *look up* and *password*.
what about: Ask a student in the class his or her name. Then turn to another student and say: *What about you? What's your name?*

Expansion

Reading Have students practice the conversation in pairs. Ask volunteers to roleplay the conversation in front of the class.

Vocabulary in Context To check comprehension, have volunteers in pairs or groups act out selected vocabulary, such as *expensive, dashes, create a password, middle initial,* and *bother*.

Financial Aid Application (Reading) CD 1, Track 15

1. Have students look at the picture of Halina and Shafia on page 50. Ask a volunteer to read the title of the reading. Ask: *Where are Halina and Shafia?* (at a computer; at home) *What are they doing?* (filling out an application) *What will the conversation be about?* (filling out applications online) Have students use the title and picture to make predictions about the reading.
2. First, have students read the dialogue silently. Then play the audio and have students read along.
3. Check students' basic comprehension. Ask *yes/no* and information questions, such as: *Where do Halina and Shafia go to get an application?* (Internet) *Are Halina and Shafia confused?* (no; It's easy.) *Is it 11 p.m.?* (no) *Do they call Dorota?* (no)

To save class time, have students do the reading for homework ahead of time.

VOCABULARY IN CONTEXT

1. Model the pronunciation of each new vocabulary word and have students repeat.
2. Make sure students understand the meaning of each vocabulary word. Review the examples in the book and create additional example sentences. For example, say: *password. People often use birthdays and names for passwords. Let's create passwords.* Go around the room and ask volunteers to make up a password. Go over each new vocabulary word similarly, using visuals and realia when appropriate. When possible, point to pictures in the book that illustrate the new vocabulary items, such as *dashes* on page 51.
3. Have students underline an example of each vocabulary item in the reading. Point out that the word *available* is not in the reading. Give students additional examples, if necessary.

DID YOU KNOW?

Say: *Most Americans have middle names, but they don't always use them.* Explain that only the middle initial is often used when filling out forms.

LISTENING ACTIVITY

🎧 **CD 1, Track 16**

1. Say: *Listen to the sentences about the Halina and Shafia's conversation. Circle* true *or* false. Play the listening selection one time without pausing. Then play it through again, pausing and replaying as necessary.
2. Go over the answers as a class. Ask students to volunteer answers.

3.3 | Let's

1. Have students look at grammar chart **3.3** on page 52. Read the examples and explanations in the chart.
2. Point out that the contraction is almost always used because *Let us* is very formal.

EXERCISE 1

1. Have students read the direction line. Say: *You have to write* let's *or* let's not *AND a verb from the box.* Go over the example in the Student Book.
2. Have students complete Exercise 1 individually. Go over the answers as a class.
3. If necessary, review grammar chart **3.3** on page 52.

Did You Know? Many Americans have a middle name.
- Nicole *Anne* Jackson
- Brian *Robert* Goldberg

🎧 **Listening Activity** Listen to the sentences about the conversation. Circle *true* or *false*.

EXAMPLE (TRUE)   FALSE

1. (TRUE)   FALSE   4. TRUE   (FALSE)
2. TRUE   (FALSE)   5. TRUE   (FALSE)
3. (TRUE)   FALSE   6. (TRUE)   FALSE

3.3 | Let's

Examples	Explanation
Let's go to the office. **Let's get** an application.	Use *let's* + base form to make a suggestion. *Let's* is a contraction for *let us*.
Let's not call now.	Use *let's not* + base form to make the negative.

EXERCISE 1 Fill in the blanks with *let's* or *let's not* and one of the verbs from the box below. Use two of the verbs twice.

| walk | fill it out | go ✓ |
| get | call | drive |

EXAMPLE   __Let's go__ to the financial aid office.

1. __Let's walk__ to the financial aid office. It's not far.
2. __Let's not walk__. It's very cold today. Let's __drive__.
3. It's not necessary to go to the office. __Let's get__ an application online.
4. This application is easy. __Let's fill it out__ now.
5. I don't understand "middle initial." Where's the telephone? __Let's call__ Dorota now.
6. It's late. __Let's not call__ now. Let's call tomorrow.

52 Unit 3

Expansion

Grammar Chart Have students work in pairs to create a schedule for the next week. Say: *Think about things you need and want to do. For each day, write down a suggestion.* Write the following example on the board: *On Monday, let's go to the Laundromat.* Circulate to observe pair work. Give help as needed.

3.4 | Compare Subject and Object Pronouns

Examples	Explanation
I am confused. Help **me**. **You** are not alone. I am here to help **you**. **He** is at home. Don't bother **him**. **She** is at home. Don't bother **her**. **It** is your date of birth. Write **it**. **We** are busy. Don't bother **us**. **They** are confused. Help **them**.	Put the subject pronoun before the verb. Put the object pronoun after the verb. Compare subject pronouns and object pronouns. | Subject Pronoun	Object Pronoun | |---|---| | I | me | | you | you | | he | him | | she | her | | it | it | | we | us | | they | them |
I am finished *with* **it**. This application is *for* **you**. This question is *about* **me**.	Use the object pronoun after a preposition: *with, for, about, to, on, in, of, at,* or *from*.

EXERCISE 2 Fill in the blanks with an object pronoun.

EXAMPLE I'm confused. Please help ___me___.

1. Dorota is helpful. Let's call ___her___.
2. I'm busy. Don't bother ___me___.
3. We are confused. Please help ___us___.
4. Simon is busy. Don't bother ___him___.
5. I'm busy. Ask your father. Ask ___him___ for help.
6. Dorota and Simon are helpful. Let's ask ___them___.
7. The application is necessary. Let's fill ___it___ out.
8. This is my password. Don't look at ___it___.
9. Are you confused? Don't worry. I'm here to help ___you___.
10. Mother knows the answer. Let's ask ___her___.

Lesson 2   53

3.4 | Compare Subject and Object Pronouns

1. Have students close their books. Elicit a list of subject pronouns and of object pronouns. Write the lists on the board.
2. Write the following sentences from the chart on the board:

   I am confused. Help me.
   We are busy. Don't bother us.

   Ask a volunteer to underline the subject pronouns and circle the object pronouns. Ask students: *Does the subject pronoun come before or after the verb?* (before) *What about the object pronoun?* (after)
3. Have students look at grammar chart 3.4 on page 53. Go over the examples and the explanations. Point out that object pronouns come after prepositions. Ask volunteers to demonstrate the meaning of *with, on,* and *in*.

EXERCISE 2

1. Have students read the direction line. Go over the example in the Student Book.
2. Have students complete Exercise 2 individually. Go over the answers as a class.
3. If necessary, review grammar chart 3.4 on page 53.

Expansion

Grammar Chart Have students rewrite the examples in the grammar chart with different pronouns. Write the following example on the board: *He's confused. Help him.*

Unit 3   53

EXERCISE 3

1. Have students read the direction line. Go over the example in the Student Book. Point out to students that the second sentence of each item repeats what the first sentence says, but in reverse order.
2. Have students complete Exercise 3 individually. Have students compare answers in pairs. Circulate to observe pair work. Give help as needed.
3. If necessary, review grammar chart **3.4** on page 53.

   ⏱ To save class time, have students do the exercise for homework ahead of time.

EXERCISE 4

1. Have students read the direction line. Go over the example in the Student Book. Ask students what *it* refers to (that). Go over #1. (It's very expensive for *us*.) Ask students what *us* refers to. (immigrants)
2. Have students complete Exercise 4 individually. Then have students compare answers with a partner. Circulate to observe pair work. Give help as needed.
3. If necessary, review grammar chart **3.4** on page 53.

   ⏱ To save class time, have students complete the exercise for homework.

EXERCISE 3 Fill in the blanks with the object or subject pronoun.

EXAMPLE We are with them. __They__ are with __us__.

1. I am with you. __You__ are with __me__.
2. She is with him. __He__ is with __her__.
3. They are with us. __We__ are with __them__.
4. You are with me. __I__ am with __you__.
5. She is with them. __They__ are with __her__.

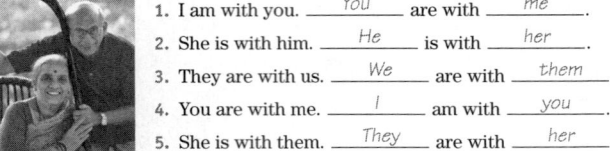

EXERCISE 4 Fill in the blanks with the object or subject pronoun.

Shafia: What's that?
Halina: __It__ (example) 's an application for financial aid. College is expensive in the U.S. We're immigrants. It's very expensive for __us__ (1).

Shafia: It's expensive for Americans too. But it's easy for __them__ (2) to fill out the application. It isn't easy for __us__ (3). I don't understand one question. I'm confused about __it__ (4).

Shafia: Let's call Dorota.
Halina: __It__ (5) 's late. It's after 10 p.m. Maybe __she__ (6) 's asleep. Let's call __her__ (7) tomorrow.

Shafia: Or call Simon.
Halina: __He__ (8) 's busy. His wife's father is sick. She's with __him__ (9) in the hospital. Simon's with his kids. He's with __them__ (10) all day.

Shafia: Let's read the application together. Maybe __we__ (11) can do __it__ (12) together.

Halina: Let's try.

Unit 3

Expansion

Exercise 4 Read the conversation out loud to the class, pausing for students to fill in the blanks.

EDITING ADVICE

1. Use *don't* to make a negative imperative.
    Don't
    ~~Not~~ write here.

2. Use *not* after *let's* to make the negative.
    not
    Let's ~~don't~~ be late.

3. Don't use *to* after *don't*.
    Don't ~~to~~ write on this line.

4. Don't use *to* after *let's*.
    Let's ~~to~~ eat now.

5. Don't forget the apostrophe in *let's*.
    Let's
    ~~Lets~~ go home.

6. Use the subject pronoun before the verb.
    They
    ~~Them~~ are good students.

7. Use the object pronoun after the verb or preposition.
    him   *them*
    Don't bother ~~he~~.   Look at ~~they~~.

EDITING QUIZ

Find the mistakes with the underlined words, and correct them. Not every sentence has a mistake. If the sentence is correct, write *C*.

EXAMPLES   Your mother is busy. Please help <u>she</u>.
                                          her

It's late. <u>Let's go</u> now.   *C*

1. <u>They</u> are busy now. Don't bother <u>~~they~~</u>.
                                           them
2. <u>She</u> is confused. Please help <u>she</u>.
                                        her
3. <u>Don't ~~to~~</u> bother Simon. <u>~~Him~~</u> is busy.
                                       He
4. <u>Let's</u> read the book together.   *C*
5. <u>Let's not</u> speak Spanish in class. <u>Let's</u> speak English now.
6. <u>Don't</u> talk about <u>me</u>.   *C*
7. This is my PIN. <u>Don't ~~to~~ look</u> at it.
8. Let's walk. Let's <u>~~don't~~</u> drive.
                      not

Lesson 2   55

Editing Advice

1. Have students close their books. Write the example sentences without editing marks or corrections on the board. For example:
    1. *Not write here.*
    2. *Let's don't be late.*

   Ask students to correct each sentence. This activity can be done individually, in pairs, or as a class. After students have corrected each sentence, tell them to turn to page 55. Say: *Now compare your work with Editing Advice in the book.*

2. Go over answers with the class. For troublespots, review the appropriate grammar chart.

Editing Quiz

1. The Editing Quiz may be used as an in-class quiz, a take-home quiz, or as a review. Have students read the direction line. Ask: *Does every sentence have a mistake?* (no) Go over the examples with the class.

2. Have students complete the quiz individually. Collect the completed quizzes for assessment or have students check each other's work. Review the answers with the class. Elicit the relevant grammar point for each correction. For example, for #1 (Answer: Don't bother ~~they~~ them.), ask: *Where are object pronouns in a sentence?* (after verbs.)

Learner's Log

1. Have students close their books. Ask: *What did you learn about Social Security cards and financial aid applications? What else do you want to know about them?* Discuss ways in which students can find out more about applications for Social Security cards and financial aid.
2. Have students open their books to complete the Learner's Log.

Expansion Activities

These expansion activities provide opportunities for students to interact with one another and further develop their speaking and writing skills. Encourage students to use grammar from this unit whenever possible.

⏱ To save class time, assign parts of the activities as homework. Then use class time for interaction and communication. If students do not need additional speaking practice, some of the activities may be assigned as writing activities for homework or skipped altogether.

WRITING ACTIVITIES

1. Say: *These are the steps you take to get a Social Security card, but the steps are out of order.* Have students read the direction line. Note that some steps can be done at different times (e.g., copying your birth certificate). Have students complete the activity individually at home or in class and collect for assessment.
2. Have students read the direction line. Do the first line in the paragraph with the class. Have students complete the activity individually at home or in class and collect for assessment.

OUTSIDE ACTIVITY

Have students bring practice applications to class and tell about their problems in filling them out.

INTERNET ACTIVITY

Have students read addresses in class. Help with pronunciation.

LEARNER'S LOG

1. What did you learn in this unit? Write three imperative sentences in your notebook about each of these topics:
   - How to fill out a Social Security card application
   - How to fill out a financial aid application
2. Write three questions you still have about Social Security cards or financial aid for students.

EXPANSION ACTIVITIES

Writing Activities

1. Rewrite these instructions in your notebook. Put the sentences in the correct order.

   How to Get a Social Security Card
   Photocopy your birth certificate.
   Take or send all your documents to the Social Security office.
   Get an application from a Social Security office or online.
   Find another identity document.
   Don't forget to sign the form.
   Fill out all the necessary information.
   Don't write the information. Print it.

2. Rewrite the following paragraph in your notebook. Change all the underlined nouns to object pronouns.

   This is a financial aid application. Read <u>the financial aid application</u> carefully. Write your name and Social Security number on <u>the financial aid application</u>. Dashes are always in a Social Security number. Don't write <u>the dashes</u> on the application. Some questions are difficult. Ask about <u>difficult questions</u>. Dorota is helpful. Ask <u>Dorota</u> for help. The man at the financial aid office is helpful too. Ask <u>the man</u> for help.

   EXAMPLE   *This is a financial aid application. Read it carefully.*

Outside Activity

Find the financial aid office at your school. Ask for a financial aid application. Practice filling it out.

Internet Activity

Go to the Social Security Web site (**www.ssa.gov**) and click on *Use Your Zip to Find our Office*. Find the address of a Social Security office near you.

Expansion

Learner's Log   Have students compare logs in pairs.

Writing Activities Variation

Have students exchange papers with a partner for proofreading.

Internet Activity Variation

Tell students that if they don't have Internet access, they can use Internet facilities at a public library. Alternatively, they can look for the Social Security Administration in the blue pages of the telephone book. Ask students who use the telephone book to find a telephone number and/or address.

UNIT

4

GRAMMAR
The Simple Present Tense
Frequency Words

CONTEXT
American Lifestyles

Unit | 4
Unit Overview

GRAMMAR

1. Briefly review Unit 3 objectives. Say: *We studied imperatives, let's, and object pronouns. Let's name examples of each one.* Write students' examples on the board Ask: *What will we study in Unit 4?* Elicit or say the objectives. (the simple present tense and frequency words)
2. Say and write on the board: *I go to the movies. I listen to music. I eat vegetables.* Underline the verb in each sentence. Say and write *Simple Present Tense* on the board. Insert *often* in the first sentence, *always* in the second sentence, and *never* in the third sentence. Point out that these frequency words go between the subject and the verb.
3. Activate students' prior knowledge. Have volunteers make similar statements about themselves. Prompt by asking: *Do you listen to music? How often?*

CONTEXT

1. Say: *Americans like to work and have fun. We go on picnics in the summer. We like to eat! We always grill hamburgers. Pizza is a favorite food.* Relate the topic to students' experience. Ask: *What's your lifestyle?*
2. Direct students' attention to the photos. Ask: *What is this family doing?* (having a picnic) *What is this man bringing to the door?* (pizza) *What are these two people doing?* (riding bikes)
3. Ask students about the lifestyles of their countries: *What's the [Venezuelan] lifestyle like?* Prompt with questions about picnics, travel, exercise, movies, dancing, and favorite foods. Have students share ideas and experiences.

Expansion

Theme The topic for this unit can be enhanced with the following ideas:
1. Pictures of family barbecues/picnics, which show typical picnic foods, such as fried chicken, hamburgers, chips, and pies
2. A flyer from a local pizzeria that delivers
3. A flyer from a local gym
4. Invitations to children's parties or other events

Unit 4   57

Lesson 1 | Overview

GRAMMAR

1. Write or point to *Simple Present Tense* on the board. Say: *In Lesson 1 we will study the simple present tense.* Say and write on the board: *I go to the movies.* Underline *go*.
2. Say: *We will also study frequency words.* Write *always* and *usually* on the board. Say: *I always go to movies. I usually go with a friend.* Elicit similar sentences from students about their free-time activities. Write verb and frequency phrases on the board. (e.g., *always go shopping, usually watch T.V.*)

CONTEXT

1. Ask: *What are we going to talk about in this lesson?* (having fun) *Americans have fun. We like music. We often go to concerts. We like art and exercise.*
2. Direct students' attention to the pictures. Ask: *What are Dorota and Halina doing? Are they at the bank?* (No, they're at the movies.) *What are these guys watching on TV?* (football) *What about this family? Are they at home?* (They're going to an art museum.)

BEFORE YOU READ

1. Go over each question as a class. Have students discuss the questions in groups. Say: *Tell what you like to do in your free time.* Write on the board: *I like to ____ in my free time.* If possible, put students in groups with people from different countries. Circulate to observe group work.
2. Ask for a few volunteers to share their answers with the class. Find out what favorite activities or hobbies students have in common.

To save class time, skip "Before You Read" or have students prepare answers for homework ahead of time.

LESSON 1

GRAMMAR
The Simple Present Tense—Affirmative Statements
Spelling of the *-s* Form
Uses of the Simple Present Tense
Frequency Words

CONTEXT
Having Fun

Before You Read
1. What are your free-time activities?
2. What is your favorite summer activity?

58 Unit 4

Culture Note
Surveys say that Americans spend much of their free time watching T.V.

---

58 *Grammar in Context Basic* Teacher's Edition

HAVING FUN

Americans **work** hard. But they **have** fun too. Americans **do** many different activities in their free time. They often **visit** with family and friends. But a visitor usually **needs** an invitation. Or the visitor **calls** first.

People sometimes **invite** their friends to their homes. Sometimes, they **watch** sports on TV. One popular game is the Super Bowl. The two best football teams in the U.S. **play** in January or February every year. Friends often **watch** this game together.

Americans **like** the movies. They often **go** to the movies on weekends. But theaters are open every day. Theaters **sell** popcorn, candy, and soft drinks. People **eat** at the movies.

People with children often **spend** time at school activities. City parks **have** many fun activities too. Americans also **enjoy** museums. Museums **have** many learning activities. A list of activities is usually on your city's Web site.

In warm weather, Americans often **go** to outdoor concerts. Many city parks **have** free concerts in the summer. People sometimes **eat** outside too. They **have** picnics. They **cook** on a grill. We **call** this kind of food "barbeque." It is very popular.

Vocabulary in Context

have fun	I **have fun** at the museum. I am happy there.
activity(ies)	City parks often have free **activities**, or fun things to do.
team	One baseball **team** has many players.
outdoor concert(s)	She likes **outdoor concerts.** She listens to music outside.
grill	I like to cook outside. I use my **grill** for cooking.
enjoy	They **enjoy** the Super Bowl. They are happy to watch this game.
spend time	She **spends** a lot of **time** with her daughter. She is with her daughter often.
invite/invitation	Americans **invite** their friends to their homes. They ask their friends to visit them. This is an **invitation.**
each other	They like **each other.** He likes her and she likes him.
best	We are a good team, but they are the **best** team.

Lesson 1   59

Having Fun (Reading)
CD 1, Track 17

1. Have students look at the title of the reading and the first sentence. Ask: *Who is the reading about?* (Americans) *What are we going to read about—work or free time?* (free time) Have students use the title and the pictures on pages 58 and 59 to make predictions about the reading.
2. Have students read the text silently. Then play the audio and have students read along silently.
3. Check students' comprehension. Ask *true* or *false* questions, such as: *Americans don't work very hard. True or false?* (false) *Visitors usually don't need an invitation. True or false?* (false) *Friends watch sports on TV together. True or false?* (true)

To save class time, have students do the reading for homework ahead of time.

VOCABULARY IN CONTEXT

1. Model the pronunciation of each new vocabulary word and have students repeat.
2. Make sure students understand the meaning of each vocabulary word. Review the examples in the book and create additional example sentences. For example, say: *have fun. I have fun in this class. I like to be with you.* Go over each new vocabulary word similarly, using visuals and realia when appropriate. When possible, point to pictures in the book that illustrate new vocabulary items, such as *activity* and *enjoy* on page 58, and *grill* on page 59.
3. Have students underline an example of each new vocabulary item in the reading. Point out that *each other* is not in the reading. Provide more examples of this phrase if students are unsure of its meaning.

Reading Variation

1. To practice listening skills, have students listen to the audio before opening their books. Ask a few comprehension questions: *When is the Super Bowl?* (in January or February) *What do theaters sell?* (popcorn, candy, and soft drinks.) Repeat the audio if necessary. Then have students open their books and read along as they listen to the audio.
2. Alternatively, have students begin by listening to the audio as they read along.

Vocabulary Teaching Ideas

Use the following ideas to teach these terms:

invite/invitation: Display an example of a child's birthday party invitation. Say: *Children invite their friends to a birthday party.*
best: Ask: *Who is the #1 soccer team in the world? Who is the best singer?*

Expansion

Vocabulary in Context Bring in objects to illustrate some of the new vocabulary items, such as posters of different sports teams. Have volunteers act out selected vocabulary items, such as *have fun, activity, team, concert, grill,* and *invite*.

Unit 4   59

DID YOU KNOW?

Say: *Movie times before 6 p.m. are often called* matinees.

LISTENING ACTIVITY

🎧 **CD 1, Track 18**

1. **Say:** *Listen to the sentences about the reading on page 59. Circle* true *or* false. Play the listening selection one time without pausing. Then play it through again, pausing and replaying as necessary.
2. Go over the answers as a class. Ask students to volunteer answers.

4.1 | The Simple Present Tense—Affirmative Statements

1. Have students cover up grammar chart 4.1 on page 60. Write the following sentences on the board:

   I like concerts.
   You like sports.
   He likes football.
   She likes tennis.
   We like English class.
   They like popcorn.

   Say: *Read these sentences. Look at the verb* like. *Point to the verb in each sentence.* Say, *Is* like *the same?* (no) *How is it different?* (There is an -s on the end when *he* and *she* are the subject.)
2. Explain that in the simple present tense, the base form of the verb is used for all subjects except for *he/she/it* and singular nouns.
3. Have students look at the grammar chart on page 60. Go over the sentences. Point out the Language Notes. **Say:** *Some verbs have irregular forms.* Go over the irregular verbs. Explain that *family* and *team* are singular nouns. Direct students' attention to the examples in chart and give more examples, such as: *My family is big. My family is fun. Their team always wins.*

Did You Know? Many theaters have cheaper tickets before 6 P.M. Senior citizens also get cheaper tickets.

🎧 **Listening Activity** Listen to the sentences about the reading. Circle *true* or *false*.

EXAMPLE (TRUE) FALSE

1. TRUE (FALSE)
2. (TRUE) FALSE
3. (TRUE) FALSE
4. (TRUE) FALSE
5. TRUE (FALSE)
6. (TRUE) FALSE
7. (TRUE) FALSE

4.1 | The Simple Present Tense—Affirmative Statements

A simple present tense verb has two forms: the base form and the -s form.

Subject	Verb (Base Form)	Complement
I	like	concerts.
You	have	a grill.
We	go	to the movies.
They	buy	popcorn at the movies.
Americans	enjoy	museums.

Subject	Verb (-s Form)	Complement
He	likes	popcorn.
She	has	a lot of friends.
Simon	enjoys	the Super Bowl.
My family	spends	a lot of time in the park.
Our team	plays	every Saturday.

Language Notes:
1. Three verbs have an irregular -s form: *go (he goes), do (she does),* and *have (it has).*
2. *Family* and *team* are singular nouns.

Expansion

Grammar Chart Have students work in pairs to rewrite the examples in the grammar chart by changing the subjects and/or the complements. (e.g., My sister likes concerts.)

EXERCISE 1 Fill in the blanks with the correct form of the affirmative simple present tense. Use the verb in parentheses ( ).

EXAMPLE He ___goes___ to the movies on the weekends.
           (go)

1. Kids ___like___ activities in parks.
   (like)
2. That family ___does___ many things together.
   (do)
3. We ___spend___ a lot of time with our friends.
   (spend)
4. My park usually ___has___ summer activities.
   (have)
5. Americans ___call___ before a visit to a friend's house.
   (call)
6. My daughter often ___invites___ her friends to our home.
   (invite)

4.2 | Spelling of the -s Form

Examples	Explanation
visit—visits like—likes	Add -s to most verbs to make the -s form.
kiss—kisses wash—washes watch—watches fix—fixes	Add -es to base forms with ss, sh, ch, or x at the end.
worry—worries try—tries	If the base form ends in a consonant + y, change y to -i and add -es.
pay—pays play—plays	If the base form ends in a vowel + y, do not change the y. Just add -s.

EXERCISE 2 Fill in the blanks with the -s form of the verb in parentheses ( ).

EXAMPLE The team ___plays___ baseball.
           (play)

1. Each football team ___tries___ to win the Super Bowl.
   (try)
2. Simon's son ___watches___ TV every night.
   (watch)
3. Dorota ___enjoys___ football games.
   (enjoy)

Lesson 1   61

EXERCISE 1

1. Have students read the direction line. Go over the example in the Student Book.
2. Have students complete Exercise 1 individually. Check the answers as a class. If necessary, review grammar chart **4.1** on page 60.

4.2 | Spelling of the -s Form

1. Have students look at grammar chart **4.2** on page 61. Go over the examples and explanations in the chart.
2. Write multiple spellings on the board for these verbs:

   carry: carrys/carries
   walk: walks/walkes
   stay: stays/staies
   mix: mixs/mixes
   splash: splashs/splashes

   Ask students which spelling is correct and why. Refer students to the rules in the grammar chart.
3. Pronounce the verbs. Have students repeat.

EXERCISE 2

1. Have students read the direction line. Go over the example in the Student Book. Point out the picture of the baseball player on page 61.
2. Have students complete Exercise 2 individually. Go over the answers as a class.
3. If necessary, review grammar chart **4.2** on page 61.

Expansion

Grammar Chart Have students work in pairs to create sentences with the verbs from grammar charts **4.1** and **4.2**. Say: *Write five sentences using the -s form.* Circulate to observe pair work. Give help as needed. Ask volunteers to read some of their sentences.

Unit 4   61

4.3 | Uses of the Simple Present Tense

1. Have students look at grammar chart **4.3** on page 62. Go over the examples and explanations.
2. Write more examples on the board and elicit rules from students.

   I have a Social Security card.
   My daughter wants a computer.
   Children get gifts at birthday parties.

EXERCISE 3

1. Have students read the direction line. Then go over the example. Say: *The ideas for the sentences are from the reading on page 59.*
2. Have students complete Exercise 3 individually. Then have students compare answers with a partner. Circulate to observe pair work. Give help as needed. If needed, go over the sentences with the class.
3. If necessary, review grammar chart **4.3** on page 62.

---

4. A new immigrant sometimes __worries__ about life here.
   (worry)
5. Only one team __wins__ the Super Bowl.
   (win)
6. Her father __washes__ the grill after a barbeque.
   (wash)
7. He __spends__ a lot of time outside in summer.
   (spend)

4.3 | Uses of the Simple Present Tense

Examples	Explanation
American movie theaters **sell** popcorn.	Use the simple present tense for facts.
We **go** to the movies once a week.	Use the simple present for repeated actions, such as customs and habits.
Americans **like** the movies.	Use the simple present with *like*, *need*, and *want*.

EXERCISE 3 Write a sentence with the correct form of the verb in the simple present tense. Use the ideas in the reading.

EXAMPLE Americans / like
Answers may vary.   *Americans like outdoor concerts.*

1. American museums / have
   American museums have many learning activities.
2. An American visitor / need
   An American visitor usually needs an invitation.
3. Two teams / play
   Two teams play in the Super Bowl.
4. People / invite
   People sometimes invite their friends to their homes.
5. An American family / go
   An American family often goes to outdoor concerts.
6. Americans / cook
   Americans cook on a grill.
7. The best football team / win
   The best football team wins the Super Bowl.

Expansion

Grammar Chart Have students come up with other examples of facts, repeated actions, and examples for *like*, *need*, and *want*.

Exercise 3 Have students work in pairs to create sentences about their own countries and cultures. (e.g., Korean families like to eat barbecue.) Circulate to help students with vocabulary.

4.4 | Frequency Words

Frequency	Frequency Word	Examples
100%	always	Americans **always** call before a visit.
↕	usually	People **usually** enjoy their free time.
	often	She **often** goes to the movies.
	sometimes	Women **sometimes** watch sports with their husbands.
	rarely	Americans **rarely** visit friends without an invitation.
0%	hardly ever	Some Americans **hardly ever** have free time.
	never	I **never** cook outside in January.

Language Note: Frequency words go before the verb. *Often, usually,* and *sometimes* can also go at the beginning or at the end of the sentence.
Sometimes we go to the movies.
We go to the movies **often**.
Usually she eats breakfast.

EXERCISE 4 ABOUT YOU Write a sentence with the words given. Add a frequency word from the chart above.

EXAMPLE speak English at home
I hardly ever speak English at home.

1. cook dinner at home
   Answers will vary.

2. watch TV in the evening

3. invite my friends to my home

4. visit my friends without an invitation

5. spend time at museums

6. work on Saturdays

Lesson 1 63

4.4 | Frequency Words

1. Have students cover up grammar chart **4.4** on page 63. Draw a similar scale on the board. Write the frequency words on the scale in a jumbled order. Say: *Try to put the frequency words in the correct order. You can use the reading on page 59 to help you.*
2. Have students look at the chart on page 63. Go over the frequency words and the examples.
3. Point out the Language Note. Say: *Some frequency words go before the verb and some words can go at the beginning or the end of a sentence.* Review the frequency words *often, usually,* and *sometimes*. Go over the example sentences.

EXERCISE 4

1. Say: *This exercise is about you.* Have students read the direction line. Go over the example in the book. Say: *Remember to write sentences about yourself.*
2. Have students complete Exercise 4 individually. Then have students compare answers with a partner. Circulate to observe pair work. Give help as needed.
3. If necessary, review grammar chart **4.4** on page 63.

Expansion

Exercises 4 Have students get into groups to discuss their statements. Then have groups report to the class. Say and write this sample statement on the board: *Two [in our group, or students' names] hardly ever cook dinner at home.* Write the results of the class discussion on the board.

Unit 4 63

EXERCISE 5

1. Say: *Dorota is talking about American customs.* Have students read the direction line. Say: *To complete the sentences, put the words in parentheses in the correct order.* Go over the example in the Student Book. Remind students to capitalize the first word of every sentence.
2. Have students complete Exercise 5 individually. Then have students compare answers with a partner. Circulate to observe pair work. Give help as needed.
3. If necessary, review grammar chart 4.4 on page 63.

EXERCISE 5 Complete the sentences in Dorota's talk about American customs. Use the words given in the correct order.

<u>Americans often invite</u> each other to dinner.
(example: Americans/invite/often)

or <u>Usually an American invites</u>
<u>An American usually invites</u> a guest for a specific day and time.
(1. an American/invite/usually)

"Let's have dinner sometime" is not an invitation.

<u>A dinner guest always comes</u> on time. It isn't polite to be more than
(2. a dinner guest/come/always)
or <u>Usually guests bring</u>
15 minutes late. <u>Guests usually bring</u> something for the host
(3. guests/bring/usually)
or <u>Sometimes they bring</u>
or hostess. <u>They sometimes bring</u> flowers.
(4. they/bring/sometimes)
or <u>Sometimes they bring</u>
<u>They sometimes bring</u> candy. At dinner,
(5. they/bring/sometimes)

<u>guests often say</u> something nice about the food or the
(6. guests/say/often)
or <u>Sometimes guests ask</u>
table. It is polite in the U.S. <u>Guests sometimes ask</u> for more
(7. guests/ask/sometimes)

food. It is common in the U.S.

64 Unit 4

Expansion

Exercise 5 Have students talk about their customs in groups. Ask: *When you are invited to dinner in your country, what are the customs? Do you bring flowers? Is it important to be on time?*

64 *Grammar in Context Basic* Teacher's Edition

EXERCISE 6 Fill in the blanks in Simon's phone conversation with Victor. Use the verbs in the box below. Use two verbs twice.

| pays | have | sells | likes |
| plays | has ✓ | need | enjoy |

Simon: Are you and Lisa busy tonight?
Victor: No, why?
Simon: The city __has__ (example) concerts in the park on Thursday evenings. Let's all go tonight.
Victor: Sure. It's a great idea.
Simon: Bring Maya. Kids __enjoy__ (1) outdoor concerts.
Victor: How much are the tickets?
Simon: The city __pays__ (2) for these concerts. They're free for all of us.
Victor: Where is it?
Simon: It's at Logan Park on Central Street. A different band __plays__ (3) there every Thursday evening from 7 to 9. The kids __have__ (4) fun with their friends. A little store in the park __sells__ (5) popcorn and ice cream. My daughter, Amy, __likes__ (6) ice cream in the summer. Marta and I __enjoy__ (7) the different kinds of music.
Victor: We __need__ (8) chairs, right?
Simon: Yes, but I __have__ (9) some extra chairs for outside. They're easy to carry. Don't worry about that. Just be at our house about 6:30.
Victor: Thanks, Simon. See you tonight!

Lesson 1   65

EXERCISE 6

1. Have students read the direction line. Go over the example. Ask a volunteer to complete the next sentence.
2. If you think students will have difficulty with the vocabulary, review or pre-teach words, such as *Maya* (a *kid*), *Lisa* (a *wife*), *Central Street* (a place), *Logan Park* (a place), *chairs* (things, what you sit in).
3. Have students complete Exercise 6 individually. Then have students compare answers with a partner. Circulate to observe pair work. Give help as needed.
4. If necessary, review grammar chart **4.1** on page 60.

Expansion

Exercise 6 Have students draw a poster advertising the concert in the conversation. Put an example on board for students to complete.

TONIGHT!
CONCERT
At _____ *on Central* _____

Date: _____ *evening*
Time: _____ - _____

Unit 4   65

Lesson 2 | Overview

GRAMMAR

1. Write the following sentences on the board:
   I *don't work* on [Sundays].
   I work *[five] days* a week.
   I *like* to relax on [Sundays].

2. Point to each example and say: *First, we're going to learn how to form the negative. Then, we're going to learn time expressions and infinitives.* Elicit more examples of each objective from volunteers.

CONTEXT

1. Say: *Some Americans do not relax. They work five days a week and weekends. They work eight hours a day.* Ask: *What will we talk about in this lesson— having fun or working in the U.S.?* (working in the U.S.)

2. Direct students' attention to the picture. Ask: *What are these places?* Point to each place. (a classroom, an office, a restaurant, a bank, a department store, a factory, and a doctor's office.)

3. Relate the topic to students' knowledge and experience. Ask: *Do you work? Where do you work? Do you work in any of these places?* Point to the picture on page 66. Have a few volunteers tell where they work.

BEFORE YOU READ

1. Go over each question as a class. Have a volunteer read the questions or read them to the class yourself. Ask students to discuss their answers in pairs.

2. Ask for a few volunteers to share their answers with the class. If they do not like their jobs, have them describe a job they want.

To save class time, skip "Before You Read" or have students prepare their answers for homework ahead of time.

LESSON 2

GRAMMAR
Simple Present Tense—Negative Forms
Expressions of Time with the Simple Present Tense
Infinitives with Simple Present Verbs

CONTEXT
Working in the U.S.

Before You Read
1. What is your job?
2. Do you like your job? Why or why not?

66 Unit 4

Expansion

Theme The topic for this unit can be enhanced with the following idea:

1. A poster with the following facts about American workers:
2. 144 million people work in the U.S.
3. 11.5 million are self-employed
4. 1.7 million workers have two jobs

---

66 *Grammar in Context Basic* Teacher's Edition

WORKING IN THE U.S.

Work is very important to Americans. They often ask each other about their jobs. But they **don't ask** each other about their salaries or wages.

Americans usually work five days a week. Most office workers and teachers **don't work** on Saturdays and Sundays. But many people have other days off. Workers in stores and restaurants hardly ever have days off on weekends. Stores and restaurants are very busy on weekends.

A day's work is usually eight hours, or 40 hours a week. But most Americans work more. Some people complain. They **don't like** to work so many hours. But others want to make more money. People with wages **get** more money for each hour of overtime work.

Many people **don't relax** on their days off. A day off **doesn't** always **mean** free time. Some people get part-time jobs on these days.

Today, the average American worker **doesn't keep** the same job for a long time. Young people change jobs often. Older people **don't like** to change jobs often. The average worker in America keeps a job for about five years.

Vocabulary in Context

salary	He is a teacher. His **salary** is $55,000 per year.
wage	They work in a store. Their **wage** is $8 an hour.
complain	She doesn't like her job. She **complains** about it a lot.
mean	A good salary **means** a worker gets a lot of money each year.
average	Most workers don't stay at one job for a long time. The **average** worker changes jobs often.
day off	Tomorrow is Tuesday. It's my **day off**. I don't work on Tuesdays.
relax	We **relax** on Sundays. We don't work.
overtime	I don't like to work **overtime**. I don't like to work more than 40 hours.
keep	They **keep** their jobs for several years. They are at the same job for several years.

Lesson 2   67

Working in the U.S. (Reading)
CD 1, Track 19

1. Have students look at the title of the reading. Ask: *Is the reading about working?* (yes) *Working where?* (in the U.S.) *What do you think it will say about working in the U.S.?* Have students use the title to make predictions about the reading.
2. First, have students read the text silently. Then play the audio and have students read along silently.
3. Check students' basic comprehension. Ask true or false questions, such as: *American workers talk about salaries. True or false?* (false) *American workers usually work six days a week. True or false?* (false) *All Americans relax on their days off. True or false?* (false)

To save class time, have students do the reading for homework ahead of time.

VOCABULARY IN CONTEXT

1. Model the pronunciation of each new vocabulary word and have students repeat.
2. Make sure students understand the meaning of each vocabulary word. Review the examples in the book and create additional example sentences. For example, say: *salary. Doctors in the U.S. have big salaries. They usually make between $90,000 and $600,000 a year.* Review each new vocabulary word similarly, using visuals and realia when appropriate.
3. Have students underline one example of each new vocabulary item in the reading.

Reading Variation
To practice listening skills, have students listen to the audio before opening their books. Ask a few comprehension questions: *Do young people often change jobs?* (yes) *How many days a week do Americans usually work?* (five) Repeat the audio if necessary. Then have students open their books and read along as they listen to the audio.

Vocabulary Teaching Ideas
Use the following ideas to teach these terms:

complain: Say: *Let's complain about the room.* Point to the problems as you say them. (e.g., *The room is too small. We need more desks. There aren't enough windows.*)

overtime: Tell students that the work week in the U.S. is 40 hours. Someone that works over 40 hours is working *overtime*.

Expansion
Vocabulary in Context Have volunteers act out selected vocabulary, such as *relax* and *complain*.

DID YOU KNOW?

Explain to students that they can find the minimum wage for each state by looking on the U.S. Department of Labor's Web site.

LISTENING ACTIVITY

🎧 *CD 1, Track 20*

1. Say: *Listen to the sentences about the reading on page 67. Circle* true *or* false. Play the listening selection one time without pausing. Then play it through again, pausing and replaying as necessary.
2. Go over the answers as a class. Ask students to volunteer answers.

4.5 | Simple Present Tense—Negative Forms

1. Have students turn to the reading on page 67. Say: *Do you see negatives? What are they?* (*don't* and *doesn't*)
2. Have students look at grammar chart 4.5 on page 68. Read the examples in the chart. Say: *There are two forms for the negative with* do. Point out that *doesn't* is used with *he, she,* and *it,* and singular nouns. *Don't* is used with all other subjects. Explain that the base form is always used with the negative.
3. Direct students to the Language Notes. Explain that irregular verbs, such as go and get, have regular negative forms. Go over the examples. Stress to students that *hardly ever, never,* and *rarely* are negative. Hence, we do not use them with a negative verb.
4. To further explain the second Language Note, say: *Two negatives = affirmative.* Give additional examples to illustrate. Write on the board: *We hardly ever don't have any days off. I never don't work on weekends.* Say: *The English is bad. Also, the meaning is affirmative: We often have days off. I always work on weekends.*

Did You Know?
- All states need to have a minimum hourly wage. It's the law in America. But each state can decide to make the minimum wage higher.
- Workers usually get time and a half (50% more per hour) for overtime work.

🎧 **Listening Activity** Listen to the sentences about the reading. Circle *true* or *false*.

EXAMPLE (TRUE)   FALSE

1. TRUE   (FALSE)
2. (TRUE)   FALSE
3. (TRUE)   FALSE
4. TRUE   (FALSE)
5. TRUE   (FALSE)
6. (TRUE)   FALSE
7. TRUE   (FALSE)

4.5 | Simple Present Tense—Negative Forms

Subject	Don't	Verb (Base Form)	Complement
I	don't	work	on Saturdays.
You	don't	live	near your work.
We	don't	enjoy	overtime work.
They	don't	spend	much money.
Those people	don't	get	wages.

Subject	Doesn't	Verb (Base Form)	Complement
He	doesn't	have	a full-time job.
She	doesn't	like	her job.
An American	doesn't	ask	about a person's salary.

Language Notes:
1. Compare the affirmative and negative forms.
   He **has** time. He **doesn't have** money.
   She **goes** to work on Friday. She **doesn't go** to work on Saturday.
   They **get** a wage. They **don't get** a salary.
2. The frequency words *hardly ever, never,* and *rarely* are not used with negative verbs. They have a negative meaning.
   We **hardly ever have** any days off.
   I **never work** on weekends.

68   Unit 4

Expansion

Grammar Chart Have students work in pairs to create new sentences for the negative verbs listed in the grammar chart. (e.g., She doesn't work on Sundays.)

---

68   *Grammar in Context Basic* Teacher's Edition

EXERCISE 1 Fill in the blanks with the negative form of the verb in parentheses ( ).

EXAMPLE He ___doesn't have___ a part-time job.
                    (have)

1. Young people ___don't keep___ their jobs a long time.
                    (keep)
2. Dorota ___doesn't complain___ about her job.
                    (complain)
3. You and I ___don't make___ a lot of money.
                    (make)
4. American workers ___don't have___ the same days off.
                    (have)
5. Simon ___doesn't talk___ about his salary.
                    (talk)
6. A day off ___doesn't mean___ free time for some people.
                    (mean)

EXERCISE 2 Write a negative sentence with the words given.

EXAMPLES Simon works on Saturday. (on Wednesday)
Simon doesn't work on Wednesday.

Simon works on Saturday. (Many Americans)
Many Americans don't work on Saturday.

1. Simon gets a salary. (an hourly wage)
   Simon doesn't get an hourly wage.
2. A *salary* means money for a year of work. (money for an hour of work)
   A salary doesn't mean money for an hour of work.
3. Some people complain about long work hours. (Dorota and Simon)
   Dorota and Simon don't complain about long work hours.
4. Workers in most stores get two days off. (weekends off)
   Workers in most stores don't get weekends off.
5. Halina works part-time. (40 hours a week)
   Halina doesn't work 40 hours a week.
6. Many Americans work overtime. (Simon and Dorota)
   Simon and Dorota don't work overtime.

Lesson 2   69

EXERCISE 1

1. Have students read the direction line. Go over the example in the Student Book.
2. Have students complete Exercise 1 individually. Go over the answers as a class.
3. If necessary, review grammar chart **4.5** on page 68.

EXERCISE 2

1. Have students read the direction line. Say: *In this exercise you rewrite each sentence. You make the verb negative, and then change the information.* Go over the examples in the book. Point out that the two examples illustrate two kinds of sentences that students might make. Point out the picture of the man holding a paycheck. Have a volunteer complete #1.
2. Have students complete the rest of Exercise 2 individually. Go over the answers as a class.
3. If necessary, review grammar chart **4.5** on page 68.

Expansion

Exercise 2 Have students work in pairs to create sentences true for them or their country. (e.g., Workers in my country don't get two days off a week.) Ask volunteers to share information with the class.

4.6 | Expressions of Time with the Simple Present Tense

1. Have students look at grammar chart **4.6** on page 70. Go over the examples. Point out the subject, verb, complement, and time expression in each example.
2. Draw a large monthly calendar on the board. Use the calendar to help illustrate the time expressions. For example, cross out five days in a week for *five days a week*.
3. Explain that time expressions only come at the end of a sentence. Illustrate with examples. Say: *Listen. Which is correct?*
   1. She doesn't on weekends work.
   2. She doesn't work on weekends.

EXERCISE 3

1. Tell students that this exercise is about them. Have students read the direction line. Go over the example in the Student Book.
2. Have students complete Exercise 3 individually. Then have students compare their answers in pairs. Circulate to observe pair work. Give help as needed.
3. If necessary, review grammar chart **4.6** on page 70.

4.6 | Expressions of Time with the Simple Present Tense

Subject	Verb (+ Complement)	Time Expression
She	works doesn't work	eight hours a day. five days a week. every day. on the weekends.
We	work overtime don't work overtime	twice a week. once a month. on Tuesdays.
They	complain don't complain	every five minutes. all the time.

Language Note: Time expressions go at the end of the sentence. They never go before the base form.

EXERCISE 3 ABOUT YOU Write a sentence about you. Use the simple present tense—affirmative or negative—and an expression of time. Add extra information where possible.

EXAMPLE take the bus
I take the bus twice a day. OR
I don't take the bus. I drive every day.

1. eat
   _____ Answers will vary. _____
2. work
3. have a day off
4. drive
5. do the laundry
6. come to this class
7. go to the supermarket

70 Unit 4

Expansion

Exercise 3 Have students compare answers to Exercise 3 in groups. Say: *Ask your group members questions, such as: How often do you eat? How often do you do the laundry?*

4.7 | Infinitives with Simple Present Verbs

We often use the infinitive form with simple present verbs. The infinitive form is always the same. Use infinitives after the following verbs: *want, need, like, expect,* and *try*.

Subject	Verb	Infinitive Form	Complement
I	like / don't like	**to relax**	on the weekends.
He	wants / doesn't want	**to take**	a day off.
She	expects / doesn't expect	**to have**	a day off.
We	try / don't try	**to do**	good work.
They	need / don't need	**to work**	on Saturday.

EXERCISE 4 Fill in the blanks with the simple present + infinitive. Use affirmative or negative and the words in parentheses ( ).

EXAMPLES We <u>don't expect to speak</u> our native language in this class.
(not expect/speak)

We <u>expect to speak</u> English in this class.
(expect/speak)

1. Some people <u>like to complain</u>.
(like/complain)

2. He <u>doesn't want to leave</u> his job.
(not want/leave)

3. We <u>need to take</u> a day off this week.
(need/take)

4. Americans <u>don't expect to</u> every day.
(not expect/work)

5. Dorota <u>doesn't like to work</u> on Sundays.
(not like/work)

6. That young man always <u>tries to do</u> a good job.
(try/do)

Lesson 2　71

4.7 | Infinitives with Simple Present Verbs

1. Write on the board: *Infinitive Form*. Ask: *What is an infinitive?* Say: *The infinitive is the base form of the verb with "to" in front.* Write an example such as *to relax*.
2. Have students look at grammar chart **4.7** on page 71. Say: *We use the infinitive after specific verbs in the simple present tense:* like, want expect, try, *and* need. Go over the examples in the chart. Point out the subject, verb, the infinitive form, and the complement in each example.
3. Explain that the infinitive form never changes. It is always the same.

EXERCISE 4

1. Have students read the direction line. Say: *You can complete the sentence with the negative or the affirmative.* Go over the examples in the Student Book. Have a volunteer complete #1.
2. Have students complete the rest of Exercise 4 individually. Then have students compare answers in pairs. Circulate to observe pair work. Give help as needed. Go over the answers with the class,
3. If necessary, review grammar chart **4.7** on page 71.

Expansion

Exercise 4 Have students work in pairs to create sentences about work. (e.g., I expect to have a day off every week.) Brainstorm topics and list them on the board. Topics might include days off/vacation, salary/wage, and insurance. Circulate to observe pair work. Give help as needed.

Unit 4　71

EXERCISE 5

1. Have students read the direction line. If necessary, clarify that students will change the verb to verb plus infinitive. Go over the examples in the Student Book.
2. Have students complete Exercise 5 individually. Then have students compare answers with a partner. Circulate to observe pair work. Give help as needed.
3. If necessary, review grammar chart **4.7** on page 71.

⏱ To save class time, have students complete the exercise for homework.

EXERCISE 6

1. Have students look at the picture on page 72. Ask: *What is this woman doing?* (looking for jobs on the Internet) Then have students read the direction line. Go over the example in the Student Book. Remind students that they are going to complete the sentences with the negative form only.
2. Have students complete Exercise 6 individually. Then have students compare answers with a partner. Circulate to observe pair work. Give help as needed.
3. If necessary, review grammar charts **4.5** on page 68 and **4.7** on page 71.

⏱ To save class time, have students complete the exercise for homework.

EXERCISE 5 Write the sentences again. Add the verbs in parentheses ( ).

EXAMPLES She takes a day off on Sunday. (want)
She wants to take a day off on Sunday.

She doesn't take a day off on Sunday. (want)
She doesn't want to take a day off on Sunday.

1. That football team wins every game. (try)
   That football team tries to win every game.
2. The workers don't make a lot of money. (expect)
   The workers don't expect to make a lot of money.
3. I don't complain about my job. (want)
   I don't want to complain about my job.
4. Simon doesn't work overtime. (need)
   Simon doesn't need to work overtime.

EXERCISE 6 Fill in the blanks in the conversation with the simple present tense. Use the negative form of the verbs in parentheses ( ).

Irma: We have a day off tomorrow. Let's go to the museum.

Sara: I'm sorry. But I __don't have__ time. I need to look for a new job.
(example: have)

Irma: You have a job.

Sara: I know. But I __don't like__ it. I __don't work__ enough
(1. like)   (2. work)
hours. And the job __doesn't pay__ enough money. My boss
(3. pay)
__doesn't like__ my work. It's not a good job for me.
(4. like)

Irma: There's a job in my company. But it's only part-time.

Sara: Thanks, Irma, but I __don't want__ to work part-time. I
(5. want)
need a full-time job.

Irma: The Web is a good place to look. But most people
__don't find__ their jobs on Web sites. They hear about them
(6. find)
from other people. So ask all of your friends.

---

72 Unit 4

Expansion

Exercise 6 Have students practice the conversation in pairs. Ask volunteers to roleplay the conversation in front of the class.

EXERCISE 7 ABOUT YOU Fill in the blanks with the simple present tense of the verbs in parentheses ( ). Use the affirmative or negative form. Write **true** sentences about work in your home town or country. Read your sentences to the class.

EXAMPLE The average worker in my home town __doesn't work__ every day.
                                                    (work)

Answers will vary.

1. A worker _____ two days off every week.
            (get)
2. Most people _____ more than eight hours a day at work.
              (spend)
3. A company _____ more money for overtime work.
             (pay)
4. People _____ to work overtime.
         (like)
5. Most people _____ about their jobs.
              (complain)
6. My country _____ a minimum hourly wage for workers.
             (have)
7. The average worker _____ a part-time job on days off.
                     (take)
8. Workers _____ four weeks off each year with pay.
          (expect/get)
9. People _____ on vacation on their weeks off.
         (go)
10. The average worker _____ jobs often.
                      (change)
11. The average worker _____ at the same job for a long time.
                      (stay)
12. Most women in my hometown _____.
                             (work)

Lesson 2   73

EXERCISE 7

1. Say: *In this exercise, you'll write true sentences about work in your town or country.* Then have students read the direction line. Go over the example in the Student Book. Have a volunteer model the example. Elicit and review difficult vocabulary, such as *minimum hourly wage*.
2. Have students complete Exercise 7 individually. Then have students compare answers with a partner. Circulate to observe pair work. Give help as needed.
3. If necessary, review grammar charts **4.5** on page 68 and **4.7** on page 71.

To save class time, have students complete the exercise for homework.

Expansion

Exercise 7 Have students compare answers in groups. If possible, put students from different countries together. Do a survey. Ask: *What country is the best to work in?*

Unit 4   73

Lesson 3 | Overview

GRAMMAR

Ask: *What tense did we study in Lesson 2?* (simple present) Write the following sentence on the board: *Do you eat hamburgers?* Repeat the question and elicit *yes* and *no* responses in complete sentences from several students. (e.g., Yes, I eat hamburgers; Yes, I do.) Then say: *In Lesson, 3, we're going to study yes/no questions in the simple present tense.*

CONTEXT

1. Say: *We're going to talk about eating customs. Many Americans eat lunch at 11:30. I usually eat dinner at 6:00. I like to get Chinese take-out.* Elicit yes/no responses. Ask: *Do you eat Chinese food? Do you get take-out?*
2. Direct students' attention to the photo. Ask: *What place is this?* (a restaurant) *Who is serving food?* (a woman; a waitress)

BEFORE YOU READ

1. Go over each question as a class. Have a volunteer read the questions or read them to the class yourself.
2. Ask volunteers to name foods and restaurants they like.

To save class time, skip "Before You Read" or have students prepare their answers for homework ahead of time.

LESSON 3

GRAMMAR
Yes/No Questions in the Simple Present Tense

CONTEXT
Eating Customs

Before You Read

Circle *yes* or *no*.

1. Do you like American food? YES   NO
2. Do you eat in American restaurants? YES   NO

74 Unit 4

Culture Note

Americans eat out more than the people of any other country. More than 65 percent eat in a restaurant one or more times a week. Getting take-out food is even more popular.

---

74   *Grammar in Context Basic* Teacher's Edition

EATING CUSTOMS

Halina: It's 1:30. It's early. **Do Americans** usually **have** lunch at this time?
Dorota: One-thirty is late. Lunch hours usually begin at 11 a.m. Americans usually have an hour for lunch. **Do you want to order** a sandwich, Halina?
Halina: Yes, I do. I'm hungry. Look. That man has a sandwich. What is it?
Dorota: It's a mushroom sandwich.
Halina: Does it have meat with the mushroom?
Dorota: I don't think so. Maybe the man's a vegetarian. Some people don't eat meat.
Halina: Do Americans often **eat** in restaurants?
Dorota: Yes, they do. They're very busy. They don't have time to cook every meal. Sometimes they go out. Sometimes they order from restaurants.
Halina: Do restaurants deliver food to your home?
Dorota: Yes, some do. And many restaurants have "take-out" food. They prepare the food for you. You take it home to eat. Supermarkets have prepared food too. It's in the deli section. They have hot and cold food. Sometimes people eat the food in the supermarkets at special tables. Most people take home prepared food. Prepared food is very popular.
Halina: Does prepared food cost more?
Dorota: Yes, it does. But it's very convenient.

Vocabulary in Context

mushroom(s)	I like **mushrooms.** They are very good for your health.
vegetarian	He's a **vegetarian.** He doesn't eat meat.
order	She wants to **order** a sandwich. She asks for a mushroom sandwich.
deliver	That restaurant **delivers** pizza. Someone brings it to your house.
take-out	Let's order **take-out.** We take the food home to eat.
deli	Let's go to the **deli** section. They have sandwiches there.
prepared food	**Prepared food** is very popular. People don't need to cook it.
convenient	Prepared food is **convenient.** It's easy because we don't have to cook it.

Lesson 3   75

Eating Customs (Reading) CD 1, Track 21

1. Have students look at the title of the reading. Ask: *What is the reading about?* (eating customs) *Is it about Indian food or American food?* (American customs) Have students use the title and the picture on page 74 to make predictions about the reading.
2. First, have students read the dialogue silently. Then play the audio and have students read along.
3. Check students' comprehension. Ask *yes/no* questions, such as: *Does lunch hour in the U.S. begin at 11:00 a.m.?* (yes) *Do supermarkets have prepared food?* (yes)

To save class time, have students do the reading for homework ahead of time.

VOCABULARY IN CONTEXT

1. Model the pronunciation of each new vocabulary word and have students repeat.
2. Make sure students understand the meaning of each vocabulary word. Review the examples in the book and create additional example sentences. For example, say: *convenient. It's convenient to eat out. I don't have to cook dinner or wash dishes.* Go over each new vocabulary word similarly, using visuals and realia when appropriate. When possible, point to pictures in the book that illustrate the new vocabulary items, such as *mushrooms* on page 75.
3. Have students underline an example of each vocabulary item in the reading.

Reading Variation

1. To practice listening skills, have students listen to the audio before opening their books. Ask a few comprehension questions: *Do Americans often eat in restaurants?* (yes) *Is prepared food popular?* (yes) Repeat the audio if necessary. Then have students open their books and read along as they listen to the audio.
2. Alternatively, have students begin by listening to the audio as they read along.

Vocabulary Teaching Ideas

Use the following ideas to teach these terms:

vegetarian: Say: *I'm a vegetarian. I don't like meat. I eat a lot of pasta and vegetables.*
order: Mimic a waiter by using a small notebook and pencil to take an order. Say: *I am a waiter. Can I take your order? What would you like to eat?*

Expansion

Reading Have students work in pairs to create a similar conversation using information about their native cultures and food customs.

Vocabulary in Context To check comprehension, have volunteers in pairs or groups act out selected vocabulary, such as *order* and *deliver*.

DID YOU KNOW?

Tell students that there are different kinds of vegetarians. For example, some vegetarians eat dairy and egg products, but don't eat meat. *Vegans* don't eat any animal products, including eggs or honey, and don't wear clothes made from animal skins or fur.

LISTENING ACTIVITY

🎧 **CD 1, Track 22**

1. Say: *This listening activity is based on the conversation about American eating customs. Listen to the instructions. Circle* true *or* false. Play the listening selection one time without pausing. Then play it through again, pausing and replaying as necessary.
2. Go over the answers as a class. Ask students to volunteer answers.

4.8 | *Yes/No* Questions in the Simple Present Tense

1. Have students look at grammar chart 4.8 on page 76. Say: *Questions in the simple present tense begin with* do or does *followed by the subject and the base form of the verb.* Say: *Do is used with I, you, we, they, and plural nouns. Does is used with he, she, it, and singular nouns.* Hold up the book and run your finger down the column of subjects and then verbs to make sure students can follow the chart.
2. Read through all the questions and short answers in the chart. Ask volunteers questions to check understanding. (e.g., *Do you like Chinese food? Yes, I do.*)
3. Review word order for questions. Then write scrambled sentences on the board, such as: *go/to a deli for lunch/she/does/?* Ask volunteers to put sentences in the correct order.

- About 10 million Americans are vegetarians. Most are young women in cities.
- The U.S. has two times more women vegetarians than men.

🎧 **Listening Activity** Listen to the statements about the conversation. Circle *true* or *false*.

EXAMPLE (TRUE)   FALSE

1. TRUE   (FALSE)   5. (TRUE)   FALSE
2. (TRUE)   FALSE   6. TRUE   (FALSE)
3. (TRUE)   FALSE   7. (TRUE)   FALSE
4. TRUE   (FALSE)

4.8 | *Yes / No* Questions in the Simple Present Tense

Do	Subject	Verb (Base Form)	Complement	Short Answer
Do	you	like	American food?	No, I don't.
Do	we	want	prepared food today?	No, we don't.
Do	they	enjoy	vegetarian food?	Yes, they do.
Do	vegetarians	eat	meat?	No, they don't.
Does	**Subject**	**Verb (Base Form)**	**Complement**	**Short Answer**
Does	he	go	to a restaurant for lunch?	Yes, he does.
Does	she	take	a long lunch hour?	No, she doesn't.
Does	this restaurant	have	take-out food?	Yes, it does.

EXERCISE 1 Fill in the blanks with *do* or *does*. Then write a short answer to each question.

EXAMPLE   __Does__ your wife cook at home?
Yes, she does.

1. __Do__ vegetarians eat meat?
   No, they don't.

2. __Do__ some restaurants deliver to your home?
   Yes, they do.

76   Unit 4

Expansion

Grammar Chart Have students go back to the reading on page 75. Say: *Find the questions in the reading. Circle* do *or* does *and the subject of each question.*

---

76   *Grammar in Context Basic* Teacher's Edition

3. __Does__ a mushroom sandwich have meat?
   No, it doesn't.
4. __Do__ supermarkets have deli sections?
   Yes, they do.
5. __Does__ the deli section have hot and cold food?
   Yes, it does.
6. __Does__ the American lunch hour usually start at 11 a.m.?
   Yes, it does.
7. __Do__ American workers take two hours for lunch?
   No, they don't.

EXERCISE 2 Complete each short conversation with a question in the simple present tense. Use the words given.

EXAMPLE A: Many Americans eat lunch outside the home. (eat in restaurants)
   B: *Do Americans eat lunch in restaurants?*

1. A: He likes meat. (like mushrooms)
   B: *Does he like mushrooms?*
2. A: She buys food in that supermarket. (buy prepared food)
   B: *Does she buy prepared food?*
3. A: That restaurant has take-out food. (have vegetarian food)
   B: *Does that restaurant have vegetarian food?*
4. A: You go to lunch early. (go at 11:00 a.m.)
   B: *Do you go to lunch at 11:00 a.m.?*
5. A: Halina and Dorota want to order some lunch. (want to order sandwiches)
   B: *Do Halina and Dorota want to order sandwiches?*
6. A: This restaurant delivers pizza. (deliver sandwiches)
   B: *Does this restaurant deliver sandwiches?*
7. A: Americans eat prepared food. (eat it in the supermarket)
   B: *Do Americans eat it in the supermarket?*

Lesson 3

EXERCISE 1

1. Have students read the direction line. Go over the example in the Student Book. Draw students' attention to the subject—*your wife*. Ask: *Is the subject singular or plural?* (singular) *Do we use* do *or* does *with a singular subject?* (does) Have a volunteer do #1.
2. Have students complete the rest of Exercise 1 individually. Check the answers as a class. If necessary, review grammar chart **4.8** on page 76.

EXERCISE 2

1. Have students read the direction line. Go over the example in the Student Book. Say: *Use the words in the parentheses to make a question.* Have a volunteer do #1.
2. Have students complete the rest of Exercise 2 individually. Check the answers as a class. If necessary, review grammar chart **4.8** on page 76.

Expansion

Exercise 2 Have students practice the short conversations in pairs. Circulate to observe pair work.

EXERCISE 3

1. Have students look at the picture. Ask: *What do you think Victor's job is?* (delivering pizza) Have students read the direction line in the Student Book.
2. Have students complete Exercise 3 individually. Have students compare answers in pairs. Circulate to observe pair work. Give help as needed. If necessary, review grammar chart **4.8** on page 76.

🕐 To save class time, have students do the exercise for homework ahead of time.

EXERCISE 4

1. Say: *This exercise is about you. You're going to ask your partner yes/no questions.* Have students read the direction line in the Student Book. Go over the example by model it with a student volunteer. Then have two other volunteers model #1.
2. Have students complete the rest of Exercise 2 in pairs. Circulate to observe pair work. Give help as needed.
3. If necessary, review grammar chart **4.8** on page 76.

EXERCISE 3 Complete the conversation with the correct question from the box.

| Do you work during the week? | Does the job pay well? |
| Do you deliver the pizzas? | Do you use your car? |

Victor: I have a new part-time job. I work for Joe's Pizza.

1. **Simon:** _Do you deliver the pizzas_ ?

   Victor: Yes, I do. I deliver them all over the city.

2. **Simon:** _Do you work during the week_ ?

   Victor: No, I don't. I work on the weekends.

3. **Simon:** _Do you use your car_ ?

   Victor: No, I don't. Joe's has a car with "Joe's Pizza" on it.

4. **Simon:** _Does the job pay well_ ?

   Victor: No, it doesn't. But people often give me extra money for the delivery.

   Simon: We call that money a "tip."

EXERCISE 4 ABOUT YOU Find a partner. Ask your partner a *yes/no* question with the words given. Give short answers and add information where possible. Then tell the class about your partner's answers.

EXAMPLE you/like to eat in restaurants
Student 1: Do you like to eat in restaurants?
Student 2: Yes, I do. I like to eat in Chinese restaurants.
Student 1: Maria likes to eat in Chinese restaurants.

1. you / like pizza _____ _Do you like pizza?_
2. you / work in a restaurant _____ _Do you work in a restaurant?_
3. you / have a part-time job _____ _Do you have a part-time job?_

78 Unit 4

Expansion

Exercise 3 Have students practice the conversation in pairs. Have volunteers roleplay the conversation in front of the class.

Exercise 4 Create two rings of students. Have half of the students stand in an outer ring around the classroom. Have the other half stand in an inner ring, facing the outer ring. Write four questions from Exercise 4 on the board. Instruct students to ask and answer the questions on the board. Call out *turn* every minute or so. Students in the inner ring should move one space clockwise. Students now ask and answer the questions with their new partner. Have students ask questions in random order. Make sure students look at each other when they're speaking.

4. you / eat only vegetarian food _Do you only eat vegetarian food?_
5. you / sometimes order take-out food _Do you sometimes order take-out food?_
6. you / eat lunch at home _Do you eat lunch at home?_
7. someone / cook for you _Does someone cook for you?_
8. restaurants in your country / deliver _Do restaurants in your country deliver?_
9. supermarkets in your country / have deli sections _Do supermarkets in your country have deli sections?_
10. many people in your country / eat vegetarian food _Do many people in your country eat vegetarian food?_

EXERCISE 5 Shafia and Ali are at Halina and Peter's house for dinner. Fill in the blanks in their conversation with a *yes/no* question in the simple present tense.

Shafia: Halina, this is a delicious meal. _Do you cook_ (example: you/cook) like this every day? _Do you have_ (1. you/have) time?

Halina: Not exactly. _Does the food taste_ (2. the food/taste) good?

Ali: The meat is very good. _Does it have_ (3. it/have) a special sauce?

Halina: Well . . . yes. But . . .

Shafia: I like the carrots. There's something different about them. _Do they have_ (4. they/have) orange in them?

Halina: Yes, I think so. I'm happy that you like them.

Ali: _Do you like to cook_ (5. you/like to cook) Halina?

Peter: Tell them about the meal, Halina.

Halina: Well . . . it's all from the supermarket!

Shafia: Of course. But you're the cook. And it's all delicious.

Halina: No, I'm not the cook. It's all prepared food.

Ali: _Does the supermarket prepare_ (6. the supermarket/prepare) hot food like this?

Halina: Yes, it does.

Shafia: _Do you and Peter eat_ (7. you and Peter/eat) prepared food often?

Halina: No, we don't. But sometimes it's very convenient.

Lesson 3 79

EXERCISE 5

1. Have students look at the picture on page 79. Ask: *What food is on the plate?* (meat and sauce) *Would vegetarians eat the food on this plate?* (no) *How do you know?* (It is meat.) Have students read the direction line. Go over the example in the Student Book.
2. Have students complete Exercise 5 individually. Then have students compare answers in pairs. Circulate to observe pair work. Give help as needed.
3. If necessary, review grammar chart **4.8** on page 76.

⏱ To save class time, have students do the exercise for homework ahead of time.

Expansion

Exercise 5 Have students practice the conversation in groups of four. Ask volunteers to roleplay the conversation in front of the class.

Unit 4 79

Lesson 4 | Overview

GRAMMAR

1. Say: *In Lesson 3 we studied yes/no questions in the simple present. In Lessons 1 and 2 we studied time expressions.* Elicit examples, such as: *Do you eat vegetables?* and *three times a week*) Write the examples on the board.
2. Say: *In Lesson 4, we will study information questions. Information questions begin with question words.* Write the two objectives on the board. Say: *Listen to the questions. Tell me the question words: Who are you? Where do you live? Why do Americans exercise?* Write the question words on the board.

CONTEXT

1. Say: *Do you exercise? I go to the gym three times a week. I run. I swim. In this lesson, we're going to read about exercise.* Ask: *Do you go to a gym? Do you run in the park? What kind of exercise do you do?*
2. Direct students' attention to the picture. Ask questions about the people in the picture: *Why is this woman wearing sneakers?* (e.g., She walks to work for exercise and wears comfortable shoes.) *What are these men doing?* (running in the park)

BEFORE YOU READ

1. Go over each question as a class. Have a volunteer read the questions or read them to the class yourself. Ask students to discuss their answers in pairs.
2. Ask for a few volunteers to share their answers with the class. Write students' answers on the board.
   To save class time, skip "Before You Read" or have students prepare their answers for homework ahead of time.

LESSON 4

GRAMMAR
Information Questions in the Simple Present Tense
Question Words as Subjects

CONTEXT
Exercise

Before You Read
1. Do you exercise every day?
2. What kind of exercise do you do?

park   sneakers   gym   bicycle   office building

80   Unit 4

Expansion

Theme The topic for this unit can be enhanced with the following ideas:
1. Pictures from magazines of people doing tai chi in a park
2. Swimming in an indoor swimming pool
3. Doing other exercises in a variety of settings

---

80   *Grammar in Context Basic* Teacher's Edition

EXERCISE

Halina: Look at that woman with a business suit and sneakers!
Dorota: That's Louisa. I know her. She walks during her lunch hour. Some Americans use their lunch hours for exercise.
Halina: **Where does she walk** in the winter?
Dorota: Maybe she goes to a gym. The building next door is a gym. Maybe her office building has a gym.
Halina: **What do you mean?**
Dorota: Some office buildings have gyms inside for their workers. They're free.
Halina: That's very interesting. I see a lot of people on bicycles too. Bicycles are great exercise. But **why does that man have** strange clothes?
Dorota: He works on his bicycle. He takes mail from one office to another here in the city. He gets a lot of exercise every day!
Halina: **Why do so many Americans exercise?**
Dorota: Most Americans don't exercise. But some do. Many people have desk jobs. They sit all day. So they try to exercise a little every day.
Halina: **What kind of exercise do you do,** Dorota?
Dorota: I walk. It's great exercise for me. I stay healthy this way.
Halina: **Where do you walk?**
Dorota: I go to a park near my house.
Halina: **How often do you exercise?**
Dorota: I try to walk every day. But I don't always have time.

Vocabulary in Context

sneaker(s)	I wear **sneakers**, not regular shoes, for exercise.
gym	I go to a **gym**. I exercise there.
next door	The building **next door** is a gym.
ride a bicycle	I have a **bicycle**. I **ride** it to work.
desk job	He has a **desk job.** He works at a desk all day.
exercise (n.)	They walk for **exercise.**
exercise (v.)	Americans don't **exercise** a lot.
park	A **park** is a good place for exercise.
during	She often walks **during** her lunch hour.
healthy	Dorota is **healthy.** She's not sick.

Lesson 4   81

Reading Variation

1. To practice listening skills, have students listen to the audio before opening their books. Ask a few comprehension questions, such as: *Where does Dorota walk?* (in a park) Repeat the audio if necessary. Then have students open their books and read along as they listen to the audio.
2. Alternatively, have students begin by listening to the audio as they read along.

Expansion

Vocabulary in Context Have volunteers act out selected vocabulary, such as *ride a bicycle* and *exercise*.

Culture Note

Many Americans have serious health problems because they overeat and they don't exercise enough. As a result, approximately 65 percent of U.S. adults are overweight or obese.

Exercise (Reading)
CD 1, Track 23

1. Have students look at the title of the reading. Ask: *What is the reading about? What are Dorota and Halina talking about?* (exercise) *What do you think they will say about exercising in America?* Have students use the title of the reading and the picture on page 80 to make predictions about the reading.
2. First, have students read the dialogue silently. Then play the audio and have students read along silently.
3. Check students' basic comprehension. Ask questions, such as: *Do some American workers exercise during their lunch hour?* (yes) *Do most Americans exercise?* (no) *Does Dorota exercise almost every day.* (yes)

To save class time, have students do the reading for homework ahead of time.

VOCABULARY IN CONTEXT

1. Model the pronunciation of each new vocabulary word and have students repeat.
2. Make sure students understand the meaning of each vocabulary word. Review the examples in the book and create additional example sentences. For example, say: *desk job. My husband has a desk job. He works at a desk in an office all day.* Go over each new vocabulary word similarly, using visuals and realia when appropriate. When possible, point to pictures in the book that illustrate new vocabulary items, such as *sneakers, gym, next door, ride a bicycle,* and *park* on page 80.
3. Have students underline one example of each vocabulary item in the reading. Note: *Bicycle* is in the reading, but not the phrase *ride a bicycle*.

Unit 4   81

DID YOU KNOW?

Explain to students that the U.S. government recommends 30 minutes a day of moderate exercise, such as walking, golfing, and water aerobics.

LISTENING ACTIVITY

🎧 **CD 1, Track 24**

1. Say: *Listen to the statements about Halina and Dorota's conversation. Circle* true *or* false. Play the audio one time without pausing. Then play it through again, pausing and replaying as necessary.
2. Go over the answers as a class. Ask students to volunteer answers.

4.9 | Information Questions in the Simple Present Tense

1. Have students look at grammar chart **4.9** on page 82. Review word order and the use of *do/does* in questions. Write on the board:

    ? word + do/does + subject + base form

    Say: *Do* is used with *I, you, we, they, and plural nouns. Does* is used with *he, she, it, and singular nouns.*

2. Go over the questions in the chart. Elicit question words from students. Write on the board:

    How often = frequency
    Why = reason
    Where = place
    When = time
    How = in what way
    What kind = type
    What = thing
    How much/many = amount
    Who = person

    Say: *Information questions ask for information about people, places, time, and other things.* Activate students' knowledge. Elicit examples of each kind of information. (e.g., place: the gym/my house/Central Park; amount: 50/$10.00)

Did You Know?
- We need only one 30-minute walk or two 15-minute walks each day for good health.
- Exercise helps lower stress levels.

🎧 **Listening Activity** Listen to the statements about the conversation. Circle *true* or *false*.

EXAMPLE TRUE (FALSE)

1. (TRUE) FALSE   4. (TRUE) FALSE
2. (TRUE) FALSE   5. (TRUE) FALSE
3. TRUE (FALSE)   6. TRUE (FALSE)

4.9 | Information Questions in the Simple Present Tense

Question Word	Do	Subject	Verb (Base Form)	Short Answer
How often	do	you	exercise?	Three times a week.
Why	do	we	exercise?	Because we want to stay healthy.
Where	do	they	exercise?	In a gym.
When	do	they	exercise?	In the morning.
How	does	he	exercise?	He walks.

Question Word	Does	Subject	Verb (Base Form)	Short Answer
What kind of exercise	does	she	do?	She rides a bicycle.
What	does	"bike"	mean?	It means bicycle.
How much	does	a bike	cost?	It costs about $200.
Who	does	Dorota	know?	She knows Louisa.
How many days	does	Dorota	exercise?	She exercises seven days a week.

Language Notes:
1. We use *because* with answers to *why* questions.
2. When we say *how often*, we want an exact number of times.
3. We use the simple present with *mean* and *cost*.

82   Unit 4

Expansion

Grammar Chart Have students go back to the reading on page 81. Have them find the information questions. Ask students to underline the question word, the subject, *do/does*, and the verb.

---

82   *Grammar in Context Basic* Teacher's Edition

EXERCISE 1 Fill in the correct question word in each short conversation. Use: *what, who, when, where, how, why, what kind of, how many,* and *how often*. The underlined words are the answers to the questions.

EXAMPLE   A: <u>How often</u> does she ride her bicycle?

B: She rides her bicycle <u>every day</u>.

1. A: <u>What</u> does *gym* mean?
   B: It means <u>a place for exercise</u>.
2. A: <u>Why</u> do they walk every day?
   B: <u>Because it's good exercise</u>.
3. A: <u>How many</u> hours do they walk every day?
   B: They walk <u>for three hours</u> every day.
4. A: <u>What kind of</u> shoes does Louisa have?
   B: She has <u>sneakers</u>.
5. A: <u>How</u> do some people get to work?
   B: <u>They ride their bicycles</u>.
6. A: <u>Who</u> does Halina see in the street?
   B: She sees <u>some people on bicycles</u>.
7. A: <u>How often</u> does Dorota walk in the park?
   B: She walks <u>four or five days a week</u>.

EXERCISE 2 Write questions with the words given. Write an answer to each question. Use the ideas from the conversation.

EXAMPLE   what / Halina / ask Dorota

What does Halina ask Dorota?

She asks Dorota about exercise in the U.S.

1. what kind of exercise / Dorota / do

   What kind of exercise does Dorota do?

   She walks.

2. where / Dorota / exercise

   Where does Dorota exercise?

   She exercises in a park.

Lesson 4   83

4.9 | Information Questions in the Simple Present Tense *(cont.)*

3. Go over short answers. Have students look at answers in the first part of the chart. Say: *Some short answers are a phrase. The phrase gives a piece of information.* Direct students' attention to the answers in the second part of the chart. Say: *Some short answers may be given in a short sentence.* Have students read the questions and answers in the chart.
4. Point out the Language Notes. Review the notes. Ask students to identify the examples in the chart.

EXERCISE 1

1. Have students read the direction line. Say: *First, look at the underlined words. Then decide what question word you need.* Go over the example in the Student Book. Have a volunteer do #1.
2. Have students complete the rest of Exercise 1 individually. Go over the answers as a class.
3. If necessary, review grammar chart **4.9** on page 82.

EXERCISE 2

1. Tell students they are going to make questions and answers. Have students read the direction line. Review meanings of questions words. Ask: *What does where mean?* (place/location) Go over the example in the Student Book. Have a volunteer complete #1.
2. Have students complete the rest of Exercise 2 individually. Then have students compare answers in pairs. Circulate to observe pair work. Give help as needed.
3. If necessary, review grammar chart **4.9** on page 82.

To save class time, have students do the exercise for homework ahead of time.

Expansion

Exercise 1 Have students practice the short conversations in pairs. Ask volunteers to roleplay the conversations in front of the class.

Unit 4   83

EXERCISE 3

1. Tell students they are going to make questions. Have students read the direction line. Review the example. Say: *The answer is:* _____. (frequency) *Look at the question word in parentheses.*
2. Point to the illustration on page 84. Write *(where)* on the board. Say: *The answer is:* Dorota goes to the park. *What is the question?* (Where does Dorota go?)
3. Have students complete Exercise 3 individually. Then have students compare answers in pairs. Circulate to observe pair work. Give help as needed.
4. If necessary, review grammar chart 4.9 on page 82.

To save class time, have students do the exercise for homework ahead of time.

---

3. when / some office workers / exercise
   When do some office workers exercise?
   They exercise during their lunch hours.

4. what / some office buildings / have for their workers
   What do some office buildings have for their workers?
   They have gyms.

5. why / some office workers / exercise
   Why do some office workers exercise?
   They sit all day. OR They have desk jobs.

6. what / mean / "bike"
   What does <u>bike</u> mean?
   It means bicycle.

EXERCISE 3 Complete the short conversation with a question in the simple present tense. Use the question word given.

EXAMPLE A: She walks for exercise. (how often)
B: How often does she walk?

1. A: She likes to wear sneakers. (why)
   B: Why does she like to wear sneakers?

2. A: She has a day off each week. (when)
   B: When does she have a day off each week?

3. A: I have some new shoes. (what kind of)
   B: What kind of shoes do you have?

4. A: They stay healthy. (how)
   B: How do they stay healthy?

5. A: She goes to the gym in the winter. (how often)
   B: How often does she go to the gym in the winter?

6. A: Halina sees some friends in the street. (how many)
   B: How many friends does Halina see in the street?

7. A: People wear special clothes for exercise. (what kind of)
   B: What kind of special clothes do people wear for exercise?

Expansion

Exercise 3 Have students practice the statements and questions in pairs.

4.10 | Question Words as Subjects

Do not use *do/does* when the question word is a subject.

Question Word (Subject)	Verb (Base Form or -s Form)	Complement	Short Answer
Who	wants	a sandwich?	I do.
Who	works	in that company?	We all do.
What kind of people	exercise	here?	Office workers.
Which company	has	a gym for workers?	My company does.
Which workers	exercise	during their lunch hours?	Louisa and two of her friends do.
How many people	wear	sneakers to exercise?	Everybody does.

Language Note: *Who* questions are singular. Answers can be singular or plural.

EXERCISE 4 Use the question words in parentheses ( ) as subjects. Write a question about each statement.

EXAMPLE Somebody needs a job. (who)
Who needs a job?

1. Somebody wants to exercise. (who)
   Who wants to exercise?

2. Some jobs pay well. (what kind of)
   What kind of jobs pay well?

3. Some people ride their bicycles to work. (how many)
   How many people ride their bicycles to work?

4. Some people take three days off a week. (who)
   Who takes three days off a week?

5. Some people exercise during their lunch hours. (which)
   Which people exercise during their lunch hours?

6. Some workers in my company sit all day. (how many)
   How many workers in your company sit all day?

7. Some exercise helps your heart. (what kind of)
   What kind of exercise helps your heart?

Lesson 4   85

4.10 | Question Words as Subjects

1. Have students look at grammar chart **4.10** on page 85. Say: *When the subject is a question word, do not use* do *or* does. Read through the questions in the chart. Point out that the verb is either the base form or the -s form. Stress that the base form is used with plural nouns (e.g., *which workers, what kind of people*), and that the -s form is used with *who* and singular nouns. (e.g., *which company*)

2. Say: *Look at the short answers. They give the subject and* do *or* does. *They do not repeat the verb.* Go over the questions and short answers. Ask: *Do you always answer with a sentence?* (No, you can answer with a phrase.) *What kind of information do these answers give?* (a piece of information about who/people, how many)

3. Point out the Language Note. Review the note. Ask students to identify the examples in the chart.

EXERCISE 4

1. Have students read the direction line. Go over the example in the Student Book.
2. Have students complete Exercise 4 individually. Go over the answers with the class.
3. If necessary, review grammar chart **4.10** on page 85.

Expansion

Exercise 4 Have students practice the statements and questions in pairs.

EXERCISE 5

1. Have students look at the photo. Ask: *Does he ride a bike for exercise?* (He rides a bike for work.) *Is he young or old?* (young) Then have students read the direction line. Go over the example in the Student Book.
2. Review #6. Elicit the difference between *when* (general time) and *what time* (specific/exact time).
3. Have students complete Exercise 5 individually. Then have students compare answers in pairs. Circulate to observe pair work.
4. If necessary, review grammar chart **4.10** on page 85.

EXERCISE 5 Match the questions on the left with the answers on the right. Put the letter of the answer on the line next to the question.

EXAMPLE Who walks five days a week? __C__

Questions

1. Where do business people work? __E__
2. How often does she walk to work? __J__
3. How does he exercise? __F__
4. What does *gym* mean? __H__.
5. Who do you exercise with? __G__
6. When does he ride his bicycle? __I__
7. What do they wear to the office? __A__
8. Why does she go to the gym? __K__
9. What kind of shoes does he wear to the gym? __B__
10. How many people exercise during their lunch hour? __L__
11. What kind of people use their bicycles for work? __D__

Answers

A. business suits

B. sneakers

C. Dorota ✓

D. Usually young people. They deliver packages.

E. in offices

F. He plays soccer.

G. my brother

H. a place for exercise

I. in the evening

J. twice a week

K. to exercise

L. about 20 from our office

Expansion

Exercise 5 Have students ask and answer questions about exercise in a partner's country. Have them ask questions, such as: *How many people in [country] exercise during their lunch hour? What do people in [country] wear to the office? Do many people in [country] ride bicycles to work?* Pair students from different countries.

EDITING ADVICE

1. Don't use the -s form after *does* or *doesn't*.
   have
   She doesn't ~~has~~ a new job.   Where does she ~~works~~?

2. Don't put time expressions before the verb.
   We ~~every day~~ go to work. →

3. Use *do / does* in all questions except subject questions.
   do you want   *wants*
   What ~~you want~~ to do?   Who ~~does want~~ to go to the gym?

4. Use the correct word order in questions.
   Where does ~~work~~ your friend? →

5. Use the normal question word order with *mean* and *cost*.
   does "Super Bowl" mean?
   What ~~means~~ "Super Bowl?"

6. Use frequency words in the correct place.
   He goes ~~always~~ to the gym.

EDITING QUIZ

Find the mistakes with the underlined words, and correct them. Not every sentence has a mistake. If the sentence is correct, write *C*.

does a grill cost?
EXAMPLE   How much ~~costs a grill~~?

1. She ~~once a week~~ likes to work overtime *once a week*.
2. He ~~doesn't likes~~ to work overtime.
   does
3. What ~~he wants~~ to cook on the grill?
4. Does he ~~enjoys~~ the museum in his city?
5. How often <u>do they eat</u> mushrooms?   *C*
   does gym mean
6. What ~~means "gym"~~?
7. How many people ~~do want to work~~ overtime?
   never
8. We eat ~~never~~ in a restaurant.

Lesson 4   87

Editing Advice

1. Have students close their books. Write the example sentences without editing marks or corrections on the board. For example:

   1. She doesn't has a new job.
   2. We every day go to work.

   Ask students to correct each sentence. This activity can be done individually, in pairs, or as a class. After students have corrected each sentence, tell them to turn to page 87. Say: *Now compare your work with Editing Advice in the book.*

2. Go over answers with the class. For troublespots, review the appropriate grammar chart.

Editing Quiz

1. The Editing Quiz may be used as an in-class quiz, a take-home quiz, or as a review. Have students read the direction line. Ask: *Does every sentence have a mistake?* (no) Go over the example with the class.

2. Have students complete the quiz individually. Collect the completed quizzes for assessment or have students check each other's work. Review the answers with the class. Elicit the relevant grammar point for each correction. For example, for #1, ask: *What's the rule for time expressions?* (Time expressions go at the end of sentences. They do not go before the verb.)

Unit 4   87

Learner's Log

1. Have students close their books. Ask: *What did you learn about free-time activities and work in the U.S? What about food and exercise in the U.S? What else do you want to know about them?* Discuss ways in which students can find out more about work and free-time activities.
2. Then have students open their books to complete the Learner's Log.

Expansion Activities

These expansion activities provide opportunities for students to interact with one another and further develop their speaking and writing skills. Encourage students to use grammar from this unit whenever possible.

To save class time, assign parts of the activities as homework. Then use class time for interaction and communication. If students do not need additional speaking practice, some of the activities may be assigned as writing activities for homework, or skipped altogether.

WRITING ACTIVITY

Have students read the direction line. Go over the example. Have students complete the activity individually at home or in class and collect for assessment.

OUTSIDE ACTIVITIES

1. Have students discuss the foods they found in a deli section with questions such as: *Do you like this _____? How often do you eat/buy it?*
2. Have students tell what foods are in the meal.
3. Have students identify the cost of food and drinks at a nearby movie theater and report to the class.

INTERNET ACTIVITIES

1. Have students research the Web site in their current towns and cities or in their hometowns.
2. Tell students that the U.S. Department of Labor has information about minimum wage by state on its Web site.

LEARNER'S LOG

1. What did you learn in this unit? Write three sentences in your notebook about each of these topics:
   - Free-time activities in the U.S.
   - Work in the U.S.
   - Food and exercise in the U.S.
2. Write three questions you still have about work and free-time activities in America.

EXPANSION ACTIVITIES

Writing Activity

Rewrite the following paragraph about Nina in your notebook. Change *I* to *she*. Change the first *she* to *Nina*.

> I live in Chicago. I like the city. Why do I like it? Because it's wonderful in the summer time. I often go to a big park downtown. It has concerts every Thursday evening. I don't pay for these concerts. They're free for all the people. I like to visit Lake Michigan. It has many free public beaches. But the water is cold. I don't swim in June or July. I swim only in August. I also visit a beautiful park on the lake. Sometimes I have dinner on one of the big ships there. I don't do that often. It's expensive. I often invite friends to visit this lovely city.

EXAMPLE   *Nina lives in Chicago.*

Outside Activities

1. Go to the deli section in a supermarket near your house. Find some prepared food that you like. Tell the class what it is. How much does the food cost?
2. Find a pizza restaurant near your house or this school. Get a take-out menu from the restaurant. Find a meal you like. Find the total price. Tell the class about it.
3. Look for a movie in a theater near you. Find the price of a regular ticket. Find the price of a ticket before 5 or 6 p.m.

Internet Activities

1. Find the Web site for your city. Look under *events* to find some fun activities in your city this week. Look under *museums* or *parks* in your city to find special activities there. Tell the class about them.
2. Search the words *United States minimum wage*. Find the minimum wage for your state. Compare it to the national minimum wage.

88   Unit 4

Expansion

Learner's Log Have students compare logs in pairs.

Writing Activity Variation

Have students exchange papers with a partner for proofreading.

Internet Activities Variation

Tell students that if they don't have Internet access, they can use Internet facilities at a public library or they can use traditional research methods to find out information including encyclopedias, magazines, books, journals, and newspapers.

UNIT

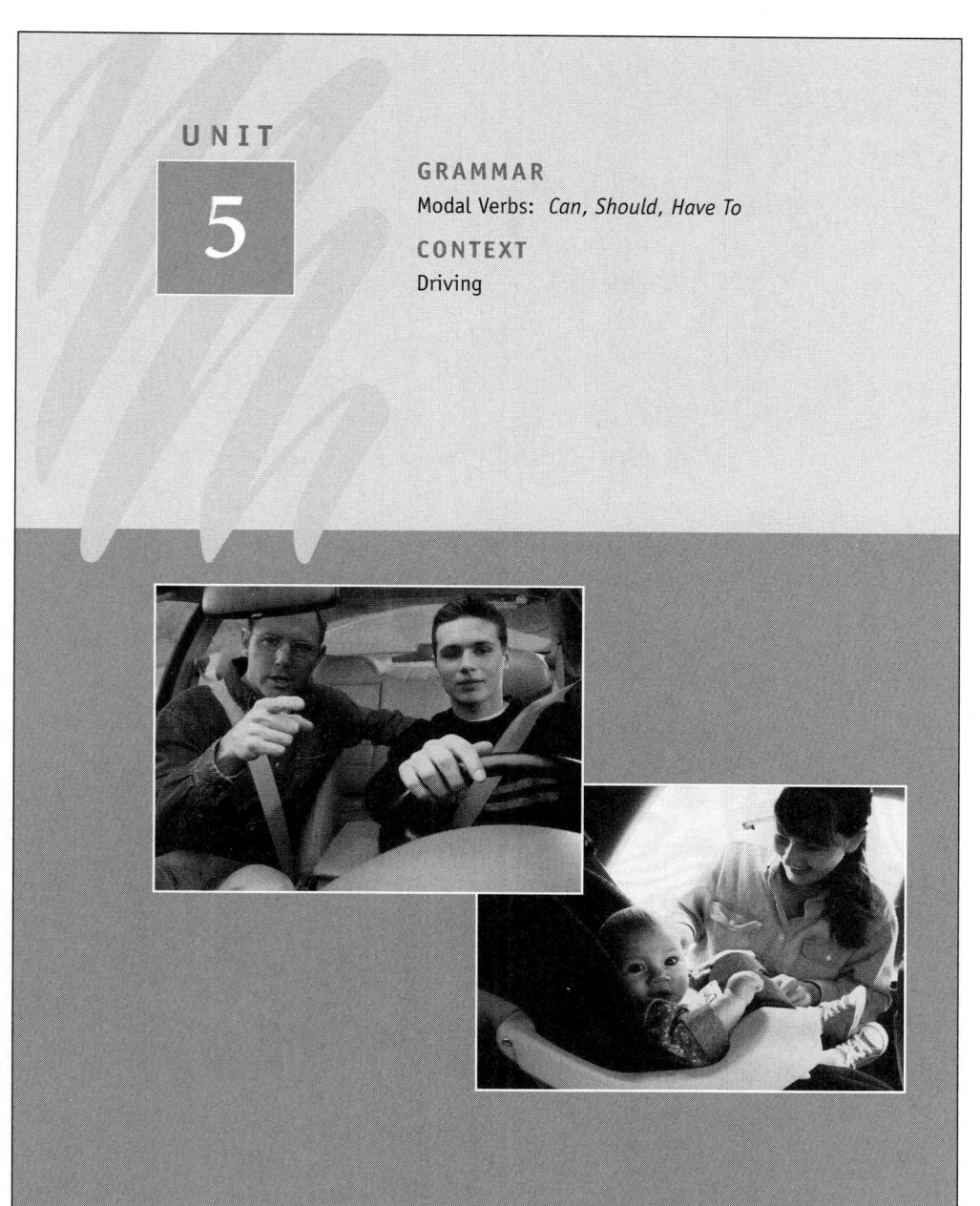

5

GRAMMAR
Modal Verbs: *Can, Should, Have To*

CONTEXT
Driving

Unit | 5
Unit Overview

GRAMMAR

1. Ask: *What did we study in Unit 4?* (the simple present tense and frequency words) Say: *In Unit 5, we will study modal verbs.* Write *Modal Verbs* on the board. Say and write on the board: *My car is old. I have to buy a new car. I should buy a new car. I have money; I can buy a new car.* Underline the modals.
2. Relate the objective to students' personal experience. Ask: *What is something you **have to** do? **Should** you do it? **Can** you do it?* Have a few volunteers answer the three questions.

CONTEXT

1. Say: *We're going to learn about driving in the U.S. We will talk about safety and driver's licenses.* Ask: *Is driving in the U.S. different from driving in your country? Can teenagers drive? Do you have to wear seatbelts?* Have students share their ideas and personal experience.
2. Direct students' attention to the photo of the teenage driver. Ask: *Is the driver young or old?* (young) *What is the boy doing?* (learning to drive) *Who's teaching him?* (his father; the man) Direct students' attention to the other photo. Say: *The mother puts her baby in an infant seat. Why?* (for safety)

Expansion

Theme The topic for this unit can be enhanced with the following ideas:

1. An infant car seat, a booster seat, or a catalog showing these items
2. A driver's license
3. A copy of a practice driving test
4. A poster or printout of common road signs

Unit 5   89

Lesson 1 | Overview

GRAMMAR

Ask: *What modal verbs will we study in Lesson 1?* (can, should, have to) Say: *I can drive. I should drive. I have to drive.* Write the sentences on the board. Underline the modals. Ask: *Is the meaning of all three sentences the same?* (no) *What is the main verb?* (drive) Say: *A modal verb adds to the meaning of the main verb.*

CONTEXT

1. Say: *We're going to learn about getting a driver's license. You have to have a license to drive in the U.S.* Activate students' knowledge. Ask: *How do you get a driver's license?*
2. Direct students' attention to the pictures. Say: *This is a driver's license. Is it the same as your license?* Have a student show his or her license and briefly compare it with the illustration. Point to the other picture of the Department of Motor Vehicles. Ask: *Where is this?* (Department of Motor Vehicles) *What are people doing here?* (getting a driver's license; taking an eye test and written test; getting license photos taken)
3. Ask: *Where do you go to take a driver's test? How many tests do you take? Are they easy or hard?* Have students share their experiences.

BEFORE YOU READ

1. Go over each statement as a class. Have a volunteer read the statements or read them to the class yourself. Ask students to circle *yes* or *no*.
2. Ask for a few volunteers to share their answers with the class.

To save class time, skip "Before You Read" or have students prepare answers for homework ahead of time.

LESSON 1

GRAMMAR
Can
Should
Have To

CONTEXT
Getting a Driver's License

Before You Read

Circle *yes* or *no*.

1. Can you drive? YES NO
2. Do you have a driver's license from this state? YES NO

90 Unit 5

Culture Note

Each state issues driver's licenses. In most states drivers have to be 16. Many states give a learner's permit to 14 and 15 year-old teens. An adult must always accompany these learners.

90 *Grammar in Context Basic* Teacher's Edition

GETTING A DRIVER'S LICENSE

Simon's son, Ed, wants to learn to drive. He is 15 years old.

Ed: Dad, I want to drive.
Simon: You **have to get** a learner's permit first.
Ed: You **can help** me with that.
Simon: No, I **can't**. In this state, drivers under age 18 **have to take** a driver's training class at school. It's the law.
Ed: A class takes a long time. I can learn faster with you.
Simon: No, you **can't**. It takes a long time to learn to drive. You **shouldn't be** in a hurry. First you **have to pass** two tests: a vision test and a written test. The written test is about the rules of driving in this state. You have to study 30 hours in the classroom. It's the law.
Ed: And then I **can get** my license. I **don't have to wait** anymore.
Simon: No. You **can get** a learner's permit. Then you **have to practice** in the car. You **should practice** many hours in a car. In this state, you **have to practice** at least six hours. And you **have to wait** three months. Then you **can take** the driving test.
Ed: Then I **can get** my license. And I **can drive** with my friends.
Simon: Not exactly.
Ed: What do you mean?
Simon: New drivers under the age of 17 don't get a full license in this state. You **have to drive** with an adult driver at night. You **can have** only one other teenager in the car. And you **can't drive** at all from 11 p.m. to 6 a.m. This law saves a lot of lives every year.

Vocabulary in Context

permit	A **permit** means the law lets you do something.
then	First I have to study. **Then** I can go out.
It takes time	It **takes** a long **time** to be a good driver.
training	People learn to drive in a driver's **training** class.
in a hurry	Ed wants his license now. He's **in a hurry.**
vision test	A **vision test** checks a person's eyes.
written test	We use pencil and paper for a **written test.**
pass a test	When you **pass** the tests, you can get the permit.
at least	He has to practice **at least** six hours. He can practice six hours or more.
law(s)	The government makes **laws.** Laws keep citizens safe.
without	He can't drive **without** a license.

Lesson 1   91

Reading Variation

1. To practice listening skills, have students listen to the audio before opening their books. Ask a few comprehension questions: *Can Ed's father help him get a learner's permit?* (no) *Does it take a long time to learn to drive?* (yes) Repeat the audio if necessary. Then have students open their books and read along as they listen to the audio.
2. Alternatively, have students begin by listening to the audio as they read along.

Vocabulary Teaching Ideas

Use the following ideas to teach these terms:

in a hurry: Start to rush out of the room and say: *I can't stay after class today—I'm in a hurry.*
training: Say: *Training means learning. To get a good job in the U.S., you need English language training.*

Expansion

Reading Have students practice the conversation in pairs. Ask volunteers to roleplay the conversation in front of the class.

Vocabulary in Context To check comprehension, have volunteers in pairs or groups act out selected vocabulary, such as *in a hurry, vision test,* and *written test.*

Getting a Driver's License (Reading) CD 1, Track 25

1. Have students look at the title of the reading. Say: *A father and son are talking about driving. The son is 15 years old.* Ask: *What do you think the son and father are saying?* Have students use the title and pictures on page 90 to make predictions about the reading.
2. Have students read the dialogue silently. Then play the audio and have students read along silently.
3. Check students' basic comprehension. Ask questions, such as: *Can Ed get a license at 15?* (No, but he can get a learner's permit.) *What does he have to do before he can practice in a car?* (pass a vision test and a written test)

To save class time, have students do the reading for homework ahead of time.

VOCABULARY IN CONTEXT

1. Model the pronunciation of each new vocabulary word and have students repeat.
2. Make sure students understand the meaning of each vocabulary word. Review the examples in the book and create additional example sentences. For example, say: *permit. I have a permit to ride a motorcycle.* Go over each new vocabulary word similarly, using visuals and realia when appropriate. When possible, point to pictures in the book that illustrate the new vocabulary items, such as *vision test* and *written test* on page 90.
3. Have students underline an example of each new vocabulary item in the reading. Point out that the word *without* is not in the reading. Provide other example sentences if students are unsure of its meaning.

DID YOU KNOW?

Ask students if males or females have more serious car crashes. Tell them that statistics (insurance and police information) say that males have more serious car crashes than females.

LISTENING ACTIVITY

🎧 **CD 1, Track 26**

1. Say: *Listen to the sentences about Simon and his son's conversation. Circle* true *or* false. Play the listening selection one time without pausing. Then play it through again, pausing and replaying as necessary.
2. Go over the answers as a class. Ask students to volunteer answers.

5.1 | Can

1. Have students look at grammar chart **5.1** on page 92. Say: *We use* can *to show ability, permission, or possibility*. Write these three examples on the board:

   ability: *I can drive a car.*
   permission: *Can I use your car?*
   possibility: *We can go to the park tomorrow. It's going to be a nice day.*

2. Go over the examples in the chart. Review word order with modals. Ask: *Where does the modal come in a sentence?* (between the subject and the base form of the verb)
3. Say: *The negative of* can *is* cannot. *The contraction, or short form, for* cannot *is* can't. Write on the board: *cannot = can't*
4. Direct students to the Language and Pronunciation Notes. Go over each note and the examples. To stress the use of *can't* to show rules, say: *can't = don't*: "*Can't park*" means "*Don't park.*" To stress the difference in pronunciation of *can* and *can't*, say five minimal sentence pairs with can and can't. (e.g., *I can go. / I can't go.; He can drive. / He can't drive.; She can speak English. / She can't speak English.*) Ask students to raise their hands if they hear *can* and to keep their hands down if they hear *can't*.

Did You Know?
- Car crashes are the number one cause of death for people ages 16 to 19. These teenagers have four times more deaths from car crashes than drivers over age 20.
- Most accidents happen at night with friends in the car.

Listening Activity Listen to the sentences about the conversation. Circle *true* or *false*.

EXAMPLE   TRUE   (FALSE)

1. (TRUE)   FALSE
2. (TRUE)   FALSE
3. TRUE   (FALSE)
4. (TRUE)   FALSE
5. TRUE   (FALSE)
6. (TRUE)   FALSE
7. (TRUE)   FALSE

5.1 | Can

Subject	Can	Verb (Base Form)	Complement
I She Simon It We You They	can cannot can't	help	him.

We use *can* to show: ability, permission, or possibility.

Language Note: We often use **can't** to show rules or laws.
You **can't** park at a bus stop. It's against the law.

Pronunciation Note: In affirmative statements, we usually pronounce *can*/kən/. In negative statements, we pronounce *can't*/kænt/. It is hard to hear the final **t**, so we use the vowel sound and stress to tell the difference between *can* and *can't*. Listen to your teacher pronounce these sentences:

I *can* go. [accent on *go*]
I *can't* go. [accent on *can't*]

92   Unit 5

Expansion

Grammar Chart Have students work in pairs to create sentences with *can* and *can't*. Have them try to use the two words to show ability, permission, possibility, and rules.

EXERCISE 1 Fill in the blanks with *can* or *can't*. Use the ideas from the conversation.

EXAMPLE Ed __can't__ drive now.

1. Drivers with a learner's permit __can__ get a license after three months in Ed's state.
2. Ed __can't__ get his permit without a driver's training class.
3. Drivers under age 17 __can't__ drive late at night in Ed's state.
4. Ed __can__ take the driver's training class now.
5. Simon __can__ help Ed practice in the car.
6. Ed __can't__ get a full license at age 16.
7. Ed __can't__ drive with a lot of his friends in the car.
8. Ed __can__ drive without a full license.

5.2 | Should

We use *should* when we give advice or make a suggestion.

Subject	Should	Verb (Base Form)	Complement
I He She We You They	should should not shouldn't	take	the test today.

EXERCISE 2 Give advice in each conversation. Use *should* or *shouldn't* and the words in parentheses ( ).

EXAMPLE A: I have my written test tomorrow.
B: __You should read__ the rules of the road again tonight.
(you/read)

1. A: My car is dirty.
B: __You should wash__ it today!
(you/wash)

Lesson 1   93

EXERCISE 1

1. Have students look at the learner's permit on page 93. Say: *This is an example of a learner's permit. People who are learning to drive can get a permit before getting their license.* Then have students read the direction line. Go over the example in the Student Book. Tell students to go back to the conversation on page 91 to help find the answers. Give help as needed.
2. Have students complete Exercise 1 individually. Check the answers as a class. If necessary, review grammar chart **5.1** on page 92.

5.2 | Should

1. Have students look at grammar chart **5.2** on page 93. Say: *We use* should *to give advice or a suggestion.*
2. Go over the examples in the chart. Review word order with modals. Ask: *Where does the modal come in a sentence?* (between the subject and the base form of the verb)
3. Say: *The negative of* should *is* should not. *The contraction, or short form, for* should not *is* shouldn't.

EXERCISE 2

1. Have students read the direction line. Go over the example in the Student Book.
2. Have students complete Exercise 2 individually. Give help as needed. Go over the answers with the class.
3. If necessary, review grammar chart **5.2** on page 93.

Expansion

Exercise 2 Have students practice the short conversations in pairs. Have volunteers roleplay the conversations in front of the class.

5.3 | Have To

1. Have students look at grammar chart **5.3** on page 94. Go over the examples in the chart. Review word order. Ask: *Where does* have to *come in the sentence?* (between the subject and the base form of the verb) Point out the use of *do*. Say: *The negative of* have to *is* doesn't have to *and* don't have to.

2. Go over the Pronunciation Note and the Language Note. Review the pronunciation rule. Say: *In relaxed speech,* have to *is pronounced /hæftə/ and* has to *is pronounced /hæstə/.* Demonstrate the pronunciation of both words. Read the examples. Have students repeat. Review the language rule. Go over the examples for affirmative and negative. Ask volunteers to give additional examples.

---

2. **A:** Drivers with a learner's permit don't have much practice.
   B: _They shouldn't drive too fast_ .
   (they/drive too fast)

3. **A:** Ed wants to learn to drive.
   B: _He shouldn't be_ in a hurry.
   (he/be)

4. **A:** Ed wants to be a safe driver.
   B: _He should practice_ a lot with a good driver.
   (he/practice)

5. **A:** Ed doesn't know the driving laws in his state.
   B: _He should learn_ them before the written test.
   (he/learn)

6. **A:** Many cars are on the roads from 4 p.m. to 7 p.m.
   B: Then _you shouldn't drive_ on those busy roads.
   (you/drive)

7. **A:** I don't have the book of driving rules, and I need to check something.
   B: _You should look_ online. The information is
   (you/look)
   on the state Web site.

5.3 | Have To

Have to shows necessity.

Subject	Have to	Verb (Base Form)	Complement
She Your teacher Simon	has to doesn't have to	take	a driver's training class.
I You We They	have to don't have to		

Pronunciation Note: In normal speech, we pronounce *have to* /hæftə/. We pronounce *has to* /hæstə/. Listen to your teacher pronounce the following sentences in normal speech:
   We *have to* take the test.   She *has to* drive safely.
   They *have to* follow the rules of the road.

Language Note: In the affirmative, **have to** shows laws or strong necessity.
   Ed **has to** get a learner's permit.
In the negative, **have to** means not necessary.
   Simon **doesn't have to** work on Saturday.

94 Unit 5

EXERCISE 3 Fill in the blanks with an affirmative or negative form of *have to*. Use the verbs in parentheses ( ) and the ideas from the conversation.

EXAMPLE Ed ___has to take___ a driver's training class.
(take)

1. Simon ___has to get___ a learner's permit.
(get)
2. All drivers ___have to pass___ the vision and written tests.
(pass)
3. Ed ___has to practice___ at least six hours to take the driving test.
(practice)
4. People over age 18 ___don't have to take___ a driver's training class.
(take)
5. An adult driver ___doesn't have to be___ with drivers under age 18 during the day.
(be)
6. All drivers ___have to have___ driver's licenses.
(have)
7. Simon ___has to teach___ Ed the driving rules.
(teach)

EXERCISE 4 ABOUT YOU Write true sentences about your English class. Fill in the blanks with the affirmative or negative form of *have to*.

EXAMPLE We ___have to speak___ English in class.
(speak)

Answers will vary.
1. We _____ homework for every class.
(do)
2. We _____ homework to the teacher every day.
(give)
3. We _____ in the same seat every day.
(sit)
4. We _____ a pen to write our exercises.
(use)
5. We _____ our book to class every day.
(bring)

Lesson 1   95

EXERCISE 3
1. Have students read the direction line. Say: *You have to decide to use an affirmative or a negative verb.* Go over the example.
2. Have students complete Exercise 3 individually. Go over the answers as a class.
3. If necessary, review grammar chart **5.3** on page 94.

EXERCISE 4
1. Say: *This exercise is about you.* Have students read the direction line. Go over the example in the Student Book. Have a volunteer model the example for the class.
2. Have students complete Exercise 4 individually. Go over the answers with the class.
3. If necessary, review grammar chart **5.3** on page 94.

Expansion

Exercise 4 Have students write sentences with *have to* and *don't have to* about another class they are currently taking of have taken in the past. Then have students compare sentences in pairs. Circulate to observe pair work. Give help as needed.

Unit 5   95

EXERCISE 5

1. Put students in pairs to complete this exercise. Have students read the direction line. Go over the example in the Student Book. Remind students that they might not be able to write two sentences about each sign. Say: *There are many ways to say the same thing. So, not everyone will have the same answer.*
2. Have students complete Exercise 5 with their partners. Circulate to observe pair work. Give help as needed.
3. If necessary, review grammar charts **5.1** on page 92, **5.2** on page 93, and **5.3** on page 94.

---

6. The teacher _____ all our exercises at home.
   (check)
7. We _____ a final test at the end of the semester.
   (take)
8. The teacher _____ us all an "A."
   (give)

EXERCISE 5 Look at the following road signs from Ed's rule book. Write an affirmative or a negative sentence about each sign. Write two sentences if possible. Use affirmative and negative forms of *can*, *should*, or *have to*.

EXAMPLES
Drivers can't go over 55 miles per hour.
Drivers have to go at least 45 miles per hour.

1. You can't ride a bicycle here.   Answers will vary, but possible answers may include:

2. Drivers can't turn right.
   Drivers have to turn left.

3. Drivers have to stop.
   All drivers at the intersection have to stop.

4. Drivers should be careful.
   Pedestrians can cross here.
   Drivers shouldn't drive fast.

96   Unit 5

Expansion

Exercise 5 Have students compare sentences in groups. Have groups choose the best sentences to present to the class. Then have the class vote on the best sentence for each road sign.

96   *Grammar in Context Basic* Teacher's Edition

5. [DO NOT ENTER sign] _Drivers can't enter._
   Drivers have to go another way.

6. [ONE WAY sign] _Drivers can only go one way._
   Drivers have to go in the direction of the arrow.

7. [WRONG WAY sign] _Drivers can't go this way._
   Drivers shouldn't enter this road.

8. [School crossing sign] _Drivers should be careful._
   Drivers shouldn't drive fast.

EXERCISE 6 ABOUT YOU With a partner, write about what you can or can't do in this class or in this school.

EXAMPLES We can _write in pen or pencil in this class._
We can't _eat in class in this school._

1. We can _____ _Answers will vary._
2. We can't _____
3. We should _____
4. We shouldn't _____
5. We have to _____
6. We don't have to _____

Lesson 1 97

EXERCISE 6

1. Say: *This exercise is about you.* Tell students that they will be writing sentences that are true for this class or this school. Put students in pairs to complete this exercise. Have students read the direction line. Go over the examples in the Student Book.
2. Have students complete Exercise 6 in pairs. Circulate to observe pair work. Give help as needed.
3. If necessary, review grammar charts **5.1** on page 92, **5.2** on page 93, and **5.3** on page 94.

🕐 To save class time, have students do this exercise for homework ahead of time.

Expansion

Exercise 6 Ask volunteers to share some of their sentences about the class or school. Write their sentences on the board.

EXERCISE 7

1. Have students read the direction line. Say: *You decide whether to use* can, should, *or* have to. Go over the example in the Student Book.
2. Have students complete Exercise 7 individually. Then have students compare answers in pairs. Circulate to observe pair work. Give help as needed.
3. If necessary, review grammar charts **5.1** on page 92, **5.2** on page 93, and **5.3** on page 94.

🕐 To save class time, have students do this exercise for homework ahead of time.

EXERCISE 7 Read the following conversations. Fill in the blanks with the affirmative or negative form of *can, should,* or *have to* and the verb in parentheses ( ).

EXAMPLE A: I don't have a car.
B: Don't worry. You __can use__ my car today.
   (use)

1. A: I don't like to drive.
   B: That's OK. You __can take__ the bus.
      (take)

2. A: Where are your keys?
   B: They're in the car.
   A: You __shouldn't leave__ your keys in the car. Someone may take them.
      (leave)

3. A: I have a new bicycle for your son.
   B: That's great, but he __can't ride__ a bicycle yet.
      (ride)

4. A: Your car is very dirty.
   B: I know. I __should get__ a car wash today, but I'm too busy.
      (get)

5. A: Let's walk to work today.
   B: We __shouldn't walk__. We don't have time. We
      (walk)
   __have to be__ at work in 30 minutes.
      (be)

6. A: I don't like to take the bus.
   B: I know. But we __have to take it__ today. We need to fix the car.
      (take)

7. A: My son wants to get his driver's license.
   B: He __should take__ classes at the new driving school. The teachers are very good there.
      (take)

98 Unit 5

EXERCISE 8 Fill in the blanks in the conversations with the correct verbs from the box.

CONVERSATION A: Ed is asking Simon about his friend from Mexico.

| doesn't have to get | should study | can drive |
| has to take | has to get | can use |

Ed: Dad, one of my friends has an international driver's license. He __can use__ it to drive in this state, right?
    (1)

Simon: Yes, he can. But he __can drive__ with an international
       (2)
license for three months. Then he __has to get__
                                    (3)
a new driver's license for this state.

Ed: What about the learner's permit?

Simon: He __doesn't have to get__ a learner's permit. But he
       (4)
__has to take__ all three of the tests. And he
(5)
__should study__ the rules of the road carefully. They are
(6)
very different from the rules in Mexico.

CONVERSATION B: The teacher, Mr. Brown, is talking to students in the high school driver's training class.

| have to wear | can't see | shouldn't worry |

Mr. Brown: Today's class is about the tests for your learner's permit. Does anyone have a question? Karl?

Karl: I'm worried about the vision test. I __can't see__
      (1)
very well.

Mr. Brown: You __shouldn't worry__. You can take the test with
           (2)
your glasses on. But then you __have to wear__ your
                               (3)
glasses in the car too. It's the law.

Lesson 1   99

EXERCISE 8

1. Have students look at the picture of the international driver's license. Ask questions about the license, such as: *Is this a U.S. driver's license? Why or why not?* Then have students read the direction line and the description of Conversation 1. Ask: *What country is Ed's friend from?* (Mexico) Have students complete the dialogue individually. Then have students read the description of Conversation 2 and complete this dialogue individually.
2. Have students compare answers to both conversations in pairs. Circulate to observe pair work. Give help as needed.
3. If necessary, review grammar charts **5.1** on page 92, **5.2** on page 93, and **5.3** on page 94.

   ⏱ To save class time, have students do this exercise for homework ahead of time.

Expansion

Exercise 8 Have students practice Conversation 1 in pairs, and Conversation 2 in groups of four (with two "silent" class members). Have students change roles. Ask volunteers to roleplay the conversations in front of the class.

Unit 5   99

Lesson 2 | Overview

GRAMMAR

1. Activate prior knowledge. Write these sentences on the board:

   He drives.
   He goes to work every day

   Dan drives to work every day. Have students make questions: *yes/no* questions (e.g., *Does he drive?*), information questions (e.g., *Where does he go every day?*), information questions with *who* and other question words as the subject (e.g., *Who drives to work every day?*).
2. Write on the board: *Modal Verbs: Yes/No questions, Information Questions,* and *Question Words as Subjects.* Say: *In this lesson we're going to learn to write these types of questions with modal verbs.*

CONTEXT

1. Say: *The U.S. has many laws about car safety. Children can't sit in the front seat. Babies have to be in car seats.* Ask: *Should there be laws for children?* Have students share their ideas.
2. Direct students' attention to the illustration. Ask: *What's this lesson about?* (Car safety for children). *How do you know?* (The pictures of car seats; the title)

BEFORE YOU READ

1. Go over each question as a class. Have a volunteer read the questions or read them to the class yourself.
2. Discuss the questions as a class.

   To save class time, skip "Before You Read," or have students prepare their answers for homework ahead of time.

LESSON 2

GRAMMAR
Modal Verbs: *Yes/No* Questions with *Can, Should,* and *Have To*
Information Questions with Modal Verbs
Question Words as Subjects

CONTEXT
Car Safety for Children

Before You Read

1. Where should children sit in a car?
2. Do you have a child in your family? What kind of car seat does the child use?

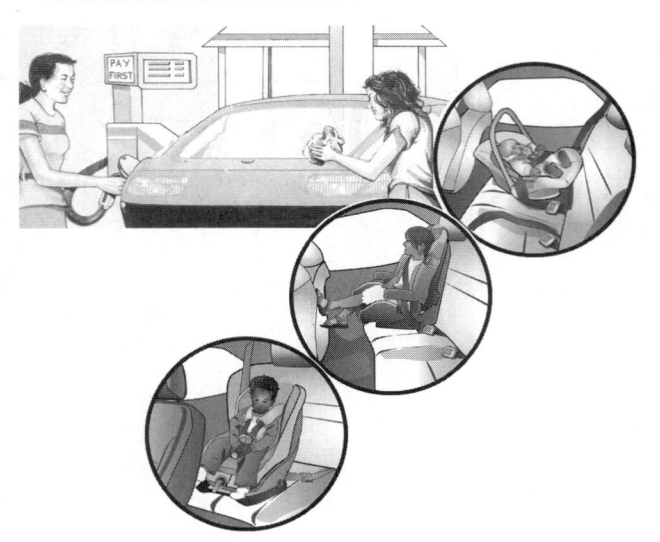

100   Unit 5

Expansion

Theme The topic for this lesson can be enhanced with the following ideas:

1. An infant carrier, a car seat, a booster seat
2. Catalogues of child car seats
3. A brochure or large newspaper ad for an outlet mall

Culture Note

Consumer Reports magazine gives ratings for many products including child and infant car seats.

CAR SAFETY FOR CHILDREN

Dorota and Halina are on the way to an outlet mall in another city. Halina asks Dorota about car seats for her daughter, Anna.

Halina: This is my first trip to an outlet mall. **Can I get** a new car seat for Anna there? She is too big for her old infant seat now. And she's still too small for a seat belt.
Dorota: Sure. And things aren't so expensive at the outlet mall.
Halina: **What kind of car seat should I get?**
Dorota: Well, she's two now. There are many different kinds of seats for older babies. We can look in several stores.
Halina: **How long does Anna have to be** in a car seat, Dorota?
Dorota: In this state, children have to be in a car seat until age eight or 57 inches tall.
Halina: **Where should I put** Anna's seat? **Can I put** it on the front passenger seat?
Dorota: No. Anna shouldn't be in the front seat. The air bag can hurt children. They should sit in the back seat until age 12.

Dorota: Halina, I have to stop for gas. Here's a gas station.
Halina: I can pay, Dorota. **Do we have to pay first?**
Dorota: Yes, the sign says "Pay First." But don't worry, Halina. I can put it on my credit card. I can pay right here at the pump.
Halina: **Should I wash** the windows?
Dorota: OK. You can wash the windows. And I can pump the gas.
Halina: **Where can I get** some water? I'm thirsty.
Dorota: Right here! This gas station has a store.

Vocabulary in Context

trip	We are in the car. We are on a **trip** out of town.
on the way	I'm **on the way** home. I'm almost home.
outlet mall	People can buy things cheaper at **outlet malls**. Outlet malls are sometimes very large with many stores.
air bag(s)	An **air bag** helps in an accident. It protects the people in the front seats.
infant	That baby is only three months old. She's an **infant.**
seatbelt	Everyone has to wear a **seatbelt** in a car. It's the law.
passenger	A **passenger** sits next to the driver.
hurt	In an accident, an airbag can **hurt** a small child.
pump (v)	We have to **pump** our own gas.
pump (n)	We can pay at the **pump** with a credit card.

Lesson 2   101

Reading Variation

To practice listening skills, have students listen to the audio before opening their books. Ask a few comprehension questions: *Should Anna be in the front seat?* (no) *Are things expensive at an outlet mall?* (no) Repeat the audio if necessary. Then have students open their books and read along as they listen to the audio.

Vocabulary Teaching Ideas

Use the following ideas to teach these terms:

on the way: Draw a simple map on the board with a house and a store, and a road between them. Draw a line from the store to the house. As you draw, say: *I'm on the way home.*
outlet mall: Try to locate a brochure or large newspaper add that shows an outlet mall.
airbag: Show a picture of airbags in a car manual.

Expansion

Reading Have students practice the conversation in pairs. Ask volunteers to roleplay the conversation in front of the class.

Vocabulary in Context To check comprehension, have volunteers in pairs or groups act out selected vocabulary, such as *seatbelt, passenger, hurt,* and *pump*.

Car Safety for Children (Reading) CD 1, Track 27

1. Have students look at the title of the reading. Say: *Halina needs to get a car seat for her daughter. What kinds of questions will she ask Dorota?* (e.g., *Where can I get a car seat?*) Have students use the title and illustrations on pages 100 and 101 to make predictions about the reading.
2. Have students read the dialogue silently. Then play the audio and have students read along silently.
3. Check students' basic comprehension. Ask questions, such as: *What does Halina want to buy?* (a car seat) *How long do children have to be in car seats?* (until age eight or 57 inches tall) *What do they have to do first at the gas station?* (pay) *What does Halina do at the gas station?* (wash the windows)

To save class time, have students do the reading for homework ahead of time.

VOCABULARY IN CONTEXT

1. Model the pronunciation of each new vocabulary word and have students repeat.
2. Make sure students understand the meaning of each vocabulary word. Review the examples in the book and create additional example sentences. For example, say: *trip. Every year I go to New York. Every year I take a trip to New York.* Go over each new vocabulary word similarly, using visuals and realia when appropriate. When possible, point to pictures in the book that illustrate words, such as *seatbelt,* and *pump* on page 100.
3. Have students underline an example of each new vocabulary item in the reading.

Unit 5   101

DID YOU KNOW?

Say: *You must put car seats in the right way. The National Highway Traffic Safety Administration says that most car seats are not put in the car correctly.*

LISTENING ACTIVITY

🎧 **CD 1, Track 28**

1. Say: *Listen to each statement about Halina and Dorota's conversation. Circle* true *or* false. Play the listening selection one time without pausing. Then play it through again pausing and replaying as necessary.
2. Go over the answers as a class. Ask students to volunteer answers.

5.4 | Yes/No Questions with *Can*, *Should*, and *Have To*

1. Have students look at grammar chart **5.4** on page 102. Go over the examples with *can* and *should*. Review word order with modals. Stress that short answers for *can* and *should* contain only the subject and the modal, and not the verb. Point out the Language Note. Review the rule. Test comprehension. Write various subjects on the board (e.g., *Mr. and Mrs. Li, the children, the family, the teacher and I*) and ask volunteers to make questions with *can* and *should*.
2. Review questions with *have to*. Ask: *Are questions with* have to *made the same?* (no) Elicit differences. (*Do/does* comes first; put *have to* after the subject.) Point out that short answers with *have to* contain only the subject and *do* or *does*, and not *have to* or the verb. Go over the examples. Direct students' attention to the Language Note. Ask: *Do you always have to use* do/does *to make questions with* have to? (yes)

- You can get information about car seats on the Internet or at a neighborhood police station.
- Tickets for not putting a child in a car seat can be up to $100 in some states.

🎧 **Listening Activity** Listen to each statement about the conversation. Circle *true* or *false*.

EXAMPLE (TRUE) FALSE

1. (TRUE) FALSE   5. TRUE (FALSE)
2. TRUE (FALSE)   6. TRUE (FALSE)
3. (TRUE) FALSE   7. TRUE (FALSE)
4. (TRUE) FALSE

5.4 | Yes/No Questions with *Can*, *Should*, and *Have To*

Modal Verb	Subject	Verb (Base Form)	Complement	Short Answer
Can	I	get	some water?	Yes, you can.
Should	we	pay	inside?	No, we shouldn't.

Language Note: Question forms and short answers with *can* and *should* are the same for all subjects.

Do/Does	Subject	Have To	Verb (Base Form)	Complement	Short Answer
Does	he	have to	get	gas now?	Yes, he does.
Does	she	have to	pay	in cash?	No, she doesn't.
Do	I	have to	pump	the gas?	Yes, you do.
Do	we	have to	pay	inside?	No, we don't.

Language Note: Use *do/does* to make questions with *have to*.

102 Unit 5

Expansion

Grammar Chart Have students ask and answer questions using *have to* about work or school. Say: *Ask your partner about his or her job. What does he or she have to do?*

EXERCISE 1 Write an affirmative or negative short answer for each question. Use the ideas from the conversation.

EXAMPLE Does Dorota have to get gas?
Yes, she does.

1. Should Halina put Anna's car seat in the passenger seat?
   No, she shouldn't.
2. Can airbags hurt children?
   Yes, they can.
3. Does Dorota have to pay in cash for her gas?
   No, she doesn't.
4. Do people have to pump their own gas at the gas station?
   Yes, they do.
5. Does Halina have to pay for the gas?
   No, she doesn't.
6. Should young children sit in the back seat of the car?
   Yes, they should.
7. Can parents hold their babies in a car?
   No, they can't.

EXERCISE 2 Fill in the blanks to make *yes/no* questions. Use the phrases from the column on the right. Write the questions on the blank.

EXAMPLE _Can I pay_ with a credit card here?   Can I pay ✓

1. _Should we pay_ for the gas?   Should we pay
2. _Can we go_ to the outlet mall?   Can I put
3. _Can I put_ the car seat in the front?   Does everyone have to use
4. _Do they have to sit_ in the back seat?   Can we go
5. _Should I pump_ first?   Should I pump
6. _Does everyone have to use_ a seatbelt?   Do they have to sit

Lesson 2   103

EXERCISE 1
1. Have students read the direction line. Say: *Make sure that the answer you give is short. Remember: Short answers for* can *and* should *have the subject plus* can *or* should. Go over the example in the Student Book.
2. Have students complete Exercise 1 individually. Go over the answers as a class.
3. If necessary, review grammar chart **5.4** on page 102.

EXERCISE 2
1. Have students read the direction line. Go over the example.
2. Have students complete Exercise 2 individually. Then have students compare answers with a partner. Circulate to observe pair work. Give help as needed.
3. If necessary, review grammar chart **5.4** on page 102.

Expansion
Exercise 2 Have students practice the questions and answers in pairs. Circulate to give help as needed.

Unit 5   103

EXERCISE 3

1. Have students read the direction line. Go over the example in the Student Book. Explain the meaning of *hold* (to keep in one's arms or lap).
2. Have students complete Exercise 3 individually. Then have students compare answers in pairs. Circulate to observe pair work. Give help as needed.
3. If necessary, review grammar chart **5.4** on page 102.

⏱ To save class time, have students do the exercise for homework ahead of time.

EXERCISE 4

1. Say: *This exercise is about you.* Tell students that they will be asking a partner about customs in his or her country. Have students read the direction line. Go over the example.
2. Have students complete Exercise 4 in pairs. Then have volunteers talk about their answers with the class.
3. If necessary, review grammar chart **5.4** on page 102.

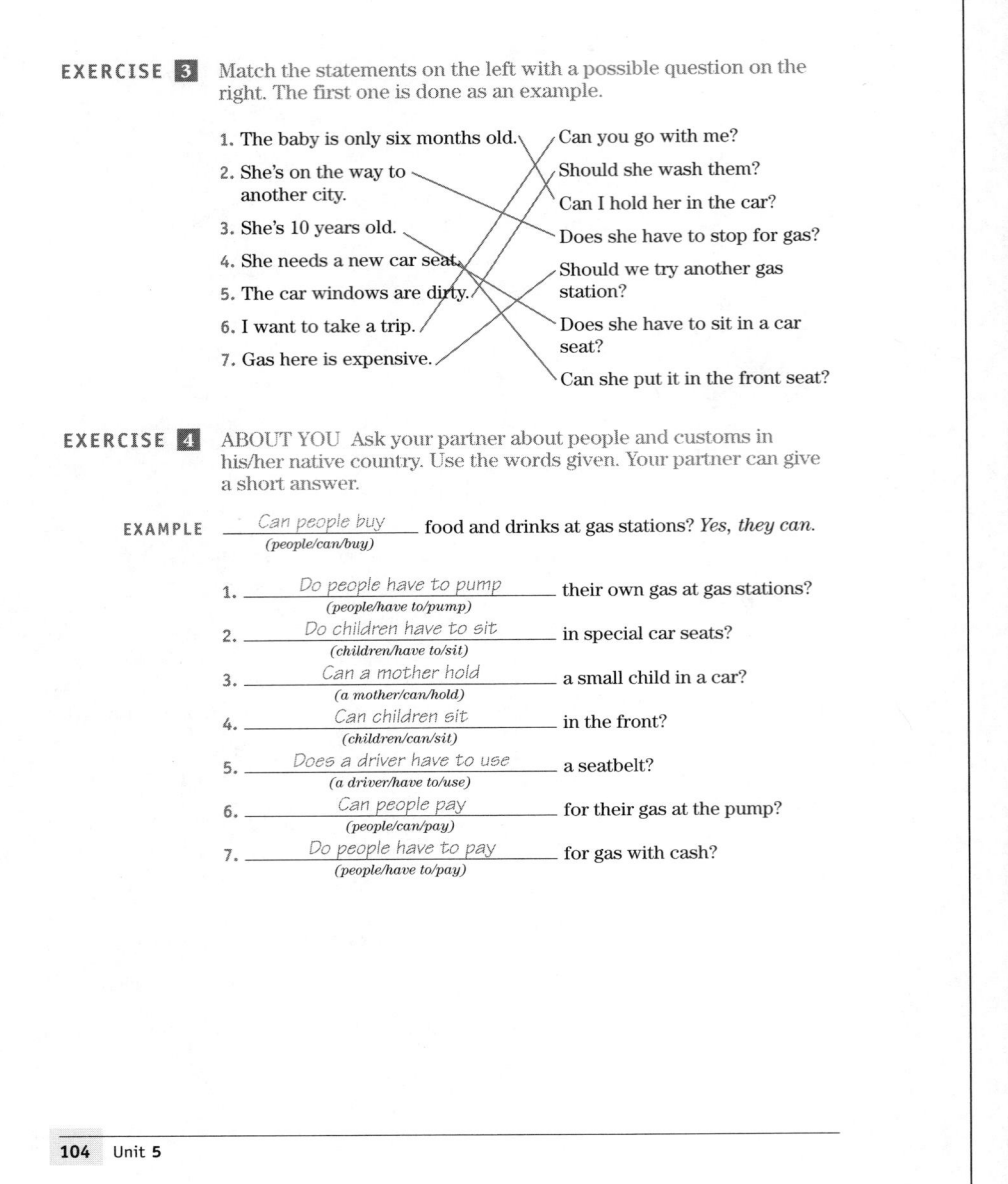

EXERCISE 3 Match the statements on the left with a possible question on the right. The first one is done as an example.

1. The baby is only six months old. — Can I hold her in the car?
2. She's on the way to another city. — Does she have to stop for gas?
3. She's 10 years old. — Can she put it in the front seat?
4. She needs a new car seat. — Does she have to sit in a car seat?
5. The car windows are dirty. — Should she wash them?
6. I want to take a trip. — Can you go with me?
7. Gas here is expensive. — Should we try another gas station?

EXERCISE 4 ABOUT YOU Ask your partner about people and customs in his/her native country. Use the words given. Your partner can give a short answer.

EXAMPLE __Can people buy__ food and drinks at gas stations? *Yes, they can.*
(people/can/buy)

1. __Do people have to pump__ their own gas at gas stations?
   (people/have to/pump)
2. __Do children have to sit__ in special car seats?
   (children/have to/sit)
3. __Can a mother hold__ a small child in a car?
   (a mother/can/hold)
4. __Can children sit__ in the front?
   (children/can/sit)
5. __Does a driver have to use__ a seatbelt?
   (a driver/have to/use)
6. __Can people pay__ for their gas at the pump?
   (people/can/pay)
7. __Do people have to pay__ for gas with cash?
   (people/have to/pay)

104 Unit 5

Expansion

Exercise 3 Have students practice the statements and questions in pairs.

Exercise 4 Write the names of countries represented in your class across the top of the board horizontally. Then write the numbers of the questions vertically down the side. Survey the class: What are the customs in the different countries? Write a check mark when a country has a particular custom. Write an *x* when it doesn't.

5.5 | Information Questions with Modal Verbs

Can/Should

Question Word	Modal	Subject	Verb (Base Form)	Complement	Short Answer
Where	can	she	get	a car seat?	At a department store.
How long	should	children	sit	in the back?	Until age 12.
How	can	parents	keep	their children safe in a car?	They can put them in a car seat.
Which car seat	should	we	use	for a small baby?	An infant seat.

Have To

Question Word	Do/Does	Subject	Have To	Verb (Base Form)	Complement	Short Answer
Where	does	your son	have to	sit?		In the back seat.
How much	do	we	have to	pay	for a car seat?	About $75.

EXERCISE 5 Answer each question. Use the ideas from the reading.

EXAMPLE How can people pay for gas?
They can pay with a credit card or cash.

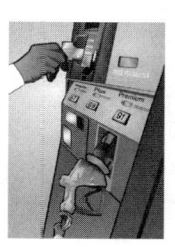

1. When can a child sit in the front passenger seat?
   A child can sit in the front passenger seat when he or she is 12.

2. Why does a small child have to sit in the back?
   A small child has to sit in the back because air bags can hurt children.

3. Why does Halina have to get a new car seat for Anna?
   She is too big for her old infant seat.

4. How long does a child have to sit in a car seat?
   A child has to fit in a car seat until age 8 or 57 inches tall.

Lesson 2   105

5.5 | Information Questions with Modal Verbs

1. Have students look at grammar chart **5.5** on page 105. Go over the word order and meaning of information questions on the board:

   Question Word + can *or* should + *Subject* + *Verb* + *Complement*

   Remind students that the verb is in the base form. Go over each example with *can* and *should*. Then review the short answers.

2. Go over the word order of information questions with *have* to on the board:

   Question Word + *do/does* + *Subject* + Have to + *Verb* + *Complement*

   Say: *We use* do *and* does *with* have to *in all questions.* Remind students that the verb is in the base form. Review each example with *have to*. Then go over the short answers.

EXERCISE 5

1. Have students look at the picture on page 105. Ask: *What is this person doing?* (paying for gas with a credit card) Have students read the direction line. Go over the example. Note the phrase *sit in the back* in #2 and elicit or explain the meaning to students. Remind students that questions with *why* are answered with *because*.

2. Have students complete Exercise 5 individually. Go over answers with the class.

3. If necessary, review grammar chart **5.5** on page 105.

Unit 5   105

EXERCISE 6

1. Have students read the direction line. Go over the example in the Student Book. Tell students not to answer the questions they write.
2. Have students complete Exercise 6 individually. Then have students compare answers in pairs. Circulate to observe pair work. Give help as needed.
3. If necessary, review grammar chart **5.5** on page 105.

⏱ To save class time, have students do the exercise for homework ahead of time.

EXERCISE 7

1. Have students look at the picture of Halina on page 107. Ask: *What is Halina doing?* (looking at a Web site on child safety) Read the direction line. Go over the example.
2. Have students complete Exercise 7 individually. Then have students compare answers in pairs. Circulate to observe pair work. Give help as needed.
3. If necessary, review grammar chart **5.5** on page 105.

---

5. What kind of seat should Halina buy?
   Halina should buy a car seat for older babies.
6. Where can people pay for gas at the gas station?
   They can pay for gas right at the pump.
7. Why does Dorota have to stop at a gas station?
   Dorota has to stop at a gas station because she needs gas.

EXERCISE 6 Ask questions about each statement using the question words given.

EXAMPLE Halina has to put Anna's car seat in the back.
Why _does Halina have to put the car seat in the back_ ?

1. They have to stop for gas on their trip.
   How often _do they have to stop for gas_ ?
2. She should drive slowly.
   Why _should she drive slowly_ ?
3. An air bag can hurt small children.
   How _can an air bag hurt small children_ ?
4. Simon has to buy some things for his car.
   How many things _does Simon have to buy for his car_ ?
5. You can use my car today.
   How long _can I use your car today_ ?
6. You should get a better car seat for your daughter.
   Why _should I get a better car seat for my daughter_ ?
7. We have to pay first at this gas station.
   Where _do we have to pay first_ ?

EXERCISE 7 Complete each short conversation with a question. Use the words given.

EXAMPLE A: Please get in the car.
B: _Where should we sit?_
(example: where/we/should sit)

106 Unit 5

Expansion

Exercise 6 Have students practice the statements and questions in pairs.

Have students give answers to the questions. Tell students that the answers are not in the reading. Say: *Create your own answers*.

Exercise 7 Have students practice the short conversations in pairs. Ask volunteers to roleplay the conversations in front of the class.

1. A: There's child safety information on the Web.
   B: _Which Web site should I check?_
      (which Web site/I/should check)

2. A: She doesn't have a car seat.
   B: _Where can she buy a good one?_
      (where/she/can buy a good one)

3. A: Their son is five years old.
   B: _Which car seat do they have to get for him?_
      (which car seat/they/have to get for him)

4. A: Car seats have different prices.
   B: _How much should we spend?_
      (how much/we/should spend)

5. A: Your seatbelt is broken.
   B: _How can I fix it?_
      (how/I/can fix it)

6. A: That new driver is only 17 years old.
   B: _When does he have to drive with an adult?_
      (when/he/have to drive with an adult)

5.6 | Question Words as Subjects

Question Word (Subject)	Modal Verb	Verb (Base Form)	Complement	Short Answer
Who	should	pay	for the gas?	Dorota should.
What	can	happen	to the baby in the front seat?	The airbag can hurt her in an accident.
How many new drivers	have to	take	the written test today?	Only three.
Which drivers	have to	get	limited licenses?	All drivers 17 and under.

Lesson 2   107

5.6 | Question Words as Subjects

1. Have students look at grammar chart **5.6** on page 107. Direct their attention to the first two questions with *should* and *can*. Write on the board:

   Question Word + can *or* should + *verb* + *complement*

   Demonstrate how to form a question with the question word as subject with the modals *can* and *should*. Remind students that the verb is in the base form. Go over the second example. Review the short answers. Note that they often don't repeat the noun in the complement, but replace it with a pronoun: *I can get it.* vs. *I can get the water for the trip.* Ask volunteers to choose a question word and make a new question. Have another volunteer answer.

2. Direct students' attention to the questions with *have to*. Say: *Do not use* do *or* does *with* have to *when the subject is a question word.* Read through the questions with *have to* in the chart.

3. Go over the short answers with *have to*. Then ask students to change the short answers to long answers. (Only three new drivers have to take the written test today. All drivers 17 and under have to get limited licenses.)

Expansion

Grammar Chart Have students work in pairs to complete the following questions:

1. *Who should pay ____?*
2. *What can happen ____?*

Tell students that the questions don't have to be about driving. They can be on any topic. Then have pairs share their questions with the class. Volunteers can answer the questions.

Unit 5   107

EXERCISE 8

1. Have students read the direction line. Go over the example in the Student Book. Then point out several of the underlined words and phrases in the exercise. Ask students what kind of question word they require.
2. Have students complete Exercise 8 individually. Go over the answers as a class.
3. If necessary, review grammar chart **5.6** on page 107.

EXERCISE 9

1. Have students read the direction line. Ask a volunteer to do #1.
2. Have students complete the rest of Exercise 9 individually. Then have students compare answers with a partner. Circulate to observe pair work. Give help as needed.
3. If necessary, review grammar charts **5.5** on page 105 and **5.6** on page 107.

    ⏱ To save class time, have students complete the exercise for homework.

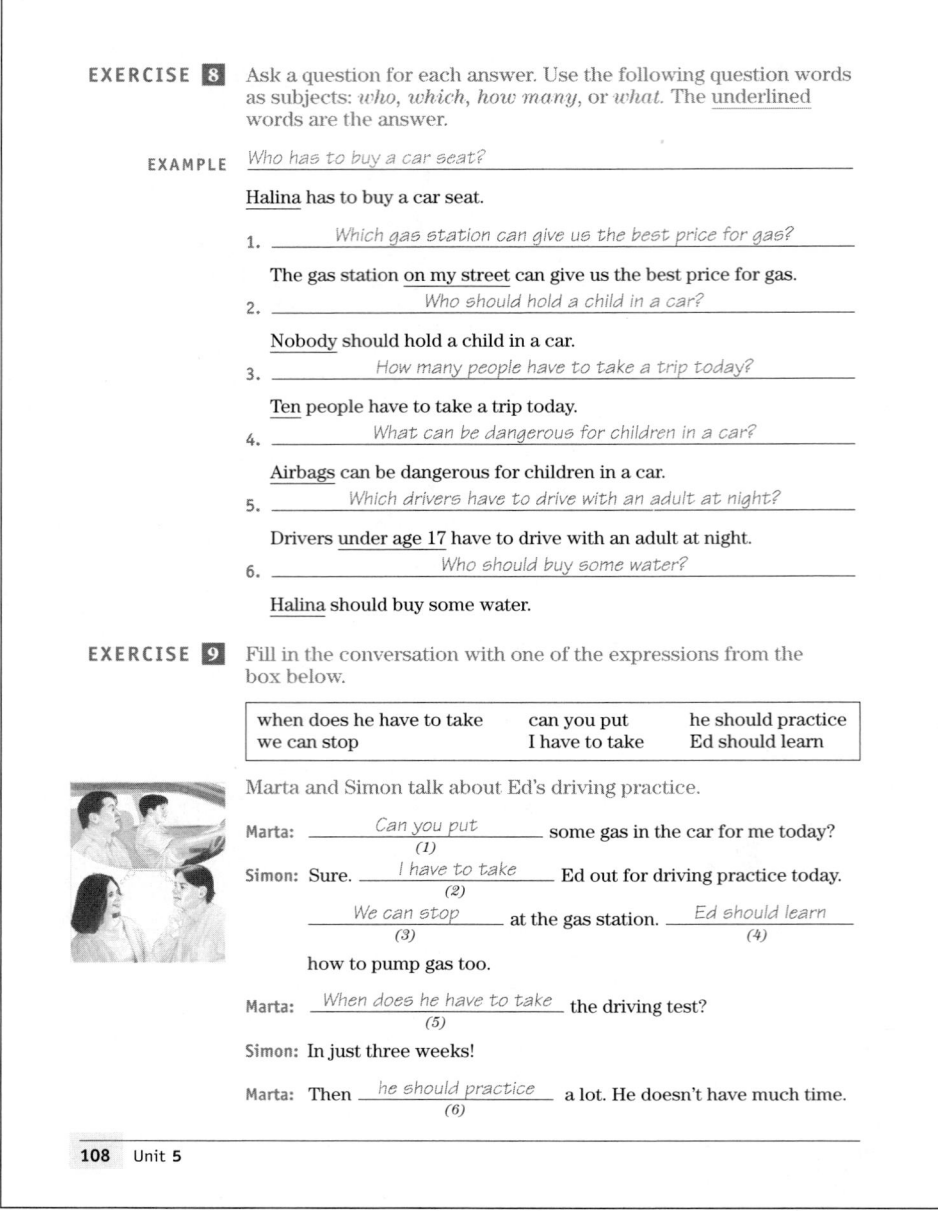

EXERCISE 8 Ask a question for each answer. Use the following question words as subjects: *who, which, how many,* or *what.* The underlined words are the answer.

EXAMPLE Who has to buy a car seat?
Halina has to buy a car seat.

1. Which gas station can give us the best price for gas?
   The gas station on my street can give us the best price for gas.
2. Who should hold a child in a car?
   Nobody should hold a child in a car.
3. How many people have to take a trip today?
   Ten people have to take a trip today.
4. What can be dangerous for children in a car?
   Airbags can be dangerous for children in a car.
5. Which drivers have to drive with an adult at night?
   Drivers under age 17 have to drive with an adult at night.
6. Who should buy some water?
   Halina should buy some water.

EXERCISE 9 Fill in the conversation with one of the expressions from the box below.

when does he have to take	can you put	he should practice
we can stop	I have to take	Ed should learn

Marta and Simon talk about Ed's driving practice.

Marta: _Can you put_ (1) some gas in the car for me today?

Simon: Sure. _I have to take_ (2) Ed out for driving practice today. _We can stop_ (3) at the gas station. _Ed should learn_ (4) how to pump gas too.

Marta: _When does he have to take_ (5) the driving test?

Simon: In just three weeks!

Marta: Then _he should practice_ (6) a lot. He doesn't have much time.

108 Unit 5

Expansion

Exercise 8 Have students change the long answers to short answers.

Exercise 9 Have students practice the conversation in pairs. Ask volunteers to roleplay the conversation in front of the class.

EDITING ADVICE

1. Always use the base form after *can*, *should*, and *have to*.

    She can ~~drives~~ *drive* the car.

2. Don't use *to* after *can* and *should*.

    She can't ~~to~~ sit in the front seat.

3. Use the correct word order in a question.

    Why (you) can't drive?

4. Don't forget to use *do* or *does* with *have to* in questions.

    Why *do* you have to get a limited license?

EDITING QUIZ

Find the mistakes with the underlined words, and correct them. Not every sentence has a mistake. If the sentence is correct, write *C*.

EXAMPLES: Why <u>~~she has to~~</u> *does she have to* take a driving class?

She <u>can drive</u> alone during the day. *C*

1. We <u>have to ~~coming~~</u> *come* to school for the class.
2. My brother <u>should takes</u> the vision test first.
3. The driving teacher <u>can ~~to~~ explain</u> the lesson very well.
4. What *do* <u>I have to do</u> to get a permit?
5. He <u>should ~~studies~~</u> *study* the rules of the road.
6. Where <u>can we practice</u>? *C*
7. What <u>~~we should to learn~~</u> *should we learn* for the written test?
8. Why *do* <u>older children have to use</u> car seats?

Lesson 2 109

Editing Advice

1. Have students close their books. Write the example sentences without editing marks or corrections on the board. For example:

    1. She can drives the car.
    2. She can't to sit in the front seat.

    Ask students to correct each sentence. This activity can be done individually, in pairs, or as a class. After students have corrected each sentence, tell them to turn to page 109. Say: *Now compare your work with Editing Advice in the book.*

2. Go over answers with the class. For troublespots, review the appropriate grammar chart.

Editing Quiz

1. The Editing Quiz may be used as an in-class quiz, a take-home quiz, or as a review. Have students read the direction line. Ask: *Does every sentence have a mistake?* (no) Go over the examples with the class.

2. Have students complete the quiz individually. Collect the completed quizzes for assessment or have students check each other's work. Review the answers with the class. Elicit the relevant grammar point for each correction. For example, for #1, ask: *What's the rule for* have to? (The main verb has to be in the base form.)

Unit 5 109

Learner's Log

1. Have students close their books. Ask: *What did you learn about driver's licenses, gas stations, and children's car seats in this unit? What else do you want to know about them?* Prompt students with questions, such as: *How many tests do you take to get a driver's license?* Write students' ideas on the board. Discuss ways in which students can find out more about driving in the U.S.
2. Have students open their books to complete the Learner's Log. Remind students to write three questions about driving in the U.S.

Expansion Activities

These expansion activities provide opportunities for students to interact with one another and further develop their speaking and writing skills. Encourage students to use grammar from this unit whenever possible.

To save class time, assign parts of the activities as homework. Then use class time for interaction and communication. If students do not need additional speaking practice, some of the activities may be assigned as writing activities for homework, or skipped altogether.

WRITING ACTIVITY

1. Say: *You are going to write an affirmative and a negative sentence about each of these pictures.* Have students read the direction line. Go over the example.
2. Have students complete the activity individually at home or in class.
3. Collect for assessment.

OUTSIDE ACTIVITY

Have volunteers tell the class how to much car seats cost.

INTERNET ACTIVITY

Write the questions on page 110 on the board. Have students who have access to the Internet to volunteer to research each question.

LEARNER'S LOG

1. What did you learn in this unit? Write three sentences in your notebook about each of these topics:
   • Driver's licenses
   • Gas stations
   • Children's car seats

2. Write three questions you still have about driving in the U.S.

EXPANSION ACTIVITIES

Writing Activity

In your notebook, write one negative and one affirmative sentence about each picture. Write about what is wrong with each picture.

EXAMPLE *This woman can't hold her baby in her arms in a car. The baby has to be in an infant seat.*

A. B. C.

Outside Activity

Go to a local department store. Find a child's car seat and an infant seat. Tell the class how much they cost.

Internet Activity

Search the words *graduated licenses* and the name of your state. Find the rules for your state about limited licenses for teenagers.
   • What is the age for a full license?
   • How many young people can be in a car with a young driver?
   • When does a young driver have to be with an adult driver?
   • What hours can he/she drive?

110 Unit 5

Expansion

Learner's Log Have students compare logs in pairs.

Writing Activity Variation

Have students exchange papers with a partner for proofreading.

Outside Activity Variation

Have students decide the best prices they found on child and infant car seats. Write the results on the board. Did anyone compare prices online?

Internet Activity Variation

Tell students that if they don't have Internet access, they can use Internet facilities at a public library. Alternatively, they can visit the nearest driver-licensing facility and request information about driving in their state.

UNIT 6

GRAMMAR
Must and *Have To*
Noncount Nouns
Quantity Expressions

CONTEXT
School

Expansion

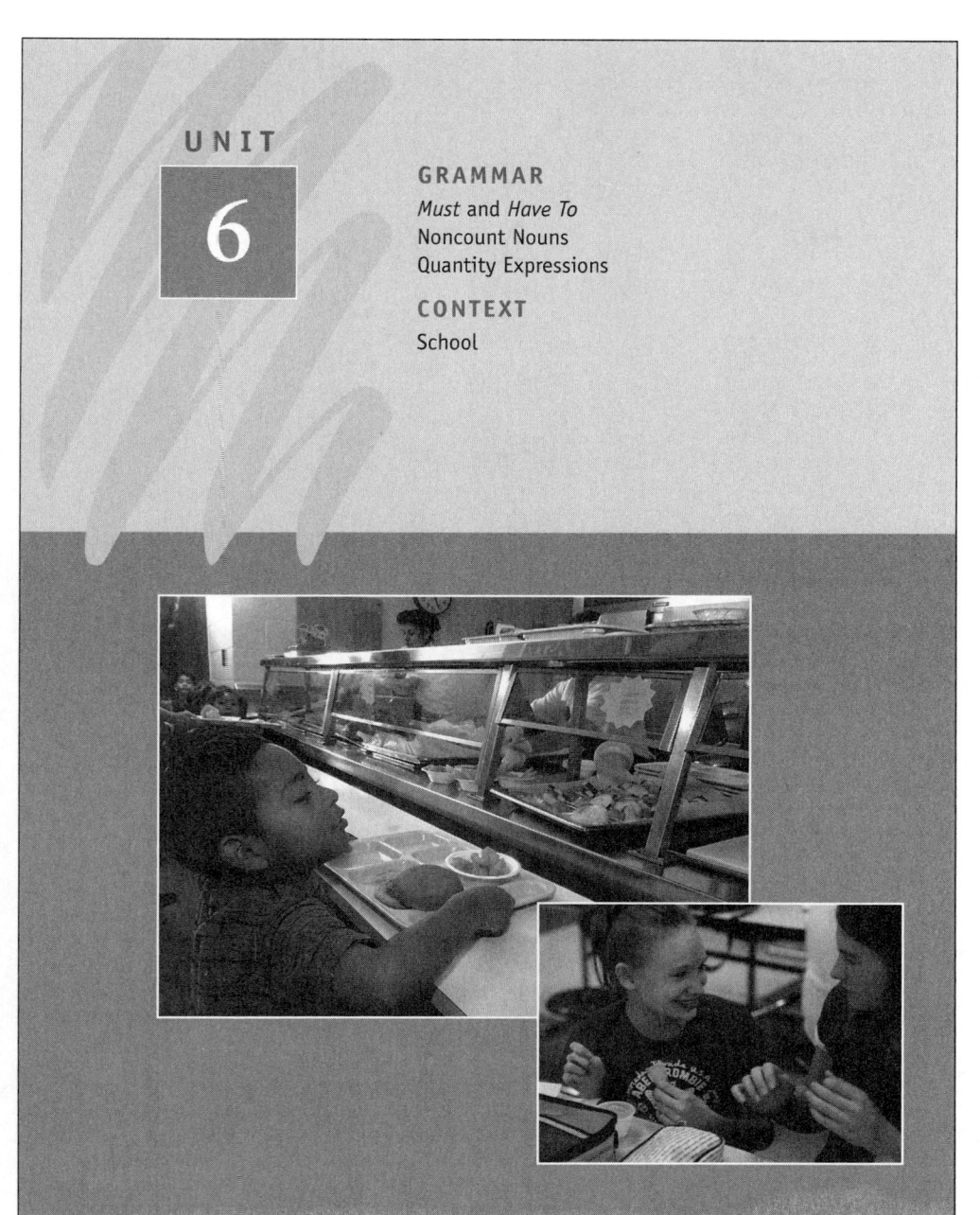

Theme The topic for this unit can be enhanced with the following ideas:

1. Menu from local elementary school cafeteria
2. Poster of food pyramid
3. Illustrations of foods in each group
4. Chart showing typical family food budget in dollars

Unit | 6
Unit Overview

GRAMMAR

1. Say: *In Unit 5 we studied* can, should, *and* have to. *In Unit 6, we're going to study* have to *and* must. Write on the board: *must = have to*. Say: Must *is a modal*. Activate students' prior knowledge. Ask: *What do you have to do to get a driver's license? What must you do?*

2. Say: *We're also going to study noncount nouns and quantity expressions*. Say and write on the board:

   a piece > candy, pizza
   1. *bottle > juice, oil*
   2. *glasses > milk*

   Point to the quantity expressions. Say: *These words tell how much.* Elicit general quantity expressions (e.g., *a lot, a little*). Write them on the board.

CONTEXT

1. Ask: *In Unit 6, we're going to talk about school lunch programs in the U.S. Lunch programs tell schools what children must eat.* Relate the topic to students. Ask: *Are school lunch programs important? Why or why not?*

2. Direct students' attention to the photos of the school lunchroom/cafeteria. Ask: *What is this boy doing?* (buying lunch; choosing food.) *What is he going to eat?* (a hamburger) *Are the girls buying lunch?* (No. They have a lunch from home.)

3. Say: *Can all families pay for a school lunch?* Have students share their knowledge and experiences.

Unit 6   111

Lesson 1 | Overview

GRAMMAR

Say: *Some families must pay the full price for a school lunch. Some have to pay a little. Some don't have to pay.* Write the sentences on the board. Say: *We're going to learn about these modals.* Underline *must, have to,* and *don't have to.* Elicit example sentences from students. Prompt with questions, such as: *What's something you must pay full price for? What's something you don't have to pay for?*

CONTEXT

1. Say: *American kids get milk, meat, vegetables, and grains in a school lunch program.* Relate the topic to students' experience. Ask: *What did you eat for lunch at school? Did you eat a lot of vegetables?*
2. Direct students' attention to the photos of the cafeteria on page 111. Ask: *Where are these children?* (in a school cafeteria/lunchroom) *What are they eating?* (lunch) Activate student's prior knowledge. Have them name specific foods.

BEFORE YOU READ

1. Go over each question as a class. Have a volunteer read the questions or read them to the class yourself. Have students discuss the questions in pairs. If possible, put students together from different countries.
2. Ask for a few volunteers to share their answers with the class.

To save class time, skip "Before You Read," or have students prepare answers for homework ahead of time.

LESSON 1

GRAMMAR
Must
Must and Have To
Must Not and Don't Have To

CONTEXT
School Lunch Programs

Before You Read

1. Do elementary schools in your native country give free lunches to children?
2. What do children like to eat for lunch?

milk

vegetables/fruits   grains/bread   meats

112   Unit 6

Culture Note
Almost 29 million students a day buy lunch or receive a free lunch in school cafeterias.

---

112   *Grammar in Context Basic* Teacher's Edition

SCHOOL LUNCH PROGRAMS

Children need good nutrition. The United States has a National School Lunch Program to give children balanced meals. Schools in this program **must** follow guidelines. They **must not** give children a lot of fat, sugar, or salt. They **must** serve food from each of these four groups:

- Meat
- Vegetables / fruits
- Grains / bread
- Milk

Children from very low-income families **don't have to** pay for a school lunch. Some families **have to** pay a small amount (less than 50¢). Some families have enough money and **have to** pay the full price. It isn't expensive. It's less than $2.00.

Parents **must** fill out an application for their children to get a free lunch. They **must** tell the truth about the family income.

Children **don't have to** eat the school lunch. They can bring a lunch from home. A popular lunch for children is a peanut butter and jelly sandwich.

Vocabulary in Context

nutrition	Children need good **nutrition** to be healthy. They need to eat good food.
balanced	A **balanced** lunch contains items from each food group.
meal(s)	Breakfast, lunch, and dinner are **meals**.
serve	Schools give children lunch. They **serve** lunch every day.
guideline(s)	The National School Lunch Program makes **guidelines**. They tell the schools what to serve.
fat	Potato chips and French fries have a lot of **fat**.
grain(s)	We use **grains** to make bread and cereal.
income	They don't get much money at their job. They have a low **income**.
amount	Fifty cents is a small **amount** of money.
less than	The lunch costs $1.75. It's **less than** $2.00.
tell the truth	**Tell the truth** on the application. Don't give false information.

Lesson 1 113

School Lunch Programs (Reading) CD 1, Track 29

1. Have students look at the title of the reading and read the first sentence. Then have them look at the picture of the sandwich. Ask: *What kind of sandwich is this?* (peanut butter) *Is this good nutrition? What's the reading about? What will it say about school lunch programs?* Have students use the title and photos on page 111 and the pictures on page 112 to make predictions about the reading.
2. Have students read the text silently. Then play the audio and have students read along silently.
3. Check students' basic comprehension. Ask questions, such as: *What kind of foods do schools have to give children?* (meat, vegetables/fruits, grains/bread, and milk) *Does everyone have to pay for lunch?* (No. Some very low-income families don't have to pay; some families pay a little; some have to pay full price.) *Do all children have to buy lunch?* (No. They can bring it from home.)

To save class time, have students do the reading for homework ahead of time.

VOCABULARY IN CONTEXT

1. Model the pronunciation of each new vocabulary word and have students repeat.
2. Make sure students understand the meaning of each vocabulary word. Review the examples in the book and create additional example sentences. For example, say: *nutrition. Good nutrition is very important to me. I don't eat a lot of candy, cake, or cookies.* Review each new vocabulary word similarly, using visuals and realia when appropriate. When possible, point to pictures in the book that illustrate the new vocabulary items, such as *grains* on page 112.
3. Have students underline an example of each new vocabulary item in the reading.

Reading Variation

1. To practice listening skills, have students listen to the audio before opening their books. Ask a few comprehension questions: *Can schools give children a lot of fat, sugar, or salt?* (no) *Do children have to eat the school lunch?* (no) Repeat the audio if necessary. Then have students open their books and read along as they listen to the audio.
2. Alternatively, have students begin by listening to the audio as they read along.

Vocabulary Teaching Ideas

Use the following ideas to teach these terms:

income: Say: *A job pays money. This money is income.* Write on the board: *$8,000, $35,000, $190,000.* Pronounce the amounts. Say: *Some people have low incomes. Others have high incomes; they make a lot of money.*

serve: Place glasses on top of a tray, or something you could use as a tray, and say: *I'm a waiter. I serve you drinks.*

Expansion

Vocabulary in Context To check comprehension, have volunteers in pairs or groups act out selected vocabulary, such as *serve* and *tell the truth*.

Unit 6 113

DID YOU KNOW?

Explain the food pyramid to students. Say: *Foods with a lot of nutrition have a wider triangular space on the food pyramid. For example,* grains *have more nutrition than* oils.

LISTENING ACTIVITY

🎧 **CD 1, Track 30**

1. Say: *Listen to the sentences about the reading on school lunch programs. Circle* true *or* false. Play the listening selection one time without pausing. Then play it through again, pausing and replaying as necessary.
2. Go over the answers as a class. Ask students to volunteer answers.

6.1 | Must

1. Have students look at grammar chart **6.1** on page 114. Explain the affirmative use of *must*. Say: *We use* must *to show rules or laws*. Go over the examples.
2. Explain the negative use of *must*. Say: *If the law says not to do something, we say* must not. Go over the examples. Give additional examples, such as: *You must use your seatbelt. It's the law. You must not drink and drive. In some states, you must not use a handheld telephone while driving.*
3. Review word order in affirmative and negative sentences with *must*. Ask: *Where does the subject go? Where does the modal* (must) *go?*

EXERCISE 1

1. Have students read the direction line. Go over the example in the Student Book. Remind students that one verb in the box will be used two times.
2. Have students complete Exercise 1 individually. Check the answers as a class.
3. If necessary, review grammar chart **6.1** on page 114.

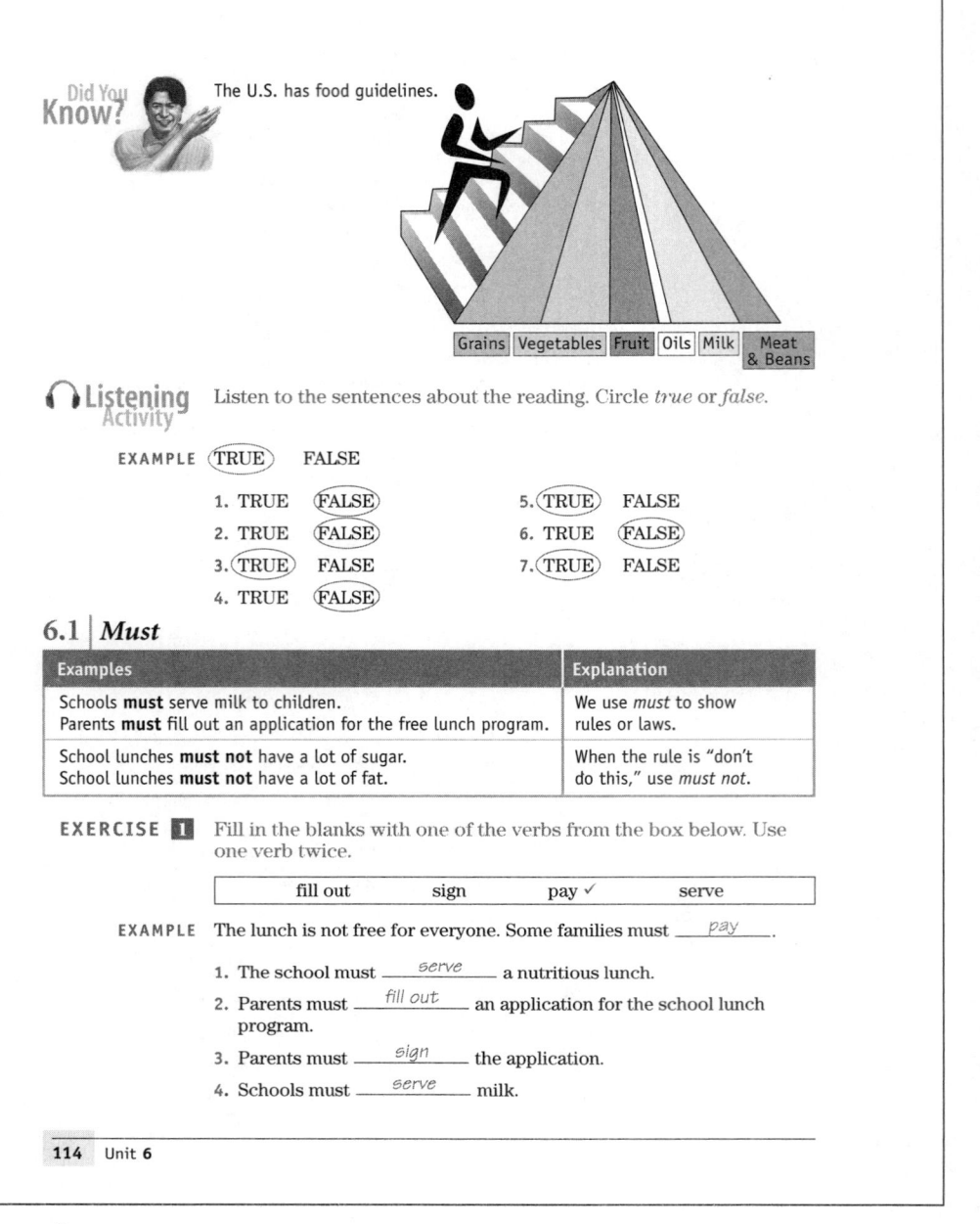

The U.S. has food guidelines.

Grains | Vegetables | Fruit | Oils | Milk | Meat & Beans

🎧 **Listening Activity** Listen to the sentences about the reading. Circle *true* or *false*.

EXAMPLE (TRUE)   FALSE

1. TRUE   (FALSE)   5. (TRUE)   FALSE
2. TRUE   (FALSE)   6. TRUE   (FALSE)
3. (TRUE)   FALSE   7. (TRUE)   FALSE
4. TRUE   (FALSE)

6.1 | Must

Examples	Explanation
Schools **must** serve milk to children. Parents **must** fill out an application for the free lunch program.	We use *must* to show rules or laws.
School lunches **must not** have a lot of sugar. School lunches **must not** have a lot of fat.	When the rule is "don't do this," use *must not*.

EXERCISE 1 Fill in the blanks with one of the verbs from the box below. Use one verb twice.

| fill out | sign | pay ✓ | serve |

EXAMPLE The lunch is not free for everyone. Some families must ___pay___.

1. The school must ___serve___ a nutritious lunch.
2. Parents must ___fill out___ an application for the school lunch program.
3. Parents must ___sign___ the application.
4. Schools must ___serve___ milk.

114 Unit 6

Expansion

Exercise 1 Ask: *What rules do we have in our class?* Brainstorm a list of rules for the class on the board using *must*.

Bayside Public Schools
Application for Free and Reduced Price Meals

To apply for free and reduced price meals for your child(ren), you must fill out this form and sign it. You must tell the truth. Use a pen.

Part 1 List the names of children at school.

Name(s) of Child(ren) Last name, First name	Age	School	Grade	Class
1. Answers will vary.				
2.				
3.				

Part 2 List the names of all household members and their monthly incomes.

Last name, First name	Monthly income
1.	
2.	
3.	

Part 3 Signature and Social Security Number

Signature of Household Member	Mailing Address
Social Security Number __ __ __ - __ __ - __ __ __ __	Phone Number ( )

For school use only
Date received _____ Date approved _____

EXERCISE 2 Look at the application for the school lunch program above. Change the sentences below from imperative statements to statements with *must*.

EXAMPLES Print your answers. You _must print your answers._
Don't use a pencil. You _must not use a pencil._

1. Fill out the application. You _must fill out the application._
2. Sign your name. You _must sign your name._
3. Don't fill out the last box. You _must not fill out the last box._
4. Write your family income. You _must write your family income._
5. Use a pen. You _must use a pen._
6. Don't use a pencil. You _must not use a pencil._
7. Don't give false information. You _must not give false information._

Lesson 1 115

EXERCISE 2

1. Have students look at the application for free and reduced meals at the top of page 115. Give students time to read through the application. Go through each part with students. Ask: *What do we put in Part 1?* (information about your children) *What goes in Part 2?* (names of people who live in your house and their income) *What do we put in Part 3?* (your signature, address, phone number, and Social Security number) You might need to explain new vocabulary, such as *grade* (Part 1) and *household* (Part 2).
2. Have students read the direction line for Exercise 2. Go over the examples. Ask: *Which statement is imperative?*
3. Have students complete Exercise 2 individually. Go over the answers with the class.
4. If necessary, review grammar chart 6.1 on page 114.

Expansion

Exercise 2 Find or create a relatively simple application to give students (e.g., for a tutoring program or a free-book program). Have students create a list of instructions for filling it out using *must* and *mustn't*.

Unit 6 115

6.2 | Must and Have To

1. Have students look at grammar chart **6.2** on page 116. To clarify and stress very formal uses of *must*, say: *We often use* must *with people who tell us or advise us what to do.* Relate the explanation to students' personal experience. Ask: *Who tells you what to do? Who gives rules and laws?* (government, parents and grandparents, doctors, schools and teachers) Say: Have to *is often used to express personal necessity. This means things only you must do.* Go over the examples.
2. Write additional examples on the board. Have students decide whether to use *must* or *have to*:
   1. I _____ call my grandmother this week. It's her birthday.
   2. I can't go into work today; I'm sick. I _____ call my boss.
3. Point out the Language Note. Say: *We don't usually use* must *in questions.* Go over the examples.

EXERCISE 3

1. Tell students they are going to complete some rules. List key words on the board, such as *slow down* and *print*.
2. Have students read the direction line. Go over the example.
3. Have students complete Exercise 3 individually. Go over the answers as a class.
4. If necessary, review grammar chart **6.2** on page 116.

EXERCISE 4

1. Have students read the direction line. Go over the example. Have a volunteer model the example.
2. Have students complete Exercise 4 individually. Then have students compare answers in pairs. Circulate to observe pair work. Give help as needed.
3. If necessary, review grammar chart **6.2** on page 116.

6.2 | Must and Have To

Must and *have to* have very similar meanings.

Examples	Explanation
You **must** write your family income. You **have to** write your family income. Schools **must** serve children milk. Schools **have to** serve children milk.	*Must* is very formal. We use *must* for rules and laws. We can also use *have to* for rules and laws.
My daughter is hungry. I **have to** make lunch for her. It's late. We **have to** leave.	Use *have to* for personal necessity. Don't use *must* for personal necessity.

Language Note: In a question, *have to* is more common than *must*.
  Do I **have to** sign the application?
  Do schools **have to** serve children milk?

EXERCISE 3 Fill in the blanks with *must* + a verb to talk about rules.

EXAMPLE Students ___must pay for___ college courses.

Answers may vary.
1. When you see a red light, you ___must stop___.
2. On an application, you ___must use a pen___.
3. Drivers ___must have a license___.
4. In a car, small children ___must be in a car seat___.
5. Immigrants ___must fill out an application___.

EXERCISE 4 Fill in the blanks to talk about personal necessities. Answers will vary.

EXAMPLE I have to ___call my mom___ every day.

Answers will vary.
1. In class, we have to _____.
2. The teacher has to _____.
3. A mother has to _____.
4. Children have to _____.
5. College students have to _____.
6. I have to _____ every day.

116 Unit 6

Expansion

Grammar Chart Ask a volunteer to tell the class something they have to do, using a complete sentence. Have students create three statements with *have to* that are true for them. (e.g., At home I have to cook dinner every night.) Next, have them create three statements with *must* that are true for their native countries. (e.g., In Colombia we must drive with our headlights on.)

6.3 | Must Not and Don't Have To

Have to and *must* have very similar meanings. *Don't have to* and *must not* have very different meanings.

Examples	Explanation
School lunches **must not** have a lot of fat. You must tell the truth. You **must not** give false information.	*Must not* gives a rule.
Children **don't have to** eat the school lunch. They can bring a lunch from home. Children of low income families **don't have to** pay for lunch. They can get a free lunch.	*Don't have to* shows that something is not necessary.

EXERCISE 5 ABOUT YOU Work with a partner. Name three things you *don't have to* do.
Answers will vary.

EXAMPLE I don't have to work on Saturdays.

EXERCISE 6 ABOUT YOU Work with a partner. Name three things students *must not do* at this school or in this class.
Answers will vary.

EXAMPLE Students must not talk in the library.

EXERCISE 7 Fill in the blanks with the negative of *must* or *have to*. Remember, they do NOT have the same meaning.

EXAMPLES Schools in the lunch program __must not__ serve a lot of sugar.

Children __don't have to__ be in the school lunch program.

1. Many families in the school lunch program __don't have to__ pay. Their children get free lunch.
2. Your son __doesn't have to__ eat at school. He can eat at home.
3. Parents __must not__ give false information on the application.
4. You __don't have to__ drink the milk. You can drink water.
5. We __don't have to__ study in the library. We can study at home.
6. You __must not__ talk loudly in the school library. It's a rule.
7. Children __must not__ come late to school.

Lesson 1 117

6.3 | Must Not and Don't Have To

Have students look at grammar chart **6.3** on page 117. Stress the very different meanings of the negatives. Say: Don't have to *means that something is not necessary.* Must not *means something is against the rules or law.* Go over the examples. Elicit more examples from students. (e.g., You mustn't be rude to a police officer; I don't have to go to class on Sunday.). Write the examples on the board.

EXERCISE 5

1. Say: *In this exercise, you tell what is true for you.* Have students read the direction line. Go over the example.
2. Have students complete Exercise 5 in pairs. Circulate to observe pair work. Give help as needed.
3. If necessary, review grammar chart **6.3** on page 117.

EXERCISE 6

1. Say: *This exercise is also about you.* Have students read the direction line. Go over the example.
2. Have students complete Exercise 6 in pairs. Circulate to observe pair work. Give help as needed.
3. If necessary, review grammar chart **6.2** on page 116.

🕐 To save class time, have students do the exercise for homework ahead of time.

EXERCISE 7

1. Have students read the direction line. Go over the example.
2. Have students complete Exercise 7 individually. Then have students compare answers in pairs. Circulate to observe pair work. Give help as needed.
3. If necessary, review grammar chart **6.2** on page 116.

🕐 To save class time, have students do the exercise for homework ahead of time.

Expansion
Exercise 5 Take a class survey. Find out what students don't have to do.

Unit 6 117

Lesson 2 | Overview

GRAMMAR

1. Ask: *What did we study in Lesson 1?* (must/mustn't, have to / don't have to). Say: *In this lesson, we are going to study count and noncount nouns. We're going to talk about quantity.* Say and write on the board: *Quantity Expressions.* Elicit examples and write them on the board. (e.g., *much, a lot, a little, some, any*)
2. Activate students' knowledge. Elicit foods and list them on the board. (e.g., pizza, cheese, potato chips, fruit, milk, juice, and fish) Ask volunteers to match a quantity expression with a food and make a sentence.

CONTEXT

1. Say: *This lesson is about what children do and don't like to eat. I don't like fish. Sometimes I throw it away. Kids often do, too.* Ask: *What foods do you love to eat?*
2. Direct students' attention to the picture of Victor and Maya on page 118. Say: *What foods do you see?* (pizza, grilled cheese sandwich, macaroni and cheese, tacos, soup, bread, coffee, water, chips, grapes, and milk) Write the names of the foods on the board.

BEFORE YOU READ

1. Go over each question as a class. Have a volunteer read the questions or read them to the class yourself. Have students discuss the questions in pairs. Ask: *Should children eat candy? Why or why not?*
2. Ask for a few volunteers to share their answers with the class.

 To save class time, skip "Before You Read," or have students prepare their answers for homework ahead of time.

LESSON 2

GRAMMAR
Count and Noncount Nouns
Quantity Expressions with Noncount Nouns
Much/A Lot of/A Little with Noncount Nouns
Some/Any with Noncount Nouns

CONTEXT
Maya's School Lunch

Before You Read
1. What foods are good for children?
2. What are some things children don't like to eat?

Culture Note
Children between the ages of three and eleven prefer pizza to any other food. Ninety-four percent of Americans eat pizza.

MAYA'S SCHOOL LUNCH

Victor: How are the lunches at your school? Do you like them?
Maya: Sometimes I do. Sometimes I don't. My favorite lunches are pizza, grilled cheese sandwiches, macaroni and cheese, and tacos. Sometimes we get **a piece of fish**, but I don't like fish.
Victor: What do you drink?
Maya: We always get **a small carton of milk**.
Victor: Do you get **any fruit**?
Maya: Yes. We always get a **piece of fruit**—an apple, an orange, a banana, or **a small bunch of grapes**. But the kids don't like the fruit. Sometimes we throw away the fruit.
Victor: That's terrible! Fruit is so good for you. Do the kids get **any soda**?
Maya: No. The teacher says that we shouldn't eat **much sugar**. But I love soda.
Victor: Your teacher's right. Sugar isn't good for you. Do all children get school lunches?
Maya: No. **Some kids** bring a lunch from home. My friend Wanda always brings her lunch to school in a lunch box. Her mother usually gives her a peanut butter and jelly sandwich and **a candy bar** or **a bag of potato chips**. She always brings **a small bottle of juice**. Juice is good for you, isn't it?
Victor: Juice contains **a lot of sugar**. Jelly contains **a lot of sugar** too. It's better to eat **a piece of fruit**. Please eat your fruit. Don't throw it away!
Maya: Dad, why do you always have **a can of soda** with you? It's better to drink **a bottle of water**.
Victor: You're right.

Vocabulary in Context

favorite	I love pizza. Pizza is my **favorite** lunch.
bunch of	We get a small **bunch of** grapes with lunch.
throw away	Don't **throw away** the fruit. It's good for you.
terrible	It isn't good to throw away fruit. It's **terrible**!
lunch box	Some people take their lunches in a **lunch box**.
contain	Soda **contains** a lot of sugar.

Lesson 2   119

Reading Variation

1. To practice listening skills, have students listen to the audio before opening their books. Ask a few comprehension questions, such as: *Does juice contain a lot of sugar?* (yes) Repeat the audio if necessary. Then have students open their books and read along as they listen to the audio.
2. Alternatively, have students begin by listening to the audio as they read along.

Vocabulary Teaching Ideas

Use the following idea to teach this term:

contain: Show students a box with objects such as pencils inside and say: *This box contains pencils.*

Expansion

Reading Have students practice the conversation in pairs. Ask volunteers to roleplay all or part of the conversation in front of the class.
Vocabulary in Context To check comprehension, have volunteers in pairs or groups act out selected vocabulary, such as *terrible* and *throw away*.

Maya's School Lunch (Reading) CD 1, Track 31

1. Have students look at the title of the reading and the picture on page 118. Ask: *What do you think Victor and Maya are talking about? Are they talking about food Maya likes? What is Victor saying?* Have students use the title and pictures to make predictions about the reading.
2. Have students read the dialogue silently. Then play the audio and have students read along silently.
3. Check students' basic comprehension. Ask questions, such as: *Does Maya like all the food at school?* (no) *Do the students like the fruit at school?* (No, sometimes they throw it away.) *What does Victor say about that?* (It's terrible that they throw fruit away.) *Does Victor drink soda?* (yes)

To save class time, have students do the reading for homework ahead of time.

Vocabulary in Context

1. Model the pronunciation of each new vocabulary word and have students repeat.
2. Make sure students understand the meaning of each vocabulary word. Review the examples in the book and create additional example sentences. For example, say: *favorite. My favorite singer is Shakira.* Go over each new vocabulary word similarly, using visuals and realia when appropriate. When possible, point to pictures in the book that illustrate new vocabulary items, such as *bunch of (grapes)* and *lunch box* on page 119.
3. Have students underline an example of each new vocabulary item in the reading.

DID YOU KNOW?

Tell students that the U.S. government has a program that helps farmers and schools. Farmers sell their produce to schools and children eat healthy fresh fruits, vegetables, and other farm products.

LISTENING ACTIVITY

🎧 **CD 1, Track 32**

1. Say: *Listen to the sentences about Victor and Maya's conversation. Circle* true *or* false. Play the listening selection one time without pausing. Then play it through again, pausing and replaying as necessary.
2. Go over the answers as a class. Ask students to volunteer answers.

6.4 | Count and Noncount Nouns

1. Have students cover up grammar chart **6.4** on page 120. Write some nouns from the chart on the board:

   sugar
   sandwich
   taco
   milk

   Ask: *Which two nouns can you count?* (*sandwich* and *taco*)

2. Have students look at grammar chart **6.4**. Say: *Count nouns have a singular form and a plural form. Noncount nouns do not have a plural form.* Go over the examples and the explanations. Review all of the noncount nouns. Point out the pictures of the food items as you go through the list.

3. Explain to students that there are exceptions. When ordering food, for example, some noncount nouns are used as count nouns. (e.g., *I'd like three pizzas. I'd like two sugars in my coffee.*)

Did You Know? The national free lunch program provides free or low-cost lunches to 28 million children in the U.S.

🎧 **Listening Activity** Listen to the sentences about the conversation. Circle *true* or *false*.

EXAMPLE TRUE (FALSE)

1. TRUE (FALSE)   5. TRUE (FALSE)
2. TRUE (FALSE)   6. (TRUE) FALSE
3. TRUE (FALSE)   7. TRUE (FALSE)
4. (TRUE) FALSE   8. TRUE (FALSE)

6.4 | Count and Noncount Nouns

Examples	Explanation
I eat two **sandwiches** a day. Do you like **tacos**? Many **children** get a free lunch.	Some nouns are *count* nouns. We can count them. We can use a number with them. They have a singular and a plural form.
The school doesn't serve **candy**. **Pizza** is very popular. The school always serves **milk**. **Juice** contains a lot of **sugar**.	Some nouns are *noncount* nouns. We don't count them. We don't use a number with them. They have no plural form.

Common noncount nouns are:

milk	bread	pizza	meat	soup
butter	jelly	coffee	tea	juice
water	chicken	soda	fruit	cheese
cream	candy	corn	peanut butter	sugar
salt	pork	fat	macaroni	fish
oil	rice	popcorn		

120 Unit 6

Expansion

Grammar Chart Have students work with a partner to create a list of five count nouns related to a single a topic such as a favorite place or game. Make a list on the board of students' nouns.

EXERCISE 1 ABOUT YOU Tell how often you eat or drink each item. Practice noncount nouns (no plural form) and the frequency words from the box below.

always	every day	often	sometimes	rarely	never

EXAMPLES fruit
I eat fruit every day.

popcorn
I never eat popcorn.

coffee
I rarely drink coffee.

Answers will vary.
1. milk
2. tea
3. coffee
4. water
5. soda
6. juice
7. bread
8. rice
9. pizza
10. meat
11. chicken
12. fish
13. pork
14. popcorn
15. candy
16. jelly

EXERCISE 2 ABOUT YOU Tell how often you eat or drink each item. Practice using count nouns and the frequency words. You can use the singular or plural form.

EXAMPLES potato(es)
I eat potatoes at least once a week.

banana(s)
I eat one banana a day.

avocado(es)
I never eat avocadoes.

Answers will vary.
1. banana(s)
2. apple(s)
3. potato chip(s)
4. cookie(s)
5. grape(s)
6. egg(s)
7. cracker(s)
8. orange(s)
9. hamburger(s)
10. hot dog(s)

Lesson 2   121

EXERCISE 1

1. Say: *In this exercise you tell what's true for you.* Direct students' attention to the list of food items. Ask: *Are these count or noncount nouns?* (noncount) Have students read the direction line. Go over the examples in the book.
2. Have students complete Exercise 1 in pairs. Circulate to observe pair work. Give help as needed.
3. If necessary, review grammar chart **6.4** on page 120.

EXERCISE 2

1. Say: *In this exercise you also tell what's true for you.* Direct students' attention to the list of foods. Ask: *Are these count or noncount nouns?* (count nouns) Have students read the direction line. Go over the examples in the Student Book.
2. Have students complete Exercise 2 in pairs. Circulate to observe pair work. Give help as needed.
3. If necessary, review grammar chart **6.4** on page 120.

Expansion

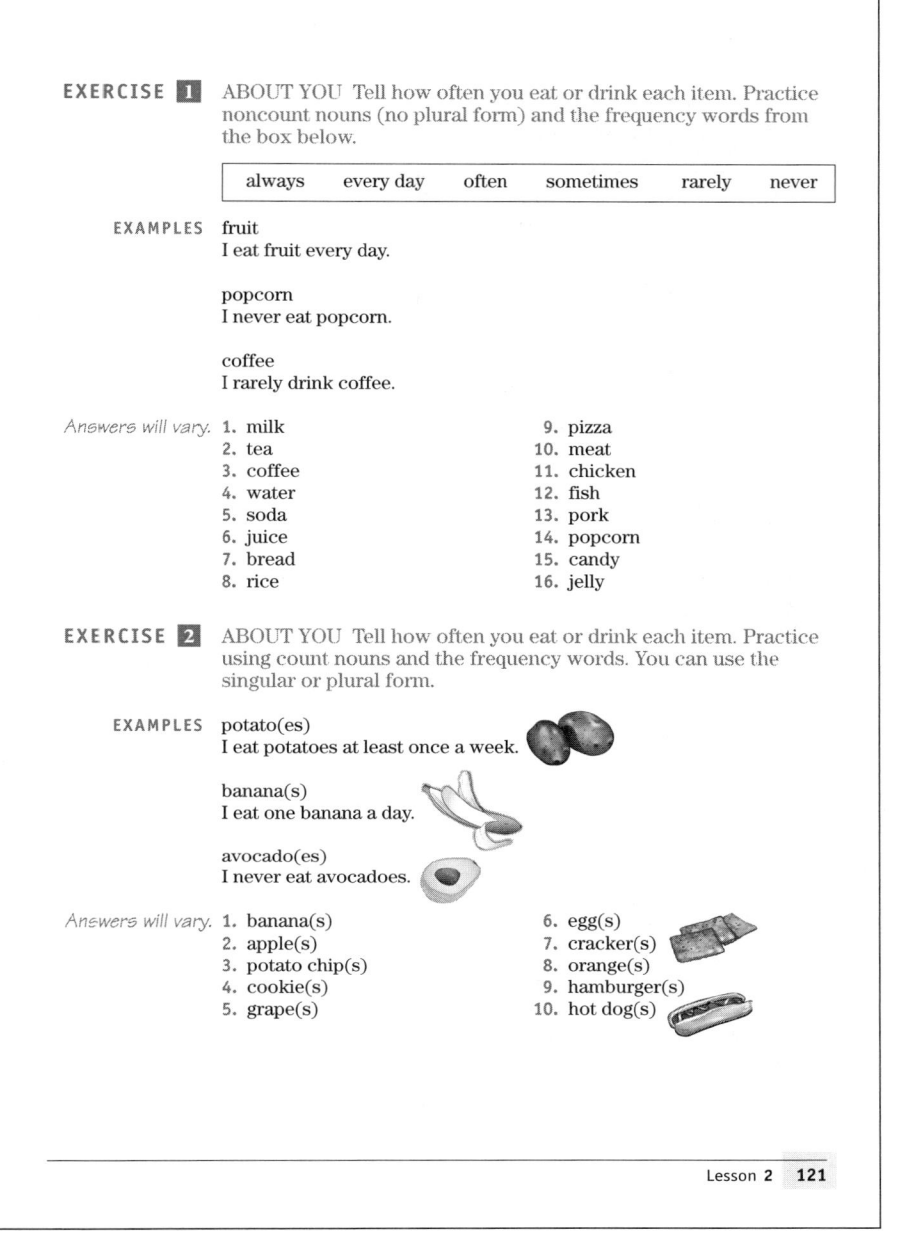

Exercise 1 and 2 Have pairs ask and answer questions. Tell partners to begin their questions with, *How often do you . . . ?*

Do a class survey. What are the most popular foods?

6.5 | Quantity Expressions with Noncount Nouns

1. Have students look at grammar chart **6.5** on page 122. Say: *To talk about quantity with noncount nouns, we use a unit of measure, such as a cup or a teaspoon, that we can count.* Go over the example sentences.
2. Read through the quantity expressions. Point out the pictures as you read through the list.
3. Have students close their books. Write a matching exercise on the board. Elicit from students ten or fifteen noncount foods and drinks and write them on the board. Write a blank in front of each item. Then list in a separate column the following quantity expressions:

    a carton
    a glass
    a bottle
    a jar
    a pound
    a piece
    a teaspoon
    a bowl
    a can
    a tablespoon

4. Have students take turns coming to the board. Ask them to match a quantity expression with a food and then make a sentence.

6.5 | Quantity Expressions with Noncount Nouns

Examples	Explanation
I eat **three pieces of fruit** a day. I drink **two cups of tea** a day. Children get **one carton of milk** with lunch.	To talk about quantity with a noncount noun, use a unit of measurement that you can count: *cup of, bowl of, carton of, teaspoon of, piece of*, etc.

Quantity Expressions with Noncount Nouns

a slice of pizza	a leaf of lettuce
a loaf of bread	a can of tuna
a slice of bread	an ear of corn
a piece of bread	a piece of fish
a slice of cheese	a piece of meat
a carton of milk	a piece of chicken
a gallon of milk	a jar of jelly
a glass of milk	a jar of peanut butter
a can of soda	a piece of candy
a cup of coffee	a piece of fruit
a pound of coffee	a teaspoon of salt
a cup of tea	a stick of butter
a glass of juice	a bowl of rice
a bottle of juice	a bowl of popcorn
a bottle of oil	a teaspoon of sugar
a bowl of soup	a jar of mayonnaise
a can of soup	a tablespoon of mayonnaise

Expansion

Grammar Chart Print names of foods on index cards. Hold up a card and ask students to write down the quantity expression that goes with the food. Ask volunteers to share their answers.

EXERCISE 3 Complete this conversation with one of the words from the box below.

| can | jar | candy ✓ | fruit | milk |

Amy: Mom. I'm hungry. Can I have a piece of __candy__ (example)?

Marta: You know it isn't good for you. Have a piece of __fruit__ (1).

Amy: Can I have a peanut butter and jelly sandwich, too? Where's the peanut butter?

Marta: You can find a __jar__ (2) of peanut butter in the cabinet next to the refrigerator.

Amy: I see a __can__ (3) of soda in the refrigerator. Can I have it too?

Marta: No. Soda has a lot of sugar. Drink a glass of __milk__ (4).

EXERCISE 4 Victor is teaching Maya to make a tuna sandwich. Fill in the blanks with a quantity expression. Answers may vary.

Victor: You can find a fresh __loaf__ (example) of bread on the table. Take two __pieces__ (1) of bread and put them on a plate. Open a __can__ (2) of tuna and put the tuna in a bowl. You can find a __jar__ (3) of mayonnaise in the refrigerator. Add two __tablespoons__ (4) of mayonnaise. Mix the tuna and mayonnaise. Put the tuna on the bread. Now you have a healthy lunch.

Maya: Dad, can I have a __can__ (5) of soda with my sandwich?

Victor: Sorry. But you can have a __glass__ (6) of water with it. And you can have a __piece__ (7) of fruit after lunch.

Lesson 2 123

EXERCISE 3

1. Have students read the direction line. Tell students the conversation is between Amy and her mother, Marta, about food. Go over the example.
2. Have students skim the conversation. Explain that clues to answers may be in information found after the blank.
3. Have students complete Exercise 3 individually. Then have students compare answers in pairs. Circulate to observe pair work. Give help as needed.
4. If necessary, review grammar chart **6.5** on page 122.

   To save class time, have students do this exercise for homework ahead of time.

EXERCISE 4

1. Have students read the direction line. Go over the example. Have students skim the reading.
2. Have students complete Exercise 4 individually. Then have students compare answers in pairs. Circulate to observe pair work. Give help as needed.
3. If necessary, review grammar chart **6.5** on page 122.

   To save class time, have students do this exercise for homework ahead of time.

Expansion

Exercise 3 Have students practice the conversation in pairs. Ask volunteers to roleplay the conversation in front of the class.

Exercise 4 Have students use Exercise 4 to tell a partner how to make a different sandwich with another food, such as turkey, ham, or egg salad.

EXERCISE 5

1. Say: *In this exercise you tell what is true for you.* Have students read the direction line. Say: *Tell exactly how much you eat or drink of an item. Tell what you don't eat or drink, too.* Elicit which example sentence gives an exact amount. (the first: *I eat two slices of bread a day.*)
2. Have students complete Exercise 5 individually. Then have students compare answers in pairs. Circulate to observe pair work. Give help as needed.
3. If necessary, review grammar chart **6.5** on page 122.

⏱ To save class time, have students do this exercise for homework ahead of time.

6.6 | Much/A Lot of/A Little with Noncount Nouns

1. Have students look at grammar chart **6.6** on page 124. Say: *We use* much, a lot, *and* a little *when we don't want or need to say exactly how much.* Review the examples and explanations. Point out that the negative example *I don't drink a lot of milk* means *I drink a little milk.*
2. Point out the Language Note. Say: *When we talk about condiments, such as salt, sugar, butter, ketchup, and pepper, we say* use, *not* eat.
3. Have students close their books. Write a food on the board and ask a students to make affirmative sentences with *a lot* or *a little.* (e.g., *He eats a lot of pizza.*) Ask volunteers to say the opposite. (e.g., *He doesn't eat much pizza.*)

EXERCISE 6

1. Say: *In this exercise you tell a partner what is true for you.* Have students read the direction line. Go over the examples.
2. Have students complete Exercise 6 in pairs. Circulate to observe pair work. Give help as needed.
3. If necessary, review grammar chart **6.6** on page 124.

EXERCISE 5 ABOUT YOU Add a quantity if possible.

EXAMPLE I eat <u>two slices</u> of bread a day. OR <u>I don't eat bread</u>.

Answers will vary.
1. I drink _____ of water a day.
2. I eat _____ of fruit a day.
3. I put _____ of sugar in my coffee or tea.
4. I buy _____ of milk a week.
5. I drink _____ of tea a day.
6. I drink _____ of juice a week.

6.6 | Much/A Lot of/A Little with Noncount Nouns

Examples	Explanation
I eat **a lot of** cheese. I don't drink **a lot of** milk. I don't use **much** sugar.	Use *a lot of* with large quantities. In negatives, you can also use *much*.
He uses **a little** sugar. He drinks **a little** tea.	Use *a little* with small quantities.

Language Note: We say *use,* not *eat,* with **sugar, salt,** and **butter.** We add these things to food.

EXERCISE 6 ABOUT YOU Tell if you eat, drink, or use a lot of this item.

EXAMPLES milk
I don't drink a lot of milk.
meat
I eat a lot of meat.
salt
I don't use much salt.

Answers will vary.
1. cheese 6. coffee
2. popcorn 7. salt
3. rice 8. sugar
4. candy 9. butter
5. milk 10. soup

Expansion

Exercise 6 Do a class survey of students' favorite and least favorite foods. Ask: *What do you eat a lot of? What do you eat a little of?* Write the results on the board.

EXERCISE 7 Fill in the blanks with *a little* and one of the words from the box below. Answers may vary.

| meat | butter | milk | salt | sugar | oil ✓ |

EXAMPLE Use _a little oil_ to cook.

1. Put _a little milk_ and _a little sugar_ in the coffee.
2. The pizza has _a little meat_ and a lot of cheese.
3. Put _a little butter_ on the bread.
4. Put _a little salt_ in the soup.

6.7 | *Some/Any* with Noncount Nouns

Examples	Explanation
A: Does the pizza have **any** meat? B: Yes. The pizza has **some** meat. A: Do kids get **any** soda with their lunches? B: No. They don't get **any** soda. A: Do you want **some** coffee? B: No. I don't want **any** coffee.	We use *any* or *some* in questions. We use *some* in affirmatives. We use *any* in negatives.

EXERCISE 8 Fill in the blanks with *some* or *any*.

EXAMPLE The pizza has __some__ meat.

1. I don't want __any__ soda.
2. The school lunch doesn't have __any__ candy.
3. Do you want __some__ milk?
4. No. I don't want __any__ milk.
5. The sandwich has __some__ mayonnaise.
6. Does the soup have __any__ salt?
7. She's a vegetarian. She doesn't eat __any__ meat.
8. I can't buy my lunch today. I don't have __any__ money.
9. You should eat __some__ fruit every day.

EXERCISE 7

1. Have students read the direction line. Go over the example.
2. Have students complete Exercise 7 individually. Go over the answers with the class. Note that for #1, two answers are possible: *Put a little milk and sugar*, or *Put a little milk and a little sugar*.
3. If necessary, review grammar chart **6.6** on page 124.

⏱ To save class time, have students do this exercise for homework ahead of time.

6.7 | *Some/Any* with Noncount Nouns

1. Have students look at grammar chart **6.7** on page 125. Review the explanations and examples. Say and write on the board the following sentences:

   Do you have some popcorn?
   I have any popcorn.
   No, I don't have some coffee.

   Have students say which sentences are incorrect and why.
2. To elicit examples of usage from the class, list count and noncount foods on the board, such as *potato chips*, *sandwiches*, and *candy*. Prompt students with the question: *Do you have any [chips] in your bag?* Have a student answer using *any* or *some*. Then have a second student ask him or her an additional question. (e.g., Do you have any candy bars?)

EXERCISE 8

1. Have students read the direction line. Go over the example. Point out the picture of the pizza slice. Ask: *What's on the pizza?* (pepperoni)
2. Have students complete Exercise 8 individually. Go over the answers with the class.
3. If necessary, review grammar chart **6.7** on page 125.

Expansion

Exercise 8 Have students write down a list of things they have in their refrigerator at home. Then have students ask and answers questions in pairs. (e.g., Do you have any milk? Yes, I have some milk.)

Lesson 3 | Overview

GRAMMAR

Say: *Look in your bags now. How many notebooks do you have? How many pens do you have? How much homework do you have? In Lesson 3, we're going to learn to ask questions with how much and how many.*

CONTEXT

1. Ask: *What do you need for your classes?* Write a volunteer's answer on the board. Ask the class if they use the same kind and/or number of items. List additional items on the board. Say: *Supplies are what you need to do something. In this lesson we're going to talk about school supplies.*
2. Direct students' attention to the picture. Ask: *What are these things for?* (school, art, writing, drawing) Go over the names of the supplies in the picture: pencils, ruler, glue stick, crayons, paper, notebook, eraser, markers, and folder.

BEFORE YOU READ

1. Go over each question as a class. Have a volunteer read the questions or read them to the class yourself.
2. Discuss the questions as a class.

To save class time, skip "Before You Read," or have students prepare their answers for homework ahead of time.

LESSON 3

GRAMMAR
Count and Noncount Nouns with *Some/Any*
Count vs. Noncount Nouns: *A Lot of/Much/Many*
Count vs. Noncount Nouns: *A Few/A Little*
Count vs. Noncount Nouns: *How Much/How Many*

CONTEXT
School Supplies

Before You Read
1. What do children need for school?
2. Should children have a lot of homework?

126   Unit 6

Expansion

Theme The topic for this unit can be enhanced with the following ideas:
1. Fliers from stores advertising school supply sales
2. Examples of various school supplies for children, such as spiral notebooks, crayons, scissors, and folders

---

Culture Note

Many stores have back-to-school sales in July and August. Students usually buy school supplies, electronics, and clothing.

SCHOOL SUPPLIES

It is September. It's the first day of school. Victor's daughter, Maya, has a list of information about school and school supplies.

Victor: What's this?
Maya: It's a note from school. It has **a lot of information** about the school. And this is my list of school supplies. I need **a lot of supplies** for school.
Victor: **How many things** do you need?
Maya: I need **two erasers, one ruler, two spiral notebooks, ten pencils, one glue stick, one pair of scissors, one large package of notebook paper, four folders, one box of tissues, and one box of crayons.**
Victor: **How many crayons** are in one box?
Maya: You can buy a box of 8, 16, 24, 36, or 48. We need at least 24.

Victor calls Simon for help.

Victor: I have **a few questions** about my daughter's school. Do you have **any time** now?
Simon: Yes, Victor. I have **a little free time** now.
Victor: My daughter has a list of school supplies. Where do I buy them?
Simon: **Many stores** sell school supplies, but the office supply store near my house has a sale on school supplies now. I have **a few coupons.** We can go together.
Victor: Do I have to buy **any books**? **How much money** do I need for books?
Simon: You don't have to buy **any books** for public school. The school gives books to the students.
Victor: That's good. The note from school has **a lot of information** about homework. Do American kids get **a lot of homework**?
Simon: Yes, they do.
Victor: One more question. Do I have to buy a uniform for my daughter?
Simon: I don't know. Children in some schools need uniforms. Read me the information from your daughter's school.
Victor: OK.

Vocabulary in Context

note	The teacher sometimes writes a **note** to parents.
information	I need **information** about the program.
school supplies	Children need **school supplies**, like pencils and paper.
coupon	Here's a **coupon.** You can get two notebooks for the price of one with this coupon.
uniform	In some schools, all the children wear the same **uniform.**

Lesson 3   127

School Supplies (Reading) CD 1, Track 33

1. Have students look at the title of the reading. Ask: *What do you think Victor and Maya are talking about this time?* (school supplies for Maya) *What is Maya saying? What's Victor saying? Do you Maya will do a lot of homework?* Have students use the title and picture on page 126 to make predictions about the reading.
2. Have students read the dialogue silently. Then play the audio and have students read along silently.
3. Check students' basic comprehension. Ask questions, such as: *What does Maya have to buy?* (school supplies) *Does Maya have to buy a uniform?* (maybe) *Does Maya have to buy books?* (no) *Do all children in public schools need uniforms?* (no)

To save class time, have students do the reading for homework ahead of time.

VOCABULARY IN CONTEXT

1. Model the pronunciation of each new vocabulary word and have students repeat.
2. Make sure students understand the meaning of each vocabulary word. Review the examples in the book and create additional example sentences. For example, say: *uniform. I don't like uniforms. I don't want to wear the same clothing every day.* Review each new vocabulary word similarly, using visuals and realia when appropriate. When possible, point to pictures that illustrate new vocabulary items, such as *school supplies* on page 126.
3. Have students underline an example of each word in the reading.

Reading Variation

1. To practice listening skills, have students listen to the audio before opening their books. Ask a few comprehension questions, such as: *Do American kids get a lot of homework?* (yes) Repeat the audio if necessary. Then have students open their books and read along as they listen to the audio.
2. Alternatively, have students begin by listening to the audio as they read along.

Vocabulary Teaching Ideas

Use the following idea to teach this term:

note: Write a quick note on a piece of paper and hand it to a student. Say: *I wrote a note to [student's name].*

Expansion

Reading Have students practice the conversation in pairs. Ask volunteers to roleplay the conversation in front of the class.

Vocabulary in Context To check comprehension, have volunteers in pairs or groups act out selected vocabulary, such as *note* and *uniform*.

Unit 6   127

DID YOU KNOW?

Explain to students that in the U.S. the number of students in a class is important. Educators think small classes are best because the teacher can give each student more attention.

LISTENING ACTIVITY

🎧 **CD 1, Track 34**

1. Say: *Listen to the sentences about the conversation about Maya's school supplies. Circle* true *or* false. Play the listening selection one time without pausing. Then play it through again, pausing and replaying as necessary.
2. Go over the answers as a class. Ask students to volunteer answers.

6.8 | Count and Noncount Nouns with *Some/Any*

1. Have students look at grammar chart 6.8 on page 128. Elicit the rule for *some* and *any* with noncount nouns. Write these examples on the board and have students say if they are correct and why or why not: *I have any coffee. I don't have some sugar.* Say: Some *and* any *are used with count nouns, too.* Some *is used in affirmative statements.* Any *is used in questions and in negative statements.* Go over the examples in the chart.
2. Point out the Language Note. Review the rule. Stress that quantity words must be used with *homework* and *information*. Say and write on the board these examples: *I have to do three homework assignments tonight. Oh, that's an interesting piece of information!*

EXERCISE 1

1. Have students read the direction line. Go over the example.
2. Have students complete Exercise 1 individually. Go over the answers with the class.
3. If necessary, review grammar chart 6.8 on page 128.

Did You Know?
- The average class in an American elementary school has 25 students.
- Most students are five years old when they start school.

🎧 **Listening Activity** Listen to the sentences about the conversation. Circle *true* or *false*.

EXAMPLE (TRUE)   FALSE

1. TRUE   (FALSE)
2. (TRUE)   FALSE
3. (TRUE)   FALSE
4. TRUE   (FALSE)
5. TRUE   (FALSE)
6. TRUE   (FALSE)
7. TRUE   (FALSE)

6.8 | Count and Noncount Nouns with *Some/Any*

Examples	Explanation
Maya has **some** information from her teacher. Victor has **some** questions.	Use *some* with noncount nouns and plural count nouns.
Does she need **any/some** glue? Does she need **any/some** pencils?	Use *any* or *some* with both noncount nouns and plural count nouns in questions.
She doesn't have **any** homework. She doesn't have **any** folders.	Use *any* with both noncount nouns and plural count nouns in negatives.

Language Note: *Homework* and *information* are noncount nouns. They have no plural form. To add a specific quantity, we can say *a homework assignment* and *a piece of information*.

EXERCISE 1 Fill in the blanks with *some* or *any*.

EXAMPLE I need __some__ paper for school.

1. Do you have __any__ homework today?
2. They have __some__ math homework.
3. I don't have __any__ problems with my homework.
4. He needs __some__ school supplies.
5. I don't need __any__ paper for my gym class.
6. Do you need __any/some__ erasers for school?
7. We need __some__ crayons for school.

Expansion

Exercise 1 Have students write responses to the questions in Exercise 1. Model this example for #1: *Do you have any homework today? Yes, I have a math assignment.*

EXERCISE 2 ABOUT YOU Answer the questions. Use *some* or *any* in your answers.

EXAMPLE Do you have any time to watch TV?
Yes. I have some time to watch TV after school.

Answers will vary.
1. Do you have any homework today?
2. Do you need any books for this course?
3. Does this class have any students from Korea?
4. Do you need any paper to do this exercise?
5. Do you have any information about universities in the U.S.?

6.9 | Count vs. Noncount Nouns: *A Lot Of/Much/Many*

	Examples	Explanation
Count	Maya needs **a lot of/many** school supplies. Does she need **a lot of/many** crayons? She doesn't need **a lot of/many** notebooks.	Use *a lot of* or *many* with count nouns.
Noncount	Does Victor have **a lot of/much** information about the school? He doesn't have **a lot of/much** money. Maya needs **a lot of** paper.	Use *a lot of* or *much* with noncount nouns in questions and negatives. In affirmative statements, use *a lot of*, not *much*.

EXERCISE 3 Circle the correct answer. In some cases, both answers are possible.

EXAMPLE I have (*much* /(*a lot of*)) paper, but I don't have ((*many*)/ *much*) pencils.

1. Some children drink (*much* /(*a lot of*)) soda, but they don't drink (*many* /(*much*)) water.
2. I eat ((*a lot of*)/ *many*) fruit, but I don't eat (*much* /(*many*)) bananas.
3. ((*Many*)/ *Much*) stores have school supply sales in August.
4. I need ((*a lot of*)/ *much*) information about schools in the U.S.
5. Children need ((*a lot of*)/ *much*) school supplies.
6. I have (*much* /(*a lot of*)) homework, but I don't have ((*much*)/ *many*) time to do it.
7. ((*Many*)/(*A lot of*)) children get a free lunch in the U.S.

Lesson 3   129

Expansion
Exercise 2 Have students practice asking and answering the questions in pairs. Circulate to help students.

EXERCISE 2

1. Say: *You are going to give answers that are true for you.* Have students read the direction line. Ask: *When do we use any?* (in questions and in negatives) Go over the example in the book. Have a volunteer model the example.
2. Have students complete Exercise 2 individually. Have students compare answers with a partner. Circulate to observe pair work. Give help as needed.
3. If necessary, review grammar chart **6.8** on page 128.

6.9 | Count vs. Noncount Nouns: *A Lot Of/Much/Many*

1. Have students look at grammar chart **6.9** on page 129. Go over the explanations and examples. Say: *A lot of and many can both be used with count nouns.*
2. Then say: *A lot of and* much *are used with noncount nouns in questions and negatives. Much is not used in affirmative statements.* Go over the statements.

EXERCISE 3

1. Have students read the direction line. Go over the example.
2. Have students complete Exercise 3 individually. Go over the answers as a class.
3. If necessary, review grammar chart **6.9** on page 129.

Unit 6   129

6.10 | Count vs. Noncount Nouns: *A Few/A Little*

Have students look at grammar chart 6.10 on page 130. Review the explanations. Say: *A few* is used with count nouns. *A little* is used with noncount nouns. Go over the examples.

EXERCISE 4

1. Have students read the direction line. Go over the example in the Student Book.
2. Have students complete Exercise 4 individually. Go over the answers with the class.
3. If necessary, review grammar chart 6.10 on page 130.

EXERCISE 5

1. Say: *In this exercise you give information that is true about you.* Go over the example. Have a volunteer model the example.
2. Have students complete Exercise 5 individually. Then have students compare answers in pairs. Circulate to observe pair work. Give help as needed.
3. If necessary, review grammar chart 6.10 on page 130.

6.11 | Count vs. Noncount Nouns: *How Much/How Many*

Have students look at grammar chart 6.11 on page 130. Review the explanations and examples. Then ask: *What do we use with count nouns?* (how many) *What do we use with noncount nouns?* (how much) Ask: *Is this sentence correct: How many does this book cost?* (no) *Why?* (because you have to use *how much* to ask about cost)

6.10 | Count vs. Noncount Nouns: *A Few/A Little*

	Examples	Explanation
Count	Maya needs **a few** erasers. She needs **a few** pencils.	Use *a few* with count nouns.
Noncount	Dorota has **a little** time on Saturday. School lunches cost **a little** money.	Use *a little* with noncount nouns.

EXERCISE 4 Fill in the blanks with *a few* or *a little*.

EXAMPLE Maya drinks __a little__ juice every day.

1. Victor has __a little__ time to help Maya with her homework.
2. Maya has __a few__ good friends at school.
3. Maya watches __a few__ TV programs after dinner.
4. She has __a little__ time to watch TV every day.
5. She needs __a few__ pencils for school.

EXERCISE 5 ABOUT YOU Fill in the blanks.

EXAMPLE I have a few __good friends__.

Answers will vary.
1. I need a little _____.
2. I know a few _____.
3. I eat a little _____ every day.
4. I eat a few _____ every week.
5. I use a little _____.

6.11 | Count vs. Noncount Nouns: *How Much/How Many*

Examples	Explanation
How many coupons do you have? **How many** crayons do you need for school?	Use *how many* with count nouns.
How much paper does she need? **How much** money do I need for books?	Use *how much* with noncount nouns.
How much does this book cost? **How much** is the school lunch?	Use *how much* to ask about cost.

130 Unit 6

Expansion

Exercise 5 Have students make questions about the statements. (e.g., for *I have a few good friends: Do you have any friends?*) Then have students work in pairs and have partners ask and answer questions.

---

130 *Grammar in Context Basic* Teacher's Edition

EXERCISE 6 ABOUT YOU Find a partner. Ask these questions about an elementary school in your partner's native country.

EXAMPLE How many days a week do kids go to school?
They go to school five days a week.

Answers will vary.
1. How many months a year do kids go to school?
2. How many kids are in an average class?
3. How much time do kids spend on homework?
4. How many hours a day are kids in school?
5. How much time do kids have for vacation?
6. How much money do kids spend on books?
7. Do kids get school lunch? How much does it cost?
8. Do kids wear a uniform? How much does a uniform cost?

EXERCISE 7 ABOUT YOU Fill in the blanks with *much* or *many*.

EXAMPLE How ___many___ lessons do we do a day?

Answers will vary.
1. How _____ classes do you have now?
2. How _____ money do you need to take one class?
3. How _____ paper do you need for your homework?
4. How _____ students in this class speak Spanish?
5. How _____ books do you need for this course?
6. How _____ time do you need for homework?
7. How _____ homework do you have with you today?
8. How _____ dictionaries do you have?

Lesson 3   131

EXERCISE 6

1. Point out the photo of children wearing school uniforms. Ask: *What are these school children wearing?* (school uniforms) Say: *In this exercise you answer questions with information that is true about elementary schools in your country.* Have students read the direction line. Go over the example. Have a volunteer model the example.
2. Have students complete Exercise 6 individually. Then have students ask and answer questions in pairs. Circulate to observe pair work. Give help as needed.
3. If necessary, review grammar chart **6.11** on page 130.

EXERCISE 7

1. Say: *In this exercise you complete the sentence with information that is true about you.* Have students read the direction line. Go over the example. Have a volunteer model the example.
2. Have students complete Exercise 7 individually. Then have students compare answers in pairs. Circulate to observe pair work. Give help as needed.
3. If necessary, review grammar chart **6.11** on page 130.

Expansion
Exercise 7 Have students practice asking and answering the questions in pairs.

Unit 6   131

EXERCISE 8

1. Say: *Marco is asking Victor some questions.* Have students read the direction line. Go over the example in the Student Book.
2. Have students complete Exercise 8 individually. Then have students compare answers in pairs. Circulate to observe pair work. Give help as needed.
3. If necessary, review Unit 6.

🕐 To save class time, have students do the exercise for homework ahead of time.

EXERCISE 8 *Combination Exercise.* Circle the correct word in parentheses ( ) to complete this conversation between Victor and his neighbor, Marco. Sometimes more than one answer is possible.

Marco: I have (*a little /* **a few**) questions. I need (**a little** */ a few*)
(example)   (1)
information. Do you have (**any**/**some**) time to answer my
(2)
questions?

Victor: Yes. I have (**a little** */ a few*) time right now.
(3)

Marco: Can my kids get into the free lunch program?

Victor: Maybe. If you don't earn (*many /* **much**) money, they can
(4)
probably get into the free lunch program.

Marco: I don't earn (*many /* **a lot of**) money. What should I do?
(5)

Victor: You have to fill out a form. The form has (**many** */ much*) questions.
(6)

Marco: How (**much** */ many*) does a school lunch cost?
(7)

Victor: The full price is $1.75. That's not (**much** */ any*) money.
(8)

Marco: I have (**a lot of** */ much*) kids in school, so for me it's (*much /* **a lot of**)
(9)   (10)
money.

Victor: How (*much /* **many**) kids do you have?
(11)

Marco: Six. Four are in school, so I really need to learn about the free lunch program.

132   Unit 6

Expansion

Exercise 8 Have students practice the conversation in pairs. Ask volunteers to roleplay the conversations in front of the class.

EDITING ADVICE

1. Don't put *a* or *an* before a noncount noun.

   I like to eat a rice.

2. Use *of* with a unit of measure.

   I want a cup ^of coffee.

3. Don't forget *of* with *a lot of*.

   I don't have a lot ^of homework today.

4. Don't confuse *much* and *many*, *a little* and *a few*.

   He doesn't have ~~much~~ ^many friends.

   I eat a little ^few grapes every day.

   Put a few ^little salt in the soup.

5. Don't use *much* in affirmative statements.

   He drinks ~~much~~ ^a lot of soda.

EDITING QUIZ

Find the mistakes with the underlined words, and correct them. Not every sentence has a mistake. If the sentence is correct, write *C*.

EXAMPLES   Do you drink <u>a lot ^of milk</u>?

   I drink <u>a little milk</u> every day.   *C*

1. I eat <u>an</u> apple every day. I don't eat <u>~~a~~ bread</u> every day.
2. Do you want a <u>can ^of soda</u>?
3. We have to read <u>a little</u> ^a few pages every day.
4. Please put <u>~~a few~~</u> ^a little sugar in my coffee.
5. I don't like to eat <u>~~a~~ grapes</u>.
6. Children need <u>a lot ^of school supplies</u>.
7. How <u>~~much~~</u> ^many cups of coffee do you drink a day?
8. I have <u>a little</u> time to help you on Saturday.   *C*

Lesson 3   133

Editing Advice

1. Have students close their books. Write the example sentences without editing marks or corrections on the board. For example:

   1. I like to eat a rice.
   2. I want a cup coffee.

   Ask students to correct each sentence. This activity can be done individually, in pairs, or as a class. After students have corrected each sentence, tell them to turn to page 133. Say: *Now compare your work with Editing Advice in the book.*

2. Go over answers with the class. For troublespots, review the appropriate grammar chart.

Editing Quiz

1. The Editing Quiz may be used as an in-class quiz, a take-home quiz, or as a review. Have students read the direction line. Ask: *Does every sentence have a mistake?* (no) Go over the examples with the class.

2. Have students complete the quiz individually. Collect completed quizzes for assessment or have students check each other's work. Review the answers with the class. Elicit the relevant grammar point for each correction. For example, for #1, ask: *What's the rule?* (*Bread* is a noncount noun. You can't use *a* with a noncount noun.)

Unit 6   133

Learner's Log

1. Have students close their books. Ask: *What did you learn about the following things in this unit: American lunch programs, healthy foods, and school supplies? What else do you want to know?* Brainstorm with students. Write ideas on the board. Discuss ways in which students can find out more about American elementary schools.
2. Have students open their books to complete the Learner's Log.

Expansion Activities

These expansion activities provide opportunities for students to interact with one another and further develop their speaking and writing skills. Encourage students to use grammar from this unit whenever possible.

To save class time, assign parts of the activities as homework. Then use class time for interaction and communication. If students do not need additional speaking practice, some of the activities may be assigned as writing activities for homework, or skipped altogether.

WRITING ACTIVITIES

1. Have students read the direction line. Go over the example. Have students complete the activity individually at home or in class. Collect for assessment.
2. Have students turn to Exercise 6 on page 131. Say: *Ask your the partner questions and then write a paragraph about schools in his or her country.*

OUTSIDE ACTIVITY

Have students get in pairs to write questions to ask an elementary school child.

INTERNET ACTIVITIES

1. Have students get into groups to exchange facts.
2. Have students get into groups and decide whose meal has the highest salt and fat counts.

LEARNER'S LOG

1. What did you learn in this unit? Write three sentences in your notebook about each of these topics:
   - Government rules for school lunch programs
   - Foods in school lunch programs
   - Healthy foods
   - School supplies
2. Write three questions you still have about American elementary schools.

EXPANSION ACTIVITIES

Writing Activities

1. In your notebook, rewrite the following paragraph. Change the underlined food to a specific amount of the food. Use the quantity expressions you learned in this unit.

   > I try to eat for good health every day. For example, I drink <u>water</u> before each meal. Then, I'm not so hungry. I don't have <u>soda</u> with every meal. I drink <u>tea</u> and not coffee after a meal. I have <u>cereal</u> for breakfast. I have salad with <u>soup</u> for lunch. In cold weather, I like <u>meat</u> for lunch. I eat <u>fruit</u> every day too. And, I try to eat <u>fish</u> once a week.

   EXAMPLE *I drink a glass of water before each meal.*

2. Use information from Exercise 6 on page 131 to write a short paragraph of five or six sentences about schools in your partner's country.

Outside Activity

Ask an elementary school child about his/her school. Tell the class the name of the child's school and some interesting facts about this child's school. What does the child like about the school?

Internet Activities

1. Go to the government's Web site on school lunches (www.fns.usda.gov/cnd/Lunch/default.htm). Click on "Program Fact Sheet." Find a few interesting facts about the program. (You can also search the name of your state with the words "school lunch program" for information in your state.)
2. Search the words *fat counter* on a search engine. Find a list of foods showing fat and sodium (salt) content. How much fat is in *one* of your meals today? How much salt?

Expansion

Learner's Log Have students compare logs in pairs.

Writing Activities Variation

Have students exchange papers with a partner for proofreading.

Internet Activities Variation

Tell students that if they don't have Internet access, they can use Internet facilities at a public library or they can use traditional research methods to find out information including looking at encyclopedias, magazines, books, journals, and newspapers.

UNIT

7

GRAMMAR
Prepositions
There Is/There Are

CONTEXT
Shopping

Expansion

Theme The topic for this unit can be enhanced with the following ideas:
1. Circulars from home improvement stores and large discount and department stores
2. Envelope of coupons for local businesses sent out in the mail, such as "Super Coups."

Unit | 7
Unit Overview

GRAMMAR

1. Ask: *What did we study in Unit 6?* (*must, have to,* noncount nouns, and quantity expressions) *What are we going to study in Unit 7?* (prepositions and *There is/There are*) Write the unit objectives on the board.
2. Activate students' prior knowledge. Ask: *What are some prepositions?* List students' answers on the board. Then write *When* and *Where.* Say: *Some prepositions show* when *and* where. Then say and write on the board examples of time and place phrases. (e.g., *at 3:00; near the store*) Say: There is/There are *tells what exists, when and where; for example: There is a movie at 2:00. There is a book on my desk.* Have students give additional examples.

CONTEXT

1. Say: *We're going to talk about shopping in this unit. I like to shop at small stores, but big stores are convenient. I can find everything I need in a big store.* Ask: *Where do you like to shop?*
2. Direct students' attention to the photos. Ask: *What kind of stores are these? Are they department stores? Supermarkets?* (home improvement store, hardware store) Point to the store on the right. *Is this a large store or a small store?* (large)
3. Ask: *Is it convenient to shop in these stores?* Have students share their personal experiences.

Unit 7   135

Lesson 1 | Overview

GRAMMAR

Say, *In Lesson 1, we are going to study prepositions in common expressions. We are also going to study prepositions in time and prepositions of place.* Write the objectives and the following sentence on the board: *There is a class at 7:30 a.m. on Saturdays in this building at the university.* Underline time phrases once and place phrases twice. Have students name the prepositions. Elicit similar expressions from students. Prompt by asking: *Do you have another class? When is it? Where is it?*

CONTEXT

1. Say: *We're going to read about convenience shopping. A lot of people have to shop after work. Some big stores are open all day and all night. Some small stores are also open 24/7.* Relate the topic to student's experience. Make sure students understand the expression *24/7.* Tell them it means 24 hours a day, seven days a week. Ask: *Do you shop 24/7?*
2. Direct students' attention to the picture of the convenience store on page 136. Ask: *What is across from the convenience store?* (the pharmacy)

BEFORE YOU READ

1. Go over each question as a class. Have a volunteer read the questions or read them to the class yourself. Have students discuss the questions in pairs. If possible, put students together from different countries.
2. Ask for a few volunteers to share their answers with the class.

 To save class time, skip "Before You Read," or have students prepare their answers for homework ahead of time.

LESSON 1

GRAMMAR
Prepositions of Time
Time Expressions Without Prepositions
Prepositions of Place
Prepositions in Common Expressions

CONTEXT
Twenty-Four/Seven

Before You Read
1. Do you ever shop late at night? Why or why not?
2. Do you ever shop at a convenience store? Why or why not?

136 Unit 7

Culture Note
Convenience stores provide more services every year. Most now have ATMs and sell money orders. Many have car washes. Some even provide Internet services.

---

136 *Grammar in Context Basic* Teacher's Edition

TWENTY-FOUR/SEVEN

Sue: Look. We're out of coffee. We need coffee for tomorrow morning. Can you go out and buy some?
Rick: Now? It's late. It's **after 9:30**. We can get it **in the morning**.
Sue: Tomorrow is Saturday. The stores are crowded **on Saturday**. I don't like to shop **on the weekend**. Anyway, we like to drink coffee **in the morning**.
Rick: But the supermarket is closed **at night**.
Sue: You're right. But the convenience store is open. It's open 24/7.
Rick: My news program is on TV **at 10 p.m.** I don't have time **before** the news program. It starts **in 20 minutes**.
Sue: You can go **after the news**.

(*Rick is now **at** the convenience store. Sue calls him **on** his cell phone.*)

Rick: Hello?
Sue: Hi. Are you **at** the convenience store now?
Rick: I'm still **in** the car. I'm **in** the parking lot.
Sue: Can you go **to** the pharmacy too and get some aspirin? I have a headache.
Rick: Can I get the aspirin **at** the convenience store?
Sue: You can, but aspirin is on sale this week **at** the pharmacy—two bottles for $5.00.
Rick: Where's the pharmacy?
Sue: It's **near** the convenience store. It's **on** the corner. It's **next to** the gas station.
Rick: Is the pharmacy open too?
Sue: Yes, it's open 24/7.
Rick: Does anyone sleep at night?

Vocabulary in Context

out of	We don't have any coffee. We're **out of** coffee.
convenience store	A **convenience store** is open late. It's a small supermarket.
24/7	**24/7** means a place is open 24 hours a day, seven days a week.
pharmacy	You can buy medicine in a **pharmacy**.
aspirin / headache	Take an **aspirin** for your **headache**.
corner	The store is on the **corner** of Main Street and Willow Street.

Lesson 1   137

Twenty-Four/Seven (Reading) CD 1, Track 35

1. Have students look at the title of the reading and the picture on page 136. Say: *Skim through the reading. What two things does Sue want?* (coffee and aspirin) *Why does she want aspirin?* (She has a headache.) See if students can make more predictions about the reading.
2. Have students read the dialogue silently. Then play the audio and have students read along silently.
3. Check students' basic comprehension. Ask questions, such as: *What does Rick want to watch on TV?* (a news program) *What is Rick going to buy?* (coffee and aspirin) *What time does the pharmacy close?* (It doesn't close; it's open 24/7.)

   To save class time, have students do the reading for homework ahead of time.

VOCABULARY IN CONTEXT

1. Model the pronunciation of each new vocabulary item and have students repeat.
2. Make sure students understand the meaning of each vocabulary item. Review the examples in the book and create additional example sentences. For example, say: *out of. I'm out of paper. Can I have a piece of paper?* (Ask a student for a piece of paper.) Go over each new vocabulary item similarly, using visuals and realia when appropriate. When possible, point to pictures in the book that illustrate the new vocabulary items, such as *convenience store, pharmacy, and corner* on page 136.
3. Have students underline an example of each new vocabulary item in the reading.

Reading Variation

1. To practice listening skills, have students listen to the audio before opening their books. Ask a few comprehension questions, such as: *How much does aspirin cost at the pharmacy this week?* (two bottles for $5.00) *What time is it?* (after 9:30) Repeat the audio if necessary. Then have students open their books and read along as they listen to the audio.
2. Alternatively, have students begin by listening to the audio as they read along.

Vocabulary Teaching Ideas

Use the following idea to teach this term:

corner: Draw a map of a local business on the corner of two well-known streets.
   Say: *[Business name] is on the corner of [street name] and [street name].*

Expansion

Reading Have students practice the conversation in pairs. Ask volunteers to roleplay the conversation in front of the class.

Vocabulary in Context To check comprehension, have volunteers in pairs or groups act out selected vocabulary, such as *headache* and *aspirin*.

DID YOU KNOW?

Tell students how much higher the cost of items are at convenience stores. Say: *Prices at a convenience store are usually 10 percent more than prices at a supermarket. If an item costs $10.00 at the supermarket, it will cost $11.00 at a convenience store.*

LISTENING ACTIVITY

🎧 **CD 1, Track 36**

1. Say: *Listen to the sentences about Rick and Sue's conversation. Circle* true *or* false. Play the listening selection one time without pausing. Then play it through again, pausing and replaying as necessary.
2. Go over the answers as a class. Ask students to volunteer answers.

7.1 | Prepositions of Time

1. Have students look at grammar chart **7.1** on page 138. Say: *Prepositions are small connecting words. We can use prepositions with time expressions.* Go over the examples. Give an additional example for each expression. (e.g., *I exercise in the morning.*)
2. Point out the Language Note. Say: *A sentence can have more than one time expression.* Go over the examples. Ask volunteers to give additional examples.

Did You Know?

- When you see a sign *Two for $5.00*, you usually don't need to buy two. You can buy one for $2.50.
- Prices at a convenience store are sometimes high. You are paying for the convenience of 24/7.

🎧 Listening Activity

Listen to the sentences about the conversation. Circle *true* or *false*.

EXAMPLE **TRUE** FALSE

1. **TRUE** FALSE
2. TRUE **FALSE**
3. TRUE **FALSE**
4. **TRUE** FALSE
5. TRUE **FALSE**
6. **TRUE** FALSE
7. TRUE **FALSE**

7.1 | Prepositions of Time

Prepositions are connecting words. We can use prepositions with time expressions.

The store is open	**in** the morning.
	in the afternoon.
	in the evening.
	at night.
The news program starts	**at** 10 p.m.
	in 20 minutes.
You can go out	**after** 9:30.
	after the news program.
	after work.
Sue goes to sleep	**before** 10:30.
The stores are crowded	**on** Saturdays.
	on the weekend.

Language Note: A sentence can have two time expressions.
I go to work **at** 7 o'clock **in** the morning.
I wake up **at** 9 a.m. **on** the weekend.

Expansion

Grammar Chart Have students work in pairs to write an example for each preposition of time (*in, at, after, before,* and *on*). Ask volunteers to share their examples.

EXERCISE 1 Fill in the blanks with the correct preposition of time: *in, on, after,* or *at.*

EXAMPLE Sue and Rick don't work __at__ night.

1. They work __on__ Monday.
2. They don't work __in__ the evening.
3. The convenience store is open __at__ night.
4. They don't work __on__ the weekend.
5. They can buy milk __in__ the morning.
6. Many stores open __at__ 9 a.m.
7. It's 9:37 now. It's __after__ 9:30 p.m.
8. We go shopping __in__ the afternoon.

EXERCISE 2 ABOUT YOU Ask a question with *When do you . . .* and the words given. Another student will answer.

EXAMPLES watch TV
A: When do you watch TV?
B: I watch TV at night.

1. drink coffee
   When do you drink coffee?
2. watch the news on TV
   When do you watch the news on TV?
3. go to sleep
   When do you go to sleep?
4. wake up
   When do you wake up?
5. go shopping
   When do you go shopping?
6. take a shower
   When do you take a shower?
7. eat lunch
   When do you eat lunch?
8. read the newspaper
   When do you read the newspaper?
9. see your friends
   When do you see your friends?
10. do your homework
    When do you do your homework?

7.2 | Time Expressions Without Prepositions

In some cases, we don't use a preposition with time.	
The store is open	24 hours a day.
The store is open	seven days a week.
We shop	three times a month.
They buy milk	once a week.
We cook	twice a day.
The convenience store is open	24/7.
The convenience store is open	all day and all night.

Lesson 1   139

EXERCISE 1

1. Have students read the direction line. Go over the example in the Student Book.
2. Have students complete Exercise 1 individually. Check the answers as a class.
3. If necessary, review grammar chart **7.1** on page 138.

EXERCISE 2

1. Say: *In this exercise, you'll ask and answer questions with a partner about when you do things.* Have students read the direction line. Go over the example. Model the example with a student.
2. Have students complete Exercise 2 in pairs. Circulate to observe pair work. Give help as needed.
3. If necessary, review grammar chart **7.1** on page 138.

7.2 | Time Expressions Without Prepositions

1. Have students look at grammar chart **7.2** on page 139. Say: *Some time expressions don't have prepositions.* Go over the examples. Give an additional example for each expression. (e.g., *The gas station on the corner is open 24 hours a day.*)
2. Write example sentences such as the following on the board: *The convenience store is open 9:30. We shop three a month. We cook every day.* Have students tell which sentences are correct and which are incorrect and why.

Expansion

Exercise 2 Take a survey. Find out how the class answered some of the questions and write the results on the board. (e.g., *In our class, [five] students wake up at 6:00 a.m.*)

Grammar Chart Have students work in pairs to write an example for each time expression. Ask volunteers to share their examples.

EXERCISE 3

1. Have students read the direction line. Go over the example in the Student Book.
2. Have students complete Exercise 3 individually. Then have students compare answers in pairs. Circulate to observe pair work. Give help as needed.
3. If necessary, review grammar chart **7.2** on page 139.

EXERCISE 4

1. Say: *In this exercise, you'll ask and answer questions with a partner about how many times you do things.* Have students read the direction line. Go over the example. Model the example with a student volunteer.
2. Have students complete Exercise 4 in pairs. Circulate to observe pair work. Give help as needed.
3. If necessary, review grammar chart **7.2** on page 139.

7.3 | Prepositions of Place

1. Have students look at grammar chart **7.3** on page 140. Say: *Prepositions can be used to show where.* Go over the examples. Use the picture on page 136 to illustrate the prepositions.
2. Point out and explain the Language Note. Say: *The prepositions* in *and* at *do not mean the same. In* means *that you are inside the building/location. At* is more general. *You could be in the store, going into the store, or even in the parking lot of the store.*

EXERCISE 3 Fill in the blanks with one of the expressions of time without a preposition. (See 7.2 on page 139).

EXAMPLE The pharmacy near Rick's house is open ___24 hours a day___.

Answers will vary.

1. Rick watches the news _____.
2. Most supermarkets in this city are open _____.
3. Most banks in this city are open _____.
4. Most people in my country shop for food _____.

EXERCISE 4 ABOUT YOU Ask a question with *how many* and the words given. Another student will answer.

EXAMPLE days a week / work
A: How many days a week do you work?
B: I work five days a week.

1. times a day / check your e-mail
   How many times a day do you check your e-mail?
2. hours a day / talk on the phone
   How many hours a day do you talk on the phone?
3. times a month / go to the library
   How many times a month do you go to the library?
4. times a day / brush your teeth
   How many times a day do you brush your teeth?
5. hours a night / sleep
   How many hours a night do you sleep?
6. times a day / cook
   How many times a day do you cook?
7. hours a day / watch TV
   How many hours a day do you watch TV?
8. times a week / shop for food
   How many times a week do you shop for food?

7.3 | Prepositions of Place

We can use prepositions with locations.

Preposition	Examples
in	Rick is **in** the car. He is **in** the parking lot.
near	The pharmacy is **near** the convenience store.
next to	The pharmacy is **next to** the gas station.
on	The convenience store is **on** the corner.
at	Rick is **at** the convenience store. Sue is **at** home. You are **at** school. My parents are **at** work.
to	Go **to** the pharmacy.

Language Note: COMPARE:
I'm **in** the store. (I'm not outside the store.)
I'm **at** the store. (I may be inside or in the parking lot, ready to go in.)

Expansion

Exercise 4 Take a survey. Find out how the class answered the questions in Exercise 4. Write the results on the board.

Grammar Chart Have students work in pairs to write an example for each preposition of place. Ask volunteers to share their examples.

EXERCISE 5 This is a phone conversation between Victor and Lisa. Lisa is at home. Victor is on his cell phone in his car. Fill in the blanks with the correct preposition: *in, on, at, near,* or *next to*.

Victor: Hello?

Lisa: Hi. It's Lisa. Where are you now?

Victor: I'm __at__ school. Where are you?
                 (example)

Lisa: I'm __at__ home. Are you __in__ class?
           (1)   (2)

Victor: No, I'm __in__ the parking lot. My class starts in ten minutes.
                 (3)

Lisa: Can you go __to__ the store on your way home?
                   (4)
We need milk. There's a sale on milk __at__ Tom's Market.
                                       (5)

Victor: Where's Tom's Market?

Lisa: It's __near__ the school. It's __on__ the corner.
            (6)   (7)
It's __next to__ the Laundromat.
      (8)

7.4 | Prepositions in Common Expressions

	We can use prepositions in many common expressions.
on	Rick is **on the phone.**
	The news program is **on TV.** You can hear the news **on the radio.**
	Aspirin is **on sale.**
for	Aspirin is on sale this week, two bottles **for** $5.00.
in	The coffee is **in** aisle three.
of	We don't have any coffee. We're out **of** coffee.

Lesson 1   141

Expansion

Exercise 5 Have students practice the conversation in pairs. Ask volunteers to roleplay the conversation in front of the class.

Grammar Chart Have students work in pairs to write an example for each expression. List the expressions on the board: *on the phone, on TV, on the radio, on sale; for* (price), *in* (location), *out of* (food or thing). Ask volunteers to share their examples.

EXERCISE 5

1. Have students read the direction line. Go over the example.
2. Have students complete Exercise 5 individually. Then have students compare answers in pairs. Circulate to observe pair work. Give help as needed.
3. If necessary, review grammar chart **7.3** on page 140.

7.4 | Prepositions in Common Expressions

Have students look at grammar chart **7.4** on page 141. Say: *There are many common expressions with prepositions.* Go over the examples. Give additional examples to illustrate the expressions. (e.g., *My daughter is on the phone 24 hours a day.*)

Unit 7   141

EXERCISE 6

1. Direct students' attention to the photo on page 142. Ask: *What is on sale at the supermarket?* Have students read the direction line. Go over the example. If necessary, explain any difficult vocabulary, such as *mangoes*.
2. Have students complete Exercise 6 individually. Then have students compare answers in pairs. Circulate to observe pair work. Give help as needed.
3. If necessary, review grammar chart **7.4** on page 141.

EXERCISE 6 This is a conversation between Simon and Marta. Fill in the blanks with *on, in, next to, of, after,* or *for*.

Simon: I'm going to the store __after__ *(example)* work. Eggs are on sale—two dozen __for__ (1) $1.89.

Marta: Buy mangoes, too. They're __on__ (2) sale—three __for__ (3) $1.49.

Simon: Anything else?

Marta: Oh, yes. Buy coffee, too.

Simon: Are we out __of__ (4) coffee? So soon?

Marta: Yes. We drink a lot of coffee.

Simon: Anything else?

Marta: No. Come home right away. Your favorite show is __on__ (5) TV at 7 p.m.

(*Simon is at the store now. He asks a store clerk for information.*)

Simon: Where's the coffee?

Clerk: It's __in__ (6) aisle four.

Simon: I don't see it. Can you help me find it?

Clerk: Sure. Here it is. It's __next to__ (7) the tea.

Expansion

Exercise 6 Have students practice the conversation in pairs. Ask volunteers to roleplay the conversation in front of the class. Have students work in pairs to create a similar conversation with their own information.

EXERCISE 7 *Combination Exercise.* This is a conversation between Rick and Sue. Fill in the blanks with the correct preposition: *in, on, at, to,* or *after*.

Sue: Hi. I'm ___on___ my cell phone.
(example)

Rick: Are you ___in___ the car?
(1)

Sue: No, I'm still ___at___ work. I can't come home right now.
(2)

___After___ work, I have to make a few stops. I can be home
(3)

___in___ about an hour and a half.
(4)

Rick: Where do you need to go?

Sue: I need to buy gas. Then I have to go ___to___ the dry cleaner.
(5)

Rick: Then can you come home?

Sue: No. Then I have to go to the post office. The post office closes ___at___ 6 p.m.
(6)

Rick: Why do you have to do all of this now? Tomorrow is Saturday. We can do these things tomorrow.

Sue: I don't like to do these things ___on___ Saturday. These
(7)

places are crowded ___on___ the weekend.
(8)

Rick: But I have dinner ___on___ the table now. Don't be too late.
(9)

Lesson 1 143

EXERCISE 7

1. Direct students' attention to the photo on page 143. *Where are they? Are they in a house or a restaurant?* (a drycleaner's) Have students read the direction line. Go over the example.
2. Have students complete Exercise 7 individually. Then have students compare answers in pairs. Circulate to observe pair work. Give help as needed.
3. If necessary, review grammar chart 7.4 on page 141.

Expansion

Exercise 7 Have students draw and label a map of locations mentioned in the conversation. Then have partners take turns telling where Sue is, where she has to go, and what she has to do. (e.g., She's at work now. She has to go to the gas station. She needs to buy gas.)

Have students work in pairs to create a similar conversation with their own information.

Unit 7   143

Lesson 2 | Overview

GRAMMAR

1. Say: *In Lesson 2 we are going to study* There is *and* There are *and quantity words.* Write the lesson's objectives on the board.
2. Activate students' prior knowledge. Elicit examples of quantity words (e.g., *some, enough, no, many*), and write them on the board. Then say and write: *There are no [flowers] in this room.* Underline *There are* and *no*. Ask volunteers to make more sentences using the quantity expressions on the board and *There is* and *There are*.

CONTEXT

1. Say: *Some stores have bad service. They do not help customers. In this lesson we're going to talk about good prices and good service.* Ask: *Do big stores have good service?* Have students share their ideas and personal experiences.
2. Direct students' attention to the pictures of Rick, Sue, and Peter on page 144. Ask: *What kind of stores are these?* (hardware stores, home improvement stores) *Do these two stores have the same prices? Do they have the same service?*

BEFORE YOU READ

1. Go over each question as a class. Have a volunteer read the questions or read them to the class yourself. Have students discuss the questions in pairs.
2. Ask for a few volunteers to share their answers with the class.
   To save class time, skip "Before You Read," or have students prepare their answers for homework ahead of time.

LESSON 2

GRAMMAR

There Is and *There Are*
Negative Forms with *There Is/There Are*
Quantity Words

CONTEXT

Good Prices or Good Service

Before You Read
1. Which is better—good service or good prices?
2. Do you prefer big stores or small stores?

144 Unit 7

Culture Note

Not all people in the U.S. want a big superstore in their town. Some people say that big chain stores take businesses away from city centers, increase traffic, and provide only badly paid jobs to people living outside of town. Other people say that these stores offer more choices, have better prices, and provide many jobs.

144   *Grammar in Context Basic* Teacher's Edition

GOOD PRICES OR GOOD SERVICE

Conversation 1—In a big store

Rick: We need lightbulbs. **There's** a coupon in the newspaper for lightbulbs. Let's go to the home supply store.

Sue: (*At the store*) **There are** so many things in this store. How can we find what we need?

Rick: **There's** a clerk over there in the lighting department. Let's ask him. Excuse me, sir. I need to find lightbulbs. **There are** lamps here, but **there are no** lightbulbs.

Clerk: Lightbulbs are in aisle three. **There's** a clerk in aisle three.

Sue: (*After visiting aisle three*) I can't find the lightbulbs. And **there's no** clerk in aisle three. Can you help us?

Clerk: Sorry. That's not my department.

Sue: (*To Rick*) **There aren't** enough clerks in this store. **There isn't** good service in this store.

Rick: But I like this store. **There are** good prices here.

Conversation 2—In a small store

Clerk: Can I help you?

Peter: Yes. I need lightbulbs.

Clerk: Lightbulbs are downstairs, but **there isn't an** elevator in the store. I can get the lightbulbs for you.

Peter: Thanks for your help. (*Thinking*) I like this store. **There's** good service here. **There are** helpful clerks here. I prefer a small store with good service.

Vocabulary in Context

service	Peter likes good **service**. He likes help in a store.
lightbulb	Rick needs a **lightbulb** for his lamp.
home supply store	A **home supply store** has many things for the home: tools, lightbulbs, paint, etc.
clerk	A **clerk** works to help people in a store.
lamp	The **lamp** is in the living room.
enough	There are a lot of shoppers, but there aren't **enough** clerks.
downstairs	We're on the first floor. Lightbulbs are **downstairs**.
elevator	Peter needs an **elevator** to go downstairs.
prefer	Peter **prefers** a store with good service.

Lesson 2 145

Reading Variation

1. To practice listening skills, have students listen to the audio before opening their books. Ask a few comprehension questions, such as: *Where are the lightbulbs in the big store?* (aisle three) *Are the clerks helpful in the small store?* (yes) Repeat the audio if necessary. Then have students open their books and read along as they listen to the audio.
2. Alternatively, have students begin by listening to the audio as they read along.

Vocabulary Teaching Ideas

Use the following idea to teach this term:

elevator: Draw a set of elevator doors on the board, with Up and Down buttons and a light over the doors. Say: *Stairs go up and down. Elevators go up and down.*

Expansion

Reading Have students practice the conversation in groups. Ask volunteers to roleplay all or part of the conversations in front of the class.

Vocabulary in Context To check comprehension, have volunteers in pairs or groups act out selected vocabulary, such as *service* and *clerk*.

Good Prices or Good Service (Reading)
CD 1, Track 37

1. Have students look at the title of the reading and the pictures on page 144. Ask: *What do you think Rick and Sue are talking about?* Have students quickly scan the reading. Ask: *What do they want to buy?* Have students use the title and pictures to make predictions about the reading.
2. Have students read the conversations silently. Then play the audio and have students read along silently.
3. Check students' basic comprehension. Ask questions, such as: *What are Rick and Sue looking for?* (lightbulbs) *Are they happy with the service at the store?* (no) *Can Peter go downstairs?* (No. There's no elevator.) *Does Peter like the small store?* (yes)

To save class time, have students do the reading for homework ahead of time.

VOCABULARY IN CONTEXT

1. Model the pronunciation of each new vocabulary item and have students repeat.
2. Make sure students understand the meaning of each vocabulary word. Review the examples in the book and create additional example sentences. For example, say: *enough. I don't have enough time to go to the gym today. I'll go tomorrow.* Go over each new vocabulary word similarly, using visuals and realia when appropriate. When possible, point to pictures in the book that illustrate the new vocabulary items,, such as *home supply store* and *clerk* on page 144, and *lamp* and *lightbulb* on page 145.
3. Have students underline an example of each new vocabulary item in the reading.

Unit 7 145

DID YOU KNOW?

Tell students the nicknames for big and small stores. Large chain stores are often called "big boxes" because the buildings that house them often look like large boxes. Small businesses are sometimes called "mom-and-pop" stores.

LISTENING ACTIVITY

🎧 **CD 1, Track 38**

1. Say: *Listen to the sentences about the picture and story. Circle* true *or* false. Play the listening selection one time without pausing. Then play it through again, pausing and replaying as necessary.
2. Go over the answers as a class. Ask students to volunteer answers.

7.5 | *There Is* and *There Are*

1. Have students look at grammar chart **7.5** on page 146. Say: *To express the existence of something we use* there is *and* there are. *We use* there is *for singular subjects and* there are *for plural subjects.* Go over the examples. Give additional examples from the classroom. (e.g., *There are four tables in the classroom.*)
2. Point out the Language Notes. Review the contraction rules. Have students close their books Write on the board: *There're six oranges. There are six oranges. There's a dog. Theres' a dog.* Ask which sentences are correct and why.

Did You Know? Some people prefer small stores because they know the owners and get personal service. Some people prefer big stores because they have a lot of items and the prices are often lower.

🎧 **Listening Activity** Listen to the sentences about the picture and story. Circle *true* or *false*.

EXAMPLE (TRUE) FALSE

1. TRUE (FALSE)   4. (TRUE) FALSE
2. TRUE (FALSE)   5. (TRUE) FALSE
3. TRUE (FALSE)

7.5 | *There Is* and *There Are*

Singular

There	is	a/an/one	Singular Subject	Prepositional Phrase
There	is	a	coupon	in the newspaper.
There	is	an	elevator	in the store.
There	is	one	clerk	in the lighting department.

Language Note: The contraction for *there is* = *there's*.

Plural

There	are	Plural Word	Plural Subject	Prepositional Phrase
There	are		good prices	in the big store.
There	are	five	clerks	in the store.
There	are	a lot of	items	in the big store.

Language Note: *There are* has no contraction.

146 Unit 7

Expansion

Grammar Chart Have students tell a partner what's in his or her apartment or house. Say and write the following examples on the board: *There are three bedrooms. There's a big kitchen.*

EXERCISE 1 Fill in the blanks with *there is* or *there are*. Use contractions where possible.

EXAMPLE __There are__ a lot of items in the big store.

1. __There is__ a sale on lightbulbs this week.
2. __There are__ lightbulbs in aisle three.
3. __There is__ a helpful clerk in the small store.
4. __There are__ many shoppers in the big store.
5. __There is__ a sign near the lightbulbs.

EXERCISE 2 This is a cell phone conversation between Simon and Victor. Fill in the blanks with *there is* or *there are*. Make a contraction whenever possible.

Simon: Hello?
Victor: Hi, Simon. It's Victor.
Simon: Are you at home?
Victor: No, I'm not. I'm at the department store with my wife. __There's__ (example) a big sale at this store—50% off all winter items. Lisa loves sales. She wants to buy a winter coat. __There are__ (1) a lot of women in the coat department, but __there's__ (2) only one clerk. Where are you?
Simon: I'm at home. __There's__ (3) a football game on TV.
Victor: I know. I think all the men are at home in front of the TV. __There's__ (4) only one man in the department—me.
Simon: That's too bad. It's a great game.
Victor: It's not so bad. __There's__ (5) a TV in the store, and __there's__ (6) a nice sofa in front of the TV. So I can watch while my wife shops.
Simon: I prefer to watch the game at home with my friends.
Victor: Me too.

Lesson 2   147

EXERCISE 1

1. Have students read the direction line. Go over the example in the Student Book. Remind students to use contractions when they can.
2. Have students complete Exercise 1 individually. Go over the answers as a class.
3. If necessary, review grammar chart **7.5** on page 146.

EXERCISE 2

1. Have students look at the picture of Victor, Lisa, and Simon on page 147. Ask: *Where are Victor and Lisa? Where is Simon?* Then have students read the direction line. Go over the example in the Student Book.
2. Have students complete Exercise 2 individually. Then have students compare answers in pairs. Circulate to observe pair work. Give help as needed.
3. If necessary, review grammar chart **7.5** on page 146.

🕐 To save class time, have students do the exercise for homework ahead of time.

Expansion

Exercise 2 Have students describe who they see in the stores where they shop. Say and write on the board the following model sentences: *There are a lot of women in the Shoe Department. There's only one clerk in the Jewelry Department.*

Unit 7   147

7.6 | Negative Forms with *There Is/There Are*

1. Have students look at grammar chart **7.6** on page 148. Say: There isn't *is the negative of* there is. *We can also write* there's no. Go over the examples. Give additional examples from the classroom. (e.g., *There isn't a dictionary in this room. There's no computer.*)
2. Say: There aren't *is the negative of* there are. *We can also write* there are no. Give additional examples. (e.g., *There aren't any dictionaries in this room. There are no computers.*)
3. Have students close their books. Write the following sentences on the board. Have volunteers come to the board and fill in the blanks:

    There's no [elevator].
    There are no [cheap TVs].
    There isn't a [good shoe department].
    There aren't any [nice clerks].

EXERCISE 3

1. Have students read the direction line. Go over the example in the Student Book.
2. Have students complete Exercise 3 individually. Then have students compare answers in pairs. Circulate to observe pair work. Give help as needed.
3. If necessary, review grammar chart **7.6** on page 148.

7.6 | Negative Forms with *There Is/There Are*

We can use *there isn't/there aren't* for the negative.

Negative Singular

There	isn't	a/an	Singular Subject	Prepositional Phrase
There	isn't	a	clerk	in aisle three.
There	isn't	an	elevator	in the big store.
There's		no	Singular Subject	Prepositional Phrase
There's		no	clerk	in aisle three.
There's		no	elevator	in the big store.

Negative Plural

There	aren't	any	Plural Subject	Prepositional Phrase
There	aren't	any	lightbulbs	in this aisle.
There	aren't	any	helpful clerks	in the big store.
There	are	no	Plural Subject	Prepositional Phrase
There	are	no	lightbulbs	in this aisle.
There	are	no	helpful clerks	in this store.

EXERCISE 3 Change to a negative statement.

EXAMPLE There's a small hardware store near my house. __There isn't__ a big store near my house.

1. There are 20 aisles in the big store. __There aren't__ 20 aisles in the small store.
2. There are lightbulbs in aisle three. __There aren't__ any lightbulbs in aisle five.
3. There's usually a clerk in aisle three. __There isn't__ a clerk in aisle three now.
4. There's an elevator in the small store. __There isn't__ an elevator in the big store.
5. There's good service in the small store. __There isn't__ good service in the big store.

148 Unit 7

Expansion

Grammar Chart Have students get into groups and describe to group members what's NOT in their neighborhood. (e.g., There's no bank in my neighborhood.)

7.7 | Quantity Words

Quantity	Examples
xxxxxx	There are **many/a lot of** lightbulbs in the store.
xxx	There are **some** lamps in aisle three.
xx	There aren't **enough** clerks in the big store.
x	There is **one/an** elevator in the small store.
0	There aren't **any** lightbulbs in aisle three. There are **no** lightbulbs in aisle three.

EXERCISE 4 ABOUT YOU Use *there is/there are* and the words given to tell about your class and your school. Use quantity words from the chart above.

EXAMPLES teacher
There's one teacher in this class.

Korean student(s)
There are some Korean students in this class.

Answers will vary.
1. desk for all students
2. elevator(s)
3. computer(s)
4. young student(s)
5. telephone(s)
6. African student(s)

EXERCISE 5 ABOUT YOU Fill in the blanks to tell about the place where you live.

EXAMPLE There are no ___old people___ in my building.

Answers will vary.
1. There's no _____ in my building.
2. There aren't many _____ in my building.
3. There are a lot of _____ in my building.
4. There are some _____ in my apartment.
5. There aren't enough _____ in my apartment.
6. There's a(n) _____ in my kitchen.
7. There aren't any _____ in my bedroom.

Lesson 2 149

7.7 | Quantity Words

Have students look at grammar chart **7.7** on page 149. Present the quantity words and examples. To check comprehension, ask volunteers to describe the contents of the room using the quantity words in the chart. (e.g., There aren't any windows in this room.)

EXERCISE 4

1. Say: *In this exercise, you're going to make and share sentences about this class and this school.* Have students read the direction line. Go over the examples in the Student Book. Have a volunteer model the examples.
2. Have students complete Exercise 4 individually. Then have students compare answers in pairs. Circulate to observe pair work. Give help as needed.
3. If necessary, review grammar chart **7.7** on page 149.

EXERCISE 5

1. Say: *In this exercise, you're going to tell about where you live.* Have students read the direction line. Go over the example in the Student Book. Have a volunteer model the example.
2. Have students complete Exercise 5 individually. Give help as needed.
3. If necessary, review grammar chart **7.7** on page 149.

Expansion
Exercise 5 Have students share their answers with a partner.

Unit 7 149

EXERCISE 6

1. Have students read the direction line. Go over the example. You might have students scan the conversation for quantity and location phrases. Then review or pre-teach terms and phrases that might be difficult, such as *batteries*, *hall closet*, and *A battery is a battery*.
2. Have students complete Exercise 6 individually. Then have students compare answers in pairs. Circulate to observe pair work. Give help as needed.
3. If necessary, review grammar chart 7.7 on page 149.

🕐 To save class time, have students do this exercise for homework ahead of time.

EXERCISE 6 This is a conversation between Rick and Sue. Fill in the blanks with *any*, *some*, *many*, *a lot of*, *enough*, *one*, *a*, or *no* to complete this conversation. In some cases, more than one answer is possible.

Sue: Where are the batteries? I need __some__ batteries for the
(example)
flashlight.

Rick: Look in the hall closet.

Sue: There aren't __any__ batteries in the closet.
(1)

Rick: Look in the kitchen. There are __some__ batteries there, I think.
(2)

Sue: There's only __one__ battery here. This flashlight needs two
(3)
batteries. We need to go to the hardware store and get more batteries.

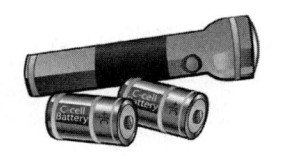

Rick: Let's go to the big store.

Sue: I prefer the small store. There's __no__ service in a big store.
(4)
There aren't __any__ clerks to help you. You have questions,
(5)
but there are __no__ clerks to answer your questions.
(6)

Rick: I don't have __any__ questions about batteries. A battery is a
(7)
battery. Look at this section of the newspaper. There are
__many / a lot of__ things on sale at the big store—hundreds of things.
(8)

Sue: We don't need hundreds of things. We just need batteries.

150 Unit 7

Expansion

Exercise 6 Have students practice the conversation in pairs. Ask volunteers to roleplay the conversation in front of the class.

Have students write a list of ten things in their refrigerator at home and then write a shopping list of five things they need. Put students into pairs. Say: *Ask your partner for something on your shopping list. Your partner will say if he or she has any.* Say and write the following model on the board:

Student A: *I need milk.*
Student B: *There isn't any milk in my refrigerator. / There's no milk in my refrigerator.*

---

150 *Grammar in Context Basic* Teacher's Edition

EXERCISE 7 This is a conversation between Rick and Sue. Fill in the blanks with the missing words from the box below. You can combine two words to fill in one blank. Make a contraction wherever possible.

there	they	is	are
it	no	isn't	aren't

Rick: Let's go to the hardware store today. __There's__ a sale on
(example)
tools. __They're__ really cheap today.
(1)

Sue: Let's go to the department store. __There's__ a sale on all
(2)
shoes. __They're__ 50 percent off. Let's go to the department store
(3)
first and then to the hardware store.

Rick: __There isn't__ enough time. It's almost 4:00. The hardware
(4)
store closes at 5:30. __It's__ Saturday today, and the
(5)
hardware store __isn't__ open late on Saturday.
(6)

Sue: The small hardware store __isn't__ open late, but the big
(7)
store is open 24/7. You know, I don't really want to go to the
hardware store with you. Tools don't interest me. I have an idea.
You can go to the hardware store, and I can go to the department
store. I need shoes.

Rick: Need or want? You have 20 pairs of shoes.

Sue: __They're__ all old. I need new shoes.
(8)

Rick: And I need new tools.

Lesson 2   151

EXERCISE 7

1. Have students look at the pictures of the tools on page 151. Have students name the tools. (hammer, screwdriver, drill) Then have students read the direction line. Do the example with the class.
2. Have students complete the rest of Exercise 7 individually. Then have students compare answers in pairs. Circulate to observe pair work. Give help as needed.
3. If necessary, review grammar chart 7.7 on page 149.

🕐 To save class time, have students do this exercise for homework ahead of time.

Expansion

Exercise 7 Have students practice the conversation in pairs. Ask volunteers to roleplay the conversation in front of the class.

Unit 7   151

Lesson 3 | Overview

GRAMMAR

1. Say: *In Lesson 3, we are going to study how to make* yes/no *and information questions with* there is *and* there are. Write the lesson's objectives on the board. Ask students to use complete sentences to answer the following questions: *Are there any students from Japan? Is there someone from Chile? How many students are there in this class?*
2. Activate students' prior knowledge. Ask: *What are some question words? (what, who, how much, how many)* Ask volunteers to make *yes/no* and information questions about the class with *There is* and *There are.*

CONTEXT

1. Say: *Stores usually offer many different things. They also offer many kinds of the same thing. When you shop, you have to choose. In this lesson, we're going to read about making choices.* Relate the topic to students' experience. Ask: *When you decide what to buy, what do you think about?*
2. Direct students' attention to the photo. Ask: *What is in this aisle?* (shampoo) *Are all the different kinds of shampoo the same price?* (no)

BEFORE YOU READ

1. Go over each question as a class. Have a volunteer read the questions or read them to the class yourself.
2. Discuss the questions as a class. Have students share their ideas and personal experiences using different brands of the same product.
   To save class time, skip "Before You Read," or have students prepare their answers for homework ahead of time.

LESSON 3

GRAMMAR
Yes/No Questions with *There Is/There Are*
Information Questions with *There Is/There Are*

CONTEXT
Choices

Before You Read
1. Is it easy to make choices in a store? Why or why not?
2. Some items, such as shampoo, are cheap and some are expensive. Is there a difference between cheap and expensive brands?

Expansion
Theme The topic for this unit can be enhanced with the following ideas:
1. Circulars from different supermarkets, drugstores, and chain stores
2. Advertisements comparing two versions of one product or two brands of the same product

Culture Note
There are many choices in supermarkets today. Most supermarkets have more than 200 kinds of fruits and vegetables. Large supermarkets may sell 24,000 items!

CHOICES

Halina and Peter are in the supermarket.

Peter: There are a lot of shampoos. **Why are there** so many shampoos? Do people need so many choices?
Halina: I don't think so. **Is there** any difference between this shampoo for $2.99 and that shampoo for $7.99?
Peter: I don't know. Let's buy the cheaper one.
Halina: OK. There's probably no difference.
Peter: **Are there** any other items on the shopping list?
Halina: Just two. We need sugar. The sugar is in aisle 6.

(in aisle 6)

Halina: This bag says 25 ounces for 89¢. That one says five pounds for $2.59. Which one is a better buy?
Peter: I don't know. What's an ounce?
Halina: It's part of a pound.
Peter: **How many ounces are there** in a pound?
Halina: Sixteen.
Peter: We need a calculator.
Halina: No, we don't. Look. There's a small sign under the sugar. The five-pound bag is about 2.9¢ an ounce. The 25-ounce bag is about 3.5¢ an ounce. The big bag is cheaper.
Peter: You're a smart shopper. Are we finished? **Is there** anything else on the list?
Halina: Yes. There's one more thing—dog food.
Peter: Wow! Look. There are over 20 kinds of dog food.
Halina: Dogs have choices too.

Vocabulary in Context

shampoo	I need to wash my hair. I need **shampoo.**
choice(s)	There are 50 shampoos. There are a lot of **choices.**
difference between	What's the **difference between** this shampoo and that one?
better buy	The large bag of sugar is a **better buy.** We can save money.
calculator	I need a **calculator** to do math.
about	This bag is 2.9¢ an ounce. It's **about** 3¢ an ounce.

Lesson 3   153

Reading Variation

1. To practice listening skills, have students listen to the audio before opening their books. Ask a few comprehension questions, such as: *Where is the sugar?* (in aisle 6) *How many kinds of dog food are there?* (over 20) Repeat the audio if necessary. Then have students open their books and read along as they listen to the audio.
2. Alternatively, have students begin by listening to the audio as they read along.

Expansion

Reading Have students practice the conversation in pairs. Ask volunteers to roleplay the conversation in front of the class.

Choices (Reading)

CD 1, Track 39

1. Have students look at the title of the reading and the photo on page 152. Ask: *Where are Halina and Peter? What are they doing?* (at the supermarket; shopping) Have students use the title, the photo, and the picture of the calculator on page 153 to make predictions about the reading. Prompt by asking: *What will Halina and Peter talk about when they choose the items?* (price, weight, size) *What is one of the items they are shopping for?* (shampoo)
2. Have students read the dialogue silently. Then play the audio and have students read along silently.
3. Check students' basic comprehension. Ask questions, such as: *Which shampoo do they buy?* (the cheaper one) *Which bag of sugar do they buy?* (the five-pound bag) *Are they going to buy a calculator?* (no)

   To save class time, have students do the reading for homework ahead of time.

VOCABULARY IN CONTEXT

1. Model the pronunciation of each new vocabulary item and have students repeat.
2. Go over the meaning of each vocabulary item. Review the examples in the book and create additional example sentences. For example, say: *difference between.* Hold up two book bags from different students. Say: *What's the difference between these two bags?* Review each new vocabulary item similarly, using visuals and realia when appropriate. When possible, point to pictures that illustrate the new vocabulary items, such as *shampoo* on page 152 and *calculator* on page 153.
3. Have students underline an example of each new vocabulary item in the reading.

Unit 7   153

DID YOU KNOW?

Explain to students that the U.S. uses the metric system for some things, such as measuring servings for food items. Say: *Two other countries also use the metric system for some things: Liberia and Myanmar. All other countries use the metric system completely.*

LISTENING ACTIVITY

🎧 **CD 1, Track 40**

1. Say: *Listen to the sentences about Peter and Halina's conversation. Circle true or false.* Play the listening selection one time without pausing. Then play it through again, pausing and replaying as necessary.
2. Go over the answers as a class. Ask students to volunteer answers.

7.8 | Yes/No Questions with *There Is/There Are*

1. Have students cover up grammar chart **7.8** on page 154. Write the following sentence on the board:

   There's an aisle of shampoo.

   Have students write a *yes/no* question for the statement. (Is there an aisle of shampoo? Is there any shampoo?) Then have students look at the chart. Say: *To make a question with* there is *and* there are, *reverse the word order.* Review each statement, question, and short answer.
2. Point out the Language Note. Review the rules. Stress the use of *any.* Have students underline *any* in the chart examples and identify the noncount noun *(cat food)* and plural count noun *(bags of sugar).*

EXERCISE 1

1. Have students read the direction line. Go over the example.
2. Have students complete Exercise 1 individually. Go over the answers with the class.
3. If necessary, review grammar chart **7.8** on page 154.

Did You Know?
- One pound = .45 kilograms
- One ounce = 28.35 grams

🎧 **Listening Activity** Listen to the sentences about the conversation. Circle *true* or *false.*

EXAMPLE (TRUE)   FALSE

1. (TRUE)   FALSE   4. TRUE   (FALSE)
2. TRUE   (FALSE)   5. (TRUE)   FALSE
3. TRUE   (FALSE)   6. (TRUE)   FALSE

7.8 | Yes/No Questions with *There Is/There Are*

Statement	Question	Short Answer
There's an aisle of shampoo.	**Is there** an aisle of tools in this store?	No, there isn't.
There are large bags of sugar.	**Are there** any small bags of sugar?	Yes, there are.
There's dog food in this aisle.	**Is there** any cat food in this aisle?	Yes, there is.

Language Notes:
1. We often add *any* to a question with noncount and plural count nouns.
2. Don't make a contraction in a singular short answer.
   Yes, there's.   Yes. There is.

EXERCISE 1 Finish the short answers.

EXAMPLE   Are there any clerks in the store? Yes, __there are__.

1. Is there a price on the shampoo bottles? No, __there isn't__.
2. Are there a lot of shoppers in the store? Yes, __there are__.
3. Is there any dog food on sale this week? Yes, __there is__.
4. Are there a lot of choices of dog food? No, __there isn't__.
5. Is there a price under the bags of sugar? Yes, __there is__.

154   Unit 7

Expansion

Exercise 1 Have students write questions about the classroom using *there is* and *there are.* Then have them ask and answer the questions with a partner. (e.g., Are there any chairs in this room? Yes, there are.)

EXERCISE 2 Finish the question.

EXAMPLE <u>Is there</u> good service in a small store? Yes, there is.

1. <u>Are there</u> any shoppers in the dog food aisle? Yes, there are.
2. <u>Is there</u> a clerk in the dog food aisle? No, there isn't.
3. <u>Is there</u> a good price on shampoo this week? No, there isn't.
4. <u>Are there</u> any coupons for shampoo in the newspaper? Yes, there are.
5. <u>Is there</u> an elevator in the supermarket? No, there isn't.
6. <u>Are there</u> a lot of shoppers today?

EXERCISE 3 ABOUT YOU Ask a question with *is there* or *are there any* and the words given. Another student will answer.

EXAMPLE an elevator / in this building

A: Is there an elevator in this building?
B: No, there isn't.

1. Mexican students / in this class
   Are there any Mexican students in this class?
2. hard exercises / in this lesson
   Are there any hard exercises in this lesson?
3. new words / in this lesson
   Are there any new words in this lesson?
4. a verb chart / in your dictionary
   Is there a verb chart in your dictionary?
5. a computer lab / at this school
   Is there a computer lab at this school?
6. public telephones / on this floor
   Are there any public telephones on this floor?
7. a gym / at this school
   Is there a gym at this school?

Lesson 3 155

EXERCISE 2

1. Point out the photo on page 155. Ask: *Where are these people?* (in a supermarket) *What does the sign in the store say?* ("Guaranteed satisfaction") *What does* guaranteed satisfaction *mean?* (If they are not happy with a product or service, they can return it.)
2. Have students read the direction line. Go over the example in the Student Book. Ask: *How do you know what to put in the blank?* (Look at the short answer.)
3. Have students complete Exercise 2 individually. Then have students compare answers with a partner. Circulate to observe pair work. Give help as needed.
4. If necessary, review grammar chart **7.8** on page 154.

To save class time, have students do the exercise for homework ahead of time.

EXERCISE 3

1. Say: *You're going to ask and answer questions with a partner.* Have students read the direction line. Go over the example in the Student Book. Then have two volunteers model the example.
2. Have students complete Exercise 3 in pairs. Circulate to observe pair work. Give help as needed.
3. If necessary, review grammar chart **7.8** on page 154.

Expansion

Exercise 2 Have a class discussion about items students have returned because they weren't satisfied. Write on the board:

Item returned:
Why:

Unit 7 155

7.9 | Information Questions with *There Is/There Are*

1. Have students look at grammar chart **7.9** on page 156. Say: *How many, what else,* and *why are common question words with* is there/are there. *The question word goes before* is there *and* are there. Go over the examples in the chart.
2. Ask: *What is the difference between* yes/no *questions and information questions?* (Information questions have question words, and short answers give a piece of information.) Review the examples in the chart. Point out the word order for both types of questions.
3. Note that in some cases the short answers to *yes/no* questions can be implied. Give examples. (e.g., *Is there any sauce? [Yes, there is. There is . . .] One can.*)

EXERCISE 4

1. Have students read the direction line. Go over the example in the Student Book.
2. Have students complete Exercise 4 individually. Go over the answers with the class.
3. If necessary, review grammar chart **7.9** on page 156.

7.9 | Information Questions with *There Is/There Are*

How much/how many, what else, and *why* are common question words with *is there/are there*. Notice question word order.

Question Word	is/are	there	Phrase	Answer
How much sugar	is	there	in the bag?	One pound.
How many ounces	are	there	in a pound?	16
What else	is	there	on the list?	Just one more thing.
Why	are	there	20 different kinds of shampoo?	I don't know.

Compare *yes/no* questions and information questions.

Yes/No Questions	Information Questions
Are there ten things on the list?	How many things **are there** on the list?
Are there different kinds of shampoo?	Why **are there** different kinds of shampoo?
Are there many kinds of dog food?	How many kinds of dog food **are there**?
Is there a difference between this shampoo and that shampoo?	Why **is there** a difference in price?

EXERCISE 4 Read the statements. Write an information question with the words in parentheses ( ).

EXAMPLE There are ten kinds of dog food. (how many / shampoo)
    How many kinds of shampoo are there?

1. There is one more thing on the list. (what else)
    What else is on the list?
2. There are 16 ounces in a pound. (how many / in two pounds)
    How many ounces are there in two pounds?
3. There are people in this line. (how many)
    How many people are there in this line?
4. There are many kinds of dog food. (why)
    Why are there many kinds of dog food?

Expansion

Grammar Chart Have students go back to the reading on page 153. Tell students to circle the information questions. Have them underline the *yes/no* questions, and put a wavy line under the short answers. (e.g., *Are there any other items on the shopping list? Just two.*)

5. There is a pharmacy in the store. (what else)
   What else is in the store?

6. There's money in my pocket. (how much)
   How much money is in your pocket?

EXERCISE 5 ABOUT YOU Use the following words to ask and answer questions about your class or school. Follow the examples.

EXAMPLES desks / in this class
A: How many desks are there in this class?
B: There are 20 desks in this class.

1. students / in this class
   How many students are in this class?
2. windows / in this room
   How many windows are in this room?
3. paper / on the floor
   How much paper is on the floor?
4. telephones / in this room
   How many telephones are in this room?
5. men's washrooms / on this floor
   How many men's washrooms are on this floor?
6. floors / in this building
   How many floors are in this building?
7. pages / in this book
   How many pages are in this book?
8. grammar information / on this page
   How much grammar information is on this page?

EXERCISE 6 Write questions and answers for the items in the box below.

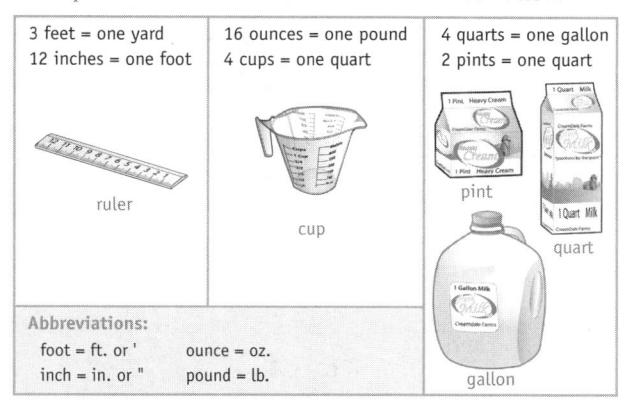

| 3 feet = one yard | 16 ounces = one pound | 4 quarts = one gallon |
| 12 inches = one foot | 4 cups = one quart | 2 pints = one quart |

ruler   cup   pint   quart   gallon

Abbreviations:
foot = ft. or '   ounce = oz.
inch = in. or "   pound = lb.

EXAMPLE How many feet are there in a yard? There are 3 feet in a yard.

1. How many inches are in a foot? There are 12 inches in a foot.
2. How many ounces are in a pound? There are 16 ounces in a pound.

Lesson 3   157

EXERCISE 5

1. Say: *In this exercise, you'll ask and answer questions about this class or school with a partner.* Go over the example. Have volunteers model the example. Tell partners to take turns asking and answering questions.
2. Have students complete Exercise 5 in pairs. Circulate to observe pair work. Give help as needed.
3. If necessary, review grammar chart **7.9** on page 156.

EXERCISE 6

1. Have students look at the pictures on page 157. Review the vocabulary for the units of measure: *feet, yard, inches; ounces, pounds, cup, pint, quart, gallon*. Then have students read the directions line. Go over the example on page 157.
2. Have students complete Exercise 6 individually. Go over the answers as a class.
3. If necessary, review grammar chart **7.9** on page 156.

Expansion

Exercise 5 Have students ask and answer questions about their homes with a partner. (e.g., How many bathrooms are there in your house?)

Unit 7   157

EXERCISE 7

1. Point out the picture of the CDs. Ask: *What are these?* (CDs). Have students read the directions line. Go over the example. Have a volunteer model the example.
2. Have students complete Exercise 7 individually. Then have students compare answers in pairs. Circulate to observe pair work. Give help as needed.
3. If necessary, review grammar chart **7.9** on page 156.

   🕐 To save class time, have students do the exercise for homework ahead of time.

---

3. **How many cups are in a quart? There are 4 cups in a quart.**
4. **How many quarts are in a gallon? There are 4 quarts in a gallon.**
5. **How many pints are in a quart? There are 2 pints in a quart.**

EXERCISE 7 Fill in the blanks with the missing words from the box below.

| there's | there is | there are |
| is there | are there ✓ | how many |

Rick: I'm going for a walk.

Sue: Wait. I need a few things at the supermarket. Let me look at my shopping list.

Rick: How many things __are there__ on the list?
                    (example)

Sue: About ten. Also go to the office store. We need CDs.

Rick: Where's the office store?

Sue: __There are__ a few office supply stores near here. __There's__ an office store next to the supermarket on Elm St. Buy a package of CDs.
     (1)   *(2)*

Rick: __How many__ CDs __are there__ in a package?
       (3)   *(4)*

Sue: You can buy a package of 50.

Rick: __Is there__ anything else on your list?
       (5)

Sue: Yes, __there is__. We need computer paper for the printer. Buy five packs of paper.
          (6)

Rick: __How many__ sheets of paper __are there__ in a pack?
       (7)   *(8)*

158   Unit 7

Expansion

Exercise 7 Have students practice the conversation in pairs. Ask volunteers to roleplay the conversation in front of the class.

Have students work in pairs to create a similar conversation using their own information.

Sue: Five hundred, I think.

Rick: I need the car. __Is there__ (9) enough gas in the tank?

Sue: I don't think so. Fill up the tank too.

EXERCISE 8 Fill in the blanks with the missing words. Use *there is/are* or *is/are there*.

Marta: The kids need new coats. Let's go shopping today. __There's__ (example) a 12-hour sale at Baker's Department Store—today only.

Simon: __Is there__ (1) a sale on men's coats too?

Marta: Yes, __there is__ (2). __There are__ (3) a lot of great things on sale: winter coats, sweaters, boots, gloves—and more.

Simon: How do you always know about all the sales in town?

Marta: It's easy. Look. __There's__ (4) an ad in the newspaper.

Simon: It says, "End of winter sale. All winter things 50% off." Why __is there__ (5) a sale on winter things? It's still winter.

Marta: Spring is almost here.

Simon: It's only January. It's so cold. __There are__ (6) two or three more months of winter.

Marta: We think it's winter. But stores need space for new things.

Lesson 3 159

EXERCISE 8

1. Have students look at the photo on page 159. Ask: *What is this woman doing?* (looking at clothes in a store) *Is she going to pay full price for these clothes? What does* clearance *mean?* (The items on are on sale for the lowest price possible. The store wants the items "cleared out" of their store.)
2. Have students read the direction line. Have a volunteer read the example. Ask: *Why is* There's *correct?* ("A sale" is singular.) Have students skim a few statements for the clue to choosing singular or plural. Remind them that *a lot* means *many*.
3. Have students complete Exercise 8 individually. Then have students compare answers in pairs. Circulate to observe pair work. Give help as needed.
4. If necessary, review grammar chart **7.8** on page 154 and **7.9** on page 156.

⏱ To save class time, have students do the exercise for homework ahead of time.

Expansion

Exercise 8 Have students practice the conversation in pairs. Ask volunteers to roleplay the conversations in front of the class.

Have students get into groups and tell about sales in their countries, saying when the big sales occur and which items are marked down. (e.g., There's a big sale in January. All winter clothes are 50% off.)

Unit 7 159

Editing Advice

1. Have students close their books. Write the example sentences without editing marks or corrections on the board. For example:

   1. Simon works five days in a week.
   2. Sue likes to shop in the night.

   Ask students to correct each sentence. This activity can be done individually, in pairs, or as a class. After students have corrected each sentence, tell them to turn to page 160. Say: *Now compare your work with Editing Advice in the book.*
2. Go over answers with the class. For troublespots, review the appropriate grammar chart.

EDITING ADVICE

1. Remember: Certain time expressions don't use prepositions.

   Simon works five days ~~in~~ a week.

2. Use the correct preposition.

   Sue likes to shop ~~in~~ the night. *(at)*

   Your favorite program begins ~~after~~ 20 minutes. *(in)*

3. Don't use *to* after *near*.

   There's a convenience store near ~~to~~ my house.

4. Don't make a contraction for *there are*.

   ~~There're~~ 20 students in the class. *(There are)*

5. Don't use *a* after *there are*.

   There are a good sales this week.

6. Don't use a double negative.

   There aren't ~~no~~ lightbulbs in this aisle. *(any)*

7. Use correct word order.

   How many batteries ~~there are~~ in the flashlight? *(are there)*

8. Don't make a contraction with a short *yes* answer.

   Is there an elevator in the store? Yes ~~there's~~. *(there is)*

EDITING QUIZ

Find the mistakes with the underlined words, and correct them. Not every sentence has a mistake. If the sentence is correct, write C.

EXAMPLES Rick and Sue are ~~in~~ *at* home now.

Shampoo is on sale this week. *C*

1. There are ~~a~~ big stores downtown.
2. Stores are crowded ~~at~~ *on* the weekend.
3. It's 8:45. The store closes at 9:00. It closes ~~after~~ *in* 15 minutes.
4. ~~There're~~ *There are* many shoppers in the afternoon.
5. There are a lot of children's programs ~~in~~ *on* TV on Saturday mornings.
6. I go to school three days ~~in~~ a week.
7. There is a big store near ~~to~~ my house.
8. Is there a clerk in aisle 3? Yes, ~~there's~~ *there is*.
9. How many convenience stores ~~there are~~ *are there* in this city?
10. There's coffee ~~at~~ *in* aisle four.
11. There aren't ~~no~~ *any* clerks on the second floor.
12. Bread is on sale: two for one. *C*

Lesson 3 **161**

Learner's Log

1. Have students close their books. Ask: *What did you learn about shopping, different types of stores, and getting good prices in the U.S.? What else do you want to know?* Write students' ideas on the board. Discuss ways in which students can find out more about shopping, stores, and prices.
2. Have students open their books to complete the Learner's Log. Remind them to write three questions about shopping in the U.S.

Expansion Activities

These expansion activities provide opportunities for students to interact with one another and further develop their speaking and writing skills. Encourage students to use grammar from this unit whenever possible.

To save class time, assign parts of the activities as homework. Then use class time for interaction and communication. If students do not need additional speaking practice, some of the activities may be assigned as writing activities for homework, or skipped altogether.

WRITING ACTIVITY

1. Brainstorm ways to describe the pictures with the class and list the ideas on the board.
2. Have students complete the activity individually at home or in class.
3. Collect for assessment.

OUTSIDE ACTIVITY

After students have completed the assignment, have them compare prices in groups, including sale prices and prices with coupons.

INTERNET ACTIVITIES

1. When assigning the tasks, do the following:
2. Remind students that they can estimate their height and weight.
3. Ask students the names of office supply stores they know. Write them on the board.

LEARNER'S LOG

1. What did you learn in this unit? Write three sentences in your notebook about each of these topics:
   - Shopping in the United States
   - Different types of stores
   - Getting a good price
2. Write three questions you still have about shopping in the U.S.

EXPANSION ACTIVITIES

Writing Activity

In your notebook, write five or six sentences to describe each picture.

Outside Activity

Check your local newspaper for ads for your favorite pharmacy or supermarket. Find a product that's on sale. What is the sale price? Find a product with a coupon. What is the sale price with the coupon? Write about the ads in your notebook.

Internet Activities

1. Search the words *metric conversion* on a search engine. Choose a Web site. Find your weight and height in both metric and American measurements.
2. Find the Web site of a big office supply store. Find the price of a package of printer paper.

Expansion

Learner's Log Have students compare logs in pairs.

Writing Activity Variation

Have students exchange papers with a partner for proofreading.

Internet Activities Variation

Tell students that if they don't have Internet access, they can use Internet facilities at a public library. Alternatively, they can calculate their height and weight on their own without using the Internet, and they can use the circular of an office supply store to find the price of a package of printer paper.

UNIT

8

GRAMMAR
The Present Continuous Tense
Time Expressions

CONTEXT
Errands

Unit | 8
Unit Overview

GRAMMAR

1. Ask: *What did we study in Unit 7?* (prepositions and *There is/There are*) *What are we going to study in Unit 8?* Say and write the objectives on the board: *the Present Continuous Tense* and *Time Expressions*.
2. Write on the board:

   be + verb -ing
   You <u>are</u> studying today.

   Point to the verb in the sentence and say: *This is the* Present Continuous Tense. Say and write on the board: *today, this week = the present = now*
3. Activate students' knowledge. Elicit more time phrases for the present. Write students' answers on the board. Ask volunteers to tell what they are doing *today* and *this week*.

CONTEXT

1. Begin by directing students' attention to the photos. Ask: *What are these places?* (bank drive-through, post office) *What is the lady in her car doing?* (getting money from her account or putting money into her account)
2. Say: *We're going to talk about errands in Unit 8. Errands are short trips we take to get a task done.* Relate the topic to students' experience. Ask: *What errands do you do?*

Expansion

Theme The topic for this unit can be enhanced with the following ideas:
1. Flyers from dry cleaners
2. Post office announcements of automated or other services giving rates for first-, second-, and third-class items
3. Magazine pictures of people doing errands
4. A weight scale

Lesson 1 | Overview

GRAMMAR

1. Say and write the following sentences on the board:

   Now, I'm writing on the board.
   Today, I'm teaching.
   This year, I'm teaching grammar.

   Write or point out the first lesson objective on the board: *Present Continuous Tense.* Say: *The present continuous tense tells what's happening in the present.* Point out the time phrases in the sentences on the board and say: *There are different kinds of present time.*

2. Elicit actions from students using different expressions of time. Prompt by asking: *What are you doing right now? What are you doing this year?*

CONTEXT

1. Begin by directing students' attention to the photo of the post office on page 164. Go over the names of the items in the post office, such as *package, letter,* and *envelope.* Say: *In this unit we are going to talk about doing errands. What will we talk about in Lesson 1?* (running an errand to the post office)

2. Relate the topic to students' experience. Ask: *How often do you go to the post office? When you go, what are people doing there?* Write students' answers on the board. (e.g., They are mailing packages. They're buying stamps.)

BEFORE YOU READ

1. Go over each question as a class. Have a volunteer read the questions or read them to the class yourself. Have students discuss the questions in pairs.

2. Ask for a few volunteers to share their answers with the class.

   To save class time, skip "Before You Read," or have students prepare their answers for homework ahead of time.

LESSON 1

GRAMMAR

Present Continuous Tense—Affirmative Statements
Spelling of the *-ing* Form of the Verb
Uses of the Present Continuous Tense
Present Continuous Tense—Negative Forms
Expressions of Time with the Present Continuous Tense

CONTEXT

At the Post Office

Before You Read

1. What services does the U.S. post office have? What items does the post office sell?
2. Do you send packages to your country? Why or why not?

Culture Note

The U.S. Post Office has been delivering mail for over 200 years. The U.S. Post office began in 1775. Benjamin Franklin was the first postmaster general.

---

164   *Grammar in Context Basic* Teacher's Edition

AT THE POST OFFICE

It is Saturday morning. People **are doing** errands. They **aren't wearing** their work clothes. They**'re wearing** casual clothes. Many things **are happening** at the post office. The postal clerks are very busy. Many people **are waiting** in line. They**'re not getting** fast service today. But they **aren't complaining.** Halina and Dorota are first in line. Halina's daughter, Anna, is with her.

A customer at the counter has two packages. The clerk **is weighing** one package. He**'s using** a scale. The man **is holding** the other package. He **isn't paying** for the postage in cash. He's **using** his credit card.

Marta **is picking up** a package. Amy is with her. Amy **is holding** Marta's hand. The clerk **is checking** Marta's identification (ID).

A customer **is using** the automated postal center. He **isn't waiting** in line. He**'s mailing** a package and he**'s weighing** the package on the scale. He**'s paying** by credit card. The machine **is printing** the postage label. Self-service is fast.

A customer **is buying** stamps from a stamp machine. He**'s paying** in cash. He**'s not using** coins. He**'s putting** a ten-dollar bill in the stamp machine. Stamp machines in the post office give coins for change. This man **is getting** some one-dollar coins in change. Nobody **is buying** phone cards or mailing supplies today.

Vocabulary in Context

do errand(s)	She's **doing errands** today. She's going to the post office and the supermarket.
customer(s)	The **customers** are waiting in the post office.
postal clerk(s)	The **postal clerks** are are helping the customers.
counter	The clerks work behind the **counter** at the post office.
casual clothes	We can play or relax in **casual clothes.**
pick up	One customer is **picking up** her package. She is getting it from the clerk.
weigh	The clerk is **weighing** a customer's package. The package **weighs** two pounds.
scale	We use a **scale** to weigh things.
postage	When we mail a package, we have to pay **postage.**
automated postal center	We can weigh our packages, print postage, and pay at the **automated postal center.** We don't need a clerk.

Lesson 1   165

Reading Variation

To practice listening skills, have students listen to the audio before opening their books. Ask a few comprehension questions, such as: *Is self-service fast?* (yes) *What day of the week is it?* (Saturday) Repeat the audio if necessary. Then have students open their books and read along as they listen to the audio.

Vocabulary Teaching Ideas

Use the following ideas to teach these terms:

customer: Say: *A customer is a person who buys something. Halina is a customer.*
counter: Run your finger along the counter in the illustration. Say: *We also have counters in kitchens.*
automated postal center: Say: *A clerk doesn't help you. You can do everything by yourself. It's like an ATM.*

Expansion

Vocabulary in Context To check comprehension, have volunteers in pairs or groups act out selected vocabulary from the reading, such as *customer, identification, pick up,* and *wait in line.*

At the Post Office (Reading) CD 1, Track 41

1. Have students look at the title of the reading and the photo on page 164. Ask: *What is happening at the post office?* Elicit some of the activities in the photo. Point to the clerk. Ask: *What is he doing?* (He is waiting on a customer; he is selling postal items.)
2. Have students read the text silently. Then play the audio and have students read along silently.
3. Check students' basic comprehension. Ask questions, such as: *What are people wearing?* (casual clothes) *Are they complaining about the slow service?* (no) *What is Marta doing?* (picking up a package) *Are people buying stamps?* (yes) *Are people buying phone cards?* (no)

To save class time, have students do the reading for homework ahead of time.

VOCABULARY IN CONTEXT

1. Model the pronunciation of each new vocabulary word and have students repeat.
2. Make sure students understand the meaning of each new vocabulary item. Review the examples in the book and create additional example sentences. For example, say: *postage.* (Hold up an envelope with stamps on it.) Say: *The postage on this envelope is [amount].* Go over each new vocabulary word using visuals and realia when appropriate. When possible, point to pictures in the book that illustrate the new vocabulary items, such as *customer, postal clerk,* and *counter* on page 164.
3. Have students underline an example of each vocabulary item in the reading.

Unit **8**   165

DID YOU KNOW?

Tell students that the first five-cent stamp pictured Benjamin Franklin. The first ten-cent stamp, also issued in 1847, pictured George Washington.

LISTENING ACTIVITY

🎧 CD 1, Track 42

1. Say: *Listen to the sentences about the reading. Circle* true *or* false. Play the listening selection one time without pausing. Then play it through again, pausing and replaying as necessary.
2. Go over the answers as a class. Ask students to volunteer answers.

8.1 | Present Continuous Tense—Affirmative Statements

1. Have students look at grammar chart 8.1 on page 166. Say: *We form the present continuous with* be *plus the verb with an* –ing *ending.* Go over the examples. Give an additional example for each expression.
2. Point out the Language Notes. Say: *Use contractions in the present continuous.* Remind students that they have already learned contractions with *be*. Explain that we don't use contractions with plural nouns.
3. Write the following sentences on the board:

   Bill is go to the store.
   The kids're playing.
   She studying now.
   Reading is my hobby.

   Have the class decide which sentences have incorrect forms for the present continuous tense and explain how to correct them. Note that in the last sentence, *reading* is a gerund and is the subject, not the verb.

The U.S. made its first stamps in 1847. They cost 5 cents. Today people send more than 202 billion pieces of mail each year.

Listening Activity Listen to the sentences about the activities in the post office. Circle *true* or *false*.

EXAMPLE TRUE (FALSE)

1. TRUE (FALSE)   5. (TRUE) FALSE
2. TRUE (FALSE)   6. (TRUE) FALSE
3. (TRUE) FALSE   7. (TRUE) FALSE
4. (TRUE) FALSE   8. TRUE (FALSE)

8.1 | Present Continuous Tense—Affirmative Statements

Subject	Be	Verb + -ing	Complement
I	am	waiting	in line.
He	is	mailing	a letter.
Nobody	is	wearing	work clothes.
We	are	using	the stamp machine.
You	are	picking up	a package.
They	are	standing	behind the counter.

Language Notes:
1. We can make contractions with a pronoun + *be*.
   I'm waiting in line.
   He's mailing a letter.
   We're using the stamp machine.
2. We can make contractions with a singular noun + *is*.
   Halina's waiting in line.
3. There is no contraction for a plural noun + *are*.
   The **clerks are** standing behind the counter.

166   Unit 8

Expansion

Grammar Chart Have students work in pairs to create sentences about the class using *wear, hold, get,* and *use*. (e.g., The teacher is wearing a sweater.)

EXERCISE 1 Fill in the blanks with the affirmative present continuous tense. Use contractions where possible. Use the ideas from the reading and the verbs in the box below. Use one verb twice.

| mail | wear | show | weigh | help | stand | buy ✓ | wait |

EXAMPLE One customer **'s buying** some stamps.

1. Dorota **'s standing** next to Halina and Anna.
2. Dorota, Halina, and Anna **are waiting** in line.
3. Marta **'s showing** her ID to the postal clerk.
4. Nobody **'s buying** phone cards.
5. The clerks **are helping** the customers.
6. A customer **'s weighing** a package at the automated postal center.
7. Everybody **'s wearing** casual clothes today.
8. Two clerks **are standing** behind the counter.

8.2 | Spelling of the *-ing* Form of the Verb

Verb	*-ing* Form	Rule
go eat look	go**ing** eat**ing** look**ing**	In most cases, add *-ing* to the base form.
sit plan	sit**ting** plan**ning**	If the verb ends in consonant + vowel + consonant, double the last consonant. Then add *-ing*.
give write	giv**ing** writ**ing**	If the verb ends in a consonant + *e*, take off the *e*. Then add *-ing*. Do not double the last consonant after you take off *e*.
show pay	show**ing** pay**ing**	Do not double final *w*, *x*, or *y*. Just add *-ing*.

Lesson 1   167

EXERCISE 1

1. Have students read the direction line. Go over the example in the Student Book.
2. Have students complete Exercise 1 individually. Check the answers as a class.
3. If necessary, review grammar chart **8.1** on page 166.

8.2 | Spelling of the *-ing* Form of the Verb

1. Have students cover up grammar chart 8.2 on page 167. Create an exercise on the board:

   go – going / eat – eating
   sit – sitting / plan – planning
   give – giving / write – writing

   Ask: *What is the spelling rule for each set of verbs?*
2. Have students look at grammar chart **8.2** on page 167. Go over the verbs and the rules.

Expansion

Grammar Chart Have students work in pairs. Ask the class to turn to the reading on page 165. Have students find all the verbs in the present continuous tense and match them to the relevant spelling rules in the chart. Go over the answers with the class.

Unit **8**   **167**

EXERCISE 2

1. Have students read the direction line. Go over the example in the Student Book. Remind students to use contractions correctly.
2. Have students complete Exercise 2 individually. Then have students compare answers in pairs. Circulate to observe pair work. Give help as needed.
3. If necessary, review grammar chart **8.2** on page 167.

8.3 | Uses of the Present Continuous Tense

1. Have students look at grammar chart **8.3** on page 168. Say: *We use the present continuous in three main ways.* Read the example sentences and explanations. Note that *stand, sleep, sit, wear, hold* and *wait* are acts without movement and therefore "no action" verbs.
2. Go over grammar chart **8.3** on page 168. Go over the examples and the explanations.

EXERCISE 2 Fill in the blanks with the present continuous of the verb in parentheses ( ). Spell the *-ing* form correctly. Use contractions where possible.

EXAMPLE She __'s mailing__ (mail) a letter.

1. They __'re getting__ (get) some stamps.
2. Halina __'s waiting__ (wait) with her daughter.
3. The clerk __'s taking__ (take) a customer's money.
4. Halina __'s talking__ (talk) to Dorota.
5. Two customers __are using__ (use) machines.
6. A man __'s putting__ (put) money in the stamp machine.
7. Nobody __'s planning__ (plan) to buy mailing supplies.
8. They __'re writing__ (write) an address on the package.

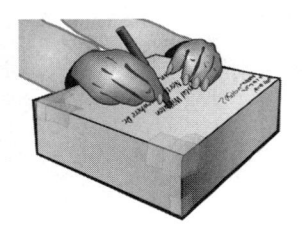

8.3 | Uses of the Present Continuous Tense

Examples	Explanation
People **are buying** stamps now.	The action is happening now, at this time.
She**'s standing** near the stamp machine. He**'s wearing** casual clothes today. They**'re holding** hands. Nobody**'s sitting** on the floor.	There is no action, but we use the present continuous with these common verbs: *stand, sleep, sit, wear, hold,* and *wait*.
I**'m working** overtime this week.	We use the present continuous when the action is happening during a specific time period.

168 Unit 8

Expansion

Exercise 2 Have students talk about the photo on page 164 in pairs. (e.g., The mail clerk is working. The is holding a package and letters.) Ask students to write as many sentences about the photo as they can without looking at the reading. Then have students share their sentences with the class.

EXERCISE 3 Write two sentences about each picture. Write about what is happening now in the picture. Use verbs from the box below.

| stand | wait | wear | play | hold | give | take | write | use |
| leave | work | pick up | go | buy | put | mail | get | sit |

EXAMPLE

This young man is going into the post office. He's wearing casual clothes today.

Answers will vary.

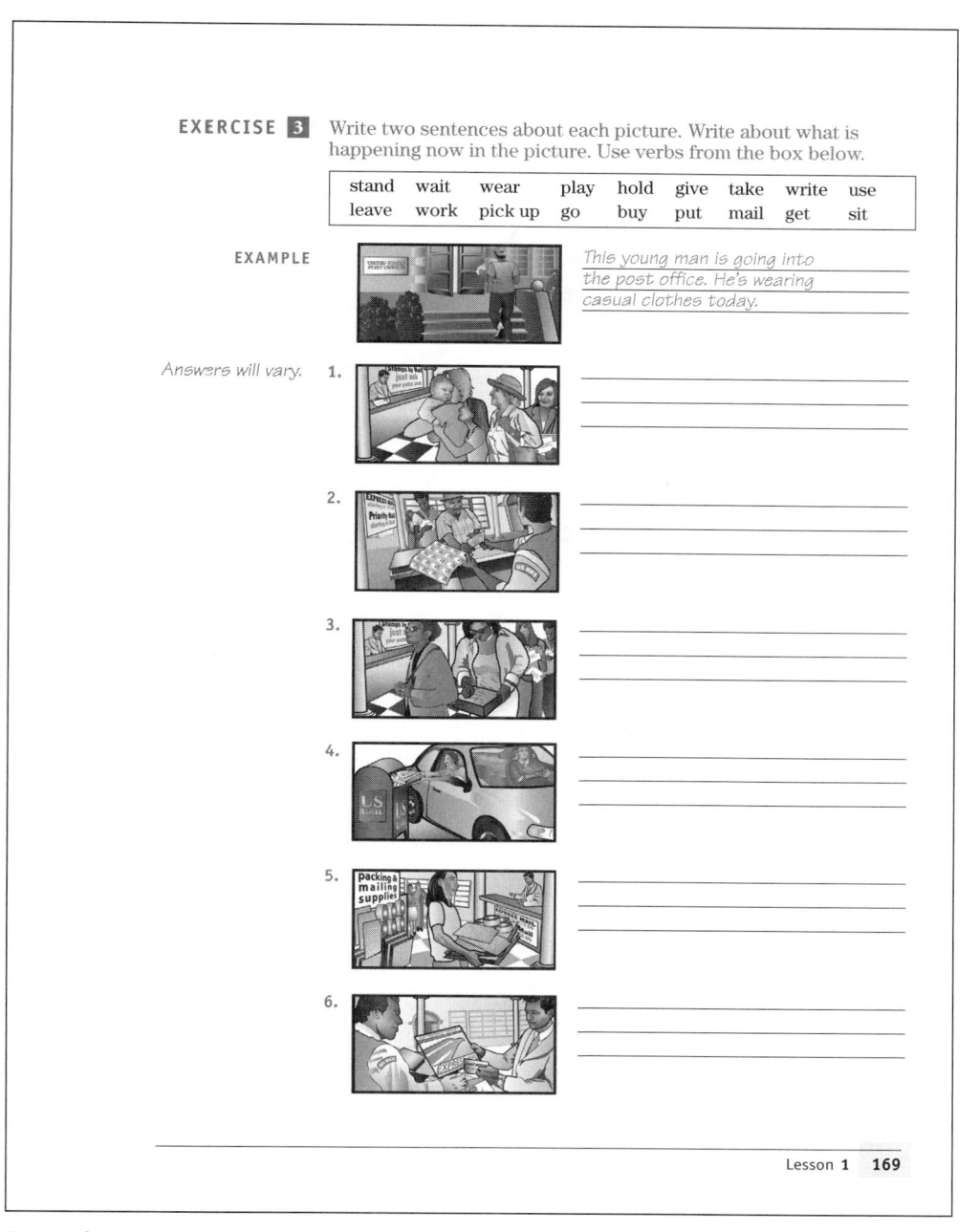

1.
2.
3.
4.
5.
6.

Lesson 1 169

Expansion

Exercise 3 Have students play a game in groups. Write a list of verbs on the board. Ask students to take turns acting out one of the verbs in front of their groups. Group members guess the action. Say: *Use sentences, such as: She's walking.* OR *She's eating.*

EXERCISE 3

1. Have students read the direction line. Go over the example. Say: *Your answers will vary.*
2. Have students complete Exercise 3 individually. Check answers with the class.
3. If necessary, review grammar charts **8.2** on page 167 and **8.3** on page 168.

Unit 8   169

8.4 | Present Continuous Tense—Negative Forms

1. Have students look at grammar chart **8.4** on page 170. Ask: *How do we make the sentence negative?* (writing *not* after the verb *be* and before the main verb) Go over the examples.
2. Point out the Language Notes. Clarify the rule for making negative contractions with *be*. Say and write on the board:
   1. *subject + be*
   2. *be + not*
3. Review the example sentences and have students match the rule with the sentence. For the second rule, remind students that plural nouns cannot be contracted with *are*. Have students read the example sentence. Ask a volunteer to rewrite the sentence on the board incorrectly by contracting the plural noun with *be*: *The women're not driving to the post office.*

EXERCISE 4

1. Have students read the direction line. Go over the examples.
2. Have students complete Exercise 4 individually. Go over the answers with the class.
3. If necessary, review grammar chart **8.4** on page 170.

8.4 | Present Continuous Tense—Negative Forms

Subject	Be	Not	Verb + -ing	Complement
I	am	not	getting	mailing supplies.
She	is	not	buying	stamps.
The woman	is	not	using	the stamp machine.
We	are	not	wearing	work clothes.
You	are	not	planning	to go to the post office.
They	are	not	writing	the correct address.
The women	are	not	driving	to the post office.

Language Notes:
1. We can make negative contractions with *be*.
   I'm not getting mailing supplies.
   The **woman's not** using the stamp machine.
   You aren't planning to go to the post office.
2. Do not make a contraction with a plural noun and *are*.
   The women aren't driving to the post office.

EXERCISE 4 Rewrite each sentence below. Make a negative sentence by changing the subject or verb. Use the words given.

EXAMPLE Marta is waiting with Amy. (talk to Amy now)
She's not talking to Amy now. OR *She isn't talking to Amy now.*

1. A man is buying stamps. (buy a phone card)
   He's not buying a phone card. OR He isn't buying a phone card.
2. Many people are waiting in line. (Marta)
   Marta's not waiting in line. OR Marta isn't waiting in line.
3. Halina and Dorota are waiting for service. (get mailing supplies)
   They're not getting mailing supplies. OR They aren't getting mailing supplies.
4. The clerks are working today. (take the day off)
   They're not taking the day off. OR They aren't taking the day off.
5. Halina is doing some errands today. (stay home)
   She's not staying home. OR She isn't staying home.

Expansion

Grammar Chart Have students go back to the reading on page 165. Say: *Rewrite some of the sentences to make them negative. Use contractions.* (e.g., People aren't doing errands.)

EXERCISE 5 ABOUT YOU Use the words below to write TRUE sentences about your activities at the present time. Make an affirmative or negative sentence. If you write a negative sentence, write a TRUE affirmative sentence also.

EXAMPLES I / write in my language
I'm not writing in my language now. I'm writing in English.

We / attend class
We're attending class now.

1. I / sit in a comfortable chair
   Answers will vary.

2. The teacher / wear casual clothes

3. We / work on a computer

4. I / use a pen

5. We / learn about the supermarket

6. All of the students / write the same sentences

7. I / spell all the words correctly

8. The teacher / help me now

8.5 | Expressions of Time with the Present Continuous Tense

Examples	Expressions of Time
I'm not cashing a check **right now**.	now (right now)
The clerk's not helping customers **at the moment**.	at the moment
We're working at home **today**. We're working at home **all day**.	today all day
They're not working overtime **this week**. I'm not working **at this time**.	this week (this month) at this time

Lesson 1   171

EXERCISE 5

1. Say: *You're going to write sentences about what is true in this class at this moment. The statements can be affirmative or negative. You must tell what is happening now.* Have students read the direction line. Go over the examples. Remind students to use contractions correctly.
2. Have students complete Exercise 5 individually. Go over the answers with the class.
3. If necessary, review grammar chart 8.4 on page 170.

8.5 | Expressions of Time with the Present Continuous Tense

Have students look at grammar chart 8.5 on page 171. Say: *Look at these common expressions of time with the present continuous tense.* Review the examples and expressions. Note that *at this time* is more formal than *now*.

Unit 8   171

EXERCISE 6

1. Have students read the direction line. Go over the examples. Remind students they may use contractions.
2. Have students complete Exercise 6 individually. Go over the answers with the class.
3. If necessary, review grammar chart **8.5** on page 171.

EXERCISE 6 Complete the short conversations with an affirmative or negative present continuous verb. Circle the expressions of time.

EXAMPLE
A: Can I use your computer?
B: Sorry, I **'m using** (use) it (at the moment). Can you wait?

1. A: Can you mail this letter for me?
   B: Sorry, I **'m staying** (stay) home all day (today).
   I **'m not going** (go) to the post office.

2. A: Dorota can't do these errands for you (now).
   B: Why not?
   A: She can't use her car (this week). She **'s having** (have) problems with it.

3. A: Victor doesn't have time to help you after work.
   B: Why not?
   A: He **'s working** (work) overtime (this week).

4. A: Please don't use the phone (right now).
   B: Why not?
   A: Because I **'m expecting** (expect) an important call.

5. A: What's wrong with this stamp machine?
   B: I don't know. But it **'s not working** (work) right (today).

6. A: This post office is very busy (right now).
   B: Yes. A lot of people **are waiting** (wait) in line at the counter.

172 Unit 8

Expansion

Exercise 6 Have students practice the short dialogues in pairs.

172 *Grammar in Context Basic* Teacher's Edition

EXERCISE 7 Marta has her package now. She's leaving the post office. She sees Dorota and Halina. Read their conversation. Then make true sentences about the conversation with the words given. Use the present continuous tense, affirmative and negative.

Marta: Hi, Dorota. It's nice to see you, Halina. How are you?
Halina: I'm fine. It's good to see you, Marta.
Dorota: Hi, Marta. I'm mailing this package to my son. He's in college now. He's living in Canada. As usual, this line is moving too slowly.
Marta: The post office has services online now. The Web site has prices for all packages. You can print the postage. You can pay for it online with your credit card. Then you can give the package to your mail carrier the next day. The cost is the same. And it's fast!
Dorota: I know. But I can't weigh the package at home. I don't have a scale. I need to send this package today.
Marta: This post office has a new automated postal center. You can weigh the package and pay for postage from a machine now. It's over there. And nobody's waiting.
Dorota: I don't know how to use it. Can you help me?

EXAMPLE Marta and Dorota / talk
Marta and Dorota are talking about post office services.
Marta and Dorota aren't talking to Amy now.

Answers will vary, but possible answers may include:

1. Dorota / tell / Marta
   Dorota is telling Marta about her son.
   Dorota isn't telling Marta about Canada.

2. Dorota / complain
   Dorota is complaining about the line.
   Dorota isn't complaining about the prices.

3. The line / move very fast
   The line isn't moving very fast.
   The line is moving very slowly.

4. Dorota / send
   Dorota is sending a package to her son.
   Dorota isn't sending a package to her mother.

5. Halina and Dorota / wait
   Halina and Dorota are waiting in line.
   Halina and Dorota aren't waiting for Marta.

Lesson 1   173

EXERCISE 7

1. Have students read the direction line. Then read the conversation as a class or have students read it silently. Go over the example. Remind students to use contractions.
2. Have students complete Exercise 7 individually. Then have students compare answers in pairs. Circulate to observe pair work. Give help as needed.
3. If necessary, review grammar chart **8.5** on page 171.

To save class time, have students complete the exercise for homework ahead of time.

Expansion

Exercise 7 Have students practice the conversation in groups of three. Ask volunteers to roleplay the conversation in front of the class.

Unit **8**   173

Lesson 2 | Overview

GRAMMAR

Write the following statement on the board: *He is going to the bank.* Ask: *Can you write a yes/no question for this statement?* (Is he going to the bank?) Then ask: *Can you write an information question for this statement?* (Where is he going?) Write the lesson objectives on the board: *Present Continuous Tense with Yes/No Questions, Information Questions, and Question Words as Subjects.*

CONTEXT

1. Say: *Drive-throughs are very convenient. They are usually fast and easy for doing errands.* Ask: *What kinds of places use drive-throughs?* (fast-food restaurants, banks, pharmacies) *Do businesses in your countries use drive-throughs? Do you think they should or shouldn't?* Have students share their knowledge and experiences.
2. Direct students' attention to the picture on page 174. Ask: *Where are Marta and Amy?* (a bank drive-through) *What do you think they are doing?* (taking out money; depositing money) Go over some of the vocabulary in the picture.

BEFORE YOU READ

1. Go over each question as a class. Have a volunteer read the questions or read them to the class yourself. Have students answer the questions in pairs.
2. Ask for a few volunteers to share their answers with the class.

To save class time, skip "Before You Read," or have students prepare their answers for homework ahead of time.

LESSON 2

GRAMMAR
Yes/No Questions with the Present Continuous Tense
Information Questions with the Present Continuous Tense
Question Words as Subjects

CONTEXT
The Drive-Through

Before You Read
1. Where are the drive-throughs in your neighborhood?
2. Which drive-throughs do you use?

tube

microphone

174 Unit 8

Culture Note

In 1946 the first drive-through was created at a bank in Chicago. They called it a "drive-in bank."

THE DRIVE-THROUGH

Americans do a lot of errands from their cars. They use drive-throughs. Marta and Amy are at their bank drive-through now.

Amy: **Are we going** home now, Mommy?
Marta: Not yet. I still have a few errands.
Amy: **Where are we going** now?
Marta: To the bank. I need some quarters for the washing machine. I can get a **roll** of 40 quarters for $10 at the bank.
Amy: **Why are you turning** here, Mommy? The bank's over there.
Marta: I'm using the drive-through, and the entrance is here.
Amy: There's someone ahead of us. **What's she doing? Is she getting** quarters, too?
Marta: She's getting money. But not quarters. She's probably cashing a check.
Amy: **Who's talking?** I hear a voice.
Marta: That's the teller. She's behind the window. She's using a microphone.
Amy: **What's that man doing** over there?
Marta: He's sending a deposit to the teller at the window. There's money or checks in that envelope.
Amy: **What's he holding?**
Marta: It's a tube. It's a place for his deposit. He can put checks or cash in the tube, and a machine takes the tube to the teller.
Amy: **Is the teller helping** both customers at the same time?
Marta: Yes.

Vocabulary in Context

drive-through	Marta and Amy are using a **drive-through**. They don't have to get out of the car for service.
tube	A customer is using a **tube** to send a deposit to the teller.
entrance	Amy's mom is going into the **entrance** of the drive-through.
roll	You can get a **roll** of 40 quarters at a bank.
turn	They are **turning** into the entrance.
teller	A **teller** is helping a customer at the bank.
microphone	The teller is using a **microphone** to talk to people.
probably	That customer is **probably** making a deposit. I'm not sure.
ahead of	Three people are **ahead of** us in line. We have to wait.

Lesson 2 175

The Drive-Through (Reading) CD 1, Track 43

1. Have students skim through the reading on page 175. Ask: *Why does Marta need to go to the bank?* (She needs a roll of quarters for the washing machine.) *Who are Marta and Amy talking about?* (the people ahead of them in the drive-through) Have students make predictions about the reading.
2. Have students read the dialogue silently. Then play the audio and have students read along silently.
3. Check students' basic comprehension. Ask questions, such as: *Where are Amy and Marta going?* (the bank) *What does Marta want to get at the bank?* (quarters) *Why does she need quarters?* (for the Laundromat) *Who does Amy hear talking?* (the teller) *Why is the man holding a tube?* (to put his deposit in it)

⏲ To save class time, have students do the reading for homework ahead of time.

VOCABULARY IN CONTEXT

1. Model the pronunciation of each new vocabulary word and have students repeat.
2. Make sure students understand the meaning of each vocabulary word. Review the examples in the book and create additional example sentences. For example, say: *entrance. The entrance to the classroom is there.* Point to the entrance. Go over each new vocabulary word similarly, using visuals and realia when appropriate. When possible, point to pictures in the book that illustrate the new vocabulary items, such as *drive-through, tube, teller, microphone,* and *ahead of* on page 174.
3. Have students underline an example of each new vocabulary item in the reading.

Reading Variation

1. To practice listening skills, have students listen to the audio before opening their books. Ask a few comprehension questions, such as: *Is the teller helping two customers at the same time?* (yes) Repeat the audio if necessary. Then have students open their books and read along as they listen to the audio.
2. Alternatively, have students begin by listening to the audio as they read along.

Vocabulary Teaching Ideas

Use the following ideas to teach these terms:

roll: Show students rolls of items, such as coins or tape.
turn: Direct a volunteer to stand up and then turn left or right.

Expansion

Reading Have students practice the conversation in groups. Ask volunteers to roleplay all or part of the conversation in front of the class.

Vocabulary in Context To check comprehension, have volunteers in pairs or groups act out selected vocabulary, such as *turn, teller, microphone,* and *ahead of*.

Unit 8 175

DID YOU KNOW?

Write *drive-thru* on the board. Ask: *Have you seen this word?* Explain that *drive-through* is often written as *drive-thru*.

LISTENING ACTIVITY

🎧 **CD 1, Track 44**

1. Say: *Listen to the following questions about Marta and Amy's conversation. Circle* true *or* false. Play the listening selection one time without pausing. Then play it through again, pausing and replaying as necessary.
2. Go over the answers as a class. Ask students to volunteer answers.

8.6 | *Yes/No* Questions with the Present Continuous Tense

1. Have students look at grammar chart 8.6 on page 176. Ask: *Where is the subject?* Then say: *To form* yes/no *questions, put the verb* be *before the subject.* Go over the examples.
2. Say: *The short answer contains just the subject and* be. *Do not include the verb in a short answer.* Go over the short answers.

EXERCISE 1

1. Have students read the direction line. Go over the example in the Student Book. Be sure students understand that the questions and answers are based on the reading.
2. Have students complete Exercise 1 individually. Go over the answers as a class.
3. If necessary, review grammar chart 8.6 on page 176.

Did You Know? Many places often have drive-throughs.
- banks
- restaurants
- pharmacies

Listening Activity Listen to the following questions about the conversation. Circle *true* or *false*.

EXAMPLE (TRUE)   FALSE

1. TRUE   (FALSE)
2. (TRUE)   FALSE
3. (TRUE)   FALSE
4. (TRUE)   FALSE
5. TRUE   (FALSE)
6. (TRUE)   FALSE
7. TRUE   (FALSE)
8. (TRUE)   FALSE

8.6 | *Yes/No* Questions with the Present Continuous Tense

Be	Subject	Verb + -ing	Complement	Short Answer
Am	I	using	the right window?	Yes, you are.
Are	you	talking	to the teller?	Yes, I am.
Is	Halina	going	into the bank?	No, she isn't.
Are	we	turning	here?	No, we're not.
Are	they	getting	some quarters?	Yes, they are.

EXERCISE 1 Make a *yes/no* question with the words given. Answer the question with a short answer. Use the ideas from the conversation.

EXAMPLE   Amy / talk to Marta
Is Amy talking to Marta? Yes, she is.

1. Marta and Amy / wait in the car
Are Marta and Amy waiting in the car? Yes, they are.
2. the man / ask for a roll of quarters
Is the man asking for a roll of quarters? No, he isn't.

176   Unit 8

Expansion

Grammar Chart Have students practice asking and answering the questions in the chart with a partner.

3. the teller / help Marta
   Is the teller helping Marta? No, she isn't.

4. the customers / complain about the service
   Are the customers complaining about the service? No, they aren't.

5. Marta and Amy / use the drive-through
   Are Marta and Amy using the drive-through? Yes, they are.

6. the tube / take a deposit to the teller
   Is the tube taking a deposit to the teller? Yes, it is.

7. the teller / talk to a customer
   Is the teller talking to a customer? Yes, she is.

8. Marta / answer Amy's questions
   Is Marta answering Amy's questions? Yes, she is.

EXERCISE 2 ABOUT YOU Use the words given to ask a partner questions about his or her present time activities. Your partner will answer with a short answer first and then add information. Write the questions and answers for practice.

EXAMPLE (you / speak English)
A: Are you speaking English now?
B: Yes, I am. I'm using the present continuous tense.

1. you / listen to the teacher
   Are you listening to the teacher now?
   Answers will vary.

2. you / practice the simple present tense
   Are you practicing the simple present tense now?
   No, I'm not.

3. you / use a Web site
   Are you using a Web site now?
   No, I'm not.

Lesson 2 177

EXERCISE 2

1. Say: *In this exercise, you're going to ask your partner questions about what he or she is doing.* Then have students read the direction line. Go over the example in the Student Book. Say: *Answers will vary.* Have two volunteers model #1. If they have difficulty, give an example answer. (e.g., *Yes, I am. I'm taking notes.*)

2. Have students complete the rest of Exercise 2 in pairs. Circulate to observe pair work. Give help as needed.

3. If necessary, review grammar chart **8.6** on page 176.

   To save class time, have students do the exercise for homework ahead of time.

Expansion

Exercise 2 Have students write three new questions to ask their partner. (e.g., Are you watching TV now?)

Unit 8   177

8.7 Information Questions with the Present Continuous Tense

1. Have students close their books. Write the following on the board:

   helping / is / How many people / the teller

   Have students unscramble the words to make a question. (*How many people is the teller helping?*) Ask: *How do you begin an information question in the present continuous tense?* (with a question word)

2. Have students look at grammar chart **8.7** on page 178. Review the word order and the examples.

3. Say: *In a short answer, do not repeat the subject and verb of the question. Compare:* "We are waiting for service," *and* "Waiting for service." Review the short answers with the class. Then say or write on the board the following question and set of answers. Ask which answers are correct and why.

   What are you doing?
   Nothing.
   Yes, you do.
   Yes, I do.
   I'm not doing anything.

---

4. your classmates / take a test
   <u>Are your classmates taking a test now?</u>
   <u>No, they aren't.</u>

5. you / write in your book
   <u>Are you writing in your book now?</u>
   <u>Answers will vary.</u>

6. your teacher / stand in front of the class
   <u>Is your teacher standing in front of the class now?</u>
   <u>Answers will vary.</u>

7. you / learn / a lot of new words today
   <u>Are you learning a lot of new words today?</u>
   <u>Answers will vary.</u>

8. your classmates / talk to you
   <u>Are your classmates talking to you now?</u>
   <u>Answers will vary.</u>

8.7 | Information Questions with the Present Continuous Tense

Question Word	Be	Subject	Verb + -ing + Complement	Short Answer
What	are	you	**doing?**	Waiting for service.
Where	is	he	**going?**	To the drive-through.
How many people	is	the teller	**helping?**	Just one right now.
Why	are	we	**waiting?**	Because the teller is busy.
Who	are	they	**talking** to?	The teller.
Why	are	Amy and Marta	**using** the drive-through?	Because it's easy and fast.

178 Unit 8

Expansion

Grammar Chart Have students write out the long answer for each question.

EXERCISE 3 Write questions for the answers given. Use the question words: *who, what, where, why, how many,* and *how.* The underlined word or phrase is the answer.

EXAMPLE *What is Amy asking Marta?*
Amy's asking Marta about the drive-through.

1. *Who is the teller talking to?*
The teller is talking to a customer.

2. *What is Marta waiting to get at the bank?*
Marta is waiting to get some quarters at the bank.

3. *What is Marta expecting to get?*
Marta is expecting to get 40 quarters.

4. *Where is the customer putting a bank deposit?*
The customer is putting a bank deposit in a tube.

5. *How is the teller talking to customers?*
The teller is talking to customers with a microphone.

6. *How many customers is the teller helping?*
The teller is helping only one customer at the moment.

7. *Who are Marta and Amy talking about?*
Marta and Amy are talking about the other customers.

EXERCISE 3

1. Have students read the direction line. Go over the example in the Student Book. Have a volunteer do #1.
2. Have students complete the rest of Exercise 3 individually. Go over the answers as a class.
3. If necessary, review grammar chart **8.7** on page 178.

Expansion
Exercise 3 Have students practice asking and answering the questions with a partner.

8.8 | Question Words as Subjects

1. Have students look at grammar chart **8.8** on page 180. Say: *The question word is the subject in each of these examples.* Go over each example.
2. Check comprehension. Have students close their books. Say or write the following short answers on the board and have students make questions:

   Amy.
   Only three.
   Students are studying English.

3. Point out the Language Notes. Review the rules. Ask: *Why must you always use a plural verb after* how many? (because *many* is plural) Clarify the rule for *who*. Explain that *who* in the question can mean one or many. You might note that a long answer with a plural subject will need a plural verb. (e.g., *Who is talking? Amy and Marta are talking.*)

EXERCISE 4

1. Say: *In this exercise, you're going to make questions. You will use a question word as subject.* Have students read the direction line. Go over the example in the Student Book.
2. Have students complete Exercise 4 individually. Go over the answers as a class.
3. If necessary, review grammar chart **8.8** on page 180.

8.8 | Question Words as Subjects

Subject	Be	Verb Phrase	Short Answer
Who	is	talking?	Amy and Marta.
What	is	happening at the bank?	Customers are doing business.
Which customer	is	waiting in line?	Marta.
How many customers	are	waiting for service?	Just one.

Language Notes:
1. Use a plural verb (*are*) after *how many*, even if the answer is singular.
2. Use a singular verb (*is*) after *who*, even if the answer is plural.

EXERCISE 4 Make questions for each answer given. The underlined word or phrase is the answer. Use the question words *who, which, what,* and *how many* as subjects.

EXAMPLE Which customer is using the tube?
A <u>man</u> is using the tube.

1. _____Who is using a microphone?_____
   The <u>teller</u> is using a microphone.
2. _____How many customers are using the tube?_____
   <u>One</u> customer is using the tube.
3. _____Which customers are getting help now?_____
   A <u>man and a woman</u> are getting help now.
4. _____What's happening at the ATM?_____
   <u>Nothing</u> is happening at the ATM.
5. _____How many customers are using the drive-through?_____
   <u>Three</u> customers are using the drive-through.
6. _____What's taking the man's deposit to the teller?_____
   A <u>tube</u> is taking the man's deposit to the teller.

180 Unit 8

Expansion

Exercise 4 Have students get into pairs. Ask them to imagine being in or at a dry cleaner. Have them describe what is happening, using the statements in Exercise 4 as a model. Finally, have them write questions for the statements using *who, which, what,* and *how many* as subjects.

EXERCISE 5 — Complete the conversation between Marta and Amy at the fast food drive-through. Use the words and expressions in the box.

| are waiting | he's asking | is putting |
| what are you getting | are we going | is it doing ✓ |

Amy: Mommy, the sign is talking. How <u>is it doing</u> that?
(example)

Marta: It's not the sign. It's the clerk. Look. He's over there at the pick-up window. <u>He's asking</u> for our order.
(1)

Amy: What are you getting, Mommy?

Marta: A burger and fries. Maybe a salad. <u>What are you getting</u>, Amy?
(2)

Amy: Ummmmmm.

Marta: Hurry, Amy, the clerk's waiting. And customers <u>are waiting</u> behind us.
(3)

Lesson 2   181

EXERCISE 5

1. Point out the pictures on page 181 amd 182. Say: *You're going to ask and answer questions based on these pictures.* Have students describe the pictures and read the direction line. Go over the example in the Student Book.
2. Have students complete Exercise 5 in pairs. Circulate to observe pair work. Tell students to take turns asking and answering questions. Give help as needed.
3. If necessary, review grammar chart **8.8** on page 180.

Expansion

Exercise 5 Have students practice asking and answering the questions with a different partner.

Unit **8**   181

Amy: Ummmm. A burger and a shake.

Marta: *(speaking to the clerk)* Two burgers, a small order of fries, and a chocolate shake, please.

Clerk: That's $7.79 with tax.

Amy: _____Are we going_____ to the pick-up window now?
(4)

Marta: Yes. Look. The clerk _____is putting_____ our lunch in a bag.
(5)

Clerk: Two dollars and 21 cents is your change. Thank you. Have a good day.

EDITING ADVICE

1. Always use a form of *be* with the present continuous tense.
   He ^is working at that store.

2. Use the correct word order in a question.
   What ~~he is~~ ^is he doing there?

3. Don't use the present continuous for usual or customary actions.
   Video stores ~~are renting~~ rent videos to many people.

4. Don't forget to put *-ing* on the end of present continuous verbs.
   They *are* go^ing to the movies today.

EDITING QUIZ

Find the mistakes with the underlined words, and correct them. If the sentence is correct, write C.

EXAMPLES   ~~He not~~ He's not going to the video store today.
           She <u>likes</u> her work.   C

1. We ~~are going~~ go to the bank every week.
2. How many packages ~~he is~~ is he weighing?
3. Many customers ^are <u>buying</u> stamps from the machine.
4. He <u>isn't writing</u> the correct address.   C
5. Why ^are <u>they waiting</u> in their car?
6. Those people ~~are mailing~~ mail letters every Saturday.
7. How much cash is he <u>~~deposit~~ depositing</u> now?

Lesson 2 183

Editing Advice

1. Have students close their books. Write the example sentences without editing marks or corrections on the board. For example:

   1. He working at that store.
   2. What he is doing there?

   Ask students to correct each sentence. This activity can be done individually, in pairs, or as a class. After students have corrected each sentence, tell them to turn to page 183. Say: *Now compare your work with Editing Advice in the book.*

2. Go over answers with the class. For troublespots, review the appropriate grammar chart.

Editing Quiz

1. The Editing Quiz may be used as an in-class quiz, a take-home quiz, or as a review. Have students read the direction line. Ask: *Does every sentence have a mistake?* (no) Go over the examples with the class.

2. Have students complete the quiz individually. Collect the completed quizzes for assessment or have students check each other's work. Review the answers with the class. Elicit the relevant grammar point for each correction. For example, for #1, ask: *What's the rule?* (Do not use the present continuous tense for customs and habits; use the simple present.)

Unit 8 183

Learner's Log

1. Have students close their books. Ask: *What did you learn about the U.S. Post Office and about drive-through windows? What else do you want to know?* Write students' ideas on the board. Discuss ways in which students can find out more about U.S. postal services and about drive-through windows.
2. Have students open their books to complete the Learner's Log. Remind students to write three questions about post offices or banks in the U.S.

Expansion Activities

These expansion activities provide opportunities for students to interact with one another and further develop their speaking and writing skills. Encourage students to use grammar from this unit whenever possible.

To save class time, assign parts of the activities as homework. Then use class time for interaction and communication. If students do not need additional speaking practice, some of the activities may be assigned as writing activities for homework, or skipped altogether.

WRITING ACTIVITY

Have students complete the activity individually at home or in class. Collect for assessment.

OUTSIDE ACTIVITIES

1. Have students share their experiences at the post office.
2. Ask students to compare post office prices with prices from other stores.
3. Ask volunteers to describe what they saw happening at the fast-food restaurant or drive-through.

INTERNET ACTIVITIES

Have students discuss their online research in groups. Then have volunteers tell the class how to open an online account, buy stamps, or send a package home.

LEARNER'S LOG

1. What did you learn in this unit? Write three sentences in your notebook about each topic.
   - U.S. post office services
   - Drive-through windows
2. Write three questions you still have about the post office or banks in the United States.

EXPANSION ACTIVITIES

Writing Activity

In your notebook, write five or six sentences about what is or isn't happening in the picture.

EXAMPLE *Simon is working on his computer. He isn't going to the post office today.*

Outside Activities

1. Go to a post office in your city. Bring a package to weigh. Ask how much it costs to send the package to your home country (you don't have to send it). If the post office has an automated postal center, use it to weigh the package and find the price.
2. Look for mailing supplies at the post office. Find out how much a small box or a large mailing envelope costs.
3. Go to a fast food restaurant in your neighborhood. Does it have a drive-through? Write some sentences about what is happening.

Internet Activities

1. Go to the Web site of a bank in your area. Find out how to open an online account.
2. Go to the United States Postal Service Web site (www.usps.gov). Find out how to buy stamps. Find out how to send a package to your country.

184 Unit 8

Expansion

Learner's Log Have students compare logs in pairs.

Writing Activity Variation

Have students exchange papers with a partner for proofreading.

Internet Activities Variation

Tell students that if they don't have Internet access, they can use Internet facilities at a public library. Alternatively, students can go to the local post office and get printed information about mailing letters and packages.

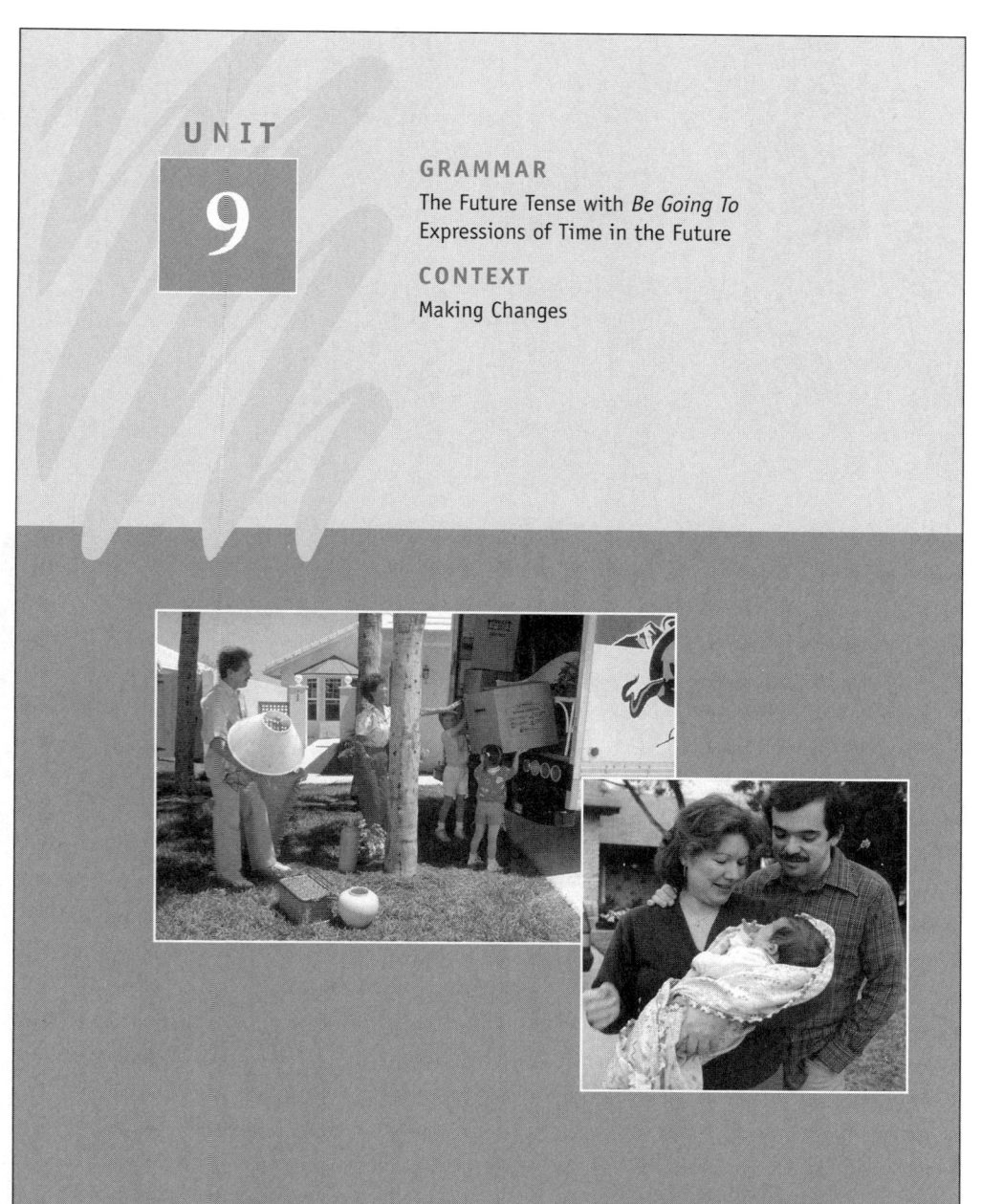

UNIT 9

GRAMMAR
The Future Tense with *Be Going To*
Expressions of Time in the Future

CONTEXT
Making Changes

Expansion

Theme The topic for this unit can be enhanced with the following ideas:
1. Mail order catalogues or store catalogues with baby equipment and baby accessories
2. Change of address forms from the post office

Unit | 9
Unit Overview

GRAMMAR

1. Briefly review the objectives for Unit 8. (the present continuous tense and time expressions) Say: *In Unit 9 we are going to study the future tense.* Write the unit objectives on the board: *The Future Tense with* Be Going To *and Expressions of Time in the Future.*
2. Say: Be going to *is future tense.* Be going *is present continuous tense.* Write these sentences on the board:
   1. John is going to go home.
   2. John is going home.
3. Ask: *When is he going home— now or later?* (In first sentence, later; in second sentence, now) Have students give additional examples of future tense sentences. Prompt by asking: *What are you going to do after school? When are you going to eat dinner?*

CONTEXT

1. Ask: *What's this unit about?* (making changes) *What big changes do people make?* Elicit examples. (e.g., going to college, moving to a new place, getting married, having a baby, changing jobs)
2. Direct students' attention to the photos. Ask: *What's happening in these two pictures?* (The family is moving to a new house and the couple is bringing home a new baby.)
3. Relate the topic to students' experience. Ask: *How many times have you moved? Do you have any children? Were these big changes?* Ask students to share their experiences.

Unit 9   185

Lesson 1 | Overview

GRAMMAR

Point out or write on the board the lesson's objectives. (*affirmative statements with* be going to, *negative statements with* be going to, *uses of the future tense with* be going to, *and expressions of time with* be going to. Say: *We use the future tense to talk about future events and to predict what will happen.* Write *to predict = to guess* on the board. Say and write on the board these example sentences: *They're going to have a baby. I think they're going to have a boy.* Ask: *Which sentence is a prediction?* Ask volunteers to give additional examples, and write them on the board. Prompt by asking questions about topics, such as moving, going to college, or other life changes.

CONTEXT

1. Ask: *What's this lesson about?* (getting ready for a baby) *How is your life going to change when you have a baby? What new things are you going to need?* Have students share their knowledge and experiences.
2. Direct students' attention to the picture of the resale shop of baby clothes and articles. Ask: *What's in this store?* (clothes and furniture for babies) Review some of the new words in the illustration.

BEFORE YOU READ

1. Go over each question as a class. Have a volunteer read the questions or read them to the class yourself. Have students discuss the questions in pairs.
2. Ask for a few volunteers to share their answers with the class.
   To save class time, skip "Before You Read," or have students prepare their answers for homework ahead of time.

LESSON 1

GRAMMAR

Affirmative Statements with *Be Going To*
Negative Statements with *Be Going To*
Uses of the Future Tense with *Be Going To*
Expressions of Time with *Be Going To*

CONTEXT

Getting Ready for a New Baby

Before You Read

1. What do parents have to buy for a new baby?
2. What changes in family life are necessary for a new baby?

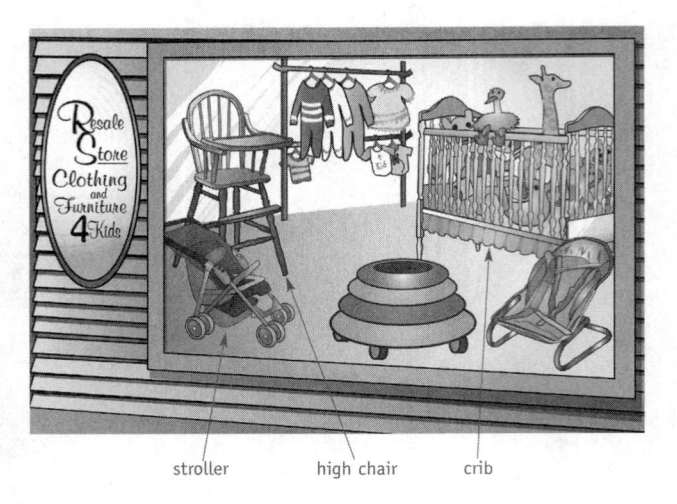

stroller   high chair   crib

186   Unit 9

Culture Note

Baby showers are small parties for new mothers usually given by a friend or relative one or two months before the baby is born. Guests bring gifts, such as baby clothing, blankets, and diapers, often chosen from the new mother's list at a department store. In the past, only women attended showers, but today men come, too.

GETTING READY FOR A NEW BABY

Shafia and her husband, Ali, **are going to have** a baby. Dorota and Halina are visiting Shafia. Ali is at work.

Shafia: My baby**'s going to arrive** in two months. I'm not ready.
Dorota: Let's see. You**'re going to need** a crib, a high chair, and a car seat.
Halina: You can use my daughter's crib. She's two now and she has a bigger bed. She**'s not going to need** the crib anymore.
Shafia: That's wonderful, Halina, thank you. I**'m not going to need** a car seat for a while. We don't have a car right now.
Dorota: Then you**'re going to need** a stroller to take the baby outside. There's a resale shop for kids in my neighborhood. You can get a high chair and a stroller there. Resale shops are not expensive.
Shafia: What's a resale shop, Dorota?
Dorota: It's a store with used items. People take their used clothing and furniture there. The shop sells them at a low price. The money often goes to a charity. Resale shops are very popular.
Shafia: That's a great idea. We can go on Thursday.
Dorota: That's fine. But don't buy too many clothes for the baby. People **are going to give** you gifts.
Shafia: You're right. We have a lot of relatives. We**'re not going to buy** too much.
Halina: You**'re** also **going to need** some help for the first weeks. New babies are a lot of work. And you**'re not going to get** much sleep.
Shafia: I know. My mother**'s going to help**. She**'s going to stay** with us for the first month. She's so excited. She**'s going to be** a grandmother for the first time.

Vocabulary in Context

used	This furniture is not new. It is **used**.
crib	Babies sleep in **cribs**.
stroller	You can take a baby for a walk in a **stroller**.
resale shop	We can buy good used items at a **resale shop**. Resale shops are sometimes called "thrift stores."
for a while	She's going to stay here **for a while**. I don't know how long.
furniture	She needs baby **furniture**: a bed and a high chair.
charity	She gives money to a **charity**. The charity helps sick children.
relative	She is my husband's sister. She is a **relative** of our family.
excited	We are **excited** about the baby. We are very happy.

Lesson 1   187

Reading Variation

1. To practice listening skills, have students listen to the audio before opening their books. Ask a few comprehension questions, such as: *How long is Shafia's mother going to stay with them?* (one month) *Is this her first grandchild?* (yes) Repeat the audio if necessary. Then have students open their books and read along as they listen to the audio.
2. Alternatively, have students begin by listening to the audio as they read along.

Expansion

Reading Have students practice the conversation in groups of three. Ask volunteers to roleplay all or part of the conversation in front of the class.

Vocabulary in Context To check comprehension, have volunteers in pairs or groups act out selected vocabulary, such as *crib*, *stroller*, and *excited*.

Getting Ready for Baby (Reading) CD 1, Track 45

1. Have students look at the title of the reading and the picture on page 186. Say: *Shafia is going to have a baby. What do you think she, Halina, and Dorota are talking about?* Have students use the title and picture to make predictions about the reading.
2. Have students read the dialogue silently. Then play the audio and have students read along silently.
3. Check students' basic comprehension. Ask questions, such as: *When is the baby going to arrive?* (in two months) *What is Halina going to give Shafia?* (a crib) *Why isn't Shafia going to buy a lot of things?* (She's going to get a lot of gifts because she and Ali have a lot of relatives.)

To save class time, have students do the reading for homework ahead of time.

VOCABULARY IN CONTEXT

1. Model the pronunciation of each new vocabulary word and have students repeat.
2. Make sure students understand the meaning of each vocabulary item. Review the examples in the book and create additional example sentences. For example, say: *used.* (Hold up a used book.) Say: *You can buy used books in the book store. They're cheaper.* Go over each new vocabulary word similarly, using visuals and realia when appropriate. When possible, point to pictures in the book that illustrate the new vocabulary items, such as *crib, furniture, stroller,* and *resale shop* on page 186.
3. Have students underline an example of each new vocabulary item in the reading.

Unit 9   187

DID YOU KNOW?

Explain to students that fewer girls are being born in the U.S. today. As a result, there will be fewer American women having children in the future.

LISTENING ACTIVITY

🎧 *CD 1, Track 46*

1. Say: *Listen to the sentences about the reading. Circle* true *or* false. Play the listening selection one time without pausing. Then play it through again, pausing and replaying as necessary.
2. Go over the answers as a class. Ask students to volunteer answers.

9.1 | Affirmative Statements with *Be Going To*

1. Have students look at grammar chart **9.1** on page 188. Review word order for affirmative statements. Say: *Put* be going to *before the verb.* Point out that the verb after *be going to* is in the base form. Go over the examples. Write the following on the board, and have students unscramble the parts and make a correct statement:

   a stroller / is / She / buy / going to

2. Point out the Language Notes. Say: *Use contractions with* be going to. Remind students that they have already learned contractions with *be*. Ask: *Can you contract a plural subject +* are? (no) Model the relaxed pronunciation of *going to*.

Did You Know? In the U.S., women between the ages of 20 and 30 have fewer babies today than in past years. But women between the ages of 35 and 44 have more.

🎧 **Listening Activity** Listen to the sentences about the conversation. Circle *true* or *false*.

EXAMPLE TRUE (FALSE)

1. TRUE (FALSE)   5. (TRUE) FALSE
2. (TRUE) FALSE   6. TRUE (FALSE)
3. (TRUE) FALSE   7. (TRUE) FALSE
4. TRUE (FALSE)   8. (TRUE) FALSE

9.1 | Affirmative Statements with *Be Going To*

Subject	Be	Going To	Verb (Base Form)	Complement
I	am	going to	need	some help.
My mother	is	going to	help	me.
We	are	going to	have	a baby.
You	are	going to	give	us a crib.
They	are	going to	buy	a used high chair.
My relatives	are	going to	give	us gifts.
There	is	going to	be	a change in Shafia's life.

Language Notes:
1. We can make contractions with the subject + *be*.
   I'm going to need some help.
   My **mother's** going to help me.
   They're going to buy us a gift.
   There's going to be a new resale shop in this area.
2. We don't make a contraction with a plural subject + *are*.
   My relatives **are** going to give us gifts.
3. In normal speech, we pronounce *going to* / gənə /. Listen to your teacher pronounce the sentences in the chart above.

188   Unit 9

Expansion

Grammar Chart Have students work in pairs to practice saying the sentences in the chart with relaxed pronunciation. Then have students think about the following situations:

meeting with a teacher
speaking to a close friend or parent
shopping at a supermarket
buying an expensive item, such as a Porsche or new home
asking questions at an art museum
taking a driving test for a license

Have students decide if they should use *gonna* or *going to* in each of these situations.

---

188   *Grammar in Context Basic* Teacher's Edition

EXERCISE 1 Fill in the blanks with the affirmative of the verb in parentheses ( ). Use the future tense with *be going to*.

EXAMPLE She <u>'s going to get</u> some things for the baby.
(get)

1. Halina and Dorota <u>are going to see</u> Shafia again on Thursday.
(see)
2. Shafia's mother <u>'s going to help</u> her with the new baby.
(help)
3. The new baby <u>'s going to arrive</u> soon.
(arrive)
4. Shafia's relatives <u>are going to bring</u> a lot of gifts for the baby.
(bring)
5. Halina and Dorota <u>are going to take</u> Shafia to the resale shop.
(take)
6. Shafia <u>'s going to need</u> a stroller for the baby.
(need)
7. Shafia and Ali <u>are going to be</u> parents for the first time.
(be)
8. With the help of her friends, Shafia <u>'s going to be</u> ready for the baby.
(be)

9.2 | Negative Statements with *Be Going To*

Subject	Form of *Be* + *Not*	Going To	Verb (Base Form)	Complement
I	am not	going to	need	help.
My father	is not	going to	help	me.
We	are not	going to	have	a boy.
You	are not	going to	give	us a stroller.
Those people	are not	going to	buy	us a gift.
There	are not	going to	be	many people at the shop.

Language Notes:
1. We can make contractions with negative forms of *be*.
   I'm not going to need help.
   My **father's not** going to help me.
   You **aren't** going to give us a stroller.
   There **isn't** going to be time to shop today.
2. We don't use a contraction with a plural noun + *are*.
   Those people **aren't** going to give us a gift.

Lesson 1 189

EXERCISE 1
1. Have students read the direction line. Go over the example in the Student Book. Remind students to use contractions when possible.
2. Have students complete Exercise 1 individually. Check the answers as a class.
3. If necessary, review grammar chart 9.1 on page 188.

9.2 | Negative Statements with *Be Going To*

1. Have students look at grammar chart 9.2 on page 189. Say: *To make negative statements write not after the verb* be.
2. Point out the Language Notes. Say: *We use contractions with negative forms of* be. Go over the examples. Ask: *What are the two ways to make contractions with negative forms of* be? (subject + *be*, *be* + *not*). Review the examples in the book. Then write additional examples on the board. (e.g., *My friend's not going to go to school tomorrow. My friend isn't going to go to school tomorrow.*) Have students identify the type of contraction in each example. Remind students not to use contractions with plural nouns and *are*.

Expansion
Grammar Chart Have students change the sentences in Exercise 1 to negative statements. Ask students to use both forms of contractions where possible. (e.g., for #2: *Shafia's mother's not going to help her with the baby. / Shafia's mother isn't going to help her with the baby.*)

Unit 9 189

EXERCISE 2

1. Have students read the direction line. Review the example in the Student Book.
2. Have students complete Exercise 2 individually. Then have students compare answers in pairs. Circulate to observe pair work. Give help as needed.
3. If necessary, review grammar chart 9.2 on page 189.

9.3 | Uses of the Future Tense with *Be Going To*

1. Have students look at grammar chart 9.3 on page 190. Say the title of the chart. Then say and write on the board:

   Two Uses:
   1. future plans
   2. predictions

   Review the examples in the chart.

   Give students the following situations and have them make three predictions with *be going to* for each situation:

   She is late today.
   He's at the bank now.

2. Point out the Language Note. Say: Going to go is *often shortened to just* going to. Go over the example and provide additional examples. (e.g., *I'm going to go to Boston next week. I'm going to Boston next week.*) Ask volunteers for additional examples.

EXERCISE 3

1. Have students read the direction line. Go over the example. Remind students to use contractions whenever possible.
2. Have students complete Exercise 3 individually. Check answers with the class.
3. If necessary, review grammar chart 9.3 on page 190.

EXERCISE 2 Fill in the blanks with the negative form of *be going to*. Use the verbs in parentheses ( ). Use contractions where possible.

EXAMPLE Shafia __isn't going to buy__ a lot of baby clothes.
(buy)

1. With a new baby, Shafia and Ali __aren't going to get__ a lot of sleep.
(get)
2. Shafia's mother __isn't going to stay__ a year.
(stay)
3. Shafia __isn't going to need__ a car seat for a while.
(need)
4. Dorota, Halina, and Shafia __aren't going to shop__ at the resale store today.
(shop)
5. There __isn't going to be__ enough space for all the baby furniture in their apartment.
(be)
6. Relatives __aren't going to give__ Shafia a crib.
(give)
7. The resale shop __isn't going to be__ open on Sunday.
(be)
8. Shafia __isn't going to buy__ a lot of baby clothes.
(buy)
9. Ali __isn't going to take__ Shafia to the resale shop.
(take)

9.3 | Uses of the Future Tense with *Be Going To*

Examples	Explanation
Shafia**'s going to buy** some things for the baby.	We use *be going to* with future plans.
You**'re not going to get** much sleep.	We use *be going to* with predictions for the future.
Language Note: We often shorten *going to go* to *going to*. We're **going to** the resale shop next week.	

EXERCISE 3 Fill in the blanks with the affirmative or negative form of *be going to* and the verb in parentheses ( ). Use the ideas from the conversation.

EXAMPLE Halina and Dorota __are going to help__ Shafia.
(help)

1. Shafia __isn't going to buy__ a crib.
(buy)
2. Shafia's mother __'s going to be__ a grandmother.
(be)

190 Unit 9

Expansion

Grammar Chart Have students work in pairs to write about future plans. Say and write the following model sentence on the board: *I'm going to a baby shower next week.*

---

190 *Grammar in Context Basic* Teacher's Edition

3. Halina __isn't going to give__ Shafia a car seat.
   (give)
4. Shafia __'s going to get__ a high chair at the resale shop.
   (get)
5. Shafia, Halina, and Dorota __are going to go__ to the resale shop on Thursday.
   (go)
6. Shafia's baby __'s going to arrive__ in two months.
   (arrive)
7. There __'s going to be__ a new person in Shafia's house.
   (be)
8. The new baby __'s going to get__ a lot of gifts.
   (get)
9. There __are going to be__ many changes in Shafia and Ali's house.
   (be)

9.4 | Expressions of Time with *Be Going To*

Time expressions in the future can go at the beginning or end of the sentence. Learn the prepositions with each expression of time.

Examples	Explanation
She's going to visit me **in** two weeks. **In** two weeks, she's going to visit me. She's going to visit me **in** January. They're going to visit **in** 2010.	We use *in* with numbers of days, weeks, months, or years in the future. It means **after**. We use *in* with names of months or years.
I'm going to visit you **on** January 12.	We use *on* with dates.
On Thursday, I'm going shopping. I'm going shopping **this** Thursday.	We use *on* or *this* with names of days. **This** means a future day in a present week.
I'm going to get some new clothes **this** week.	We use *this* with future time in the same week, month, or year.
Tomorrow I can help you. I can't help you **tonight**.	We use *tomorrow* for the day after today. *Tonight* means this night.
They're going to visit us **next week**.	We use *next* with weeks, months, or years after the present week, month, or year.
She's going to stay with us **for a while**.	*For a while* means for an indefinite amount of time.
She's going to live here **for** a month.	We use *for* with a specific amount of time.
We're going to see our relatives **soon**.	We use *soon* for a near future time that is not specific.

Lesson 1   191

9.4 | Expressions of Time with *Be Going To*

1. Have students look at grammar chart 9.4 on page 191. Say: *Time expressions can go at the beginning or end of the sentence.* Point out the prepositions in the time expressions. (*in*, *on*, and *for*) Go over the examples and explanations.
2. Say the following rules. Ask the class to name the appropriate time expressions:

   with a date (on)
   with names of months (in)
   with a specific amount of time (for)
   for the day after today (tomorrow)
   with names of days (on/this)

3. Write the answers on the board. Add *soon* and *for a while*. Ask volunteers to make sentences with the expressions.

Expansion

Grammar Chart Have students write five sentences that are true for them using the time expressions in the chart.

Unit 9   191

EXERCISE 4

1. Have students read the direction line. Review the example.
2. Have students complete Exercise 4 individually. Go over the answers with the class.
3. If necessary, review grammar chart 9.4 on page 191.

EXERCISE 5

1. Say: *You're going to write about what is true for you.* Have students read the direction line. Go over the example.
2. Have students complete Exercise 5 individually. Then have students compare answers in pairs. Circulate to observe pair work. Give help as needed.
3. If necessary, review grammar chart 9.4 on page 191.

  To save class time, have students complete the exercise for homework ahead of time.

EXERCISE 4 Fill in the blanks with the correct preposition for each expression of time.

EXAMPLE I'm going to be 23 years old ___on___ February 16.

1. Shafia's going to have her baby ___in___ two months.
2. Shafia's going to visit the resale shop ___next___ week.
3. Shafia and Ali are going to stay in their apartment ___for___ a while.
4. Shafia's mother is going to stay ___for___ a month.
5. We're going to take a vacation ___in___ August.
6. I'm going to do the laundry ___on___ Saturday.
7. He's going to go back to his country ___in___ 2020.
8. Their relatives are going to arrive ___on___ September 22.

EXERCISE 5 ABOUT YOU Write a sentence about your future plans. Use the verbs given in the future with *be going to*. Use an expression of time.

EXAMPLE have dinner with my Mom
I'm going to have dinner with my Mom next Sunday.

1. do my homework for this class
   _____Answers will vary._____
2. get a (different) job
3. finish this book
4. go to the supermarket
5. come to English class again
6. have a test in this class
7. use a computer

192 Unit 9

Expansion

Exercise 5 Have students tell their partner three more things that they are going to do in the future. (e.g., I'm going to go to the movies with friends on Saturday. / I'm going to the movies with friends on Saturday.)

8. go to my next class

9. speak English very well

EXERCISE 6 ABOUT YOU Make predictions about your future. Think about your life in ten years. Use the verbs given in the affirmative or negative with *be going to*. Add information where possible.

EXAMPLE live in an apartment
In ten years, I'm not going to live in an apartment.
I'm going to have a house.

1. live in this city
   Answers will vary.

2. be a student

3. work in an office

4. have a big family

5. be a U.S. citizen

6. forget my language

Lesson 1 193

Exercise 6 Variation
Have students make predictions about a friend or family member's life in ten years.

Expansion
Exercise 6 Survey the class. What are students' predictions for their future? Write the results on the board.

EXERCISE 6

1. Point out the picture of the man on page 193. Ask: *What is this man doing? What do you think he is going to be in the future?* (a doctor) Say: *Now you're going to make predictions about your future.* Have students read the direction line. Go over the example.
2. Have students complete Exercise 6 individually. Then have students compare answers in pairs. Circulate to observe pair work. Give help as needed.
3. If necessary, review grammar chart **9.4** on page 191.

To save class time, have students complete the exercise for homework ahead of time.

Unit 9 193

EXERCISE 7

1. Tell students they are going to complete two conversations. Point out the picture of Halina and Shafia. Ask: *What do you think they're talking about?* (the baby's room) Have students read the direction line. Have a volunteer complete #1 in Conversation 1.
2. Have students complete both conversations in Exercise 7 individually. Then have students compare answers in pairs. Circulate to observe pair work. Give help as needed.
3. If necessary, review grammar chart **9.1** on page 188 and **9.2** on page 189. To save class time, have students complete the exercise for homework ahead of time.

---

7. return to my country to live
   _____
   _____

8. have a different car
   _____
   _____

EXERCISE 7 Complete the conversations. Use the verbs given in the affirmative or negative with *be going to*.

Conversation A:
Halina and Shafia are talking about the new baby's room.

Halina: Where is the new baby's room?

Shafia: We have an extra room. It's small. But there __is going to be__ (example: be) enough space for a crib.

Halina: What's in the room now?

Shafia: There's a desk and a computer. But we __aren't going to keep__ (1. keep) them there. Ali __'s going to move__ (2. move) them to the living room next month. His brother __'s going to help__ (3. help) him. The desk is very heavy.

Halina: What about the color of the walls?

Shafia: We __'re going to paint__ (4. paint) the room pink. But not now. There's __not going to be__ (5. be) enough time.

194   Unit 9

Exercise 7 Variation
Have students complete the first dialogue as a conversation about a different situation, such as making room for a guest, a boarder, or new pet.

---

194   *Grammar in Context Basic* Teacher's Edition

Conversation B:

Halina, Dorota, and Shafia are talking about the baby's name.

Halina: Shafia, do you have a name for the baby?

Shafia: No. Ali and I <u>are going to choose</u> a name later. We
(1. choose)
<u>'re not going to hurry</u>. It's very important to choose the right
(2. hurry)
name. After the baby's birth, we <u>'re going to ask</u> some of
(3. ask)
our relatives for ideas.

Dorota: There are long lists of names on the Web. Just search "baby names." You can even find the meaning of each name.

Shafia: That's interesting. But the baby <u>isn't going to have</u> an
(4. have)
American name. We <u>'re going to give</u> the baby a name
(5. give)
from our country.

Dorota: There are names from other countries on the Web too. There are thousands of names for boys and girls.

Shafia: Thanks, Dorota. But we <u>'re going to wait</u> to see the baby
(6. wait)
first.

Lesson 1 195

Expansion

Exercise 7 Have students practice the conversations in pairs. Ask volunteers to roleplay the conversations in front of the class.

Unit **9**   **195**

Lesson 2 | Overview

GRAMMAR

1. Say: *In Lesson 1, we studied the future tense and time expressions with* be going to. Write the objective for Lesson 2 on the board: *Yes/No Questions with* Be Going To, *Information Questions with* Be Going To, *Questions with* How Long *and* Be Going To, *and Subject Questions with* Be Going To.
2. Write this statement on the board: *Hui is going to be a doctor.* As a class, make each type of question for the statement. (e.g., Is he going to be a doctor? Why is he going to be a doctor? How long is he going to be in medical school? Who is going to be a doctor?)

CONTEXT

1. Take a quick survey of the class. Ask: *How many times do people usually move? I have moved [number of times] in the last ten years. It's a lot of work to move!*
2. Direct students' attention to the picture of Simon and Victor on page 196. Go over new vocabulary in the picture. Ask: *What are Victor and Simon doing?* (Victor is moving. Simon is helping him.) Point to the change of address card. Ask: *What do you write on this card?* (your old address and your new address)

BEFORE YOU READ

1. Go over each question as a class. Have a volunteer read the questions or read them to the class yourself. Have students answer the questions in pairs.
2. Ask for a few volunteers to share their answers with the class.

To save class time, skip "Before You Read," or have students prepare their answers for homework ahead of time.

LESSON 2

GRAMMAR

Yes/No Questions with *Be Going To*
Information Questions with *Be Going To*
Questions with *How Long* and *Be Going To*
Subject Questions with *Be Going To*

CONTEXT

Moving to a New Apartment

Before You Read
1. Are you going to move soon? Why or why not?
2. How do people prepare for a move?

196   Unit 9

Culture Note

Many Americans use professional movers who supply boxes, pack the contents of the house or apartment, and transport the belongings to the new address. Others rent trucks and pack their own belongings.

---

196   *Grammar in Context Basic* Teacher's Edition

MOVING TO A NEW APARTMENT

Victor: I'm going to move in two weeks. There's so much to do!
Simon: You're right. **Are you going to hire** a mover?
Victor: No, I'm not. I'm going to rent a truck. We don't have a lot of things. But I'm going to need some help. **Are you going to be** available on the 25th of this month?
Simon: Sure. I can help you.
Victor: Thanks, Simon. What should I do about my mail?
Simon: You can fill out a change-of-address card at the post office. Or, you can fill it out online. It's easy to do. The post office sends your mail to your new address for one year.
Victor: **What's going to happen** with my phone?
Simon: You have to call the phone company. **Is your new apartment going to be** in the same neighborhood?
Victor: Yes, it is. Why?
Simon: Then you can probably keep the same phone number.
Victor: That's good. **How long is it going to take** for the new service?
Simon: You can usually get it on the same day. There's a fee to change phone service from one place to another. But it's not usually more than $50.
Simon: **When are you going to pack? Are you going to need** boxes?
Victor: I'm starting to pack now. I have some boxes, but not enough.
Simon: Go to some stores in your neighborhood. You can ask them for their old boxes.
Victor: That's a good idea. I also have a lot of old things. **What am I going to do** with them? I don't want to move them.
Simon: You can give them to charity. There's a resale shop in this neighborhood.

Vocabulary in Context

move	Our apartment is too small. We're going to **move** to a bigger apartment.
mover	A **mover** can help you move things from one building to another.
hire	He isn't going to **hire** movers. He doesn't want to pay money to move.
pack	I'm going to **pack** my things. I'm going to put them in boxes.
truck	You can move all your furniture in a moving **truck**.
rent	I can **rent** a truck for one day. It's not expensive.
neighborhood	Victor is moving close to his old apartment. His new apartment is in the same **neighborhood**.
fee	He pays a **fee** for service.

Lesson 2   197

Moving to a New Apartment (Reading)

CD 1, Track 47

1. Have students look at the title of the reading and the picture on page 196. Say: *Victor is moving. He asks Simon lots of questions. What does he want to know? Skim the reading and find out.* (Is Simon going to be available to help? What should he do about his mail? What's going to happen with his phone? What should he do with the things he doesn't want?)
2. Have students read the dialogue silently. Then play the audio and have students read along silently.
3. Check students' basic comprehension. Ask questions, such as: *Who is moving?* (Victor) *When is he going to move?* (in two weeks) *Who is going to help him?* (Simon) *Where is Victor's new apartment going to be?* (in the same neighborhood) *Is he going to have the same phone number?* (yes, probably.) *Does Victor have boxes?* (Yes, but he doesn't have enough.) *Where is he going to get more boxes?* (at some stores in the neighborhood)

To save class time, have students do the reading for homework ahead of time.

VOCABULARY IN CONTEXT

1. Model the pronunciation of each new vocabulary word and have students repeat.
2. Make sure students understand the meaning of each vocabulary word. Review the examples in the book and create additional example sentences. For example, say: *move. We're going to move to a new classroom next semester.* Review each new vocabulary word similarly, using visuals and realia when appropriate. When possible, point to pictures in the book that illustrate the new vocabulary items, such as *pack* on page 196.
3. Have students underline an example of each new vocabulary item in the reading.

Reading Variation

1. To practice listening skills, have students listen to the audio before opening their books. Ask a few comprehension questions, such as: *What can Victor do with his old things?* (give them to charity) Repeat the audio if necessary. Then have students open their books and read along as they listen to the audio.
2. Alternatively, have students begin by listening to the audio as they read along.

Expansion

Reading Have students practice the conversation in groups. Ask volunteers to roleplay all or part of the conversation in front of the class.

Vocabulary in Context To check comprehension, have volunteers in pairs or groups act out selected vocabulary, such as *move, mover, hire,* and *pack*.

DID YOU KNOW?

Tell students some reasons why Americans might be moving less:

- More people commute.
- More people buy houses.
- More husbands and wives have careers that make moving difficult.

LISTENING ACTIVITY

🎧 **CD 1, Track 48**

1. Say: *Listen to the sentences about Victor and Simon's conversation. Circle true or false.* Play the listening selection one without pausing. Then play it through again, pausing and replaying as necessary.
2. Go over the answers as a class. Ask students to volunteer answers.

9.5 | *Yes/No* Questions with *Be Going To*

1. Have students look at grammar chart **9.5** on page 198. Say: *To form yes/no questions with* be going to, *put the subject after* be *and before* going to. *The verb in the base form follows* going to. Go over the examples.
2. Say: *The short answer contains just the subject and* be. *Do not include the verb in the short answer.* Review the short answers.

Did You Know? Many Americans move every year. But the number is going down. Only 14 percent of Americans moved in 2003. It was the lowest number since 1948.

🎧 **Listening Activity** Listen to the sentences about the conversation. Circle *true* or *false*.

EXAMPLE (TRUE)   FALSE

1. TRUE   (FALSE)
2. (TRUE) FALSE
3. (TRUE) FALSE
4. TRUE   (FALSE)
5. (TRUE) FALSE
6. TRUE   (FALSE)
7. TRUE   (FALSE)

9.5 | *Yes/No* Questions with *Be Going To*

Be	Subject	Going To	Verb (Base Form)	Complement	Short Answer
Am	I	going to	need	a change of address form?	Yes, you are.
Is	Victor	going to	move	out of town?	No, he isn't.
Are	we	going to	get	a new phone number?	No, you aren't.
Are	Victor and Lisa	going to	hire	a moving company?	No, they aren't.
Is	there	going to	be	a fee?	Yes, there is.
Are	there	going to	be	any problems?	Yes, there are.

198   Unit 9

Expansion

Grammar Chart Have students practice the questions and short answers in the chart with a partner.

EXERCISE 1 Write *yes/no* questions about Victor and Simon's conversation. Use *be going to* and the words given. Give a short answer.

EXAMPLE Victor / move soon

Is Victor going to move soon? Yes, he is.

1. Victor / rent a truck
   Is Victor going to rent a truck? Yes, he is.
2. Victor / buy some boxes
   Is Victor going to buy some boxes? No, he isn't. OR No, he's not.
3. Victor's new apartment / be in his old neighborhood
   Is Victor's new apartment going to be in his old neighborhood? Yes, it is.
4. Victor / change his phone number
   Is Victor going to change his phone number? No, he isn't. OR No, he's not.
5. it / take a long time to get new phone service
   Is it going to take a long time to get new phone service? No, it isn't. OR No, it's not.
6. the post office / send Victor's mail to his new address
   Is the post office going to send Victor's mail to his new address? Yes, it is.
7. there / be / a fee to change phone service
   Is there going to be a fee to change phone service? Yes, there is.
8. Victor / move / all his things
   Is Victor going to move all his things? No, he isn't. OR No, he's not.

EXERCISE 2 Complete the short conversations. Write a *yes/no* question with *be going to*. Use the words in parentheses ( ).

EXAMPLE A: We're going to move.
B: Are you going to move this week?
   (this week)

1. A: I'm going to change my address.
   B: Are you going to change your phone number too?
      (your phone number too)
2. A: He's going to pay for that service.
   B: Is he going to pay more than $50?
      (more than $50)

Lesson 2 199

EXERCISE 1

1. Have students read the direction line. Go over the example in the Student Book.
2. Have students complete Exercise 1 individually. Go over the answers as a class.
3. If necessary, review grammar chart **9.5** on page 198.

EXERCISE 2

1. Have students read the direction line. Go over the example in the book. Have two volunteers model #1.
2. Have students complete the rest of Exercise 2 individually. Then have students compare answers. Circulate to observe pair work. Give help as needed.
3. If necessary, review grammar chart **9.5** on page 198.

   To save class time, have students do the exercise for homework ahead of time.

Expansion

Exercise 2 Have students practice the short dialogues in pairs.

9.6 | Information Questions with *Be Going To*

1. Have students look at grammar chart **9.6** on page 200. Say: *Information questions begin with a question word followed by* be *plus the subject plus* going to *plus the verb in the base form.* Go over the examples.
2. Say: *The short answer does not include the subject or the verb.* Compare: *We're going to hire the movers next week. Next week.* Go over the other short answers in the chart.
3. Have students close their books. Write the following phrases on the board:
   When he move to California
   Why Mi Son buy a new car
   How many there be
4. Ask volunteers to come to the board and write complete questions with *be going to* with the phrases.

---

3. A: They're going to move.
   B: _Are they going to move to a new house?_
   (to a house)
4. A: We're going to visit our relatives.
   B: _Are you going to visit your relatives on Saturday?_
   (on Saturday)
5. A: She's going to get some used furniture.
   B: _Is she going to get some used clothing too?_
   (used clothing too)
6. A: I'm going to look for a new apartment.
   B: _Are you going to look for a new apartment in this same neighborhood?_
   (in this same neighborhood)
7. A: Victor's going to fill out a change-of-address card.
   B: _Is he going to fill out a change-of-address card online?_
   (online)

9.6 | Information Questions with *Be Going To*

Question Word	Be	Subject	Going To	Verb (Base Form) + Complement	Short Answer
Why	are	you	going to	move?	Because I need a bigger apartment.
Where	is	she	going to	live?	In California.
Who	is	he	going to	hire?	Ace Moving Company.
When	are	they	going to	hire the movers?	Next week.
How much	are	they	going to	pay them?	About $500.
How many boxes	are	there	going to	be?	Maybe 50 or more.
What kind of fee	is	there	going to	be?	A service fee of $50.

200 Unit 9

Expansion
Grammar Chart Have students write out the long answer for each question.

EXERCISE 3 Ask an information question about each statement. Use the question words in parentheses ( ).

EXAMPLE A: He's going to fill out a change-of-address card. (Where)
B: _Where is he going to fill it out?_

1. A: She's going to hire movers. (How many)
   B: _How many movers is she going to hire?_
2. A: I'm going to get a new phone. (What kind of)
   B: _What kind of phone are you going to get?_
3. A: There are going to be some problems. (What kind of)
   B: _What kind of problems are there going to be?_
4. A: Her relatives are going to come here. (Why)
   B: _Why are her relatives going to come here?_
5. A: You're going to pay a lot for this service. (How much)
   B: _How much am I going to pay for this service?_
6. A: He's going to talk to someone about a new apartment. (Who)
   B: _Who is he going to talk to about a new apartment?_
7. A: They're going to help you. (How)
   B: _How are they going to help me?_
8. A: We're going to change our phone service. (When)
   B: _When are you going to change your phone service?_

Lesson 2   201

EXERCISE 3

1. Have students read the direction line. Go over the example in the Student Book. Have a volunteer do #1.
2. Have students complete the rest of Exercise 3 individually. Go over the answers as a class.
3. If necessary, review grammar chart **9.6** on page 200.

Expansion

Exercise 3 Have students practice asking and answering the questions from Exercise 3 with a partner.

Unit 9   201

EXERCISE 4

1. Have students read the direction line. Go over the example in the Student Book. Have a volunteer do #1.
2. Have students complete the rest of Exercise 4 individually. Then have students compare answers with a partner. Circulate to observe pair work. Give help as needed.
3. If necessary, review grammar chart 9.6 on page 200.

🕐 To save class time, have students do the exercise for homework ahead of time.

9.7 | Questions with *How Long* and *Be Going To*

Have students look at grammar chart 9.7 on page 202. Say: *We use* How Long *to ask about specific times. When we answer with a specific time we use* until *and* for. Until *means up to or before a particular time.* Review the examples and the explanations. Have students give additional example questions and answers. Prompt by writing on the board topics, such as *be in the U.S., study at this school,* and *be at work today.* Ask two volunteers to make questions and answers.

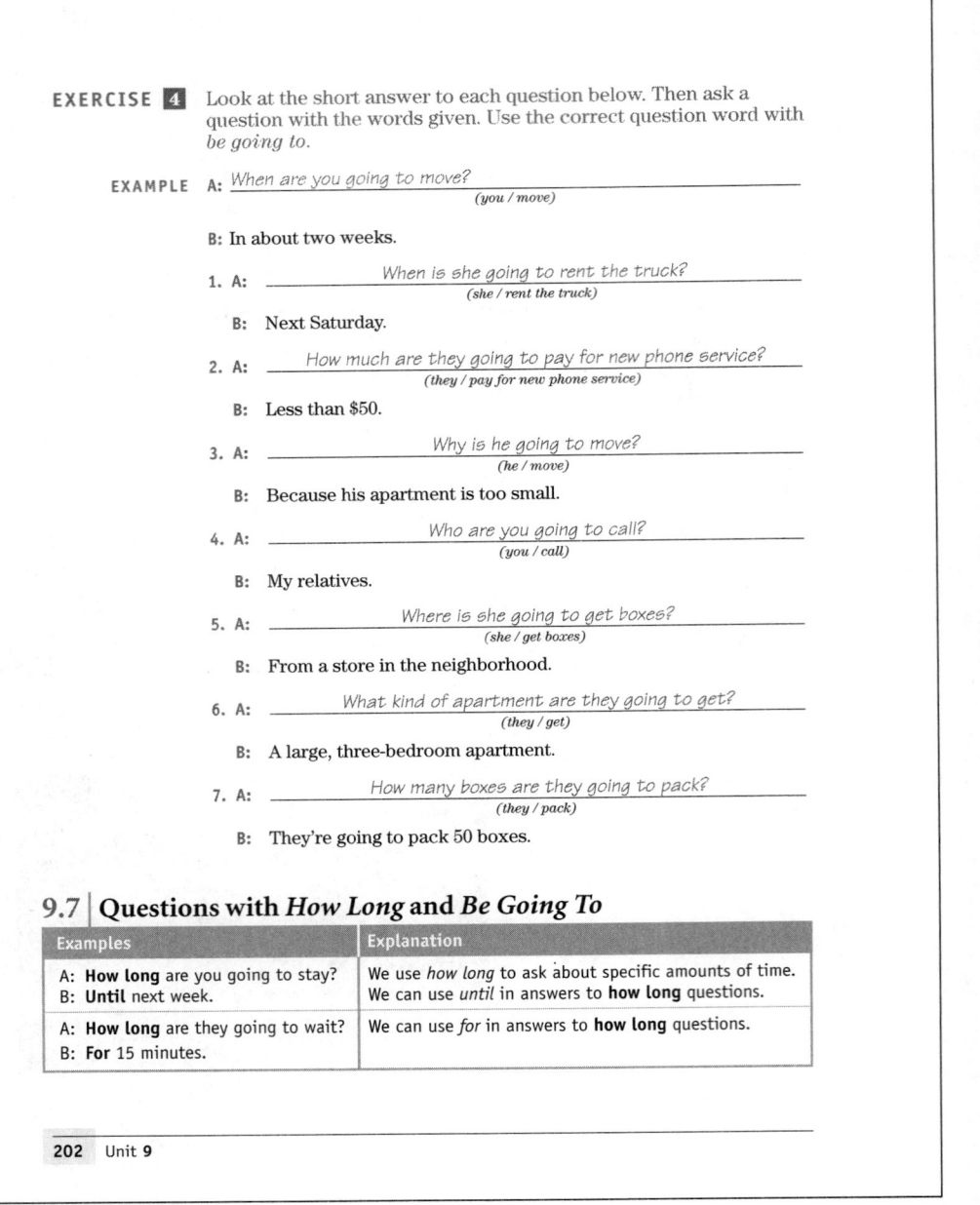

EXERCISE 4 Look at the short answer to each question below. Then ask a question with the words given. Use the correct question word with *be going to*.

EXAMPLE A: When are you going to move?
(you / move)
B: In about two weeks.

1. A: When is she going to rent the truck?
(she / rent the truck)
B: Next Saturday.

2. A: How much are they going to pay for new phone service?
(they / pay for new phone service)
B: Less than $50.

3. A: Why is he going to move?
(he / move)
B: Because his apartment is too small.

4. A: Who are you going to call?
(you / call)
B: My relatives.

5. A: Where is she going to get boxes?
(she / get boxes)
B: From a store in the neighborhood.

6. A: What kind of apartment are they going to get?
(they / get)
B: A large, three-bedroom apartment.

7. A: How many boxes are they going to pack?
(they / pack)
B: They're going to pack 50 boxes.

9.7 | Questions with *How Long* and *Be Going To*

Examples	Explanation
A: **How long** are you going to stay? B: **Until** next week.	We use *how long* to ask about specific amounts of time. We can use *until* in answers to **how long** questions.
A: **How long** are they going to wait? B: **For** 15 minutes.	We can use *for* in answers to **how long** questions.

202 Unit 9

Expansion

Exercise 4 Have students practice asking and answering the questions with another partner.

Have students take turns making up short answers and questions. Ask a student to make up an answer and have the class make up the question for the answer.

EXERCISE 5 ABOUT YOU Ask your partner a question with *How long* for each statement given. Your partner can give an answer with *for* or *until*. Write the questions and answers.

EXAMPLE you / be in this course

How long are you going to be in this course?

I'm going to be in this course until the end of the semester.

1. we / work on this exercise

   How long are we going to work on this exercise?
   Answers will vary.

2. we / use this book

   How long are we going to use this book?
   Answers will vary.

3. you / stay at school today

   How long are you going to stay at school today?
   Answers will vary.

4. you / work today

   How long are you going to work today?
   Answers will vary.

5. this school / be open today

   How long is this school going to be open today?
   Answers will vary.

6. you / watch TV tonight

   How long are you going to watch TV tonight?
   Answers will vary.

Lesson 2

EXERCISE 5

1. Point to the photo on page 203. Ask: *How long is she going to watch TV?* (for a while, until the next program comes on) Then say: *Now you're going to ask and answer questions with a partner about how long you do something.* Have students read the direction line. Go over the example in the Student Book. Have volunteers model the example.
2. Have students first write only the questions to Exercise 5 individually. Then have them ask their partner the questions. Circulate to observe pair work. Give help as needed.
3. If necessary, review grammar chart 9.7 on page 202.

Expansion

Exercise 5 Have students write three more questions to ask their partner.

9.8 | Subject Questions with *Be Going To*

1. Have students look at grammar chart **9.8** on page 204. Ask: *What is the subject of these questions?* (a question word) Say: *To form the question, write the question word or phrase plus the verb be plus going to plus the verb in the base form.* Write on the board:

    ? word + be + going to + *verb* + *complement*

    Review the examples and the short answers.

2. Have students write a question using the formula on the board. Then have several students share their questions with the class.

EXERCISE 6

1. Have students read the direction line. Go over the example.
2. Have students complete Exercise 6 individually. Then go over the answers with the class.
3. If necessary, review grammar chart **9.8** on page 204.

9.8 | Subject Questions with *Be Going To*

Question Word (Subject)	Be	Going To	Verb (Base Form)	Complement	Short Answer
Who	is	going to	move?		Victor is.
How many friends	are	going to	help	Victor?	Two.
What kind of people	are	going to	work	with you?	Young people.
Which services	are	going to	change?		Only the phone service.
What	is	going to	happen?		I'm going to move!

EXERCISE 6 Write an information question for each statement. Use the question word in parentheses ( ) as a subject.

EXAMPLE Somebody is going to visit me. (Who)
Who is going to visit you?

1. Something is going to change. (What)
   What is going to change?
2. Many people are going to move this year. (How many)
   How many people are going to move this year?
3. Some services are going to be expensive. (Which)
   Which services are going to be expensive?
4. Somebody is going to give me some boxes. (Who)
   Who is going to give you some boxes?
5. Something is going to happen on Thursday. (What)
   What is going to happen on Thursday?
6. A moving company is going to help me. (Which)
   Which moving company is going to help you?
7. Some apartments are going to be available. (What kind of)
   What kind of apartments are going to be available?

Expansion

Exercise 6 Have students practice saying the statements and asking the questions in pairs.

EXERCISE 7 Victor is calling a truck rental company. He wants to rent a truck for his move. Complete Victor's conversation using yes/no and information questions with *be going to*. Use the words in parentheses ( ).

Clerk: Avery Truck Rental. How can I help you?

Victor: I need to rent a truck. I'm going to move, and I'm checking prices.

Clerk: <u>Are you going to use</u> the truck in the city or out of town?
(example: you / use)

Victor: Here in the city.

Clerk: O.K. <u>What kind of truck are you going to need</u>?
(1. what kind of truck / you / need)

Victor: I don't know.

Clerk: Well, <u>how many rooms are you going to move</u>?
(2. how many rooms / you / move)

Victor: It's a two-bedroom apartment.

Clerk: A 15-foot truck is big enough.

Victor: <u>How much is it going to cost</u>?
(3. how much / it / cost)

Clerk: <u>Are you going to move</u> on
(4. you / move)
the weekend or during the week?

Victor: Is there a difference in price?

Clerk: Yes. It's $20 a day more on the weekends.
<u>When are you going to need the truck</u>?
(5. when / you / need the truck)

Victor: Next week. Wednesday or Thursday.

Clerk: <u>How long are you going to need</u> it?
(6. how long / you / need)

Victor: Just one day.

Clerk: O.K. Then it's going to cost $39.00 a day and 99 cents a mile.

Lesson 2 205

EXERCISE 7

1. Tell students they are going to complete Victor's conversation. Have students read the direction line. Ask: *Who is Victor speaking to?* (a clerk at the truck rental company) *What are they talking about?* (Victor wants to rent a truck.) Go over the example. If necessary, clarify to students that they are going to make questions with the words in parentheses.
2. Have students complete Exercise 7 individually. Then go over the answers with the class.
3. If necessary, review all the grammar charts in Lesson 2.

To save class time, have students do the exercise for homework ahead of time.

Expansion

Exercise 7 Have students practice the conversation in pairs. Have volunteers roleplay the conversation in front of the class.

Unit 9 205

EXERCISE 8

1. Direct student's attention to the photo on page 206. Ask: *What do you see? What's happening?* (Someone is moving.) Have students read the direction line. Have a volunteer complete #1.
2. Have students complete the rest of Exercise 8 individually. Then have students compare answers in pairs. Circulate to observe pair work. Give help as needed.
3. If necessary, review all the grammar charts in Unit 9.

🕒 To save class time, have students do the exercise for homework ahead of time.

EXERCISE 8 Complete the conversation between Victor and Simon. Use questions and statements with *be going to*. Use the verbs from the box below.

| are going to help | I'm going to finish | I'm going to invite |
| are you going to pack | are going to move out | are you going to be |

Simon: When __are you going to pack__ the rest of your things?
                           (1)

Victor: __I'm going to finish__ next week.
            (2)

Simon: Ed and I can help you on Thursday. I have the day off.

Victor: Thanks. But __are you going to be__ available on Sunday?
                              (3)
The people in my new apartment __are going to move out__ on
                                            (4)
Sunday. We can take some of my things there on Sunday night.

Simon: We're available then. How many other people
__are going to help__ you?
        (5)

Victor: Just two of my friends. Then later, __I'm going to invite__ you
                                                       (6)
all for dinner.

206   Unit 9

Expansion

Exercise 8 Have students practice the conversation in pairs. Have volunteers roleplay the conversation in front of the class.

EDITING ADVICE

1. Don't write *gonna*. Write *going to*.
   > We're ~~gonna~~ [going to] get jobs.

2. Always use a form of *be* with *going to*.
   > We [']re[^] going to shop at a resale shop.

3. Always use the correct word order in questions.
   > Where ~~they are~~ [are they] going to work?

4. Use the correct preposition with time expressions.
   > We are going to move ~~on~~ [in] two weeks.

EDITING QUIZ

Find the mistakes with the underlined words, and correct them. Not every sentence has a mistake. If the sentence is correct, write *C*.

EXAMPLES How long <u>you're going</u> [are you going] to live here?

He's going to live here until next year. *C*

1. Shafia's relatives <u>going</u> [are going] to give her many gifts.
2. My family's <u>gonna</u> [going to] move in April.
3. When <u>she's</u> [is she] going to have the baby?
4. He's going to fill out a change-of-address card. *C*
5. We're going to move <u>in</u> [on] January 29.
6. It's going to take a long time. *C*
7. She's going to stay here <u>on</u> a while.
8. What kind of apartment <u>those people going to get</u>? [are]

Lesson 2 207

Editing Advice

1. Have students close their books. Write the example sentences without editing marks or corrections on the board. For example:
   1. *We're gonna get jobs.*
   2. *We going to shop at a resale shop.*

   Ask students to correct each sentence. This activity can be done individually, in pairs, or as a class. After students have corrected each sentence, tell them to turn to page 207. Say: *Now compare your work with Editing Advice in the book.*

2. Go over answers with the class. For troublespots, review the appropriate grammar chart.

Editing Quiz

1. The Editing Quiz may be used as an in-class quiz, a take-home quiz, or as a review. Have students read the direction line. Ask: *Does every sentence have a mistake?* (no) Go over the examples with the class.

2. Have students complete the quiz individually. Collect the completed quizzes for assessment or have students check each other's work. Review the answers with the class. Elicit the relevant grammar point for each correction. For example, for #1, ask: *What's the rule?* (Use *be* with *going to*.)

Unit 9 207

Learner's Log

1. Have students close their books. Ask: *What did you learn about resale shops, moving, renting a truck, and getting ready for a baby? What else do you want to know?* Write students' ideas on the board. Discuss ways in which students can find out more about these topics.
2. Have students open their books to complete the Learner's Log. Remind students to write three questions about moving to a new home or about preparing for a baby.

Expansion Activities

These expansion activities provide opportunities for students to interact with one another and further develop their speaking and writing skills. Encourage students to use grammar from this unit whenever possible.

To save class time, assign parts of the activities as homework. Then use class time for interaction and communication. If students do not need additional speaking practice, some of the activities may be assigned as writing activities for homework, or skipped altogether.

WRITING ACTIVITY

Have students complete the activity individually at home or in class. Collect for assessment.

OUTSIDE ACTIVITIES

Have students report their information to the class. Ask volunteers to explain how to rent a truck and how to get the best buy at a resale store.

INTERNET ACTIVITIES

1. Have students discuss the moving tips they found online in groups. Then ask groups to share with the class some of the best tips.
2. Discuss baby names with the class. Ask volunteers to discuss the names they liked or didn't like and why.

LEARNER'S LOG

1. What did you learn in this unit? Write three sentences in your notebook about each topic.
   • Resale / thrift shops
   • Preparing to move
   • Renting a truck
   • Preparing for a new baby
2. Write three questions you still have about moving to a new apartment or house or about preparing for a new baby.

EXPANSION ACTIVITIES

Writing Activity

In your notebook, write a paragraph of six to eight sentences about the picture. Write about what is going to happen.

EXAMPLE *Victor is coming out of his apartment building. He is going to put some boxes on the truck.*

Outside Activities

1. Call a truck rental company in your city and find out how much it costs to rent a 15-foot truck next Saturday.
2. Find a resale or thrift shop in your neighborhood. Visit the shop and tell the class about your experience.

Internet Activities

1. Search the words *moving tips*. Find some advice about moving. Write three sentences. Share them with the class.
2. Search the words *baby names* or *names*. Find an interesting name (or your name) and read about it. What does it mean? Where does it come from? Tell the class about the name.

Expansion

Learner's Log Have students compare logs in pairs.

Writing Activity Variation

Have students exchange papers with a partner for proofreading.

Internet Activities Variation

1. Tell students that if they don't have Internet access, they can use Internet facilities at a public library.
2. Alternatively, students can visit a truck rental company for a list of moving tips. They can also ask librarians or bookstore clerks for help in finding books with baby names.

UNIT 10

GRAMMAR
Comparatives
Superlatives

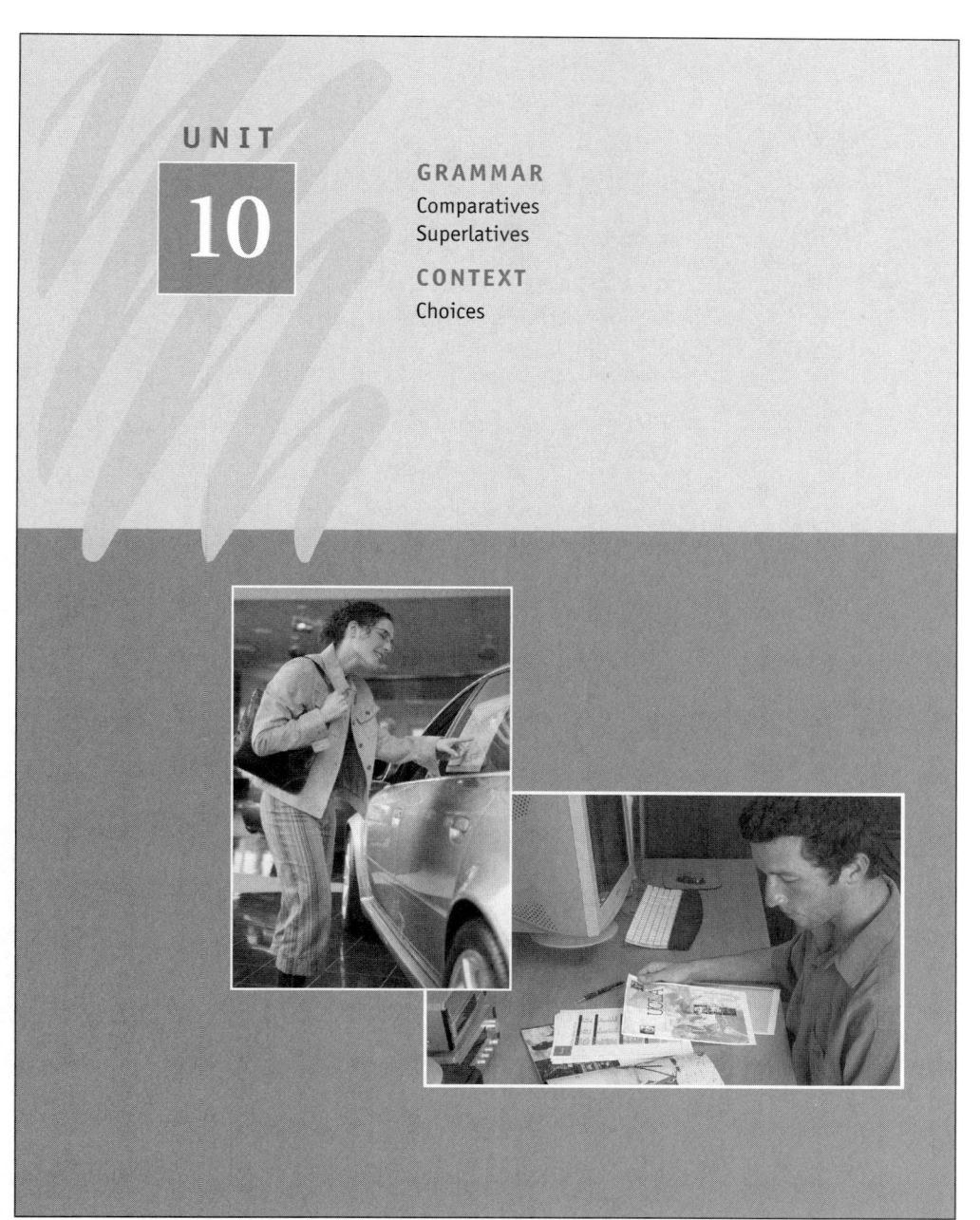

CONTEXT
Choices

Expansion

Theme The topic for this unit can be enhanced with the following ideas:
1. College catalogues
2. Car magazines; a consumer report magazine with car ratings

Unit | 10
Unit Overview

GRAMMAR

1. Ask: *What did we study in Unit 9?* (the future tense with *be going to* and expressions of time in the future) *What are we going to study in Unit 10?* (comparatives and superlatives) Write *Comparatives and Superlatives* on the board.
2. Activate students' knowledge. Ask: *What are some ways to make comparisons in English?* (add *-er, more, -est, most*) Say and write these comparisons on the board:

    Boston is smaller than New York.
    New York is more exciting.
    I think New York is the most exciting city in the U.S.

    Underline the comparatives and superlatives.
3. Relate the objective to students' personal experience. Ask several students to compare two of their favorite cities.

CONTEXT

1. Say: *In Unit 9, we talked about making big changes. Now, we're going to talk about making big choices.* Activate students' knowledge. Ask: *What big choices do people make?*
2. Direct students' attention to the photos. Say: *These people are making big choices. What are they choosing?* (The woman is choosing a car. The man is choosing a college.)
3. Say: *It's very important to go to a good school. Why is it important to choose a good school?* Ask students to share their ideas.

Unit **10**   **209**

Lesson 1 | Overview

GRAMMAR

Ask: *What is comparing?* (telling how things are alike and different) Say: *In Lesson 1, we are going to study adjectives called comparatives, such as* nicer, older, better, *and* smaller. *How are these adjectives the same?* (They end in *-er.*) Point to two books and say: *This book is bigger than that book.* Write the sentence on the board. Elicit more comparative sentences from volunteers.

CONTEXT

1. Begin by directing students' attention to the picture of Shafia at the computer. Ask: *What is Shafia looking at?* (information about different colleges) *Why is Shafia looking at college brochures?* (She's comparing colleges. She's going to choose a college.)
2. Ask: *When you choose a college, what do you need to know about the college?* Have students share their knowledge and experience.

BEFORE YOU READ

1. Go over each question as a class. Have a volunteer read the questions or read them to the class yourself. Have students discuss the questions in pairs.
2. Ask for a few volunteers to share their answers with the class.

To save class time, skip "Before You Read," or have students prepare their answers for homework ahead of time.

LESSON 1

GRAMMAR
Comparative Forms of Adjectives
Spelling of the *–er* Form
Comparisons with Nouns and Verbs

CONTEXT
Community Colleges

Before You Read
1. Where is the state university in this state?
2. What community colleges do you know about in this area?

210 Unit 10

Culture Note
Community colleges are an American invention. The first community colleges were started over 100 years ago, and now there are 1,166 community colleges in the U.S.

210   *Grammar in Context Basic* Teacher's Edition

COMMUNITY COLLEGES

In the U.S., many students choose to go to a community college. Students can get a two-year certificate or a degree. Some students start at a community college. Then they go to a four-year college or university to get a bachelor's degree.

A four-year university is **more expensive than** a community college. The average tuition at a community college is $2,000 a year. At a four-year state university, it is $11,000 a year. A community college is often **closer** to home **than** a four-year college. Community colleges in big cities often have several campuses.

There are other differences too. A community college often has **smaller** classes than a university. Some university classes can have more than 100 students. And students at a community college are usually **older than** students at a four-year college. The average age of students at a community college is 29. At a university, most students are between the ages of 18 and 24.

Community college students are often **busier** too. Many students have full- or part-time jobs and families. Community colleges are **more convenient than** universities for students with small children. Many community colleges provide child-care services. There are more night and weekend classes too.

An educated person has a **better** chance of finding a good job. Which is **better** for you: a community college or a four-year college?

Vocabulary in Context

bachelor's degree	My brother has four years of college. He has a **bachelor's degree** in French.
certificate	My cousin has a **certificate** from a community college to work with children.
tuition	Students have to pay **tuition** to go to college.
campus	My college has several **campuses.** There is a **campus** near my house. There is another campus downtown.
educated	My father is an **educated** person. He has a bachelor's degree.
provide	The college **provides** many services.
chance	He's very busy this week. He doesn't have a **chance** to rest.

Lesson 1 211

Reading Variation

1. To practice listening skills, have students listen to the audio before opening their books. Ask a few comprehension questions, such as: *Which has more night and weekend classes—a community college or a four-year college?* (a community college) Repeat the audio if necessary. Then have students open their books and read along as they listen to the audio.
2. Alternatively, have students begin by listening to the audio as they read along.

Vocabulary Teaching Ideas

Use the following ideas to teach these terms:

certificate: Bring in certificates of achievement of different types.
tuition: Print on the board:
   Courses: $500.00 per semester hour. Elicit from students the tuition for your school.
campus: Show students a map of the campus at your institution.
educated: Ask students to describe an educated person.
chance: Say: Chance *means opportunity.* Ask: *Do you have any chance to exercise during the week? When?*

Community Colleges (Reading) CD 1, Track 49

1. Have students skim the reading and look at the picture on page 210. Ask: *What is the reading about? What are community colleges being compared to?* (four-year colleges) Have students use the title and picture to make predictions about the reading.
2. Have students read the text silently. Then play the audio and have students read along silently.
3. Check students' basic comprehension. Ask questions, such as: *Are community colleges four-year colleges?* (No. They're two-year colleges.) *On average, how much does it cost to go to a community college?* ($2,000 a year) *Do community colleges have large or small classes?* (small) *Why are community college students busier?* (Students usually have a full- or part-time job and a family)

To save class time, have students do the reading for homework ahead of time.

VOCABULARY IN CONTEXT

1. Model the pronunciation of each new vocabulary word and have students repeat.
2. Make sure students understand the meaning of each vocabulary item. Review the examples in the book and create additional example sentences. For example, say: *bachelor's degree. I have a bachelor's degree in Teaching English as a Second Language. I studied at [college name] for four years.* Go over each new vocabulary word similarly, using visuals and realia when appropriate. When possible, point to pictures in the book that illustrate the new vocabulary, such as *certificate* on page 211.
3. Have students underline an example of each vocabulary item in the reading.

Unit 10 211

DID YOU KNOW?

Ask: *Did you know that nursing is the most popular degree program in community colleges?*

LISTENING ACTIVITY

🎧 **CD 1, Track 50**

1. **Say:** *Listen to the sentences about the reading on community colleges. Circle* true *or* false. *Play the listening selection one time without pausing. Then play it through again, pausing and replaying as necessary.*
2. Go over the answers as a class. Ask students to volunteer answers.

- Not all students at a community college want to get a degree. Some students go there just to learn more English. Others go to attend a certificate program, such as a certified nursing assistant program. Others go to improve their skills, such as computer skills.
- There are different levels of college degrees: associate's degree, bachelor's degree, master's degree, and PhD (or doctorate).

Listening Activity — Listen to the sentences about the reading. Circle *true* or *false*.

EXAMPLE (TRUE)   FALSE

1. (TRUE)   FALSE   4. TRUE   (FALSE)
2. TRUE   (FALSE)   5. TRUE   (FALSE)
3. (TRUE)   FALSE   6. (TRUE)   FALSE

10.1 | Comparative Forms of Adjectives

We can compare two people or things. There are two patterns of comparison and a few irregular forms. We use *than* to complete the comparison.

Pattern	Simple	Comparative	Examples
Pattern 1: After a one-syllable adjective, add *-er*	old tall	old**er** tall**er**	Community college students are **older than** university students.
Pattern 1 with a spelling change: After a two-syllable adjective that ends in *–y*, change *y* to *i* and add *–er*.	busy happy	bus**ier** happ**ier**	Community college students are often **busier than** university students.
Pattern 2: With other two-syllable adjectives and all three-syllable adjectives add *more* before the adjective.	helpful expensive	**more** helpful **more** expensive	University tuition is **more expensive than** community college tuition.
Irregular Adjectives: We change the word completely.	good bad	better worse	A community college is **better** for me **than** a university. My grade in Biology is **worse than** my grade in Math.

Language Notes:
1. We omit *than* if we do not mention the second item of comparison.
   She is richer than I am, but I am happier.
2. Some two-syllable words can follow both Pattern 1 or Pattern 2.
   common—**more** common OR common**er**
3. We can put *much* before a comparative form.
   Those students are **much younger** than we are.

10.2 | Spelling of the *-er* Form

Simple Adjective	Comparative Adjective	Explanation
old cheap	old**er** cheap**er**	Add *-er* to most adjectives.
big hot	big**ger** hot**ter**	If the adjective ends with consonant-vowel-consonant, double the final consonant before adding *-er*.
nice late	nic**er** lat**er**	If the adjective ends in *e*, add *-r* only.
busy easy	bus**ier** eas**ier**	If a two-syllable adjective ends in *y*, change *y* to *i* and add *-er*.

Lesson 1

Expansion

Grammar Chart Have students go back to the reading on page 211. Have students say what pattern each comparative form follows.

10.1 | Comparative Forms of Adjectives

1. Have students look at grammar chart **10.1** on page 213. Say: *We compare two things or two people. We usually compare using one of two forms.* Activate students' knowledge. Ask: *What are the two forms?* (add *-er* or add *more*) Review the patterns and examples.
2. Write on the board: *Pattern 1: add -er.* Go over both rules and example words. Read the example sentences. Repeat the procedure for Pattern 2 and then for irregular adjectives.
3. Explain the order of parts in a comparative sentence. Write the following on the board:

   A+ Comparative + *than* + *B.*
   Explain that A and B are the people or things being compared. Have students look at the example sentences again and identify the terms being compared. (e.g., for Pattern 1, A = *community college students;* B= *university students*)
4. Point out the Language Notes. For #1, ask: *Who is being compared?* (She and I) Write this sentence on the board: *She is richer than I am, but I am happier _____.* Ask the class to fill in the blank. (than she is) Explain that *much* means *very.*

10.2 | Spelling of the *-er* Form

1. Have students cover up grammar chart **10.2** on page 213. Write the following adjectives on the board:
   1. *old/older; cheap/cheaper*
   2. *big/bigger; hot/hotter*
   3. *nice/nicer; late/later*
   4. *busy/busier; easy/easier*
2. Say: *Here are the spelling rules for comparatives.* Then read out the spelling rules in random order and ask students to match the adjectives to the rules.
3. Have students look at grammar chart **10.2** on page 213. Go over the adjectives and the explanations.

EXERCISE 1

1. Have students read the direction line. Go over the example in the Student Book.
2. Have students complete Exercise 1 individually. Check the answers as a class.
3. If necessary, review grammar charts **10.1** and **10.2** on page 213.

EXERCISE 2

1. Tell students they are going to compare a community college and a university. Have students read through the information on the colleges in the chart. You might pre-teach terms that may be unfamiliar to students, such as *day-care center* and *credit hour*. Then have students read the direction line. Go over the example in the Student Book.
2. Have students complete Exercise 2 individually. Then have students compare answers in pairs. Circulate to observe pair work. Give help as needed.
3. If necessary, review grammar charts **10.1** and **10.2** on page 213.

EXERCISE 1 Write the comparative forms of the adjectives. Use correct spelling.

1. convenient — *more convenient*
2. big — *bigger*
3. fine — *finer*
4. lazy — *lazier*
5. hard — *harder*
6. funny — *funnier*
7. expensive — *more expensive*
8. friendly — *friendlier*
9. hot — *hotter*
10. good — *better*
11. kind — *kinder*
12. mad — *madder*
13. late — *later*
14. bad — *worse*

EXERCISE 2 Compare Wilson College and Jackson University using the information below. The numbers in the table go with the numbers in the exercise.

	Wilson College	Jackson University
Example:	Has night and weekend classes	Doesn't have night or weekend classes
1.	$60 per credit hour	$450 per credit hour
2.	Average class size = 16 students	Average class size = 30 students
3.	80 percent of students have jobs	10 percent of students have jobs
4.	Has a day-care center	Doesn't have a day-care center
5.	All classes are in one building.	The campus has more than 60 buildings.
6.	College opened in 1985.	University opened in 1910.
7.	Teachers have a bachelor's degree or master's degree.	Teachers have a master's degree or PhD.

Use the comparative form of one of the adjectives from the choices below.

| busy | good | big | convenient ✓ |
| old | small | expensive | educated |

EXAMPLE Wilson College is *more convenient than* Jackson University for people with day jobs.

1. Jackson University is *more expensive than* Wilson College.
2. Classes at Wilson College are *smaller than* classes at Jackson University.

Expansion

Exercise 2 Have students give explanations for each comparison. (e.g., Wilson College is more convenient because they have night and weekend classes.)

3. Most students at Wilson College work full-time. Students at Wilson College are ___busier than___ students at Jackson University.
4. Wilson College is ___better than___ Jackson University for parents with small children.
5. Jackson University is ___bigger than___ Wilson College.
6. Jackson University is ___older than___ Wilson College.
7. Teachers at Jackson University are ___more educated than___ teachers at Wilson College.

EXERCISE 3 Fill in the blanks with the comparative form of the word in parentheses ( ). Add *than* where necessary.

EXAMPLE A: I'm going to start my education at a community college.

B: Why?

A: It's ___cheaper than___ a four-year college.
       (cheap)

1. A: Which college do you prefer? Truman College or Northeastern University?

   B: I'm going to go to Truman College. It's ___more convenient___ for
                                              (convenient)
   me. It's ___closer___ to my home and the tuition is less.
             (close)
   What about you?

   A: I'm going to study math. Northeastern has a good math program, so it's ___better___ for me.
                                                                      (good)

2. A: Are you going to buy new textbooks or used books?

   B: I prefer used books. They're ___cheaper than___ new books.
                                    (cheap)

   A: I prefer new books. They're ___cleaner___. I don't like to
                                   (clean)
   see another student's answers in my book.

Lesson 1   215

EXERCISE 3

1. Tell students they are going to complete short conversations that compare two schools. Have students read the direction line. Go over the example in the Student Book.
2. Have students complete Exercise 3 individually. Then have students compare answers in pairs. Circulate to observe pair work. Give help as needed.
3. If necessary, review grammar charts **10.1** and **10.2** on page 213.

🕐 To save class time, have students complete the exercise for homework ahead of time.

Exercise 3 Variation

Have students write similar short dialogues, comparing two schools they know, including courses of study, teachers, used vs. new textbooks, types of students, and location.

Unit 10   215

3. A: Some of the students in my class are married with children and have full-time jobs. They're much ___busier than___ I am.
   (busy)
   B: You're only 18. You live with your parents, so going to college is much ___easier___ for you.
   (easy)

4. A: I'm going to the bookstore to buy my books.
   B: I'm going to buy my books online. Books in the bookstore are ___more expensive than___ books online.
   (expensive)
   A: But it's ___faster___ to get your books at the bookstore.
   (fast)
   B: You're right. It's ___slower___ to get books from an online bookstore. But it only takes four or five days.
   (slow)

5. A: What are your plans for your education?
   B: I'm going to get my general education at the community college. Tuition is ___cheaper___ there. Then I'm going to go to a four-year college. But I'm going to feel a little strange there.
   (cheap)
   A: Why?
   B: Because I'm 34 years old. I'm ___older than___ most of the other students.
   (old)

6. A: My math teacher, Ms. Woods, is never in her office. Next semester I'm going to take Mr. Riley's math class.
   B: Why?
   A: He's much ___more available than___ Ms. Woods.
   (available)

7. A: My grades this semester are ___worse than___ my grades last semester.
   (bad)
   B: Why?
   A: I'm much ___busier___ now. I have 12 credit hours and a full-time job. And my classes are much ___harder___.
   (busy)   (hard)

216   Unit 10

Expansion

Exercise 3 Have students practice the conversations in pairs. Ask volunteers to roleplay the conversation in front of the class.

EXERCISE 4 ABOUT YOU Compare yourself to your best friend.

EXAMPLE tall *I am taller than my best friend.*

1. responsible _____ Answers will vary. _____
2. educated _____
3. busy _____
4. funny _____
5. friendly _____
6. polite _____
7. tall _____
8. strong _____

10.3 | Comparisons with Nouns and Verbs

Examples	Explanation
Part-time students need **more time** to finish college.	We can use *more* before nouns to make a comparison statement.
You spend **less money** at a community college. My math class has **fewer students** than my biology class.	We can use *less* or *fewer* with nouns to make a comparison. Use *less* with noncount nouns. Use *fewer* with count nouns.
I prefer the city college because it costs **less**. You pay much **more** at a university. I study **harder** on the weekends.	We can use a comparative form after verbs.

EXERCISE 5 ABOUT YOU Find a partner and get information from him/her. Write sentences about you and your partner with the words given. Read your sentences to the class.

EXAMPLE have books *I have more books than Max.*

1. work hard _____ Answers will vary. _____
2. take classes _____
3. drive _____
4. have time to relax _____
5. study _____
6. have brothers and sisters _____

Lesson 1   217

Expansion

Exercise 4 Have students work with a partner to compare their favorite singers or actors. Say: *You can use the adjectives from the list or your own ideas.* Ask volunteers to share some of their comparisons with the class.

Exercise 5 Ask volunteers to share some of their comparisons with the class.

EXERCISE 4

1. Say: *Now you're going to compare you and your best friend.* Have students read the direction line. Go over the example in the Student Book. Have a volunteer model the example.
2. Have students complete Exercise 4 individually. Then have students compare answers in pairs. Circulate to observe pair work. Give help as needed.
3. If necessary, review grammar charts **10.1** and **10.2** on page 213.

   To save class time, have students complete the exercise for homework ahead of time.

10.3 | Comparisons with Nouns and Verbs

1. Have students look at grammar chart **10.3** on page 217. Go over the examples and explanations.
2. For comparisons with nouns, stress nouns as *who* and *what*. Write *more _____* on the board. Ask: *What do you need* more *of?* Write students' answers on the board. Repeat the procedure for *less* and *fewer*, noting their use with noncount and count nouns. For comparisons with verbs, stress the location of the comparative form after verbs. Note that these comparatives are adverbs.
3. Relate the objective to students' ideas and experience. Have students make sentences. Prompt by asking questions, such as: *What do you think students need?*

EXERCISE 5

1. Say: *Now you're going to compare you and your partner.* Have students read the direction line. Go over the example in the Student Book. Have volunteers model the example.
2. Have students complete Exercise 5 in pairs. Circulate to observe pair work. Give help as needed.
3. If necessary, review grammar chart **10.3** on page 217.

   To save class time, have students complete the exercise for homework ahead of time.

EXERCISE 6

1. Have students look at the pictures and read through the information on the colleges in the chart. Then have students read the direction line. Go over the example in the Student Book.
2. Have students complete Exercise 6 individually. Then have students compare answers in pairs. Circulate to observe pair work. Give help as needed.
3. If necessary, review grammar chart 10.3 on page 217.

⏱ To save class time, have students complete the exercise for homework ahead of time.

EXERCISE 6 Compare Wilson College and Jackson University using the information below. The numbers in the table go with the numbers in the exercise.

	Wilson College	Jackson University
Example: number of students	2,000	10,000
1. cost per credit hour	$50	$145
2. night classes	150	50
3. books in library	8,000	50,000
4. number of campuses	5	2
5. number of students in a class	30	16
6. students over the age of 40	215	77
7. married students	800	200

EXAMPLE Jackson University has ___more students___ than Wilson College.

1. Wilson College costs ___less___ per credit hour.
2. Wilson College has ___more night classes___ than Jackson University.
3. Wilson College has ___fewer books___ in its library.
4. Wilson College has ___more campuses___ than Jackson University.
5. Wilson College has ___more students___ in a class.
6. Wilson College has ___more students___ over the age of 40.
7. Jackson University has ___fewer married students___ than Wilson College.

218 Unit 10

Expansion

Exercise 6 Have students explain comparisons. (e.g., for the example: *Jackson University has 10,000 students and Wilson College has only 2,000.*)

EXERCISE 7 Shafia is in college. She is comparing herself to Simon's daughter, Tina. Tina is in high school. Fill in the blanks to complete this story.

Answers may vary.

Tina is in high school, and I'm in college. I have ___more___ (example) responsibilities than she does. Tina doesn't have to work, but I do. I have a part-time job, and I'm taking 12 credit hours. I have ___to___ (1) work but ___I still have___ (2) time to study.

College classes are ___more difficult than___ (3) high school classes. Tina studies only two hours a day. I study four hours a day. I have much ___more___ (4) homework than she does.

The class size is different too. My classes are ___bigger than___ (5) Tina's classes. Her classes have 25 students. Some of my classes at college have 200 students.

Students at my college are all ages. Many students in my class are much ___older than___ (6) I am. Some of them are my parents' age. In high school, all the students are about the same age.

Lesson 1   219

EXERCISE 7

1. Have students read the direction line. Go over the example in the Student Book. Say: *In this exercise, you can fill in the blanks with* more, less, *and comparative forms of adjectives. Include* than *when necessary.*
2. Have students complete Exercise 7 individually. Go over the answers as a class.
3. If necessary, review grammar chart **10.3** on page 217.

🕐 To save class time, have students complete the exercise for homework ahead of time.

Expansion

Exercise 7 Have students write a similar paragraph, comparing their life in school to another student's.

Unit **10**   219

Lesson 2 | Overview

GRAMMAR

Say: *In Lesson 1, we learned how to compare two items. Now we're going to learn to compare three or more items.* Write on the board:

Superlatives

Then write the following statement on the board:

*Mt. Everest is the **highest** mountain in the world.*

Elicit more examples from volunteers.

CONTEXT

1. Ask: *What are we going to read about in this lesson?* (choosing a used car) Say: *I usually buy the cheapest car, but it's important to buy a good car. There are many things to think about: mileage, economy, safety.* Ask: *How do you choose a car? What do you think about?* Have students share their ideas.
2. Direct students' attention to the picture of Simon and Victor on page 220. Ask: *What kind of Web site are Victor and Simon looking at?* (They're looking at a Web site about cars.) Point to the Web page showing the fuel economy of two cars. Ask: *What's on the Web site?* (car comparisons)

BEFORE YOU READ

1. Go over each question as a class. Have a volunteer read the questions or read them to the class yourself. Have students answer the questions in pairs.
2. Ask for a few volunteers to share their answers with the class.

🕐 To save class time, skip "Before You Read," or have students prepare their answers for homework ahead of time.

LESSON 2

GRAMMAR
Superlative Forms of Adjectives
Spelling of the *–est* Forms
Superlatives with Nouns and Verbs

CONTEXT
Choosing a Used Car

Before You Read

1. Do you have a car? Is it a new car or a used car? What kind of car is it?
2. In your opinion, what are the best cars?

220   Unit 10

Culture Note

Consumer Reports Magazine compares many used and new cars in a special list every year. The magazine compares price, mileage, performance, and much more.

220   *Grammar in Context Basic* Teacher's Edition

CHOOSING A USED CAR

Victor: I want to buy a used car. My co-worker, Sam, wants to sell me his 1999 car. He wants $4,000. Is that a good price?
Simon: I don't know. **The best** way to get information about used car prices is in the "blue book."
Victor: What's the "blue book"?
Simon: The "blue book" shows prices and other information about new and used cars. It can help you make a decision. We can look at it online.

After Simon goes online:
Simon: Look. Here's your co-worker's car.
Victor: There are three prices for the same car. Why?
Simon: The price depends on several things: condition of the car, mileage, and extras. Cars in **the best** condition with **the lowest** miles and the **most** extras are **the most expensive.** Cars with **the highest** mileage and **the most** problems are **the least expensive.**
Victor: Sam says his car is in good condition.
Simon: **The best** way to know for sure is to take it to a mechanic. You need a good car. Repairs are very expensive.
Victor: But it costs money to go to a mechanic.
Simon: It's better to lose $200 than $4,000. But the price of the car is not the only thing to consider. Also consider fuel economy. There's a Web site that compares fuel economy. Here it is. Look. Your co-worker's car gets only 22 miles per gallon (mpg). Look at these other two cars. This car gets 30 miles per gallon. This one gets 35 miles per gallon. Your co-worker's car is **the cheapest** to buy but it isn't **the most economical** to use.
Victor: There's a lot to know about buying a used car!

Vocabulary in Context

co-worker	Victor works with Sam. Sam is Victor's **co-worker.**
condition	My car is in good **condition.** I have no problems with it.
depends on	The price of the car **depends on** miles, condition, etc.
mileage	How many miles does the car have? What is its **mileage?**
consider	You have to **consider** a lot of things before you buy a car.
fuel economy/ economical	This car doesn't use a lot of gas. This car has good **fuel economy.** It is very **economical.**
extras	This car has a lot of **extras:** air-conditioning, a CD player, etc.
mechanic	A **mechanic** fixes cars.
repair	An old car needs a lot of **repairs.**
decision	There are many choices. He has to make a **decision.**

Lesson 2   221

Choosing a Used Car (Reading) CD 1, Track 51

1. Direct students' attention to the title of the reading on page 221. Ask the following questions and have students scan the reading for the answers: *Who is buying a used car?* (Victor) *What does the price of a used car depend on?* (the condition of the car, mileage, and extras) Ask: *What do you think Victor will ask Simon? What will Simon say?* Have students make predictions about the reading.
2. Have students read the dialogue silently. Then play the audio and have students read along silently.
3. Check students' basic comprehension. Ask questions, such as: *What costs $4,000?* (the car Victor wants to buy) *What is the "blue book"?* (a book that gives information about cars) *What kind of information does the blue book have?* (prices and other information on new and used cars) *Why does Simon tell Victor to take the car to a mechanic?* (so the mechanic can find out if it's in good condition.) *What else does Simon think Victor should consider before buying the car?* (fuel economy)

To save class time, have students do the reading for homework ahead of time.

VOCABULARY IN CONTEXT

1. Model the pronunciation of each new vocabulary item and have students repeat.
2. Make sure students understand the meaning of each vocabulary item. Review the examples in the book and create additional example sentences. For example, say: *co-worker. [NAME of another English teacher] is my co-worker. [He/She] teaches here, too.* Go over each new vocabulary word similarly, using visuals and realia when appropriate. When possible, point to pictures in the book that illustrate the new vocabulary items, such as *co-worker* on page 240.
3. Have students underline an example of each vocabulary item in the reading.

Reading Variation

To practice listening skills, have students listen to the audio before opening their books. Ask a few comprehension questions, such as: *How many miles per gallon does Victor's co-worker's car get?* (22 miles per gallon) Repeat the audio if necessary. Then have students open their books and read along as they listen to the audio.

Vocabulary Teaching Ideas

Use the following ideas to teach these terms:

depends on: Say: *The price of a used book depends on condition and age.*
consider: Mime the action by tilting your head to one side and looking thoughtful.
repair: Give examples. (e.g., The car won't start; the window is broken.)
decision: Act out making a decision. Put books on your desk, and act out choosing one.

Expansion

Reading Have students practice the conversation in pairs. Ask volunteers to roleplay all or part of the conversation in front of the class.

Vocabulary in Context To check comprehension, have volunteers in pairs or groups act out selected vocabulary, such as *consider, mechanic,* and *decision.*

Unit 10   221

DID YOU KNOW?

Explain to students that the price the car dealership advertises is called the *asking price* or the *ticket price*.

LISTENING ACTIVITY

🎧 **CD 1, Track 52**

1. Have students look at the photo on page 222. Ask: *What do they sell here?* (used cars) Say: *Listen to the sentences about the conversation. Circle* true *or* false. Play the listening selection one time without pausing. Then play it through again, pausing and replaying as necessary.
2. Go over the answers as a class. Ask students to volunteer answers.

Did You Know? When you buy a new or used car, you do not have to pay the asking price. The buyer can try to get a lower price from the seller.

Listening Activity Listen to the sentences about the conversation. Circle *true* or *false*.

EXAMPLE   TRUE   (FALSE)

1. (TRUE)   FALSE
2. (TRUE)   FALSE
3. TRUE   (FALSE)
4. TRUE   (FALSE)
5. TRUE   (FALSE)
6. (TRUE)   FALSE
7. (TRUE)   FALSE

---

222   *Grammar in Context Basic* Teacher's Edition

10.4 | Superlative Forms of Adjectives

We use the superlative form to point out the number one item in a group of three or more. Add *the* before the superlative form.

Pattern	Simple Adjective	Comparative Adjective	Examples
Pattern 1: After a one-syllable adjective, add *-est*.	low tall	low**est** tall**est**	Car A has **the lowest** mileage.
Pattern 1 with a spelling change: After a two-syllable adjective that ends in *-y*, change *y* to *i* and add *-est*.	easy happy	eas**iest** happ**iest**	**The easiest** way to compare prices is with the "blue book."
Pattern 2: With other two-syllable adjectives and all three-syllable adjectives, add *the most* before the adjective.	helpful expensive	**the most** helpful **the most** expensive	Car A is **the most expensive** car.
Irregular Adjectives: We change the word completely.	good bad	**the best** **the worst**	Which car is in **the best** condition? Car C is in **the worst** condition.

Language Notes:
1. We often add a prepositional phrase after a superlative form.
   Your car is the oldest car **in the parking lot.**
2. You can use *one of the* with a superlative form. The noun it describes is plural.
   Lexus **is one of the** most expensive car**s**.
3. Omit *the* after a possessive form.
   My best friend has a 1995 Toyota.

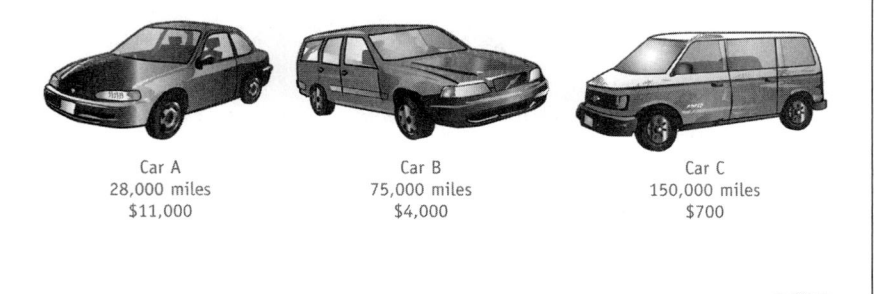

Car A
28,000 miles
$11,000

Car B
75,000 miles
$4,000

Car C
150,000 miles
$700

Lesson 2   223

10.4 | Superlative Forms of Adjectives

1. Have students look at grammar chart **10.4** on page 223. Say: *Superlatives name the number one item in a group. We usually make superlatives in two ways.* Activate students' knowledge. Ask: *What are the two ways?* (Add *-est* or add *the most*.) Review the patterns and examples.
2. Write on the board: *Pattern 1: add -est*. Go over both rules and example terms. Read the example sentences. Repeat the procedure for Pattern 2 and then for irregular adjectives.
3. Go over the Language Notes. Review the rules and example sentences. For Note 1, explain that a prepositional phrase after a superlative often identifies the group. Give an additional example: *My mother is the best mother in the world.* Ask: *What is the group?* (all the mothers in the world) For Note 2, explain that *one of the* is used to describe a top item in a group of top items, best or worst. Give additional examples. (e.g., *This show is one of the worst shows on TV. That is one of the best songs ever written.*)

Expansion

Grammar Chart Have students go back to the reading on page 221. Ask them to circle all the superlatives and decide the pattern each form follows. Then ask several students to share their decisions with the class.

10.5 | Spelling of -est Forms

1. Have students look at grammar chart **10.5** on page 224. Review the examples of simple and superlative adjectives and the explanations.
2. Check comprehension by asking students the superlative form of familiar and unfamiliar adjectives. Tell students they do not need to know what the words mean. Say the words as you write them on the board:

   fast (fastest)
   dry (driest)
   handy (handiest)
   sad (saddest)
   young (youngest)
   early (earliest)
   weird (weirdest)
   strange (strangest)

   Elicit the answers from the class and write them on the board. Ask volunteers to identify the spelling rule for each word.

EXERCISE 1

1. Have students read the direction line. Have a volunteer do #1.
2. Have students complete Exercise 1 individually. Go over the answers as a class.
3. If necessary, review grammar charts **10.4** on page 223 and **10.5** on page 224.

EXERCISE 2

1. Have students read the direction line. Have a volunteer create a superlative statement about the cars in the chart.
2. Have students complete Exercise 2 individually. Then have students compare answers in pairs. Circulate to observe pair work. Give help as needed.
3. If necessary, review grammar chart **10.5** on page 224.

   ⏲ To save class time, have students do the exercise for homework ahead of time.

10.5 | Spelling of -est Forms

Simple Adjective	Superlative Adjective	Explanation
old cheap	old**est** cheap**est**	Add *-est* to most adjectives.
big hot	big**gest** hot**test**	If the adjective ends with consonant-vowel-consonant, double the final consonant before adding *-est*.
nice late	nice**st** late**st**	If the adjective ends in *e*, add *-st* only.
busy easy	bus**iest** eas**iest**	If a two-syllable adjective ends in *y*, change *y* to *i* and add *-est*.

EXERCISE 1 Write the superlative form of the adjectives below. Use correct spelling.

1. convenient — *most convenient*
2. big — *biggest*
3. fine — *finest*
4. lazy — *laziest*
5. funny — *funniest*
6. expensive — *most expensive*
7. friendly — *friendliest*
8. hot — *hottest*
9. good — *best*
10. kind — *kindest*
11. mad — *maddest*
12. late — *latest*
13. helpful — *most helpful*
14. busy — *busiest*

EXERCISE 2 Victor is comparing three cars. Write superlative sentences about these three cars, using the information in the table and the words in parentheses ( ). The numbers in the table go with the numbers in the exercise.

Car A	Car B	Car C
Example: 28 mpg	25 mpg	20 mpg
1. big enough for 4 passengers	big enough for 5 passengers	big enough for 6 passengers
2. 1998	2004	2001
3. $4,000	$8,000	$10,000
4. needs work	in very good condition	in average condition

224 Unit 10

Expansion

Exercise 2 Have students get into groups to compare cars, trucks, bicycles, or other vehicles. Brainstorm brands and write them on the board. Then list the qualities to compare: cost, size, condition, age, and fuel economy/mileage. Tell students to use both comparative and superlative adjective forms. Write this example sentence on the board: *Hondas are the best cars in the world.*

EXAMPLE Car A is <u>the most economical</u>.
            (economical)

1. Car C is <u>the biggest</u> inside.
            (big)

2. Car A is <u>the oldest</u>. Car B is <u>the newest</u>.
            (old)   (new)

3. Car C is <u>the most expensive</u>. Car A is <u>the cheapest</u>.
            (expensive)   (cheap)

4. Car B is in <u>the best</u> condition. Car A is in <u>the worst</u> condition.
               (good)   (bad)

EXERCISE 3 Fill in the blanks with the superlative form.

1. *on the phone*

    Shafia: I need your help. I want to buy a car. This is one of <u>the biggest</u>
    (big)
    decisions of my life. What's <u>the best</u> car?
    (good)

    Dorota: I can't answer that question. It depends on your needs.

2. *at home*

    Marta: You're going to graduate from high school next year. Let's talk about college for you. I prefer the city college for you because it's <u>the closest</u> to our home. It's also <u>the most economical</u>.
    (close)   (economical)

    Tina: I want to go to <u>the best</u> college in the U.S. I want to be a doctor.
    (good)

    Marta: You are choosing one of <u>the hardest</u> professions.
    (hard)

    Tina: I know, but I really want to be a doctor.

3. *at the bike shop*

    Lisa: Let's choose a bike for you. This one looks good, but it's <u>the heaviest</u>.
    (heavy)

    Maya: I don't like that one. I prefer this one. It's <u>the most beautiful</u> of
    (beautiful)
    all the bikes.

Expansion

Exercise 3 Have students practice the short dialogues with a partner. Ask volunteers to roleplay the conversations in front of the class.

EXERCISE 3

1. Have students read the direction line. Go over the example in the Student Book.
2. Have students complete Exercise 3 individually. Go over the answers as a class.
3. If necessary, review grammar charts **10.4** on page 223 and **10.5** on page 224.

EXERCISE 4

1. Say: *You're going to talk about your family members. Who's the most intelligent? Who's the most beautiful?* Have students read the direction line. Go over the example in the book. Have a volunteer model the example.
2. Have students complete the rest of Exercise 4 individually. Then have students compare answers with a partner. Circulate to observe pair work. Give help as needed.
3. If necessary, review grammar charts **10.4** on page 223 and **10.5** on page 224.

 To save class time, have students do the exercise for homework ahead of time.

10.6 | Superlatives with Nouns and Verbs

1. Have students look at grammar chart **10.6** on page 226. Activate students' prior knowledge. Ask: *How do we use* more, less, *and* fewer *in comparative statements?* (They go before a noun; *less* is used with noncount nouns, *fewer* is used with count nouns.) Ask: *What are the superlatives we use with nouns and verbs?* (*the most, the least, the fewest*) Review the examples and explanations. Point out that the superlative form can also be used after verbs.
2. Have students give additional examples. Prompt by asking questions, such as: *Who eats the most candy in your family? Who watches the least TV?*

---

4. *at the electronics store*

Halina: I need to buy a new computer. I want to buy ___the fastest___ one.
(fast)

How about this one?

Peter: This one is probably ___the most expensive___
(expensive)

5. *at the post office*

Halina: What's ___the most economical___ way to send this package?
(economical)

Clerk: You can send it by third-class mail.

Halina: What's ___the fastest___ way to send this package?
(fast)

Clerk: You can use express mail.

EXERCISE 4 ABOUT YOU Write about the number one person in your family for each of these items.

EXAMPLE tall *My brother Tim is the tallest person in our family.*

1. intelligent _____ *Answers will vary.* _____
2. beautiful _____
3. interesting _____
4. serious _____
5. funny _____
6. old _____
7. good cook _____
8. bad cook _____

10.6 | Superlatives with Nouns and Verbs

Examples	Explanation
Which car uses **the most gas**?	We can use *the most* before nouns to make superlative statements.
I want to spend **the least money** possible. This car has **the fewest** extras.	We can use *the least* and *the fewest* before nouns. Use *the least* with noncount nouns. Use *the fewest* with count nouns.
Which car costs **the most**? Who drives **the best** in your family?	We can use a superlative form after verbs.

226   Unit 10

Expansion

Exercise 4 Have students create three more superlative statements about family members. (e.g., My sister [name] is the most athletic.)

---

226   *Grammar in Context Basic* Teacher's Edition

EXERCISE 5 Victor and Simon are looking at car prices online. Fill in the blanks with the superlative form of the words in parentheses ( ).

Victor: Look at these ten cars. Maybe I should get __the cheapest__ car.
(example: cheap)

Simon: __The cheapest__ is sometimes __the most expensive__.
(1. cheap) (2. expensive)

Victor: How is that possible?

Simon: The cheapest car sometimes needs __the most repairs__.
(3. repairs)
You should also consider fuel economy. This car gets 35 miles per gallon. It's __the most economical__.
(4. economical)

Victor: But I like this one __the best__.
(5. good)

Simon: That one gets only 22 miles per gallon.

Victor: But it has __the most extras__: air-conditioning, power windows, sunroof, and more.
(6. extras)

Simon: You want my advice, right? This is __the best__ advice I can give you.
(7. good)

EXERCISE 6 ABOUT YOU Form a group with three classmates. Discuss the answers to these questions. Report your answers to the class.

Answers will vary.
1. Who speaks the most languages?
2. Who's the youngest?
3. Who's the best student?
4. Who has the longest last name?
5. Who's the newest immigrant?
6. Who's the tallest?
7. Who's the shortest?
8. Who's wearing the most jewelry?

Lesson 2   227

EXERCISE 5
1. Have students read the direction line. Go over the example in the Student Book.
2. Have students complete Exercise 5 individually. Give help as needed. Go over the answers as a class.
3. If necessary, review grammar chart 10.6 on page 226.

EXERCISE 6
1. Say: *Now you're going to make superlative statements about the students in the class.* Have students read the direction line.
2. Have students complete Exercise 6 in groups of three if possible. Go over the answers as a class.
3. If necessary, review grammar chart 10.6 on page 226.

Expansion

Exercise 5 Have students practice the conversation in pairs. Then have volunteers roleplay the conversation in front of the class.

Unit 10   227

EXERCISE 7

1. Have students read the direction line. Say: *Remember, you're going to be completing sentences with both comparatives and superlatives.* Have a volunteer do #1.
2. Have students complete Exercise 7 individually. Then go over the answers with the class.
3. If necessary, review the grammar charts in **Unit 10**.

---

9. Who has the largest family?
10. Who lives the closest to the school?
11. Who's taking the most classes?
12. Who has the longest hair?
13. Who talks the most in class?

EXERCISE 7 *Combination Exercise* Fill in the blanks with the comparative or superlative form of the word in parentheses ( ). Add *than* or *the* where necessary.

1. Gas in Europe is __more expensive than__ gas in the U.S.
   (expensive)

2. There are three kinds of gas. Premium gas is __the most expensive__.
   (expensive)

3. I'm going to buy a car. I want to get __the best__ price, so I'm going to compare a lot of cars.
   (good)

4. Can you help me buy a used car? You have __more experience than__ I do.
   (experience)

5. I have many choices. I'm thinking of buying __the most economical__ car.
   (economical)

6. Which car should I buy? I want to get __the best__ car possible for $4,000.
   (good)

7. Is a Japanese car __better than__ an American car?
   (good)

8. This car is __cheaper than__ that car.
   (cheap)

9. I'm looking at three cars. This car is __the prettiest__ of all of them. And it is in __the best__ condition. It probably needs __fewer__ repairs.
   (pretty) (good) (few)

10. My new car is __more beautiful than__ my old car.
    (beautiful)

11. A car is __more convenient than__ a bicycle.
    (convenient)

EDITING ADVICE

1. Don't use -er and *more* together.
   My new car is ~~more~~ better than my old car.

2. Don't use -est and *most* together.
   I want to buy the ~~most~~ cheapest car.

3. Use *than* before the second item of comparison.
   This car is more expensive ^than^ that car.

4. Don't confuse *then* and *than*.
   My English class is easier ~~then~~^than^ my math class.

5. Use *the* before a superlative form.
   Which is ^the^ best college?

6. Don't use *more* in superlative statements.
   My brother is the ~~more~~^most^ interesting person in my family.

EDITING QUIZ

Find the mistakes with the underlined words, and correct them. Not every sentence has a mistake. If the sentence is correct, write *C*.

EXAMPLES Which is the ~~most~~ fastest car in the world?
My new car is <u>bigger than</u> my old car. *C*

1. Of these four cars, which one is <u>the ~~more~~^most^ economical</u>?
2. My car gets ~~more~~ better mileage than your car.
3. Max is <u>the most intelligent</u> student in this class. *C*
4. The teacher speaks English <u>better</u>^than^ I do.
5. The blue car costs <u>more ~~then~~^than^</u> the green car.
6. Her son is ^the^<u>best</u> student in his class.
7. Community college students are <u>~~oldest~~^older^ than</u> university students.
8. What is your ~~most~~ worst subject in school?
9. Who is the <u>~~more~~^most^ intelligent</u> student in this class?

Lesson 2   229

Learner's Log

1. Have students close their books. Ask: *What did you learn about community colleges and four-year universities? What did you find out about buying a used car? What else do you want to know?* Write students' ideas on the board. Discuss ways in which students can find out more about these topics.
2. Have students open their books to complete the Learner's Log. Remind students to write three questions about colleges or buying a used car.

Expansion Activities

These expansion activities provide opportunities for students to interact with one another and further develop their speaking and writing skills. Encourage students to use grammar from this unit whenever possible.

To save class time, assign parts of the activities as homework. Then use class time for interaction and communication. If students do not need additional speaking practice, some of the activities may be assigned as writing activities for homework, or skipped altogether.

WRITING ACTIVITIES

Have students complete the activities individually at home or in class. If in class, you might have students do the activity in small groups. Collect for assessment.

OUTSIDE ACTIVITY

Ask several students to share their comparisons.

INTERNET ACTIVITIES

1. Have students discuss the used cars they found online in groups. Then have groups share their information with the class.
2. Compare students' information as a class. Make a chart on the board and write in car names and miles per gallon.

LEARNER'S LOG

1. What did you learn in this unit? Write three sentences in your notebook about each topic.
   • Community colleges and four-year universities
   • Buying a used car
2. Write three questions you still have about colleges or buying a used car.

EXPANSION ACTIVITIES

Writing Activities

1. In your notebook, write six or seven sentences about the pictures. Compare Shafia's and Halina's English classes. Compare the room, the desks, the teachers, the time of class, and the homework.

   EXAMPLE *Shafia's class has fewer students than Halina's class.*

2. In your notebook, compare three classes you are taking (for example: math, grammar, and reading). Write six or seven superlative sentences about your classes. Write about: hours of class each week, price of books, how easy the classes are, your grades in the classes, the amount of homework, how many students are in the classes, and how important each class is for you.

   EXAMPLE *My chemistry class has the most credit hours.*

Outside Activity

Compare your family car to another car in your neighborhood. Or compare the cars of two friends. Tell the class the names of the cars. Compare age, condition, price, comfort, and how much you like each car.

   EXAMPLE *My car is older than my brother's car.*

Internet Activities

1. Search the words *blue book* and *used car prices*. Find the prices of three used cars. Tell the class the names of the cars, the condition, and the prices.
2. Search the words *compare fuel economy*. Find two cars you like. Tell the class about them.

Expansion

Learner's Log Have students compare logs in pairs.

Writing Activities Variation

Have students exchange papers with a partner for proofreading.

Internet Activities Variation

Tell students that if they don't have Internet access, they can use Internet facilities at a public library. Alternatively, have students look in the classifieds section of a newspaper to look for used cars.

UNIT 11

GRAMMAR
The Past Tense of *Be*
Regular Verbs in the Simple Past Tense
Irregular Verbs in the Past Tense
Time Expressions with the Past Tense

CONTEXT
Getting a Job

Unit | 11
Unit Overview

GRAMMAR

1. Say: *In Unit 10, we studied adjectives in the comparative and superlative forms. In Unit 11, what kind of words will we study?* (verbs) *What tense?* (past) Write the unit objectives on the board: *the past tense of* Be, *regular verbs, and irregular verbs; and time expressions with the past tense.*

2. Say and write on the board: *I was at the doctor's office. I wasn't at work.* Underline the verbs. Activate students' knowledge. Ask for examples of past-time expressions and write them on the board. (e.g., *ago, yesterday, last night*) Elicit example sentences from students. Say: *I was at the doctor's office yesterday. Where were you yesterday?*

CONTEXT

1. Begin by directing students' attention to the photos. Ask: *What's the man doing? What is he writing?* (He's filling out a job application.) *What about the woman? What's she doing? Why is she smiling?* (She's in a job interview. She feels good about the interview. She's going to get the job.)

2. Ask: *What are we going to talk about in this unit?* (getting a job) *How do you get a job? What do you do?* Have students share their knowledge and experience.

Expansion

Theme The topic for this unit can be enhanced with the following ideas:
1. Job applications
2. Lists of typical interview questions

Unit 11 231

Lesson 1 | Overview

GRAMMAR

1. Say: *In Lesson 1, we're going to learn expressions of time in the past, and statements and questions with* be. Ask: *What kind of statements are we going to study?* (affirmative and negative) *What kind of questions?* (yes/no, information, and subject) Write the lesson objectives on the board.
2. Elicit example questions with *be* for each objective. Give the following statement and have students make questions: *I was at a used car dealership today.* (example questions: *Were the cars in good condition? What kind of cars were there? What was the cheapest car?*)

CONTEXT

1. Begin by directing students' attention to the photo of the department store. Then direct students' attention to the photo insert of people waiting in line. Ask: *What do you think they are they doing?* (applying for a job)
2. Say: *Now, we're going to talk about applying for a job. I worked [in a bank] many years ago. The interview wasn't easy.* Say: *Think about your job interviews. Were they easy? What were the questions?* Have students share their experiences.

BEFORE YOU READ

1. Go over each question as a class. Have a volunteer read the questions or read them to the class yourself. Have students discuss the questions in pairs.
2. Ask for a few volunteers to share their answers with the class.

To save class time, skip "Before You Read," or have students prepare their answers for homework ahead of time.

LESSON 1

GRAMMAR
Affirmative and Negative Statements with *Be*
Expressions of Time in the Past
Yes/No Questions with *Be*
Information Questions with *Be*
Subject Questions with *Be*

CONTEXT
Applying for a Job in a Store

Before You Read
1. What jobs can people get in stores?
2. How do people look for jobs?

232 Unit 11

Culture Note
Jobs in Retail There are many different kinds of careers involved in selling goods to the public:
finance
human resources
information systems
inventory control
management
marketing
merchandising and buying

232   *Grammar in Context Basic* Teacher's Edition

APPLYING FOR A JOB IN A STORE

Halina is talking to Dorota on the phone.

Halina: I **was** at Baker's Department Store today.
Dorota: **Were** there any good sales?
Halina: I **wasn't** there for the sales. I **was** there to apply for a job. Positions are available now for work during the holidays. A lot of people **were** there. They **weren't** happy. There **was** a long line to apply for jobs.
Dorota: **Were** there interviews today too?
Halina: There **were** no interviews. I **was** surprised. The application **was** on a computer.
Dorota: Many big stores have job applications on the computer now. Employers usually interview people later. How **were** the questions on the application? **Were** they hard to answer?
Halina: They **weren't** difficult at all. The first questions **were** about my job history and education. There **were** questions about references. You **were** one of my references, Dorota.
Dorota: You can use me as a reference anytime. What **were** some other questions?
Halina: There **were** some funny questions. One **was**: "Your job starts at 8:00. Where should you be at 8:00? A) In the parking lot, B) In the employees' check-in room, or C) In your department.
Dorota: That's interesting. What **was** your answer?
Halina: It **wasn't** A. Time is important here. It **was** C, of course.

Vocabulary in Context

apply for	I want to **apply for** a new job. I have to fill out an application.
position	There are jobs available at Baker's. What **position** do you want to apply for?
interview (v.) interview (n.)	People from the store are going to talk to me. They are going to **interview** me. The **interview** is tomorrow.
surprised	I am **surprised**. He doesn't work at Baker's anymore.
reference	Can I use you as my **reference**? Employers are going to call you. They're going to ask you questions about me.
as	He used his employer **as** a reference. She works **as** a cashier. He wants a job **as** a salesman.
employer employee	My **employer** has a big business. He hires new people each year. These people are his **employees**.
check in	I have to **check in** at 8 a.m. for work.

Lesson 1   233

Reading Variation

1. To practice listening skills, have students listen to the audio before opening their books. Ask a few comprehension questions, such as: *Were there interviews today?* (no) Repeat the audio if necessary. Then have students open their books and read along as they listen to the audio.
2. Alternatively, have students begin by listening to the audio as they read along.

Expansion

Reading Have students practice the conversation in pairs. Ask volunteers to roleplay the conversation in front of the class.

Vocabulary in Context To check comprehension, have volunteers in pairs or groups act out selected vocabulary, such as *interview, surprised, employer,* and *employee*.

Applying for a Job in a Store (Reading)
CD 1, Track 53

1. Have students look at the title of the reading and the photos on page 232 to make predictions about the reading. Say: *Halina is talking to Dorota on the phone. What are they talking about? Why was Halina at the store?* (They're talking about applying for a job at the store. Halina was at the store to apply for a job.)
2. Have students read the dialogue silently. Then play the audio and have students read along silently.
3. Check students' basic comprehension. Ask questions, such as: *What store was Halina at?* (Baker's Department Store) *Why were the people there not happy?* (There was a long line to apply for jobs.) *Why did Halina write Dorota's name on the application?* (Dorota was one of her references.) *What were the application questions about?* (job history and education)

To save class time, have students do the reading for homework ahead of time.

VOCABULARY IN CONTEXT

1. Model the pronunciation of each new vocabulary item and have students repeat.
2. Review each vocabulary item. Make sure students understand the examples in the book and create additional example sentences. For example, say: *apply for. My daughter is going to apply for a job as a waitress in a restaurant.* Go over each new vocabulary word similarly, using visuals and realia when appropriate. When possible, point to pictures in the book that illustrate the new vocabulary, such as *interview* on page 231.
3. Have students underline an example of each vocabulary item in the reading.

Unit 11   233

DID YOU KNOW?

Tell the class about different kinds of job interviews:

selection interview: the employer knows you're qualified but wants to find out if you would work well in the company

group interview: the employer interviews you and other candidates at once to separate leaders from followers

panel interview: several interviewers interview you at one time

LISTENING ACTIVITY

🎧 CD 1, Track 54

1. Say: *Listen to the sentences about Dorota and Halina's conversation. Circle* true *or* false. Play the listening selection one time without pausing. Then play it through again, pausing and replaying as necessary.
2. Go over the answers as a class. Ask students to volunteer answers.

11.1 | Affirmative and Negative Statements with *Be*

1. Have students look at grammar chart 11.1 on page 234. Say: *When the subject is singular, use* was. *When the subject is plural, use* were. Go over the affirmative examples. Ask: *What form of* be *in the past do we use with* he *or* she? (was)
2. Direct students' attention to the negative statements in the chart. Remind students that adding *not* to the verb negates the verb. Ask: *What words are contracted in the examples?* (be + not) *What is the plural form?* (weren't) *What is the singular form?* (wasn't)

Did You Know? Almost all stores and small businesses have at least one interview with future employees. Professional jobs often have two and sometimes three interviews.

🎧 **Listening Activity** Listen to the sentences about the conversation. Circle *true* or *false*.

EXAMPLE **(TRUE)** FALSE

1. TRUE **(FALSE)**
2. **(TRUE)** FALSE
3. TRUE **(FALSE)**
4. TRUE **(FALSE)**
5. **(TRUE)** FALSE
6. TRUE **(FALSE)**
7. **(TRUE)** FALSE

11.1 | Affirmative and Negative Statements with *Be*

Subject	Be (Affirmative)	Complement
I	was	on time for work.
An employee	was	late today.
We	were	references for Halina.
You	were	at home today.
All the employees	were	busy.
There	was	a problem at work.
There	were	two new employees.

Subject	Be (Negative)	Complement
I	wasn't	in the office.
Her office	wasn't	open.
We	weren't	busy last night.
You	weren't	on the phone.
The employees	weren't	late for work.
There	wasn't	enough time.
There	weren't	any calls for you.

234 Unit 11

Expansion

Grammar Chart Have students return to the reading on page 233. Ask students to review each use of *was* and *were* and underline the subject.

EXERCISE 1 Fill in the blanks with the affirmative or negative form of *be* in the past. Use the ideas from the conversation.

EXAMPLE Halina __was__ at Baker's Department Store today.

1. Halina's job application __was__ on a computer.
2. Some of the questions __were__ funny.
3. Dorota __wasn't__ at the store with Halina today.
4. The questions on the application __weren't__ hard to answer.
5. Dorota __was__ a reference for Halina.
6. There __were__ questions about Halina's job history on the application.
7. Halina __wasn't__ at Baker's for a sale.
8. People __were__ in line for jobs at Baker's today.

11.2 | Expressions of Time in the Past

Examples	Explanation
I was in Chicago two days **ago**.	We use *ago* with numbers of minutes, hours, days, weeks, months, or years. It means *before now*.
He wasn't at work **yesterday**.	Yesterday is the day before today.
We were there **last week**. They weren't with us **last night**.	We use *last* with the words *night, week, month,* and *year*. It means the night, week, month, or year before the present one.

EXERCISE 2 ABOUT YOU Make statements about you. Use the words given. Use the affirmative or negative form of *be* in the past.

EXAMPLE at home last night
I wasn't at home last night.

1. in this class yesterday

   Answers will vary.

2. on a bus this morning

Lesson 1   235

EXERCISE 1

1. Have students read the direction line. Go over the example in the Student Book.
2. Have students complete Exercise 1 individually. Check the answers as a class.
3. If necessary, review grammar chart 11.1 on page 234.

11.2 | Expressions of Time in the Past

Have students look at grammar chart 11.2 on page 235. Say: *Ago, yesterday, and last are expressions we use with the past.* Go over the examples and the explanations. Give additional examples. (e.g., *This is October. My mother was in the hospital a month ago, in September. We didn't have class yesterday. I wasn't at work last month. I was on vacation.*)

EXERCISE 2

1. Say: *You're going to make the following statements true for you.* Have students read the direction line. Go over the example in the Student Book. Ask a volunteer to model the example.
2. Have students complete Exercise 2 individually. Then have students compare answers in pairs. Circulate to observe pair work. Give help as needed.
3. If necessary, review grammar chart 11.2 on page 235.

Expansion

Grammar Chart Have students write three additional sentences using the time expressions in the chart.

11.3 | Yes/No Questions with Be

1. Have students look at grammar chart **11.3** on page 236. Say: *When making a yes/no question with the past tense of* be, *write* was *or* were *before the subject*. Go over the examples.
2. Say: *Short answers contain the subject and* was *or* were. *They don't contain the complement*. Go over the questions and short answers. Check students' comprehension. Point to various example answers and ask students to name the implied complement. (e.g., For the first example, ask: *You were* what? *On time today*.)

EXERCISE 3

1. Say: *In this exercise, you're going to write* yes/no *questions and short answers*. Have students read the direction line. Go over the example in the Student Book.
2. Have students complete Exercise 3 individually. Go over the answers with the class.
3. If necessary, review grammar chart **11.3** on page 236.

---

3. on time for class today

4. an employee of a store last year

5. an employer in my country

6. in my country two years ago

7. a teenager five years ago

11.3 | Yes/No Questions with Be

Be	Subject	Complement	Short Answer
Was	I	on time today?	Yes, you were.
Was	the new employee	at work today?	No, she wasn't.
Were	you	on a bus today?	Yes, I was.
Were	the new employees	late today?	No, they weren't.
Was	there	an interview today?	Yes, there was.
Were	there	any jobs available?	No, there weren't.

EXERCISE 3 Write a *yes/no* question about each statement. Use the words in parentheses ( ). Answer with a short answer. Use the ideas in the conversation.

EXAMPLE Halina was at Baker's Department Store today. (at a job interview)
Was she at a job interview? No, she wasn't.

1. Many people were at Baker's. (to apply for jobs)
   Were many people at Baker's to apply for jobs?

2. There were questions on Halina's application. (about her job history)
   Were there questions about her job history?

3. The job application was on a computer. (easy to fill out)
   Was the job application easy to fill out?

4. Halina was surprised. (about the positions at Baker's)
   Was Halina surprised about the positions at Baker's?

Expansion

Grammar Chart Have students practice answering the questions in the chart with long answers.

5. Many people were in line. (for interviews)
   Were many people in line for interviews?

6. Dorota was helpful. (a reference for Halina)
   Was Dorota a reference for Halina?

11.4 | Information Questions with *Be*

Question Word	Be	Subject	Complement/Time Expression	Short Answer
Why	was	Dorota's name	on Halina's job application?	Because Dorota was a reference.
Where	were	you	today?	At Baker's.
Who	was	your last employer?		Baker's Department Store.
How	was	your job interview	last week?	It was great!
Why	were	there	a lot of people at Baker's?	To apply for holiday positions.

EXERCISE 4 Complete the short conversations. Ask an information question about each statement. The underlined words are the answers.

EXAMPLE A: I wasn't at work today.
B: *Where were you?*
A: I was <u>at a job interview</u>.

1. A: My employer was <u>surprised</u>.
   B: _____*Why was he surprised?*_____
   A: <u>Because</u> I was an hour early for work.

2. A: There were a lot of questions on the application.
   B: _____*How were they?*_____
   A: They were <u>easy</u>.

Lesson 1 237

11.4 | Information Questions with *Be*

1. Have students look at grammar chart **11.4** on page 237. Say: *When making an information question with the past tense of be, write the question word plus was or were before the subject.* Go over the examples in the chart.

2. Say: *Short answers only contain the information requested. They don't contain the subject or be.* Review the questions and short answers. Note the example: *It was great!* Remind students that some short answers can be in complete sentences if they give a very general piece of information as an answer. If necessary, have students review similar grammar rules for question words in chart **4.9** on page 82.

EXERCISE 4

1. Have students read the direction line. Go over the example in the Student Book.
2. Have students complete Exercise 4 individually. Have students share their answers with the class.
3. If necessary, review grammar chart **11.4** on page 237.

Expansion

Exercise 4 Have students practice the short conversations in pairs. Ask volunteers to roleplay the conversation in front of the class.

Unit 11   237

11.5 | Subject Questions with *Be*

1. Have students look at grammar chart **11.5** on page 238. Remind students that in subject questions, the subject is the question word and the question word can be a word or phrase. Review the examples and short answers. Say: *Short answers do not state the complement. They go back to the subject.* Write the following short answers on the board:

   The student by the window.
   Three or four.

2. Ask students to write questions that could be answered by these short answers. Ask several students to share their questions with the class.

EXERCISE 5

1. Say: *In this exercise, you're going to complete questions about statements.* Have students read the direction line. Go over the example in the book. Note the answer. Ask: *Who does* Who *mean?* (some employees) *What does* there *mean?* (at the office) Have volunteers model the example.
2. Have students complete Exercise 5 individually. Have students share and discuss their answers with the class.
3. If necessary, review grammar chart **11.5** on page 238.

---

3. A: There was a new employee in the store yesterday.
   B: _Who was the new employee in the store?_
   A: It was a young woman. I don't know her name.
4. A: They were out of town for the holidays.
   B: _Where were they?_
   A: In Florida.
5. A: I was at Baker's several days ago.
   B: _When were you at Baker's?_
   A: On December 23.
6. A: Many positions were available at Baker's.
   B: _What kind of positions?_
   A: Sales positions.

11.5 | Subject Questions with *Be*

Question Word (Subject)	Be	Complement	Short Answer
How many employees	were	late today?	Only one.
Which employee	was	late?	The new employee.

EXERCISE 5 Complete the short conversations with information questions as subjects. Use *be* in the past.

EXAMPLE A: Some employees were at the office yesterday.
B: Who _was there_ ?

1. A: Many questions were on the application.
   B: What kind of _questions were on the application_ ?
2. A: Some people were surprised.
   B: Who _was surprised_ ?
3. A: Positions were available in that company last month.
   B: How many _positions were available_ ?
4. A: Something was wrong with your application.
   B: What _was wrong with my application_ ?
5. A: Some of the questions were funny.
   B: Which _questions were funny_ ?

238 Unit 11

Expansion

Exercise 5 Have students write answers to the questions, giving specific information. (e.g., for #1: What kind of questions were on the application? There were questions about work experience.) Then have students take turns asking and answering the questions in pairs.

EXERCISE 6 Shafia is very interested in Halina's job application. She is asking a lot of questions. Fill in their conversation with an expression from the box below. Use two of the expressions twice.

| there were | were | was | what was |
| were there | weren't | wasn't | were you ✓ |

Shafia: So, your application was on a computer. <u>Were you</u> (example) comfortable with that?

Halina: Sure. I know a lot about the computer. The computer was an important part of my job in Poland.

Shafia: <u>What was</u> (1) your job in Poland?

Halina: I was in sales. Part of my job was to write sales reports.

Shafia: <u>Were there</u> (2) a lot of questions about your job history? American employers are very interested in that.

Halina: No. I have a very short job history.

Shafia: <u>Was</u> (3) it difficult to find references? I worry about that. I don't know many people here.

Halina: Dorota was one reference for me. The other two <u>were</u> (4) friends of Peter's. It <u>wasn't</u> (5) difficult to find references. People are happy to be a reference for you.

Shafia: <u>Were there</u> (6) any questions about American work customs? Those are difficult. I don't know much about work customs here.

Halina: <u>There were</u> (7) some questions. But they <u>weren't</u> (8) difficult to answer. There were three possible answers. It <u>was</u> (9) easy to choose the correct answer most of the time.

Lesson 1   239

EXERCISE 6

1. Have students read the direction line. Review the example in the Student Book. Remind students that two of the expressions will be used twice. Remind students that the first word in a sentence must be capitalized.
2. Have students complete Exercise 6 individually. Then have students compare answers in pairs. Circulate to observe pair work. Give help as needed.
3. If necessary, review the grammar charts in **Lesson 1**.

   To save class time, have students complete the exercise for homework ahead of time.

Exercise 6 Variation

Do the exercise as a class. Have various students read the dialogue out loud and complete Shafia's questions or Halina's statements. Ask the class to explain why the answer is correct or incorrect.

Lesson 2 | Overview

GRAMMAR

1. Write the following statement on the board: *The teacher asked a lot of questions.* Say: *In the last lesson, we learned how to form the past tense of* be *and how to make questions with the past tense of* be. *Now we're going to learn how to form the past of regular and irregular verbs.*
2. Elicit prior knowledge. Ask: *What regular verbs do you know? What irregular verbs do you know?* Write a few regular verbs on the board. (e.g., *talk, live, ask*) Ask volunteers to give the past tense form and make a sentence with the verb.

CONTEXT

1. Say: *In the last lesson, we read about applying for a job in a store. Now Halina is applying for an office job.* Have students share their opinions. Ask: *When you apply for an office job, what questions do employers ask you? What do they want to know?*
2. Direct students' attention to the picture of Halina in a job interview on page 240. Ask: *What is going on in this picture?* (Halina is speaking with two people about her last job. She is in a job interview.) Point to the woman. Ask: *What is she thinking about?*

BEFORE YOU READ

1. Go over each question as a class. Have a volunteer read the questions or read them to the class yourself. Have students answer the questions in pairs.
2. Ask for a few volunteers to share their answers with the class.

   To save class time, skip "Before You Read," or have students prepare their answers for homework ahead of time.

LESSON 2

GRAMMAR

Affirmative Forms of Regular Past Tense Verbs
Spelling of the Regular *-ed* Form
Irregular Forms of the Simple Past Tense
Negative Forms of Regular and Irregular Past Tense Verbs

CONTEXT

Applying for a Job in an Office

Before You Read
1. Do you want a job in an office? Why or why not?
2. Where do you want to work? Why?

My old job was very difficult.

240 Unit 11

Expansion

Theme The topic for this unit can be enhanced with the following ideas:

1. A chart or pre-reading discussion about office work in the U.S. today listing features such as the ability to work from home and casual Friday
2. A list of interviewing *Do's & Don'ts* from a magazine article
3. Various types of résumés

APPLYING FOR A JOB IN AN OFFICE

Halina and Dorota are talking about another job application.

Halina: I **had** a job interview today.
Dorota: Great! Was it at Baker's Department Store?
Halina: No. I **applied** for a job in an office. I **saw** an ad online for a sales position a few weeks ago. I **sent** my résumé. And they **called** me yesterday. I **went** for the interview this morning.
Dorota: That was fast. How was the interview?
Halina: Well, **I didn't get** there on time. I **didn't find** parking close to the office building. I **had to park** three blocks away.
Dorota: How late were you?
Halina: Only 15 minutes.
Dorota: Next time, go to the building the day before the interview. You can check travel time and parking then.
Halina: I **didn't like** the interview, Dorota. It **took** an hour. There were two people. They **asked** me a lot of questions. And I was nervous.
Dorota: What were some of the questions?
Halina: Well, one question was, "Why do you want this job?" I told them my last job was too hard. I **worked** long hours. I **didn't make** enough money.
Dorota: You shouldn't complain about your past jobs. Instead, say positive things about this new company.
Halina: I **did**. I **told** them some good things. Their company isn't too far from my neighborhood. It's easy to get there. I **didn't complain** about the parking.
Dorota: But you **didn't say** anything about the company. Find some information on the company's Web site. What does the company do? What do you like about it? It's important to know something about the company.
Halina: I **made** a lot of mistakes in this interview. I **said** the wrong things.
Dorota: Don't worry. It was good practice. The next time is going to be easier.

Vocabulary in Context

résumé	My **résumé** is very important. It has my job history and my education history on it.
ad	There are **ads** for jobs in the newspaper and online.
block	There's an office building three **blocks** from my house.
instead	I don't want coffee. I want tea **instead**.
positive	Don't complain. Say something **positive** instead.
make mistakes	Some of her answers on the test were wrong. She **made mistakes**.

Lesson 2 241

Applying for a Job in an Office (Reading)
CD 1, Track 55

1. Have students use the title and picture to make predictions about the reading. Say: *Halina is telling Dorota about another job interview. What is Halina going to say about the interview? Did she like it?* (No. She made a lot of mistakes.)
2. Have students read the dialogue silently. Then play the audio and have students read along silently.
3. Check students' basic comprehension. Ask questions, such as: *Did Halina get to the interview on time?* (No. She was 15 minutes late.) *How long was the interview?* (one hour) *Why didn't she like the interview?* (They asked her a lot of questions and she was nervous.) *What did she say about her last job?* (She had to work too hard and they didn't pay her enough money.) *What did she say about the company she was interviewing with?* (The company isn't too far away and the parking is good.)

To save class time, have students do the reading for homework ahead of time.

VOCABULARY IN CONTEXT

1. Model the pronunciation of each new vocabulary item and have students repeat.
2. Make sure students understand the meaning of each vocabulary item. Review the examples in the book and create additional example sentences. For example, say: *instead. I don't want to drive to work. I want to walk instead.* Review each new vocabulary item similarly, using visuals and realia when appropriate.
3. Have students underline an example of each new vocabulary item in the reading.

Reading Variation

1. To practice listening skills, have students listen to the audio before opening their books. Ask a few comprehension questions, such as: *Should you complain about your past jobs in an interview?* (no) Repeat the audio if necessary. Then have students open their books and read along as they listen to the audio.
2. Alternatively, have students begin by listening to the audio as they read along.

Expansion

Reading Have students practice the conversation in pairs. Ask volunteers to roleplay all or part of the conversation in front of the class.

Vocabulary in Context To check comprehension, have volunteers in pairs or groups act out selected vocabulary, such as *résumé, positive,* and *instead*.

Unit 11 241

DID YOU KNOW?

Tell students about personnel agencies. Explain that some agencies charge fees. If you accept a job and then quit before a specific time period (e.g., six months), you may have to pay the agency.

LISTENING ACTIVITY

🎧 **CD 1, Track 56**

1. Say: *Listen to the questions about Halina and Dorota's conversation. Circle* true *or* false. Play the listening selection one time without pausing. Then play it through again, pausing and replaying as necessary.
2. Go over the answers as a class. Ask students to volunteer answers.

11.6 | Affirmative Forms of Regular Past Tense Verbs

1. Have students look at grammar chart 11.6 on page 242. Ask: *How do you form the past tense of regular verbs?* (add *-ed* to the base form)
2. Review the Pronunciation Note. Write on the board: -ed= /d/, /t/, /ɪd/. Read the rule and then read out the example sentences for each sound. Have students look at the verbs in the chart. Pronounce each verb and ask students to name the sound. (/d/: *complained, filled out*; /t/ *parked, asked*; /ɪd/: *needed, wanted*)

Did You Know? Sometimes companies hire people for 90 day trial periods. If the employee does good work, he or she usually gets the job permanently after the 90 days.

🎧 **Listening Activity** Listen to the sentences about the conversation. Circle *true* or *false*.

EXAMPLE (TRUE) FALSE

1. TRUE (FALSE)
2. TRUE (FALSE)
3. (TRUE) FALSE
4. (TRUE) FALSE
5. TRUE (FALSE)
6. (TRUE) FALSE
7. (TRUE) FALSE

11.6 | Affirmative Forms of Regular Past Tense Verbs

We add *-ed* to the base form of the verb to form the past tense of many verbs. We use the past tense with actions completed in the past.

Subject	Verb + -ed	Complement
I	complained	about my last job.
He	filled out	the application.
Halina	needed	a job application.
We	parked	close to our work.
You	wanted	a better job.
The employers	asked	me a lot of questions.

Pronunciation Note: The affirmative ending *-ed* has three sounds: /d/, /t/, and /ɪd/. We pronounce the /ɪd/ sound if the verb ends in a *t* or *d* sound. Listen to your teacher pronounce the following sentences:

/d/ He played football.
We used a computer.

/t/ She washed the dishes.
You cooked the meal.

/ɪd/ They wanted a new car.
I decided to get a job.

242   Unit 11

Expansion

Grammar Chart Have students practice the pronunciation of the words in the grammar chart and other past tense verbs in pairs. Write these additional verbs on the board for practice: *worked* (/t/), *filed* (/d/), *graded* (/ɪd/), *clashed* (/t/), *bagged* (/d/) Circulate to give help with pronunciation.

EXERCISE 1 Fill in the blanks with the past tense of the verb in parentheses ( ). Use the ideas in the conversation.

EXAMPLE Halina __parked__ far from the office building.
(park)

1. Halina __filled out__ an application for a sales job.
(fill out)
2. A sales company __called__ Halina for an interview.
(call)
3. Two people __interviewed__ Halina.
(interview)
4. The people __asked__ Halina about her job history.
(ask)
5. Halina __complained__ about her old job.
(complain)
6. Dorota and Halina __talked__ about the interview.
(talk)
7. Halina __needed__ to say something positive about the new company during her interview.
(need)

11.7 | Spelling of the Regular -ed Form

Examples	Explanation
work/worked We **worked** there for three years.	For most verbs, add -ed to the base form.
live/lived She **lived** near her new work place.	If the verb ends in e, add -d only.
study/studied She **studied** for many years to get this job.	If the verb ends in consonant + y, change y to i and add -ed.
play/played The team **played** well.	If the verb ends in a vowel + y, do not change the y to i.
shop/shopped s h o p C V C She **shopped** for food yesterday.	Double the final consonant if a single syllable word ends in consonant (C) + vowel (V) + consonant (C).

Lesson 2 243

EXERCISE 1

1. Have students read the direction line. Go over the example in the Student Book.
2. Have students complete Exercise 1 individually. Go over the answers with the class.
3. If necessary, review grammar chart **11.6** on page 242.

11.7 | Spelling of the Regular -ed Form

1. Have students look at grammar chart **11.7** on page 243. Review the examples and explanations.
2. Write additional examples on the board. Ask students what the spelling rule is. (e.g., *carry/carried, pray/prayed, drop/dropped, fire/fired, talk/talked*)

Expansion

Exercise 1 Have students practice the pronunciation of the words in Exercise 1. Circulate to give help with pronunciation.

EXERCISE 2

1. Have students read the direction line. Go over the example.
2. Have students complete Exercise 2 individually. Go over the answers as a class.
3. If necessary, review grammar chart **11.7** on page 243.

11.8 | Irregular Forms of the Simple Past Tense

1. Have students look at grammar chart **11.8** on page 244. Say: *You have to memorize the past tense forms of irregular verbs.* Go over the verbs in the chart.
2. Read and review the Language Notes.
3. Have students close their books. Check comprehension by asking students to give the past tense form of some of the verbs in the chart. Write the verbs on the board. (e.g., *take, make, give, do, say, know*) Ask various students to say and spell the past tense form. Ask volunteers to make sentences.

EXERCISE 3

1. Have students read the direction line. Go over the example.
2. Have students complete Exercise 3 individually. Then have students compare answers in pairs. Circulate to observe pair work. Give help as needed.
3. If necessary, review grammar chart **11.8** on page 244.
   🕐 To save class time, have students do the exercise for homework ahead of time.

EXERCISE 2 Fill in the blanks with the past tense of the verb in parentheses ( ). Use the spelling rules from chart 11.7.

EXAMPLE   I __liked__ my job in that company.
(like)

1. Many people __applied__ for the sales job.
   (apply)
2. Employees in that company probably __studied__ for a long time.
   (study)
3. You __stopped__ in front of the office building.
   (stop)
4. Those women __planned__ to work on Saturday.
   (plan)
5. We __stayed__ at the interview for half an hour.
   (stay)
6. The company __hired__ some new workers for the holidays.
   (hire)

11.8 | Irregular Forms of the Simple Past Tense

Base Form	Past Form	Base Form	Past Form	Base Form	Past Form
take	took	say	said	send	sent
have	had	tell	told	go	went
get	got	make	made	see	saw
know	knew	give	gave	do	did

Language Notes:
1. We use irregular past tense forms in the affirmative only.
2. Look for a complete list of irregular past tense forms in Appendix D.

EXERCISE 3 Fill in the blanks with the past tense of a verb from the box below. Use chart 11.8 to check for irregular past tense forms.

see ✓	have	send	give
go	get	tell	take

EXAMPLE   Halina __saw__ two people at her interview.

1. Halina __had__ a job interview last week.
2. She __sent__ her résumé to a company.
3. She __went__ to the office building for an interview.
4. The interview __took__ an hour.

Expansion

Exercise 2 and 3 Have students practice the pronunciation of the past tense verbs in both exercises. Have students work in pairs. Circulate to help with pronunciation.

5. Halina ___got___ information about the job online.
6. Dorota ___told___ Halina how to find information about the company.
7. Dorota ___gave___ Halina some good advice.

11.9 | Negative Forms of Regular and Irregular Past Tense Verbs

We use *didn't* + the base form for the negative of both regular and irregular verbs in the past.

Subject	Didn't	Verb (Base Form)	Complement
I	didn't	work	at Baker's last year.
Halina	didn't	arrive	on time.
My employer	didn't	hire	any new employees.
You	didn't	apply	for the job.
We	didn't	know	all the answers.
They	didn't	give	the right answer.
Those ads	didn't	tell	the truth.

Language Note: Compare the affirmative and the negative.
She **worked** on Saturday. She **didn't work** on Sunday.
They **went** by car. They **didn't go** by bus.

EXERCISE 4 Use the words in parentheses ( ) to make a negative statement about the sentence given.

EXAMPLE Halina said many things. (positive things about the company)
But _she didn't say positive things about the company._

1. Halina parked her car. (close to the office building)
   But _she didn't park close to the office building._

2. Halina interviewed for an office job. (at Baker's)
   But _she didn't interview for a job at Baker's._

3. Dorota went with Halina to the supermarket. (to her job interview)
   But _she didn't go with Halina to her job interview._

4. The new employees worked during the week. (on weekends)
   But _they didn't work on weekends._

5. Halina used Dorota as a reference on her application. (Simon)
   But _she didn't use Simon as a reference._

Lesson 2   245

11.9 | Negative Forms of Regular and Irregular Past Tense Verbs

1. Have students look at grammar chart 11.9 on page 245. Say: *We use didn't plus the base form for the negative of regular and irregular verbs in the past.* Write on the board:

   didn't + base form of verb

   Go over the examples in the chart.

   Stress that *didn't + the base form* is used for all verbs in the past, both regular and irregular.

2. Review the Language Note. Give additional examples for *went.* (e.g., *Jay went yesterday. He didn't go last week.*) Write the past tense form of a few irregular verbs on the board (e.g., *knew, gave, told*) and ask volunteers to give an affirmative and negative sentence for each one.

EXERCISE 4

1. Have students read the direction line. Review the example in the Student Book.
2. Have students complete Exercise 4 individually. Go over the answers as a class.
3. If necessary, review grammar chart 11.8 on page 244 and 11.9 on page 245.

Expansion

Grammar Chart Have students go back to Exercise 3 on page 244. Say: *Make the sentences in this exercise negative.*

Unit 11   245

EXERCISE 5

1. Have students read the direction line. Go over the examples in the book. Remind students to use *didn't* + the base form for both regular and irregular verbs in negative statements. Have students skim the reading first. Explain any unfamiliar terms. (e.g., *out of town on business* = to go to another city for business)
2. Have students complete Exercise 5 individually. Then have students compare answers with a partner. Circulate to observe pair work. Give help as needed.
3. If necessary, review grammar chart **11.9** on page 245.

To save class time, have students do the exercise for homework ahead of time.

EXERCISE 5 Complete the short conversations with the affirmative or negative past tense of the verb in parentheses ( ).

EXAMPLES
A: I used you as a reference on a job application.
B: Yes, I know. The company ___called___ me yesterday.
(call)

A: I used you as a reference on a job application.
B: I'm surprised. The company ___didn't call___ me.
(call)

1. A: Halina applied for a job at Baker's last month.
   B: Yes, but she ___didn't get___ the job. She's looking for another job now.
   (get)

2. A: You look nervous. What's wrong?
   B: I ___made___ a big mistake at work today.
   (make)

3. A: You didn't apply for the sales position. Why?
   B: I ___didn't have___ time. I'm going to apply next week.
   (have)

4. A: I was surprised by the news.
   B: We were all surprised. We ___didn't expect___ this news.
   (expect)

5. A: I don't work at that company now.
   B: Why? It's a good company.
   A: Yes. But they ___sent___ me out of town on business too often. I ___didn't see___ my family enough.
   (send) (see)

6. A: You have a new job now.
   B: Yes. How do you know?
   A: Your friend, Jesse, ___told___ me.
   (tell)

246 Unit 11

Expansion

Exercise 5 Have students practice the short conversations in pairs. Ask volunteers to roleplay the dialogues in front of the class. Have the class listen for and, when needed, correct pronunciation of past tense regular verbs in the affirmative.

EXERCISE 6 ABOUT YOU Use the words given to tell about your activities. Use an affirmative or negative past tense sentence.

EXAMPLE stay home all day yesterday
I didn't stay home all day yesterday. OR I stayed home all day yesterday.

Answers will vary.
1. apply for a new job last week
2. use a computer yesterday
3. give the teacher my homework today
4. make a lot of mistakes on the last test
5. take a bus to school today
6. shop at a supermarket last week
7. talk to my teacher before class

EXERCISE 7 Complete the conversation between Dorota and Halina about another job interview three weeks later. Use the affirmative or negative past tense of the verb in parentheses ( ).

Halina: Thanks for your advice about interviews, Dorota. Unfortunately, I __didn't get__ *(example: get)* the sales job. But I __had__ *(1. have)* another interview this morning. It was for a position in another company. The interview __went__ *(2. go)* very well this time.

Dorota: That's good.

Halina: I was on time. And I was prepared. I __learned__ *(3. learn)* about the company on the Web first. I __told__ *(4. tell)* the interviewers positive things about their company. I __didn't complain__ *(5. complain)* about my old job. I was lucky too. They __didn't ask__ *(6. ask)* about Anna. I'm not sure about child care for her yet.

Dorota: Don't worry, Halina. They can't ask any personal questions in a job interview. It's against the law.

Halina: Really? I __didn't know__ *(7. know)* that.

Lesson 2   247

EXERCISE 6

1. Say: *You're going to make these statements true for you by using the affirmative or the negative.* Have students read the direction line. Go over the example in the book. Have a volunteer model #1.
2. Have students complete Exercise 6 individually. Then have students compare answers in pairs. Circulate to observe pair work. Give help as needed.
3. If necessary, review grammar chart **11.9** on page 245.

⏱ To save class time, have students do the exercise for homework ahead of time.

EXERCISE 7

1. Say: *Halina is talking to Dorota about another job interview.* Have students read the direction line. Be sure that students understand this is Halina's third interview. Have a volunteer complete the first sentence.
2. Have students complete the rest of Exercise 7 individually. Then have students compare answers in pairs. Circulate to observe pair work. Give help as needed.
3. If necessary, review the grammar charts in **Lesson 2**.

⏱ To save class time, have students do the exercise for homework ahead of time.

Expansion

Exercise 6 Do a quick survey of students' answers. Record the results on the board.

Exercise 7 Have students practice the conversation in pairs. Then have volunteers roleplay the conversation in front of the class.

Have students work in pairs to create their own conversation about a successful or unsuccessful job interview.

Unit 11   247

Lesson 3 | Overview

GRAMMAR

1. Briefly review the objectives of Lessons 1 and 2. Give examples of present and past tense forms of some verbs taught in the lessons (e.g., *be, go, talk, do, say, work*) and of affirmative and negative sentences in the past. (e.g., *I went to class. I didn't go to class.*) Say: *In Lesson 3, we're going to study more irregular verbs and more questions in the past tense.* Write the lesson objectives on the board.
2. Activate students' knowledge. Ask students to make questions in the past tense based on statements. Prompt with statements, such as: *Jenny was a waitress many years ago; Tim only worked there for one day.* Elicit and list question words on the board if necessary.

CONTEXT

1. Say: *We're going to read about jobs of the future. Nowadays, many people choose to work in medicine.* Point out the fastest-growing jobs listed in the Culture Note. Ask: *Why do people choose these jobs?* Have students' share their ideas.
2. Direct students' attention to the picture of the professionals. Ask: *What careers or professions do you see here?* Then ask: *How long does it take to prepare for these jobs?*

BEFORE YOU READ

1. Go over each question as a class. Have a volunteer read the questions or read them to the class yourself. Have students discuss the questions in pairs.
2. Ask for a few volunteers to share their answers with the class.

   To save class time, skip "Before You Read," or have students prepare their answers for homework ahead of time.

LESSON 3

GRAMMAR

Yes/No Questions in the Past—Regular and Irregular Verbs
More Irregular Verbs in the Past Tense
Information Questions in the Past
Subject Questions

CONTEXT

Jobs of the Future

Before You Read

1. Do you know some people with interesting jobs? What kind of jobs do they have?
2. In your opinion, what are the jobs of the future?

248 Unit 11

Culture Note

According to the U.S. Department of Labor, these are the top ten fastest-growing jobs in the U.S:

Medical assistants
Network systems and data communications analysts
Physician assistants
Social and human service assistants
Home health aides
Medical records and health information technicians
Physical therapist aides
Computer software engineers, applications
Computer software engineers, systems software
Physical therapist assistants

---

248 *Grammar in Context Basic* Teacher's Edition

JOBS OF THE FUTURE

Matt is visiting Simon and Marta for the first time. Matt helped Marta's father in the hospital. Simon and Marta are talking about Matt's job.

Simon: So, Matt, you have an interesting career. You are a physical therapist, right?
Matt: Well, not exactly. I'm a PT assistant. I help the physical therapists in the hospital.
Marta: **Why did you choose** this career, Matt?
Matt: Well, I like physical activity. I like to help people. And a job in health services is a good job for the future. One in four new jobs is going to be in health services. **Did you know** that?
Simon: Yes. We read something about it last week.
Marta: **What did you do** to prepare for this job?
Matt: First, I took classes at a community college. I was in a special program for PT assistants.
Simon: **How long did it take?**
Matt: Two years. I got a certificate from the college.
Marta: **Did you have** on-the-job training also?
Matt: Yes. We had training at the hospital for some time. I worked with several physical therapists and their patients. I was so busy in those days. I had another job too.
Marta: **What did you do?**
Matt: I was a part-time fitness instructor at an athletic club. I thought about a career in fitness.
Simon: **How long did you stay** there?
Matt: Only a year. Two jobs took too much time.

Vocabulary in Context

career	One **career** of the future is health services. Another **career** of the future is employment services.
patient	Marta's father was in the hospital. He was a **patient**.
physical therapist (PT)	A **physical therapist** helps patients move and exercise after an accident or injury.
training	Companies often give new employees on-the-job **training**. The employees learn about the job during **training**.
athletic club (health club)	People go to an **athletic club** to exercise. Sometimes we call it a health club.
fitness instructor	A **fitness instructor** works at a health club. He or she helps people with exercise and exercise machines.
temporary	His job is **temporary**. He is going to work for only four months.

Lesson 3   249

Reading Variation

1. To practice listening skills, have students listen to the audio before opening their books. Ask a few comprehension questions, such as: *Who was in the hospital?* (Marta's father) Repeat the audio if necessary. Then have students open their books and read along as they listen to the audio.
2. Alternatively, have students begin by listening to the audio as they read along.

Vocabulary Teaching Ideas

Use the following ideas to teach these terms:

career: Ask: *What's the difference between a career and a job? A career is a profession that you have training for. A job is an activity you do to earn money.*
patient: Say: *When you receive medical care, you are a patient.*

Expansion

Reading Have students practice the conversation in groups of three. Ask volunteers to roleplay the conversation in front of the class.

Vocabulary in Context To check comprehension, have volunteers in pairs or groups act out selected vocabulary, such as *patient, physical therapist,* and *fitness instructor.*

Jobs of the Future (Reading) CD 1, Track 57

1. Have students look at the title of the reading and the picture on page 248. Have them read the direction line. Tell students to make predictions about the reading. Ask: *What is the reading about? What questions will Marta and Simon ask Matt?*
2. Have students read the dialogue silently. Then play the audio and have students read along silently.
3. Check students' basic comprehension. Ask questions, such as: *Is Matt a physical therapist?* (No. He's a physical therapist assistant.) *What does he like about the career?* (He likes the physical activity and he likes to help people.) *What other kind of job did he have?* (He was a fitness instructor at an athletic club.)

To save class time, have students do the reading for homework ahead of time.

VOCABULARY IN CONTEXT

1. Model the pronunciation of each new vocabulary item and have students repeat.
2. Make sure students understand the meaning of each vocabulary item. Review the examples in the book and create additional example sentences. For example, say: *career. I started my teaching career 15 years ago after graduating from college.* Go over each new vocabulary item similarly, using visuals and realia when appropriate. When possible, point to pictures in the book that illustrate the new vocabulary, such as *patient* on page 248.
3. Have students underline an example of each new vocabulary item in the reading. Explain that although *temporary* is not in the reading, this term describes many work positions.

DID YOU KNOW?

Tell students that most college students in the U.S. work. About 80% of undergraduates have jobs.

LISTENING ACTIVITY

🎧 *CD 1, Track 58*

1. Say: *Listen to the sentences about Simon and Marta's conversation with Matt. Circle* true *or* false. Play the listening selection one time without pausing. Then play it through again, pausing and replaying as necessary.
2. Go over the answers as a class. Ask students to volunteer answers.

11.10 | *Yes/No* Questions in the Past—Regular and Irregular Verbs

1. Have students look at grammar chart **11.10** on page 250. Say: *To make* yes/no *questions in the past, we use* did *plus the base form of the verb.* Remind students that the pattern is the same for regular and irregular verbs. Go over the example questions and short answers.
2. Read and review the Language Note. Model the pronunciation of *did you* and *did he* in Note 1. For Note 2, elicit additional examples of affirmative and question forms for verbs in the chart, such as *stay*, *have*, and *make*.

Part-time or temporary work is a good way to find a job. Many people get their full-time job that way.

Listening Activity Listen to the sentences about the conversation. Circle *true* or *false*.

EXAMPLE TRUE (FALSE)

1. (TRUE) FALSE   5. TRUE (FALSE)
2. TRUE (FALSE)   6. (TRUE) FALSE
3. (TRUE) FALSE   7. TRUE (FALSE)
4. (TRUE) FALSE

11.10 | *Yes/No* Questions in the Past—Regular and Irregular Verbs

The question pattern for regular and irregular verbs is the same. We use *did* + the base form.

Did	Subject	Verb (Base Form)	Complement	Short Answer
Did	I	make	a mistake?	Yes, you did.
Did	Matt	choose	a job in a health club?	No, he didn't.
Did	she	get	the job?	No, she didn't.
Did	we	do	the right thing?	Yes, you did.
Did	you	have	an interview?	No, I didn't.
Did	they	stay	with that company?	Yes, they did.

Language Note:

1. In normal speech, we pronounce *did you* as /dɪdʒə/, and *did he* as /dɪdi/. Listen to your teacher pronounce the following sentences:
   Did you see that man?   Did he get the job?
   Did you know that?   Did he have any training?
2. Compare the affirmative and question forms.
   He **worked** on Saturday. **Did** he **work** on Sunday?
   She **got** the job. **Did** she **get** a good salary?

Expansion

Grammar Chart Have students write three *yes/no* questions in the past to ask their partner.

EXERCISE 1 Write yes/no questions with the words given. Answer them with a short answer. Use the ideas in the conversation.

EXAMPLE Matt / need / an education for his job
Did Matt need an education for his job? Yes, he did.

1. Matt / study / at a university
Did Matt study at a university? No, he didn't.

2. Matt / choose / a good career for the future
Did Matt choose a good career for the future? Yes, he did.

3. Matt / help / Marta's father in the hospital
Did Matt help Marta's father in the hospital? Yes, he did.

4. Simon and Marta / ask Matt a lot of questions
Did Simon and Marta ask Matt a lot of questions? Yes, they did.

11.11 | More Irregular Verbs in the Past Tense

Base Form	Past Form	Base Form	Past Form	Base Form	Past Form
eat	ate	spend	spent	come	came
choose	chose	keep	kept	meet	met
reac	read*	feel	felt	leave	left
write	wrote	think	thought	hear	heard

*Pronunciation Note: The past tense of **read** sounds like the color **red**.

EXERCISE 2 Fill in the blanks about the conversation with affirmative past tense verbs. Choose from the verbs above.

EXAMPLE Matt __spent__ two years at a community college.

1. Marta __met__ Matt in the hospital.
2. Matt __came__ to visit Simon and Marta.
3. Matt __chose__ a career in health services.
4. Matt __thought__ about a career as a fitness instructor.
5. Simon __read__ about careers in health services last week.
6. Matt __left__ his job at the athletic club.

Lesson 3   251

EXERCISE 1

1. Have students read the direction line. Go over the example in the Student Book.
2. Have students complete Exercise 1 individually. Check the answers as a class.
3. If necessary, review grammar chart **11.10** on page 250.

11.11 | More Irregular Verbs in the Past Tense

1. Have students close their books. Write the following verbs from the chart on the board: *eat, choose, read, write, spend, keep, leave, hear*. Have students say and spell the past tense forms.
2. Have students open their books and look at grammar chart **11.11** on page 251. Have them check to see how many forms they got correct. Then review all of the verbs in the chart and the Pronunciation Note. Ask volunteers to write short sentences using a past tense form and share the sentence with the class.

EXERCISE 2

1. Have students read the direction line. Ask a volunteer to do #1.
2. Have students complete the rest of Exercise 2 individually. Go over the answers with the class.
3. If necessary, review grammar chart **11.11** on page 251.

Expansion

Grammar Chart Have students write three questions in past tense form to ask their partner. Tell students to use the verbs from the grammar chart.

11.12 | Information Questions in the Past

1. Have students close their books. Write on the board:

    ? word + *did* + subject + base form of verb + complement

    Then write the following scrambled sentences:

    did / at her last job / Susie / ? / work / How long

    ? / What kind of job / Mr. Woods / find / did

    Ask: *What is the order of an information question in the past with* did? Have the class work together to put the questions and punctuation in order. Rewrite the questions correctly on the board. (*How long did Susie work at her last job? / What kind of job did Mr. Woods find?*)
2. Have students look at grammar chart **11.12** on page 252. Review the example questions and short answers.

EXERCISE 3

1. Have students read the direction line. Go over the example.
2. Have students complete Exercise 3 individually. Go over the answers with the class.
3. If necessary, review grammar chart **11.12** on page 252.

11.12 | Information Questions in the Past

Question Word	Did	Subject	Verb (Base Form)	Complement	Short Answer
Why	did	I	get	that job?	Because you had a lot of training.
What kind of job	did	Matt	find?		A job as a PT assistant.
Where	did	you	go	to school?	I went to a community college.
How many jobs	did	he	apply for?		Five.
How long	did	they	work	at their last job?	For five years.

EXERCISE 3 Write an information question for each answer in the short conversation. The underlined words are the answers.

EXAMPLE A: How many jobs did he apply for?
         B: He applied for three jobs.

1. A: Where did you take classes?
   B: I took classes at a community college.
2. A: How did she feel yesterday at work?
   B: She felt sick yesterday at work.
3. A: How many PT assistants did Matt know in that hospital?
   B: Matt knew four PT assistants in that hospital.
4. A: Where did they hear about the job?
   B: They heard about the job from friends.
5. A: How long did Marta's father stay in the hospital?
   B: Marta's father stayed in the hospital for three weeks.
6. A: What kind of part-time job did Matt get?
   B: Matt got a part-time job as a fitness instructor.
7. A: What kind of job did Matt choose?
   B: Matt chose a career as a PT assistant.

252 Unit 11

Expansion

Exercise 3 Have students practice the short conversations in pairs.

11.13 | Subject Questions

Use the verb in the past form with a subject question.

Question Word (Subject)	Verb -ed or Irregular Form	Complement	Short Answer
Which patient	needed	the doctor?	The woman in room 321.
How many patients	came	to the hospital?	Only one.
Who	wrote	about health careers?	A doctor.
What	happened	to her?	She got sick.

EXERCISE 4 Make questions with the words given. Use the question word as the subject. Use regular and irregular past tense verbs.

EXAMPLE Who / take / those people to the hospital
Who took those people to the hospital?

1. What / happen / at the health club yesterday
   What happened at the health club yesterday?
2. Who / tell / you about that job
   Who told you about that job?
3. How many people / apply for / the job as a fitness instructor
   How many people applied for the job as a fitness instructor?
4. Which patient / spend / two weeks at the hospital
   Which patient spent two weeks at the hospital?
5. Which student / choose / a job in health services
   Which student chose a job in health services?

11.14 | More Irregular Verbs in the Past Tense

Base Form	Past Form	Base Form	Past Form	Base Form	Past Form
put	put*	fall	fell	pay	paid
break	broke	hurt	hurt*	cost	cost*
find	found	understand	understood	buy	bought
drive	drove	lose	lost	sell	sold

Language Note: *Some verbs use the base form as the irregular past.

Lesson 3   253

11.13 | Subject Questions

1. Have students look at grammar chart **11.13** on page 253. Say: *Subject questions begin with the question word followed by the verb in the past tense.* Go over the examples.
2. Review the short answers. Remind students that short answers for subject questions usually contain just the subject.

EXERCISE 4

1. Have students read the direction line. Go over the example. Tell students that they will make questions. They will not answer the questions.
2. Have students complete Exercise 4 individually. Go over the answers with the class.
3. If necessary, review grammar chart **11.13** on page 253.

11.14 | More Irregular Verbs In the Past Tense

Have students look at grammar chart **11.14** on page 253. Point out that some verbs use the base form as the past. Go over the verbs and ask volunteers to write sentences in the past on the board using the verbs.

Expansion

Grammar Chart Have students write three questions to ask their partner using verbs from grammar chart **11.14** on page 253.

Unit 11   253

EXERCISE 5

1. Have students read the direction line. Go over the example. Remind students to use the words in parentheses to answer the questions.
2. Have students complete Exercise 5 individually. Then have students compare answers in pairs. Circulate to observe pair work. Give help as needed.
3. If necessary, review grammar charts **11.13** and **11.14** on page 253.

EXERCISE 5 Write a question and an answer with the words given. Use the words in parentheses ( ) in the answer.

EXAMPLE Where / she / hurt her arm (at the health club)
Where did she hurt her arm?
She hurt it at the health club.

1. Which arm / she / break (her right arm)
   Which arm did she break?
   She broke her right arm.

2. How much / his classes / cost ($55 per credit hour)
   How much did his classes cost?
   They cost $55 per credit hour.

3. What kind of books / she / buy for school (science books)
   What kind of books did she buy for school?
   She bought science books for school.

4. How / you / find that job (on the Internet)
   How did you find that job?
   I found that job on the Internet.

5. When / they / lose their jobs (last week)
   When did they lose their jobs?
   They lost their jobs last week.

6. Who / fall (the patient)
   Who fell?
   The patient fell.

7. Which college / he / choose (a community college)
   Which college did he chose?
   He chose a community college.

8. How much / the students / pay for training (a lot of money)
   How much did the students pay for training?
   They paid a lot of money for training.

9. Who / drive / her to the hospital (her husband)
   Who drove her to the hospital?
   Her husband drove her to the hospital.

254   Unit 11

Expansion

Exercise 5 Have students write three to five questions to ask their partner. Tell students that the questions should be in the past tense. Ask students to share their questions and answers with the class.

EDITING ADVICE

1. Don't use the past tense after *to* (the infinitive).
   He wanted to ~~spent~~ *spend* all the money.

2. Use the base form after *did* and *didn't*.
   Where did they ~~went~~ *go* after class?
   They didn't ~~found~~ *find* the answer.

3. Don't use *did* in subject questions. Use the past form.
   What ~~did happen~~ *happened* at school today?

4. Remember to change the spelling of the *-ed* forms for certain verbs.
   She ~~applyed~~ *applied* to that school.

5. Don't forget to change irregular verbs to the correct past tense form.
   I ~~hurted~~ *hurt* my leg.   He ~~breaked~~ *broke* his arm.

EDITING QUIZ

Find the mistakes with the underlined words, and correct them. Not every sentence has a mistake. If the sentence is correct, write *C*.

EXAMPLES The employees didn't ~~arrived~~ *arrive* on time.
          He chose a career in health services. *C*

1. Did they ~~had~~ *have* an interview today?
2. He ~~keeped~~ *kept* that job for three years.
3. What ~~they said~~ *did they say* to her?
4. Who ~~did make~~ *made* a mistake?
5. We felt good after the interview. *C*
6. She didn't ~~understood~~ *understand* the company rules.
7. They ~~tryed~~ *tried* to get a good job.

Lesson 3   255

Editing Advice

1. Have students close their books. Write the example sentences without editing marks or corrections on the board. For example:
   1. *He wanted to spent all the money.*
   2. *Where did they went after class?*
   Ask students to correct each sentence. This activity can be done individually, in pairs, or as a class. After students have corrected each sentence, tell them to turn to page 255. Say: *Now compare your work with Editing Advice in the book.*
2. Go over answers with the class. For troublespots, review the appropriate grammar chart.

Editing Quiz

1. The Editing Quiz may be used as an in-class quiz, a take-home quiz, or as a review. Have students read the direction line. Ask: *Does every sentence have a mistake?* (no) Go over the examples with the class.
2. Have students complete the quiz individually. Collect the completed quizzes for assessment or have students check each other's work. Review the answers with the class. Elicit the relevant grammar point for each correction. For example, for #1, ask: *What's the rule?* (Use *did* plus the base form for *yes/no* questions in the past.)

Unit 11   255

Learner's Log

1. Have students close their books. Ask: *What did you learn about applying for a job, interviews, and jobs of the future? What else do you want to know?* Write students' ideas on the board. Discuss ways in which students can find out more about these topics.
2. Have students open their books to complete the Learner's Log. Remind students to write three questions about jobs in the U.S.

Expansion Activities

These expansion activities provide opportunities for students to interact with one another and further develop their speaking and writing skills. Encourage students to use grammar from this unit whenever possible.

To save class time, assign parts of the activities as homework. Then use class time for interaction and communication. If students do not need additional speaking practice, some of the activities may be assigned as writing activities for homework, or skipped altogether.

WRITING ACTIVITY

Have students complete the activity individually at home or in class. Collect for assessment.

OUTSIDE ACTIVITIES

1. Have students exchange information about health clubs in groups. Find out which ones are the most economical.
2. Ask students to bring their job applications to class. Have them compare and correct applications with classmates in pairs or groups.

INTERNET ACTIVITY

Have students discuss the jobs they researched in groups and decide which seem the best. Have groups share their ideas with the class.

LEARNER'S LOG

1. What did you learn in this unit? Write three sentences in your notebook about each topic:
   • applying for a job
   • a job interview
   • jobs of the future
2. Write three questions you still have about jobs in the United States.

EXPANSION ACTIVITIES

Writing Activity

In your notebook, rewrite the following conversation between Matt and a new patient, Tracy. Change *now* to *last year*. Make the necessary changes to the verbs.

Tracy: Now I work in the employment services department at Baker's Department Store.

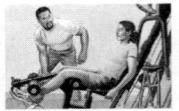

Matt: What do you do there?

Tracy: I keep information about employees. I help employees with their taxes and health insurance. And I write reports.

Matt: How do you get a job like that?

Tracy: Well, it isn't difficult. It takes two years to get a certificate in business.

Matt: Do you like your job?

Tracy: No, I don't. I don't want to work in business. I want a career in health services like you.

Outside Activities

1. Find a health or exercise club in your city or town. Call or visit it. Ask how much it costs to be a member. Ask about the activities at the club. Tell the class about the club.
2. Go to a store near you. Ask for a job application and fill it out for practice.

Internet Activity

Search the words *Occupational Outlook Handbook*. Look for an interesting job. Find it in the handbook. Find the answers to these questions about the job. Tell the class about the job.
   • What education is necessary?
   • What is the average pay for this job?
   • Are jobs like this growing faster than average?

256   Unit 11

Expansion

Learner's Log Have students compare logs in pairs.

Writing Activity Variation

Have students exchange papers with a partner for proofreading.

Internet Activity Variation

1. Tell students that if they don't have Internet access, they can use Internet facilities at a public library.
2. Alternatively, they can ask a librarian for the *Occupational Outlook Handbook* or another reference book with similar data.

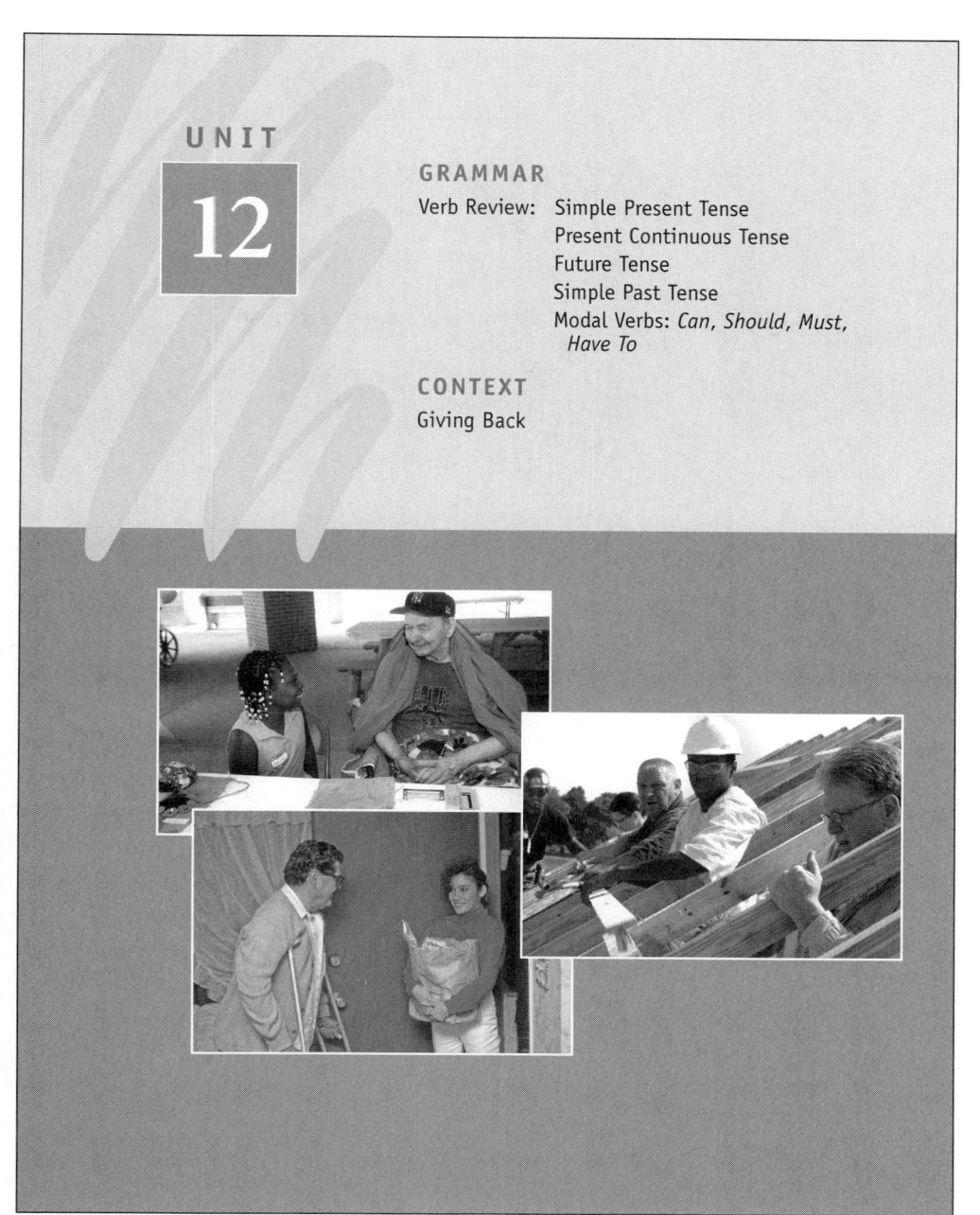

UNIT 12

GRAMMAR
Verb Review: Simple Present Tense
Present Continuous Tense
Future Tense
Simple Past Tense
Modal Verbs: *Can, Should, Must, Have To*

CONTEXT
Giving Back

Expansion

Theme The topic for this unit can be enhanced with the following ideas:

1. Announcements of local volunteer opportunities in flyers and brochures, and Web site addresses of volunteer organizations
2. Information about volunteer organizations and the groups they help

Unit | 12
Unit Overview

GRAMMAR

Say: *In Unit 12, we will review what you learned in Units 1-11.* Activate students' prior knowledge: Ask: *What verb tenses did we study?* Write them on the board: *Simple Present, Present Continuous, Future, Simple Past, Modal Verbs:* can, should, must, have to. Say: *We also studied time expressions.* Write the unit objective on the board: *Verb Review.* Ask volunteers to give a sentence for each tense using a time expression. Ask: *What else did you learn?* (affirmative and negative statements; *yes/no*, information, and subject questions) Ask volunteers to give examples.

CONTEXT

1. Begin by directing students' attention to the photos. Ask: *Who do you see in these pictures? Where are they? What are they doing?* (Top left: A little girl seems to be visiting an older man in a medical care facility. Bottom left: A young girl is bringing groceries to a man on crutches at his house. Right: Three men are building a house.)
2. Ask: *What do you think this unit is going to be about?* (helping people; giving back to the community) Say: *Look at the pictures again. How do people give back to the community?* (do things for people who need help–do their errands for them, visit them to cheer them up, help build them a new home)
3. Ask: *Should everyone give back? Who should we help?* Have students share their ideas and experience.

Unit 12   257

Lesson 1 | Overview

GRAMMAR

Say: *In Lesson 1, we're going to review verb tenses. What else are we going to review?* (infinitives, modal verbs, and time expressions) Point out or write the lesson objectives on the board. Activate students' knowledge. Ask for examples of infinitives and time expressions. Write the examples on the board.

CONTEXT

1. Say: *We're going to read about helping people. Do you volunteer? What's a volunteer?* (a person who helps people in need but doesn't get paid for his/her work) Ask: *Do you like to help people? Who do you help? What do you do?* Have students share their experiences.
2. Direct students' attention to the pictures of Simon and Victor. Ask: Activate students' prior knowledge. Ask: *How did Simon and Dorota help newcomers to the U.S.?* (e.g., showed them how to use the Laundromat, find a new apartment, move, fill out applications, get a job, get a Social Security Card, take a driver's test, buy an infant car seat)

BEFORE YOU READ

1. Go over each question as a class. Have a volunteer read the questions or read them to the class yourself. Have students discuss the questions in pairs.
2. Ask for a few volunteers to share their answers with the class.
   To save class time, skip "Before You Read," or have students prepare their answers for homework ahead of time.

LESSON 1

GRAMMAR
Review of Verb Tenses—Affirmative and Negative
Review of Infinitives
Review of Modal Verbs—Affirmative and Negative
Review of Time Expressions

CONTEXT
Helping Others

Before You Read
1. What help did you need as a newcomer?
2. What do you do to help other newcomers?

258   Unit 12

Culture Note
Most volunteering in the U.S. is done for religious organizations (34%) or educational/youth service organizations (27%). People also volunteer for social or community organizations (12.4%) and for hospital/health organizations (7.5%).

---

258   *Grammar in Context Basic* Teacher's Edition

HELPING OTHERS

Simon, Dorota, Victor, Lisa, and Halina are in a coffee shop.

Victor: Simon, thanks for your help on moving day. With your help, it **didn't take** us so long. You **gave** me some good advice about used cars too. But I **don't have** a car yet. **I'm** still **looking**.
Simon: How is your new apartment?
Lisa: We **are** very comfortable there. It's big and sunny. Our daughter **likes** her new school too. She **doesn't have to walk** far. **We're all enjoying** life in the U.S. now. We **don't feel** like newcomers anymore. Thanks for all your help.
Simon: No problem. Any time.
Halina: I **want to thank** you, Dorota. With your help, I **learned** about many important places in this city. Also, you **helped** me with my Social Security card. And your advice about job interviews **was** very helpful. I really **like** my new job. **I'm going to stay** with this company for a while.
Dorota: I **was** happy to help, Halina.
Halina: My life **is** easier now. I **don't feel** so confused. Maybe I **can help** you in your work with newcomers. I **can be** a volunteer. **I'm not going to be** so busy from now on.
Victor: You **can count on** my help too.
Simon: That's good. Marta and I **are going to have** a meeting for volunteers next week. You **should come**. It **isn't going to take** a long time. And you **can learn** about other volunteer activities too. There are many opportunities to help others.

Vocabulary in Context

volunteer (n.) volunteer (v.)	I'm a **volunteer** for newcomers. I also **volunteer** at a day care center. They do not pay me for my work.
newcomer	My friend just arrived in the U.S. He is a **newcomer**.
really + verb	He **really needed** a new TV. It was very important to get a new TV. His old TV broke.
from now on	This is my last day to take the bus to work. **From now on**, I'm going to drive.
opportunity	I have an **opportunity** to work at Baker's Department Store. I can work there if I want to.
count on	We can help you. We are available all day Saturday. You can **count on** us to help you on Saturday.

Lesson 1   259

Reading Variation

1. To practice listening skills, have students listen to the audio before opening their books. Ask a few comprehension questions, such as: *Does Halina like her new job?* (yes) Repeat the audio if necessary. Then have students open their books and read along as they listen to the audio.
2. Alternatively, have students begin by listening to the audio as they read along.

Vocabulary Teaching Ideas

Use the following idea to teach this term:

count on: Write on the board: *Count on me = I will do it. / I will be there.*

Expansion

Reading Have students practice the conversation in groups of five. Ask volunteers to roleplay the conversation in front of the class.

Vocabulary in Context To check comprehension, have volunteers in pairs or groups act out selected vocabulary, such as *volunteer* and *newcomer*.

Helping Others (Reading)
CD 1, Track 59

1. Have students look at the title of the reading and the picture on pages 257 and 258. Say: *Quickly skim the reading. What do Halina and Victor say they want to do now?* (help Dorota and Simon with other newcomers) Have students use the title and pictures to make predictions about the reading.
2. Have students read the dialogue silently. Then play the audio and have students read along silently.
3. Check students' basic comprehension. Ask questions, such as: *Who do Victor and Lisa thank?* (Simon) *What did Simon do?* (helped them move, gave advice about used cars) *Did Victor buy a car?* (no) *Who thanked Dorota?* (Halina) *What did Dorota do?* (taught her about places in the city, helped with getting a Social Security Card, gave advice about job interviews) *How can Halina help Dorota?* (She can be a volunteer.) Are Victor and Lisa going to volunteer? (Victor is; Lisa doesn't say.)

To save class time, have students do the reading for homework ahead of time.

VOCABULARY IN CONTEXT

1. Model the pronunciation of each new vocabulary word and have students repeat.
2. Make sure students understand the meaning of each vocabulary item. Review the examples in the book and create additional example sentences. For example, say: *really plus verb. I really wanted to play tennis today, but it's raining.* Go over each new vocabulary item similarly, using visuals and realia when appropriate. When possible, point to pictures in the book that illustrate the new vocabulary.
3. Have students underline an example of each vocabulary item in the reading.

DID YOU KNOW?

Tell students that *mentoring* is a popular type of volunteer work in the U.S. Adults work with young people in need. They help out with homework, give advice, offer emotional support, and much more.

12.1 | Review of Verb Tenses—Affirmative and Negative

1. Have students look at grammar chart **12.1** on pages 260-261. Review the information about each tense.
2. Have students close their books. Write sentences on the board and ask students to tell you what tense each verb is.

Did You Know? The number of American volunteers goes up every year. Between 60 and 65 million Americans volunteer each year. They volunteer at least one hour a week.

12.1 | Review of Verb Tenses—Affirmative and Negative

The Simple Present Tense

	Examples	Explanation
Be	a. Dorota **is** 40 years old. b. Victor **isn't** a volunteer yet. c. Dorota **is** from Poland. d. Simon and Marta **aren't** Polish. e. The five friends **are** in a coffee shop. f. It **isn't** cold today. g. It **is** 3:00 p.m. h. Halina and Victor **are** happy. Their lives **aren't** as difficult now.	a. Age b. Occupation/work c. Place of origin d. Nationality e. Location f. Weather g. Time h. Description
There + Be	a. **There is** a need for volunteers. b. **There aren't** many newcomers here today.	Use *there is* and *there are* to talk about a subject for the first time.
Other Verbs	a. Halina **works** in an office. b. Dorota **doesn't work** every day.	a. Facts b. Habits, customs, regular activity

The Present Continuous Tense

Examples	Explanation
a. Halina **is thanking** Dorota. b. Halina **isn't looking** for a job at this time.	a. Actions at the present moment b. Actions at a present time period

260 Unit 12

Expansion

Grammar Chart List one or more explanations on the board for each tense. Have students say or write an example sentence. You might write this example on the board:

Simple Present: Age.
Brett is six years old.

Make a list of many verbs on the board, mixing all of the tenses in the chart. Put students in pairs or groups. Have them sort out the verbs by tense and then share their answers with the class.

The Future Tense with *Be Going To*

	Examples	Explanation
Be	Halina and Victor **are going to be** volunteers.	Future plans Predictions for the future
There + Be	**There isn't going to be** a volunteer meeting tomorrow.	
Other Verbs	Halina **is going to help** newcomers. Halina **is going to have** more free time soon.	

The Simple Past Tense

	Examples	Explanation
Be	Halina **was** a salesperson in Poland.	Actions completed in the past
There + Be	There **weren't** many people in the coffee shop yesterday.	
Regular Verbs	Victor **moved** to a new apartment two weeks ago. He **didn't move** far away.	
Irregular Verbs	Halina **didn't get** a job in a store. She **got** a job in an office.	

EXERCISE 1 Complete each sentence about the conversation with the correct tense of the verb in parentheses ( ). Use affirmative verbs.

EXAMPLE Halina __is talking__ to Dorota now.
(talk)

1. Simon, Dorota, Halina, Lisa, and Victor __are sitting__ together in a coffee shop.
(sit)
2. Victor's family __found__ a bigger apartment.
(find)
3. Victor __likes__ his new apartment.
(like)
4. Victor and Halina __are enjoying__ American life now.
(enjoy)
5. Simon __gave__ Victor good advice about used cars.
(give)

Lesson 1   261

EXERCISE 1

1. Have students read the direction line. Go over the example in the Student Book.
2. Have students complete Exercise 1 individually. Check the answers as a class.
3. If necessary, review grammar chart **12.1** on pages 260-261.

Expansion

Grammar Chart Have students give additional examples for the following:

Simple Present Tense: *Be*
Simple Present Tense: *There + Be*
Present Continuous Tense: *go* / affirmative and negative
Future Tense with *Be Going To: Be*
Future Tense with *Be Going To: There + Be*
Future Tense with *Be Going To: Write*
Simple Past Tense: *Be*
Simple Past Tense: *There + Be*
Simple Past Tense: *Work*
Simple Past Tense: *Have*

EXERCISE 2

1. Have students read the direction line. Go over the example in the Student Book.
2. Have students complete Exercise 2 individually. Go over the answers with the class.
3. If necessary, review grammar chart 12.1 on pages 260-261.

---

6. Victor __is going to buy__ a used car soon.
   (buy)
7. Halina and Victor __were__ newcomers several months ago.
   (be)
8. Halina __has__ a Social Security card.
   (have)
9. Dorota __helped__ Halina get her Social Security card.
   (help)
10. Halina __is going to help__ Dorota with other newcomers from now on.
    (help)

EXERCISE 2 Read each sentence. Write the negative form with the words in parentheses ( ).

EXAMPLE The five friends are having coffee now. (lunch)
They aren't having lunch.

1. Victor and Halina are talking about their lives now. (their problems)
   They aren't talking about their problems now.
2. Victor wanted to move. (stay in his old apartment)
   He didn't want to stay in his old apartment.
3. His old apartment was too small. (big enough for his family)
   It wasn't big enough for his family.
4. Victor feels comfortable in America now. (strange anymore)
   He doesn't feel strange anymore.
5. Simon gave Victor advice. (about jobs)
   He didn't give him advice about jobs.
6. Halina and Victor had a lot to do at first. (much free time then)
   They didn't have much free time then.
7. Halina's life is easier now. (so difficult)
   It isn't so difficult now.
8. She is going to work in her company for a while. (look for another job soon)
   She isn't going to look for another job soon.

262 Unit 12

Exercise 2 Variation

Do the exercise as a listening and speaking activity. Put students into pairs and have one partner close his or her book. The other partner reads the sentence then the term in parentheses. The first partner listens and makes the sentence negative with the substitute term.

12.2 | Review of Infinitives

Examples	Explanation
Halina started **to work** for a new company. She expects **to stay** there for a while. It's fun **to be** a volunteer. Halina wants **to be** a volunteer. Victor is trying **to buy** a used car.	• The infinitive is formed by *to* and the base form of the verb. • Infinitives can go after adjectives or verbs. • The tense is always in the verb before the infinitive.

EXERCISE 3 Complete each sentence with an infinitive expression.

EXAMPLE It's good *to help other people*

Answers will vary.
1. Victor wants *to buy a used car*.
2. Halina needed *to get a Social Security card*.
3. Halina learned *to apply for jobs*.
4. It's not easy *to be a newcomer*.
5. Simon and Marta like *to volunteer*.
6. Simon and Marta are trying *to plan a meeting*.
7. Halina and Victor are expecting *to help newcomers*.

Lesson 1 263

12.2 | Review of Infinitives

Have students look at grammar chart **12.2** on page 263. Say: *The infinitive form is to plus the base form of a verb.* Review the explanations. Ask: *Can you remember the verbs we use with the infinitive? (want, need, like, expect,* and *try)* Give an example sentence. (e.g., I *want to go to the movies on Saturday.*) Write the example on the board. Remind students that expressions with *it* are often followed by an infinitive.

EXERCISE 3

1. Have students read the direction line. Go over the example in the Student Book. Tell students to base their sentences on information they have learned about Victor, Halina, Simon, and Marta in their book. Say: *Your answers will vary.*
2. Have students complete Exercise 3 individually. Go over answers with the class.
3. If necessary, review grammar chart **4.7** on page 71 and **12.2** on page 263.

Expansion

Exercise 3 Have students complete the sentences in Exercise 3 so that they are true for them or someone they know. Have students share their answers in small groups.

Unit 12 263

12.3 | Review of Modal Verbs

1. Have students look at grammar chart **12.3** on page 264. Review the examples and explanations.
2. Have students close their books. Give students additional examples and ask students to explain what the sentences mean. For example, write on the board: *I can build a house.* Ask: *What does this mean?* (I have the ability to build a house. OR It's OK to build a house; I have permission.)

EXERCISE 4

1. Say: *In this exercise, you're going to make the sentences true for you by using affirmative or negative modals.* Have students read the direction line. Go over the examples in the book. Have volunteers model the examples.
2. Have students complete Exercise 4 individually. Go over the answers with the class.
3. If necessary, review grammar chart **12.3** on page 264 or grammar charts **5.1–5.3** in Unit 5 and **6.1–6.3** in Unit 6.

12.3 | Review of Modal Verbs
Can, Should, Must, Have To

Examples	Explanation
a. Victor **can speak** English better now. b. He doesn't have his driver's license. He **can't drive** now. c. Victor and Halina **can volunteer** now.	a. Ability—no ability b. Permission—not permitted c. Possibility—impossibility
a. We **should help** other people. b. You **shouldn't arrive** late to an interview.	Advice, suggestion
a. Everyone **must get** a Social Security card in order to work. b. You **must not drive** without a driver's license.	a. Strong obligation from a rule or law b. Strong obligation not to do something because of a rule or law
a. Victor's daughter **has to go** to school. b. She **doesn't have to go** to a public school.	a. Strong necessity or obligation (by law, custom, rule, or personal necessity) b. Not necessary

EXERCISE 4 ABOUT YOU Fill in the blanks with the affirmative or negative form of the modals in parentheses ( ). Make sentences that are true about you.

EXAMPLES: __I have to__ (have to) work tonight.
__I don't have to__ (have to) work on weekends.

Answers will vary.

1. _____ (should) speak English every day.
2. _____ (have to) go to school.
3. _____ (can) speak English like an American.
4. _____ (should) speak my language in this class.
5. _____ (must) drive without a license.
6. _____ (have to) pay for classes at this school.

264   Unit 12

Expansion

Grammar Chart Have students change the affirmative sentences to negative, and vice versa, for each example sentence in the chart.

Have students write an affirmative and negative sentence for each modal verb phrase in the chart.

EXERCISE 5 Halina, Victor, Simon, and Dorota continue their conversation. Fill in the blanks with the correct forms of the verbs in parentheses ( ). Use the different tenses, infinitives, and modals.

Part 1:

Dorota: There's a lot to do. Sometimes we __don't get__ enough
(1. get, negative)
volunteers to help.

Victor: What else do volunteers do?

Simon: Well, many newcomers __don't know__ how to drive. They
(2. know, negative)
__aren't sure__ sure about the rules on American roads.
(3. be, negative)
Volunteers __can help__ people get their driver's
(4. can / help)
licenses. Tomorrow, Dorota and I __are going to meet__ with a
(5. meet)
group of newcomers. One young man __needs to drive__ to
(6. need / drive)
work every day. I __practiced__ with him yesterday. But
(7. practice)
I __'m going to be__ out of town next weekend.
(8. be)

Victor: I __want to help__ him. But I __don't have__ a car yet.
(9. want / help)   (10. have, negative)

Part 2:

Dorota: Next Thanksgiving, we __'re going to prepare__ a holiday dinner
(1. prepare)
for newcomers. We __'re going to look for__ volunteers now. It's
(2. look for)
difficult __to find__ people right before a holiday.
(3. find)
Everyone is so busy then.

Halina: Peter and I __want to help__ you. I __can cook__.
(4. want / help)   (5. can / cook)

Dorota: Thanks, Halina. My friend Nancy __works__ with new-
(6. work)
comers from all over the world. She __prepares__ holiday
(7. prepare)
meals every year at a school in her neighborhood. You can help.

EXERCISE 5

1. Have students read the direction line. Have a volunteer do #1.
2. Have students complete Exercise 5 individually. Then have students compare answers in pairs. Circulate to observe pair work. Give help as needed.
3. If necessary, review grammar chart **12.1** on pages 260-261.

🕐 To save class time, have students complete the exercise for homework ahead of time.

Expansion

Exercise 5 Have students practice the conversation in groups. Ask volunteers to roleplay the conversations in front of the class.

12.4 | Review of Time Expressions

Have students look at grammar chart **12.4** on page 266. Activate students' knowledge. Ask students to separate the expressions by their use. Begin by having students give examples of expressions that mean habit or custom. *(always, never, from now on, often, usually, hardly ever, sometimes, rarely, every week)* Repeat the procedure for expressions used to show something happening *(right now, at the moment)*, future plans or predictions *(in a few weeks, next week, soon, tomorrow, right away)*, past events *(yesterday, last year, two weeks ago)*, and events thought of as present, past, or future *(this week: I go this week; I went this week; I'm going to go this week).*

EXERCISE 6

1. Have students read the direction line. Then go over the example.
2. Have students complete Exercise 6 individually. Go over the answers with the class.
3. If necessary, review the grammar charts on time expressions, including **4.4** on page 63, **8.5** on page 171, **9.4** on page 191, **11.2** on page 235, and **12.4** on page 266.

12.4 | Review of Time Expressions

always	sometimes	this week	right away
never	hardly ever	in a few weeks	yesterday
from now on	rarely	next week	last year
often	right now	soon	two weeks ago
usually	at the moment	tomorrow	every week

EXERCISE 6 Circle the time expressions in the following sentences. Then fill in the blanks in the sentences with an affirmative verb from the box. Use the correct tense. Two verbs are used twice.

help	move	tell ✓	write	give	have
know	enjoy	come	teach	find	invite

EXAMPLE At the coffee shop (yesterday,) Dorota ___told___ Halina about her friend, Nancy.

1. Nancy (often) ___helps___ newcomers.
2. These newcomers (hardly ever) ___have___ all the items necessary for their new life in America.
3. Nancy ___gives___ them clothes and household items.
4. The items (usually) ___come___ from Nancy's friends and co-workers and charities.
5. (Last year) five new families from Africa ___moved___ into Nancy's neighborhood.
6. Nancy ___gave___ them enough items for a comfortable home.
7. She ___found___ jobs for them too.
8. These families ___enjoy___ their new life in America (now.)
9. (These days) Nancy ___teaches___ these families about American life.
10. She ___is going to invite___ the newcomers to her famous Thanksgiving dinner (later this year.)
11. (Last year) after the dinner, a city newspaper ___wrote___ a story about Nancy's work with newcomers.
12. (Now) everyone ___knows___ about Nancy's work.
13. She ___found___ many new volunteers to help her (in the future.)

266 Unit 12

Expansion

Grammar Chart Have students work in pairs to write six to ten sentences in the four tenses. Tell students to use time expressions.

EXERCISE 7 Look at the picture below. Write a paragraph about the picture. Use all the tenses you learned in this book: simple present, present continuous, future (*be going to*), simple past, and modal verbs. Use affirmative and negative sentences.

EXAMPLES Newcomers are going to have an American Thanksgiving dinner.

There's a turkey on each table. Volunteers prepared the turkey.

Answers will vary, but possible answers may include:
Dorota is cooking in the kitchen. She's wearing a chef's hat. She isn't eating any food now. Volunteers are cutting the turkey and bringing out more food on trays. Everyone is having a good time. They're going to eat a lot of food. They shouldn't be hungry for hours.

Lesson 1   267

EXERCISE 7

1. Have students look at the picture of the Thanksgiving dinner. Ask: *What's happening in this picture?* (People are eating Thanksgiving dinner.) Ask: *Are these Americans or are they newcomers?* (newcomers) Then have students read the direction line. Go over the examples.
2. Have students complete Exercise 7 individually. Then have partners exchange paragraphs to compare. Ask volunteers to read some of their sentences.
3. If necessary, review grammar chart **12.1** on pages 260-261.

Expansion

Exercise 7 Have students get into groups to talk about how they're going to spend their next Thanksgiving or other important holiday. Say and write on the board: *Tell your group where you are going to be, who you are going to be with, what you're going to do, and what you're going to eat.*

Unit **12**   267

Lesson 2 | Overview

GRAMMAR

1. Write the following questions on the board:
   Do you do any volunteer activities? What do you do?
2. Ask: *What's the difference between these two questions?* (The first is a *yes/no* question. The second is an information question.) Have students provide more examples of each type of question.

CONTEXT

1. Talk with students about any volunteer activities you do. (e.g., *I volunteer my time at the public library teaching ESL.*) Encourage students to ask *yes/no* and information questions about your work. (e.g., *How many hours a month do you work in the library?*)
2. Direct students' attention to the photos on page 268. Ask: *What are these people doing?* (They're unloading food and supplies to give to people who need them.)

BEFORE YOU READ

1. Go over each question as a class. Have a volunteer read the questions or read them to the class yourself. Have students answer the questions in pairs.
2. Ask for a few volunteers to share their answers with the class. Ask if anyone in the class volunteers.

   To save class time, skip "Before You Read," or have students prepare their answers for homework ahead of time.

LESSON 2

GRAMMAR
Yes/No Questions
Review of Information Questions

CONTEXT
Volunteer Activities

Before You Read
1. What volunteer activities do you know about?
2. Why do people volunteer?

268 Unit 12

Culture Note

Reasons why people volunteer:
   It's an important thing to do.
   Other people respect you.
   It helps you become a better person.
   You can help many people.
   You can help create change.
   You can make friends.

268   *Grammar in Context Basic* Teacher's Edition

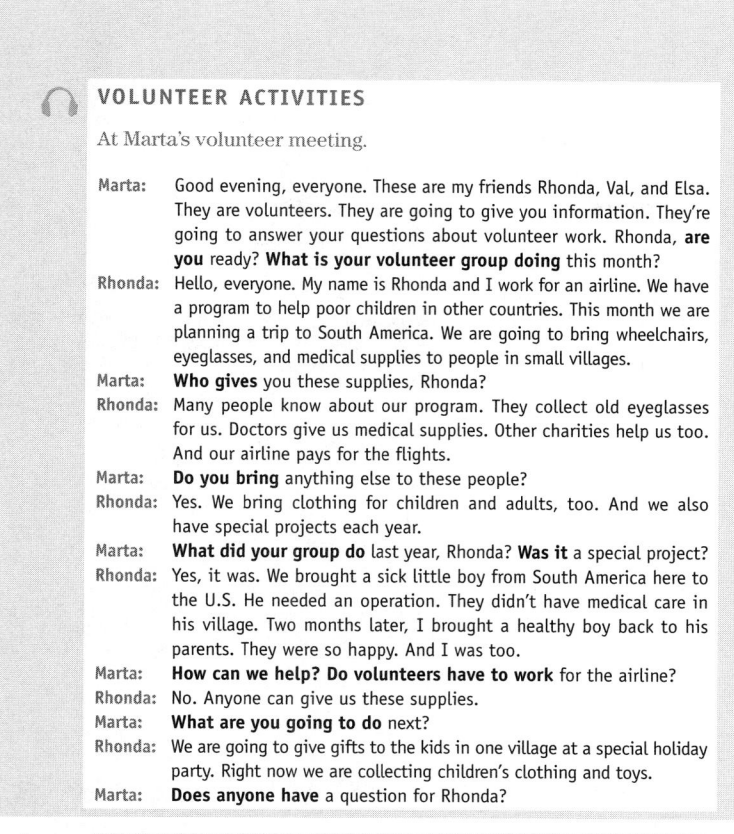

VOLUNTEER ACTIVITIES

At Marta's volunteer meeting.

Marta: Good evening, everyone. These are my friends Rhonda, Val, and Elsa. They are volunteers. They are going to give you information. They're going to answer your questions about volunteer work. Rhonda, **are you** ready? **What is your volunteer group doing** this month?

Rhonda: Hello, everyone. My name is Rhonda and I work for an airline. We have a program to help poor children in other countries. This month we are planning a trip to South America. We are going to bring wheelchairs, eyeglasses, and medical supplies to people in small villages.

Marta: **Who gives** you these supplies, Rhonda?

Rhonda: Many people know about our program. They collect old eyeglasses for us. Doctors give us medical supplies. Other charities help us too. And our airline pays for the flights.

Marta: **Do you bring** anything else to these people?

Rhonda: Yes. We bring clothing for children and adults, too. And we also have special projects each year.

Marta: **What did your group do** last year, Rhonda? **Was it** a special project?

Rhonda: Yes, it was. We brought a sick little boy from South America here to the U.S. He needed an operation. They didn't have medical care in his village. Two months later, I brought a healthy boy back to his parents. They were so happy. And I was too.

Marta: **How can we help? Do volunteers have to work** for the airline?

Rhonda: No. Anyone can give us these supplies.

Marta: **What are you going to do** next?

Rhonda: We are going to give gifts to the kids in one village at a special holiday party. Right now we are collecting children's clothing and toys.

Marta: **Does anyone have** a question for Rhonda?

Vocabulary in Context

fly (v.) flight (n.)	I'm going to **fly** from New York to Miami today. My **flight** leaves at 5 p.m.
airline	What **airline** are you taking to Miami?
wheelchair	Peter can't walk. He needs a **wheelchair.**
bring— brought	A: What did you **bring** to class today? B: I **brought** my book.
project	Rhonda's **project** is to collect clothing for newcomers to the U.S.
village	Only 500 people live in his **village.**
operation	Tom broke his leg. He needed an **operation** in the hospital.
collect	I **collect** old clocks. I have 20 of them now.

Lesson 2 269

Reading Variation

1. To practice listening skills, have students listen to the audio before opening their books. Ask a few comprehension questions, such as: *Was the little boy healthy after his operation?* (yes) *How long did he stay in the U.S.?* (two months) Repeat the audio if necessary. Then have students open their books and read along as they listen to the audio.
2. Alternatively, have students begin by listening to the audio as they read along.

Vocabulary Teaching Ideas

Use the following ideas to teach this term:

airline: Write the names of various countries' airlines on the board, such as *British Airways, Air France, Japan Airlines,* and *Korean Airlines.* Ask students the names of their countries' airlines and write them on the board.

Expansion

Reading Have students practice the conversation in pairs. Ask volunteers to roleplay all or part of the conversation in front of the class.

Volunteer Activities (Reading) CD 1, Track 60

1. Have students look at the title of the reading and the photo on page 268. Then ask students to scan the reading. *What did the volunteers do last year?* (They brought a sick little boy from South America to the U.S. He needed an operation)
2. Have students read the dialogue silently. Then play the audio and have students read along silently.
3. Check students' basic comprehension. Ask questions, such as: *What do the three women do?* (They are volunteers.) *What does Rhonda's volunteer group do?* (They have a program to help poor children in other countries.) *Where are they going this month?* (to South America) *What are they going to bring?* (medical supplies, wheelchairs, eyeglasses) *What did Rhonda's group do last year?* (They brought a sick little boy from South America to the U.S. for an operation.) *What are they going to do next?* (bring gifts to the kids of one village at a special holiday party)

To save class time, have students do the reading for homework ahead of time.

VOCABULARY IN CONTEXT

1. Model the pronunciation of each new vocabulary word and have students repeat.
2. Make sure students understand the meaning of each vocabulary word. Review the examples in the book and create additional example sentences. For example, say: *fly. I don't like to fly in airplanes. I prefer to drive.* Go over each new vocabulary word similarly, using visuals and realia when appropriate. When possible, point to pictures in the book that illustrate the new vocabulary.
3. Have students underline an example of each new word in the reading.

Unit 12 269

DID YOU KNOW?

Say: *More women than men in the U.S. volunteer regardless of age, economic status, or educational level.*

12.5 | *Yes/No* Questions

1. Have students look at grammar chart **12.5** on pages 270-271. Review the questions and short answers.
2. Play a game. Prepare a list of 20-30 verbs that students have learned. Divide the class into two to four teams. Write a verb and a verb tense on the board. (e.g., *talk / present continuous*) Someone from each team must go to the front of the board to write a *yes/no* question using the verb in the given tense. The next team member has to write a logical (but not necessarily true) answer.

Did You Know? Most volunteers in America are women between the ages of 35 and 44. But volunteers over age 60 give the most hours of their time.

12.5 | *Yes/No* Questions

The Simple Present Tense

	Yes/No Questions	Short Answers
Be	**Is** she at home?	Yes, she is.
	Are the volunteers from South America?	No, they aren't.
There + Be	**Is there** a meeting at your house?	Yes, there is.
	Are there any volunteers at the meeting?	No, there aren't.
Other Verbs	**Does** Dorota **work** for an airline?	No, she doesn't.
	Do charities **help** the volunteers?	Yes, they do.

The Present Continuous

Yes/No Questions	Short Answers
Is Rhonda **talking** to the group?	Yes, she is.
Are you **learning** about volunteer activities?	No, I'm not.
Are the volunteers **asking** for money?	No, they aren't.

The Future with *Be Going To*

Yes/No Questions	Short Answers
Am I **going to need** help?	Yes, you are.
Is there going to be a meeting?	No, there isn't.
Are the people **going to ask** questions?	Yes, they are.

270 Unit 12

Expansion

Grammar Chart Have students work in pairs to write *yes/no* questions for another pair. Then have pairs ask and answer questions. Tell students to use the simple present, the present continuous, the future with *be going to*, the simple past, and modals.

The Simple Past Tense

	Yes/No Questions	Short Answers
Be	**Were** you a volunteer last year? **Was** he in South America last week? **Were** the volunteers helpful last year?	No, I wasn't. Yes, he was. Yes, they were.
There + Be	**Was there** a problem with the volunteers last year? **Were there** enough volunteers to help people?	No, there wasn't. Yes, there were.
Regular and Irregular Verbs	**Did** Rhonda **help** someone? **Did** they **bring** toys to the children?	Yes, she did. No, they didn't.

Modal Verbs

	Yes/No Questions	Short Answers
Should	**Should** we volunteer for that project?	Yes, we should.
Can	**Can** I volunteer?	Yes, you can.
Have to	**Does** she **have to** volunteer today? **Do** doctors **have to** come to the meeting?	No, she doesn't. Yes, they do.

Language Note: Questions with *must* are not common. We use *have to* for questions.

EXERCISE 1 Ask a *yes/no* question about the conversation. Use the words given. Use the same tense as in the statement. Answer your question with a short answer.

EXAMPLE Rhonda has a job. (with an airline)

Does Rhonda have a job with an airline? Yes, she does.

1. Rhonda is talking. (about her job with the airline)

    Is Rhonda talking about her job with the airline? Yes, she is.

2. Rhonda brings medical supplies to poor children. (wheelchairs)

    Does Rhonda bring wheelchairs to poor children? Yes, she does.

3. A little boy needed medical care last year. (an operation)

    Did a little boy need an operation last year? Yes, he did.

Lesson 2

EXERCISE 1

1. Have students read the direction line. Remind students to use the same tense that's in the affirmative statement. Go over the example in the Student Book.
2. Have students complete Exercise 1 individually. Go over the answers with the class.
3. If necessary, review grammar chart **12.5** on pages 270-271.

12.6 | Review of Information Questions

1. Have students look at grammar chart **12.6** on pages 272-274. Say: *Let's look at how to form information questions.* Review how to form questions and short answers for each tense and go over all examples.
2. For simple present, write the following on the board to begin the review:

    question word + *be*
    question word + *be* + *there*
    question word + *do* + complement + verb
    question word + verb

    Say: *These are the four ways to make questions with* in the present tense. Remind students not to use *do* or *does* in subject questions. Have students cover their books. Give a formula and ask volunteers to make a question using that formula.

---

4. The sick boy was in a village. (in the United States)
   Was the sick boy in the United States? No, he wasn't.
5. Rhonda brought the boy to the United States. (back to his parents)
   Did Rhonda bring the boy back to his parents? Yes, she did.
6. The volunteers are going to have a party. (in the United States)
   Are the volunteers going to have a party in the United States? No, they aren't.
7. There are many people at Marta's house today. (any volunteers)
   Are there any volunteers at Marta's house today? Yes, there are.
8. People should give Rhonda toys for the holiday party. (medical supplies)
   Should people give Rhonda medical supplies for the holiday party? No, they shouldn't.
9. People can ask Rhonda questions. (about other projects)
   Can people ask Rhonda about other projects? Yes, they can.

12.6 | Review of Information Questions

Simple Present Tense

	Information Questions	Answers
Be	Who **is** Rhonda? Where **are** Rhonda, Val, and Elsa?	She's a volunteer. They're at Marta's house.
There + Be	Why **is there** a meeting today at Marta's house? How many people **are there** at the meeting?	To give information about volunteer work. About 20.
Other Verbs: Questions about the Complement	Where **does** Rhonda **work**? How **do** doctors **help**?	With an airline. They give medical supplies.
Subject Questions	Who **collects** eyeglasses? Which airline **helps** people?	Many people. Rhonda's airline.

272 Unit 12

Expansion

Grammar Chart Play a game. Prepare a list of 20-30 verbs that students have learned. Divide the class into two to four teams. Write a verb and a verb tense on the board. (e.g., *talk / present continuous*) Someone from each team must go to the front of the board to write an information question using the verb in the given tense. The next member must write a logical (but not necessarily true) answer to the question.

Present Continuous Tense

	Information Questions	Answers
Questions About the Complement	Who **is** Rhonda **talking** to? What **are** volunteers **collecting** now?	New volunteers. Children's clothing and toys.
Subject Questions	How many volunteers **are speaking** at the meeting?	Three.

Future Tense

	Information Questions	Answers
Be	What **is** the special project **going to be**? When **are** you **going to be** a volunteer?	A holiday party for kids. Next month.
There + Be	When **is there going to be** another meeting? How many meetings **are there going to be**?	Next week. Only two more.
Questions About the Complement	What **is** Rhonda **going to do** with the toys? When **are** the volunteers **going to give** the toys to the children?	She's going to give them to kids. In December.
Subject Questions	Which children **are going to get** the gifts? Who **is going to be** at the meeting?	The children in one small village. Many new volunteers.

Lesson 2 273

12.6 | Review of Information Questions (cont.)

3. For the present continuous tense, ask: *How do you form a verb in this tense?* (*be* + verb-*ing*) Ask: *Can you use* do *with the -ing verb?* (no)
4. Have students compare information questions about the complement and information questions about the subject in the chart. (Both begin with question words, but in subject questions there is no noun or pronoun for the subject. The question word or phrase is the subject.) Go over examples in the present continuous tense to illustrate.
5. Direct students' attention to the future tense in the bottom part of the chart on page 273. Ask: *What form of the verb do we use after* be going to *in questions?* (the base form)

Expansion

Grammar Chart Have students turn to the reading on page 137 in Unit 7. Say: Write information questions about the reading. Then have students take turns asking and answering questions about the reading. (e.g., *What is Rick going to buy? Coffee and aspirin.*)

Unit 12   273

12.6 | Review of Information Questions (cont.)

6. For questions in the simple past tense, remind students that *did* is used with both regular and irregular verbs except *be*.
7. For modal verbs, say: *Questions with* can *and* should *are formed the same. To form questions with* have to, *use* does *or* do *followed by the subject plus* have to. *All information questions begin with a question word*. Point out the Language Note. Say: *Must isn't usually used in questions.*

Simple Past Tense

	Information Questions	Answers
Be	Where **was** the meeting? Why **were** the parents worried?	We don't know. Because there was no medical care in the village.
There + Be	Why **was there** a special project last year? What kind of help **was there** for the boy?	Because a little boy was sick. Medical help.
Questions About the Complement: Regular and Irregular Verbs	What kind of help **did** the boy **need**? When **did** the boy **have** his operation?	He needed an operation. He had it last year.
Subject Questions	Which volunteers **brought** the boy to the U.S.?	The women from the airline.

Modal Verbs

	Information Questions	Answers
Questions About the Complement	When **can** we help Rhonda? How **should** we help her? When **does** Rhonda **have to** get the toys?	You can help right now. You can give her clothing and toys. A week before the holiday trip.
Subject Questions	Who **can** help Rhonda? How many children **had to** get help in that village last year?	All of us can help her. Two or three.

Language Note: Questions with *must* are not common. Use *have to* for questions.

EXERCISE 2 Write an information question about each sentence. Use the question words in parentheses ( ).

EXAMPLE Rhonda has a job (What kind)

What kind of job does she have?

She works for an airline.

Answers will vary, but possible answers may include:

1. Rhonda does volunteer work. (What kind)
   What kind of volunteer work does Rhonda do?
   She helps poor children in other countries.

2. Rhonda went to South America last year. (Why)
   Why did Rhonda go to South America last year?
   She brought a little sick boy here to the U.S.

3. Someone pays for the flights to South America. (Who)
   Who pays for the flights to South America?
   The airline pays for the flights.

4. The volunteers are going to have a party for children. (When)
   When are the volunteers going to have a party for children?
   They are going to have a party for children on a special holiday.

5. A sick boy had to come to the U.S. (Why)
   Why did a sick boy have to come to the U.S.?
   He needed an operation.

6. People should help with the holiday project. (How)
   How should people help with the holiday project?
   They should give clothing and toys.

7. Rhonda is explaining something to the new volunteers. (What)
   What is Rhonda explaining to the new volunteers?
   She's explaining the volunteer work.

EXERCISE 2

1. Have students read the direction line. Say: *Use the ideas from the reading on page 269 to complete this exercise.* Go over the examples. Say: *You're going to write a question and an answer.*

2. Have students complete Exercise 2 individually. Then have students take turns asking and answering the questions. Circulate to observe pair work. Given help as needed.

3. If necessary, review grammar chart **12.6** on pages 272–274.

EXERCISE 3

1. Say: *In this exercise, you're going write questions about the picture.* Have students read the direction line. Go over the examples.
2. Have students complete Exercise 3 individually. Then have students ask and answer questions about the picture with a partner. Circulate to observe pair work. Given help as needed.
3. If necessary, review grammar chart **12.5** on pages 270-271 and **12.6** on pages 272-274.

EXERCISE 3 Look at the picture below. Rhonda is at the special Christmas party for the children. Write six questions about the picture. Use *yes/no* questions and information questions. Use all the tenses: simple present, present continuous, future, past, and modal verbs. Write the short answers.

EXAMPLES
Is there a Christmas tree at the party.
What is the little girl asking Santa?

Answers will vary, but possible answers may include:
1. Is there a Christmas tree? Yes, there is.
2. Who are the children waiting for? For Santa.
3. Are the children going to talk to Santa? Yes, they are.
4. Did all the children already sit on Santa's lap? No, they didn't.
5. Should Santa be nice to the children? Yes, he should.
6. What will Santa ask the children? What they want.

276 Unit 12

Exercise 3 Variation

Have students choose a different illustration in the book and make six questions about the picture. Then have students ask and answer questions about the picture with a partner.

EXERCISE 4 Val, a second volunteer at Marta's meeting, tells the group about her activities. People are asking her questions about her volunteer activities. Write their questions with the words given. Use the answer to help you with the tense.

EXAMPLE Man: Where __do you volunteer__?
(you / volunteer)

Val: I volunteer in my neighborhood. My volunteer job is very interesting. I also work with children. I work at a day care center for single moms. I work there once a week. There are other volunteers too. We help with the children. We also plan special projects.

1. Woman: How __does the center help single moms__?
(the center / help single moms)

   Val: Mothers pay half the cost of regular day care centers.

2. Woman: How many __children are there__ in the class?
(children / there)

   Val: Every day is different. There are usually about 15 or 20 kids.

3. Man: How many __hours does each volunteer__?
(hours / each volunteer / work)

   Val: Each volunteer works four hours on their day.

4. Man: What day __did you work__ last week?
(you / work)

   Val: I worked on Thursday last week.

5. Woman: What __did you do?__?
(you / do)

   Val: I helped with the art activities, I served the meals, and I played with the children a lot.

6. Man: How __did you find out__ about this day care center?
(you / find out)

   Val: It was on our city's Web site. That's a good place to look for volunteer opportunities.

7. Woman: What special project __are the volunteers planning__ now?
(the volunteers / plan)

   Val: We're planning an art show and sale of the children's art.

Lesson 2   277

EXERCISE 4

1. Say: *Val is being interviewed about her volunteer activities. The answer will help you write the question.* Have students read the direction line. Go over the example.
2. Have students complete Exercise 4 individually. Then have students compare answers in pairs. Circulate to observe pair work. Give help as needed.
3. If necessary, review grammar chart **12.5** on pages 270-271 and **12.6** on pages 272-274.

   ⏱ To save class time, have students do the exercise for homework ahead of time.

Expansion

Exercise 4 Have students practice the conversation as a class. Ask one student to play Val. The rest of the students can take turns asking the questions.

Unit 12   277

EXERCISE 5

1. Say: *Now Elsa is being interviewed about her volunteer activities.* Have students read the direction line. Go over the example.
2. Have students complete Exercise 5 individually. Then have students compare answers in pairs. Circulate to observe pair work. Give help as needed.
3. If necessary, review grammar chart **12.5** on pages 270-271 and **12.6** on pages 272-274.

   To save class time, have students do the exercise for homework ahead of time.

---

8. **Man:** What kind of art ___are the children learning___ ?
   (children / learn)

   Val: We're teaching them to paint.

9. **Man:** When ___is the sale going to be___ ?
   (the sale / be)

   Val: In three months. I can tell you the date later.

10. **Woman:** What ___should we do___ to help?
    (we / should do)

    Val: You should come to the sale. The money is for the kids.

11. **Man:** What ___is the center going to do___ with the money?
    (center / do)

    Val: We are going to buy books for the new children's library.

EXERCISE 5 Elsa is talking now. People are asking Elsa questions. Complete each question with the words given. Use the answers to help you with the tense.

Marta: This is Elsa. She volunteers to help older people. She works with a neighborhood group. She works one week each month.

Woman: ___Are you going to work___ this week, Elsa?
(example: you / work)

Elsa: Yes, I am. I'm going to help an older woman in my neighborhood. She can't see very well and she lives alone.

Man: How ___are you going to help her___ ?
(1. you / help her)

Elsa: I'm going to take her to a doctor's appointment tomorrow, and I'm going to get her groceries on the weekend.

Woman: What ___does this woman do___ all day?
(2. this woman / do)

Elsa: She goes to the gym two days a week. A volunteer takes her. She exercises in a swimming pool.

Woman: ___Can she swim___ ?
(3. she / can swim)

Elsa: She doesn't exactly swim. She takes a special class for seniors. It's exercise in the water.

Woman: When ___did she start___ these classes?
(4. she / start)

Elsa: She started the classes 20 years ago. She says, "This class is responsible for my long life." Last week she turned 90.

278   Unit 12

Expansion

Exercise 5 Have students practice the conversation as a class. Ask one student to play Elsa. The rest of the students can take turns asking the questions.

EDITING ADVICE

1. Always use the base form after *doesn't*, *don't*, *didn't*, *to*, and modals.

   They didn't ~~went~~ *go* to the meeting today.

   He wanted to ~~fixed~~ *fix* the car for her.

   He should ~~to~~ go to work on time.

2. Don't use a form of *be* with the simple present or past tenses.

   I ~~am~~ go to the store every week. She ~~was go~~ *went* to the store yesterday.

3. Don't use *do*, *does*, or *did* in a subject question.

   Who ~~does work~~ *works* as a volunteer?

4. Don't forget to use *do*, *does*, or *did* in a question about the complement.

   Where ~~he worked~~ *did he work*?

5. Use the correct word order in questions.

   When ~~he is~~ *is he* going to drive her to the supermarket?

EDITING QUIZ

Find the mistakes with the underlined words, and correct them. Not every sentence has a mistake. If the sentence is correct, write *C*.

EXAMPLES   She should <u>helps</u> Marta.
Where did <u>you go</u>? *C*

1. Does that volunteer <u>has</u> a full-time job? *have*
2. Why <u>I should</u> volunteer? *should I*
3. She <u>have to worked</u> extra hours last week. *had to work*
4. Marta didn't <u>invited</u> too many people to her house. *invite*
5. They shouldn't <u>to complain</u> about their job.
6. How many volunteers <u>did worked</u> at the day care center last week?
7. Val <u>can count</u> on the new volunteers. *C*

Lesson 2   279

Learner's Log

1. Have students close their books. Ask: *What did you learn about Val's, Elsa's, and Rhonda's volunteer jobs? What else do you want to know?*
2. Have students open their books to complete the Learner's Log. Remind students to write three questions about volunteering in the U.S.

Expansion Activities

These expansion activities provide opportunities for students to interact with one another and further develop their speaking and writing skills. Encourage students to use grammar from Units 1–12 whenever possible. To save class time, assign parts of the activities as homework. Then use class time for interaction and communication. If students do not need additional speaking practice, some of the activities may be assigned as writing activities for homework, or skipped altogether.

WRITING ACTIVITY

Have students complete the activity individually at home or in class. Collect for assessment.

OUTSIDE ACTIVITY

Have students get into groups to share the information about the volunteers they spoke with. Ask: *What were their reasons for volunteering? Were they the same or different?*

INTERNET ACTIVITIES

Have students discuss in groups the volunteer opportunities they found in their area. Then ask groups to share with the class the opportunities they found most interesting. Ask students if they're going to volunteer.

LEARNER'S LOG

1. Write three sentences in your notebook about each topic. Use a different tense in each sentence.
   - Val's volunteer job
   - Elsa's volunteer job
   - Rhonda's volunteer job
2. Write three questions you still have about volunteers.

EXPANSION ACTIVITIES

Writing Activity
In your notebook, write five to six true sentences about the picture. Write at least one sentence with each tense you learned in this book: the present continuous, simple present, future, past, and a modal verb.

Outside Activity
Ask some Americans about their volunteer work. What do they do? How often? Tell the class what you learned.

Internet Activities
1. Search the words *volunteer opportunities* and the name of your city. Find an interesting volunteer activity. Tell the class about it.
2. Go to the Web site: *www.usafreedomcorps.gov*. This site offers volunteer jobs for the U.S. government. Find an interesting volunteer opportunity and tell the class about it.

280   Unit 12

Expansion

Learner's Log Have students compare logs in pairs.

Writing Activity Variation

Have students exchange papers with a partner for proofreading.

Internet Activities Variation

Tell students that if they don't have Internet access, they can use Internet facilities at a public library. They can also ask a librarian to help them find information on volunteering.

Appendices

APPENDIX A

The Calendar

Months	Days	Seasons
January (Jan.)	Sunday (Sun.)	Winter
February (Feb.)	Monday (Mon.)	Spring
March (Mar.)	Tuesday (Tues.)	Summer
April (Apr.)	Wednesday (Wed.)	Fall or Autumn
May	Thursday (Thurs.)	
June (Jun.)	Friday (Fri.)	
July (Jul.)	Saturday (Sat.)	
August (Aug.)		
September (Sept.)		
October (Oct.)		
November (Nov.)		
December (Dec.)		

Dates

January 6, 1999 or Jan. 6, 1999 or 1/6/99 or 1-6-99
October 27, 2004 or Oct. 27, 2004 or 10/27/04 or 10-27-04

Numbers

Cardinal Numbers	Ordinal Numbers
1 = one	first
2 = two	second
3 = three	third
4 = four	fourth
5 = five	fifth
6 = six	sixth
7 = seven	seventh
8 = eight	eighth
9 = nine	ninth
10 = ten	tenth
11 = eleven	eleventh
12 = twelve	twelfth
13 = thirteen	thirteenth
14 = fourteen	fourteenth
15 = fifteen	fifteenth
16 = sixteen	sixteenth
17 = seventeen	seventeenth
18 = eighteen	eighteenth
19 = nineteen	nineteenth
20 = twenty	twentieth
30 = thirty	thirtieth
40 = forty	fortieth
50 = fifty	fiftieth
60 = sixty	sixtieth
70 = seventy	seventieth
80 = eighty	eightieth
90 = ninety	ninetieth
100 = one hundred	hundredth
1,000 = one thousand	thousandth
1,000,000 = one million	millionth

Appendix A / The Calendar

APPENDIX B

Spelling Rules for Verbs and Nouns

Spelling of the -s Form of Verbs and Nouns

Verbs	Nouns	Rule
visit—visit**s** need—need**s** like—like**s** spend—spend**s**	chair—chair**s** bed—bed**s** truck—truck**s** gift—gift**s**	Add **-s** to most words to make the *-s* form.
mi**ss**—miss**es** wa**sh**—wash**es** cat**ch**—catch**es** fi**x**—fix**es**	dress—dress**es** dish—dish**es** match—match**es** box—box**es**	Add **-es** to base forms with *ss, sh, ch,* or *x* at the end.
wor**r**y—worr**ies** t**r**y—tr**ies** stu**d**y—stud**ies**	par**t**y—part**ies** ci**t**y—cit**ies** ber**r**y—berr**ies**	If the word ends in a consonant + *y*, change **y** to *-i* and add **-es**.
p**ay**—pay**s** pl**ay**—play**s** enj**oy**—enjoy**s**	b**oy**—boy**s** d**ay**—day**s** k**ey**—key**s**	If the word ends in a vowel + *y*, do not change the *-y*. Just add **-s**.
	lea**f**—lea**ves** kni**fe**—kni**ves**	If the noun ends in ***f*** or ***fe***, change to **ves**.

Irregular -s Forms of Verbs

have—ha**s**
go—go**es**
do—do**es**

Irregular Plural Forms of Nouns

man—men woman—women child—children mouse—mice	foot—feet tooth—teeth person—people (or persons) fish—fish

Spelling of the -ing Forms of Verbs

Verbs	Rule
go—go**ing** eat—eat**ing** spend—spend**ing**	Add **-ing** to most verbs to make the **-ing** form.
tak<u>e</u>—tak**ing** writ<u>e</u>—writ**ing** mak<u>e</u>—mak**ing**	If a verb ends in silent **e**, drop the **e** and add **-ing**. Do NOT double the final consonant. WRONG: writting
pa<u>y</u>—pa**ying** bu<u>y</u>—bu**ying** worr<u>y</u>—worr**ying** stud<u>y</u>—stud**ying**	If a verb ends in a **y**, just add **-ing**. WRONG: studing
s<u>to</u>p—sto**pping** r<u>u</u>n—ru**nning** sp<u>i</u>t—spi**tting**	If a one-syllable verb ends in consonant + vowel + consonant, double the final consonant and add **-ing**.
beg<u>í</u>n—begi**nning** perm<u>í</u>t—permi**tting** occ<u>ú</u>r—occu**rring**	If a two-syllable word ends in consonant + vowel + consonant, double the final consonant and add **-ing** only if the last syllable is stressed.
ó<u>pe</u>n—open**ing** há<u>ppe</u>n—happen**ing** devé<u>lo</u>p—develop**ing**	If a two or more syllable word ends in consonant + vowel + consonant and the final syllable is not stressed, do NOT double the final consonant. Just add **-ing**.

Spelling of the -ed Forms of Regular Past Tense Verbs

Verbs	Rule
listen—listen**ed** look—look**ed**	Add **-ed** to most regular verbs to form the past tense.
bak<u>e</u>—bake**d** smil<u>e</u>—smile**d** sav<u>e</u>—save**d**	If a verb ends in silent **e**, just add **d**. Do NOT double the final consonant. WRONG: smilled
wor<u>ry</u>—worr**ied** stu<u>dy</u>—stud**ied**	If a verb ends in a consonant + **y**, change the **y** to **i** and add **-ed**. WRONG: worryed
enj<u>oy</u>—enjoy**ed** del<u>ay</u>—delay**ed**	If a verb ends in a vowel + **y**, just add **-ed**. WRONG: enjoied
st<u>op</u>—sto**pped** dr<u>ag</u>—dra**gged** sl<u>am</u>—sla**mmed**	If a one-syllable verb ends in consonant + vowel + consonant, double the final consonant and add **-ed**.
perm<u>ít</u>—permi**tted** occ<u>úr</u>—occu**rred**	If a two-syllable word ends in consonant + vowel + consonant, double the final consonant and add **-ed** only if the last syllable is stressed.
ópen—open**ed** háppen—happen**ed** devélop—develop**ed**	If a two or more syllable word ends in consonant + vowel + consonant and the final syllable is not stressed, do NOT double the final consonant. Just add **-ed**.

APPENDIX C

Spelling of Comparative and Superlative Forms of Adjectives

Simple Adjective	Comparative Adjective	Superlative Adjective	Rule
old cheap	older cheaper	oldest cheapest	Add *-er* and *-est* to most adjectives.
big hot	bigger hotter	biggest hottest	If the adjective ends with consonant-vowel-consonant, double the final consonant before adding *-er* or *-est*.
nice late	nicer later	nicest latest	If the adjective ends in *e*, add *-r* or *-st* only.
busy easy	busier easier	busiest easiest	If the adjective ends in *y*, change *y* to *i* and add *-er* or *-est*.

APPENDIX D

Alphabetical List of Irregular Past Forms

Base Form	Past Form	Base Form	Past Form
be	was/were	cut	cut
become	became	do	did
begin	began	draw	drew
bend	bent	drink	drank
bet	bet	drive	drove
bite	bit	eat	ate
blow	blew	fall	fell
break	broke	feed	fed
bring	brought	feel	felt
build	built	fight	fought
buy	bought	find	found
catch	caught	fit	fit
choose	chose	fly	flew
come	came	forget	forgot
cost	cost	get	got

Continued

Base Form	Past Form	Base Form	Past Form
give	gave	run	ran
go	went	say	said
grow	grew	see	saw
have	had	sell	sold
hear	heard	send	sent
hide	hid	shake	shook
hit	hit	shoot	shot
hold	held	shut	shut
hurt	hurt	sing	sang
keep	kept	sit	sat
know	knew	sleep	slept
lead	led	speak	spoke
leave	left	spend	spent
lend	lent	spread	spread
let	let	stand	stood
lie	lay	steal	stole
light	lit (or lighted)	swim	swam
lose	lost	take	took
make	made	teach	taught
mean	meant	tear	tore
meet	met	tell	told
mistake	mistook	think	thought
pay	paid	throw	threw
put	put	understand	understood
quit	quit	wake	woke
read	read	wear	wore
ride	rode	win	won
ring	rang	write	wrote

APPENDIX E

Capitalization Rules

- The first word in a sentence: **M**y friends are helpful.
- The word "I": My sister and **I** took a trip together.
- Names of people: **J**ulia **R**oberts; **G**eorge **W**ashington
- Titles preceding names of people: **D**octor (**D**r.) **S**mith; **P**resident **L**incoln; **Q**ueen **E**lizabeth; **M**r. **R**ogers; **M**rs. **C**arter
- Geographic names: the **U**nited **S**tates; **L**ake **S**uperior; **C**alifornia; the **R**ocky **M**ountains; the **M**ississippi **R**iver

    NOTE: The word "the" in a geographic name is not capitalized.

- Street names: **P**ennsylvania **A**venue (**A**ve.); **W**all **S**treet (**S**t.); **A**bbey **R**oad (**R**d.)
- Names of organizations, companies, colleges, buildings, stores, hotels: the **R**epublican **P**arty; **H**einle **T**homson; **D**artmouth **C**ollege; the **U**niversity of **W**isconsin; the **W**hite **H**ouse; **B**loomingdale's; the **H**ilton **H**otel
- Nationalities and ethnic groups: **M**exicans; **C**anadians; **S**paniards; **A**mericans; **J**ews; **K**urds; **E**skimos
- Languages: **E**nglish; **S**panish; **P**olish; **V**ietnamese; **R**ussian
- Months: **J**anuary; **F**ebruary
- Days: **S**unday; **M**onday
- Holidays: **C**hristmas; **I**ndependence **D**ay
- Important words in a title: **G**rammar in **C**ontext; **T**he **O**ld **M**an and the **S**ea; **R**omeo and **J**uliet; **T**he **S**ound of **M**usic

    NOTE: Capitalize "the" as the first word of a title.

APPENDIX F

Glossary of Grammatical Terms

- **Adjective** An adjective gives a description of a noun.
    It's a *tall* tree.   He's an *old* man.   My sisters are *nice*.

- **Adverb** An adverb describes the action of a sentence or an adjective or another adverb.
    She speaks English *fluently*.   I drive *carefully*.
    She speaks English *extremely* well.   She is *very* intelligent.

- **Affirmative** means *yes*.

- **Apostrophe** ' We use the apostrophe for possession and contractions.
    My *sister's* friend is beautiful.   Today *isn't* Sunday.

- **Article** The definite article is *the*. The indefinite articles are *a* and *an*.
    I have *a* cat.   I ate *an* apple.   *The* president was in New York last weekend.

- **Base Form** The base form, sometimes called the "simple" form, of the verb has no tense. It has no ending (-s or -ed): *be, go, eat, take, write*.
    I didn't *go* out.   He doesn't *know* the answer.
    You shouldn't *talk* loudly in the library.

- **Capital Letter** A B C D E F G . . .

- **Comma** ,

- **Comparative Form** A comparative form of an adjective or adverb is used to compare two things.
    My house is *bigger* than your house.
    Your car is *better* than my car.

- **Complement** The complement of the sentence is the information after the verb. It completes the verb phrase.
    He works *hard*.   I slept *for five hours*.   They are *late*.

- **Consonant** The following letters are consonants: *b, c, d, f, g, h, j, k, l, m, n, p, q, r, s, t, v, w, x, y, z*.
    NOTE: *y* is sometimes considered a vowel, as in the world *syllable*.

- **Contraction** A contraction is made up of two words put together with an apostrophe.
    He's my brother.   *You're* late.   They *won't* talk to me.
    (*He's = he is*)   (*You're = you are*)   (*won't = will not*)

- **Count Noun** Count nouns are nouns that we can count. They have a singular and a plural form.

    1 pen — 3 pens   1 table — 4 tables

- **Frequency Words** Frequency words are *always, usually, often, sometimes, rarely, seldom, never.*

    I *never* drink coffee.   We *always* do our homework.

- **Imperative** An imperative sentence gives a command or instructions. An imperative sentence omits the word *you*.

    Come here.   *Don't be* late.   Please *sit* down.

- **Infinitive** An infinitive is *to* + base form.

    I want *to leave.*   You need *to be* here on time.

- **Modal** The modal verbs are *can, could, shall, should, will, would, may, might, must.*

    They *should* leave.   I *must* go.

- **Negative** means no.

- **Nonaction Verb** A nonaction verb has no action. We do not use a continuous tense (*be* + verb *-ing*) with a nonaction verb. The nonaction verbs are: *believe, cost, care, have, hear, know, like, love, matter, mean, need, own, prefer, remember, see, seem, think, understand, want.*

    She *has* a computer.   We *love* our mother.

- **Noncount Noun** A noncount noun is a noun that we don't count. It has no plural form.

    She drank some *water.*   He ate some *rice.*

    I need *money.*

- **Noun** A noun is a person (*brother*), a place (*kitchen*), or a thing (*table*). Nouns can be either count (*1 table, 2 tables*) or noncount (*money, water*).

    My *brother* lives in California.   My *sisters* live in New York.

    I get *mail* from them.

- **Object** The object of the sentence follows the verb. It receives the action of the verb.

    He bought *a car.*   I saw *a movie.*   I met *your brother.*

- **Object Pronoun** Use object pronouns (*me, you, him, her, it, us, them*) after the verb or preposition.

    He likes *her.*   I saw the movie. Let's talk about *it.*

- **Parentheses ( )**

- **Participle, Present** The present participle is verb + *-ing*.

    She is *sleeping.*   They were *laughing.*

Appendix F / Glossary of Grammatical Terms

- **Period** .
- **Phrase** A group of words that go together.
    Last month my sister came to visit.
    There is a strange car *in front of my house*.
- **Plural** Plural means more than one. A plural noun usually ends with *-s*.
    She has beautiful *eyes*.
- **Possessive Form** Possessive forms show ownership or relationship.
    Mary's coat is in the closet.   *My* brother lives in Miami.
- **Preposition** A preposition is a connecting word: *about, above, across, after, around, as, at, away, before, behind, below, by, down, for, from, in, into, like, of, off, on, out, over, to, under, up, with.*
    The book is *on* the table.
- **Pronoun** A pronoun takes the place of a noun.
    I have a new car. I bought *it* last week.
    John likes Mary, but *she* doesn't like *him*.
- **Punctuation** Period . Comma , Colon : Semicolon ; Question Mark ? Exclamation Mark !
- **Question Mark** ?
- **Regular Verb** A regular verb forms its past tense with *-ed*.
    He *worked* yesterday.   We *listened* to the radio.
- ***s* Form** A present tense verb that ends in *-s* or *-es*.
    He *lives* in New York.   She *watches* TV a lot.
- **Sentence** A sentence is a group of words that contains a subject[1] and a verb (at least) and gives a complete thought.
    SENTENCE: She came home.
    NOT A SENTENCE: When she came home
- **Simple Form of Verb** The simple form of the verb, also called the "base" form, has no tense; it never has an *-s, -ed,* or *-ing* ending.
    Did you *see* the movie?   I can't *find* his phone number.
- **Singular** Singular means one.
    She ate a *sandwich*.   I have one *television*.
- **Subject** The subject of the sentence tells who or what the sentence is about.
    My sister bought a new car. *The car* is beautiful.

---

[1] In an imperative sentence, the subject *you* is omitted: *Sit down. Come here.*

Appendix **F** / Glossary of Grammatical Terms

- **Subject Pronouns** Use subject pronouns (*I, you, he, she, it, we, you, they*) before a verb.

    They speak Japanese.   *We* speak Spanish.

- **Superlative Form** A superlative form of an adjective shows the number one item in a group of three or more.

    January is the *coldest* month of the year.

    You have the *best* seat in the room.

- **Syllable** A syllable is a part of a word that has only one vowel sound. (Some words have only one syllable.)

    change (one syllable)   after (af·ter = 2 syllables)
    look (one syllable)   responsible (re·spon·si·ble = 4 syllables)

- **Tense** A verb has tense. Tense shows when the action of the sentence happened.

    SIMPLE PRESENT: She usually *works* hard.
    FUTURE: She *will work* tomorrow.
    PRESENT CONTINUOUS: She *is working* now.
    SIMPLE PAST: She *worked* yesterday.

- **Verb** A verb is the action of the sentence.

    He *runs* fast.   I *speak* English.

- **Vowel** The following letters are vowels: *a, e, i, o, u. Y* is sometimes considered a vowel (for example, in the word *syllable*).

APPENDIX G

The United States of America: Major Cities

AL	Alabama	HI	Hawaii	MA	Massachusetts	NM	New Mexico	SD	South Dakota
AK	Alaska	ID	Idaho	MI	Michigan	NY	New York	TN	Tennessee
AZ	Arizona	IL	Illinois	MN	Minnesota	NC	North Carolina	TX	Texas
AR	Arkansas	IN	Indiana	MS	Mississippi	ND	North Dakota	UT	Utah
CA	California	IA	Iowa	MO	Missouri	OH	Ohio	VT	Vermont
CO	Colorado	KS	Kansas	MT	Montana	OK	Oklahoma	VA	Virginia
CT	Connecticut	KY	Kentucky	NE	Nebraska	OR	Oregon	WA	Washington
DE	Delaware	LA	Louisiana	NV	Nevada	PA	Pennsylvania	WV	West Virginia
FL	Florida	ME	Maine	NH	New Hampshire	RI	Rhode Island	WI	Wisconsin
GA	Georgia	MD	Maryland	NJ	New Jersey	SC	South Carolina	WY	Wyoming
								DC*	District of Columbia

*The District of Columbia is not a state. Washington, D.C. is the capital of the United States.
Note: Washinton, D.C., and Washington state are not the same.

Index

A
A little, 124
   count *vs.* noncount nouns with, 130
A lot (of), 124, 149–151
   count *vs.* noncount nouns with, 129
A/an, 38–40, 149–151, AP9
About, 153
Account, 35
Activity(ies), 59
Ad, 241
Adjectives, 18–19, AP9
   comparative forms of, 213
      spelling, 213–217, AP6
   possessive, 27
   superlative forms of, 223
Adverb, AP9
Affirmative imperatives, 46–47
Affirmative statements
   with *be*, 37
      negatives statements compared with, 16
   with *be going to*, 188–189
   in present continuous tense, 166–167
   in simple past tense, 242–243
   in simple present tense, 37, 60–61
Ahead of, 175
Air bag(s), 101
Airline, 269
Always, 29
Amount, 113
An. See A/an
Answers
   short, *be* in, 30–32. *See also Yes/no* questions
   to *who* questions, 85
Any, 149–151
   with count nouns, 128–129
   with noncount nouns, 125, 128–129

Apostrophe ('), AP9
   use with *be* contractions, 10–12
Application, 45
Apply for, 233
Appointment, 29
Article, AP9. *See also A/an; The*
As, 233
Aspirin, 137
At least, 91
Athletic club, 249
ATM, 35
Automated postal center, 165
Automatic checkout, 15
Available, 51
Average, 67

B
Bachelor's degree, 211
Balanced, 113
Bank, 3
Be
   affirmative statements with, 37
   in simple past tense, 234–235
   in simple present tense, 260
   contractions with, 10–11
   with descriptions, 18
   forms of, 5–7
   information questions with, 36–37, 237–238
   it expressions with, 19–20
   negative statements with
      and affirmative statements compared, 16
      long and short forms, 16–17
      in simple past tense, 234–235
      in simple present tense, 260
   with present continuous tense, 170–171
   simple past tense of, 234–235
      time expressions, 235–236
   with simple present tense, 260

   with *this/that/these/those*, 12–13
   in *yes/no* questions, 30–32, 236–237
Be going to
   affirmative statements with, 188–189
   future tense with, 190–191, 261, 270
   with *how long* questions, 202–203
   information questions with, 200–202
   negative statements with, 189–190
   yes/no questions with, 198–200
Behind schedule, 29
Best, 59
Better buy, 153
Birth certificate, 45
Birthday, 45
Blanket(s), 9
Block, 241
Both, 3
Bother, 51
Bring, 269
Broken, 25
Brought, 269
Bunch of, 119

C
Calculator, 153
Calendar, names and abbreviated forms on, AP1
Campus, 211
Can, 92–93, 264–265
   information questions with, 105–107
   with question word as subject, 107–108
   yes/no questions with, 102–104, 271
Cannot/can't, 92–93

Index   **I1**

Capital letters, AP9
   rules for using, AP8
Cardinal numbers, AP2
Career, 249
Cash, 35
Cashier(s), 15
Casual clothes, 165
Certificate, 211
Chance, 211
Charity, 187
Check in, 233
Choice(s), 153
Cities, major U.S., AP13
Citizen, 3
Clean, 9
Clerk, 145
Clock, 25
Clothes, 9
Code, 15
Coin(s), 9
Collect, 269
Common expressions, prepositions in, 141–143
Comparatives, 213, AP9
   with nouns and verbs, 217–219
   spelling of, 213–217, AP6
Complain, 67
Complement, AP9
Condition, 221
Confused, 3
Consider, 221
Consonant, AP9
Contain, 119
Contractions, AP9
   with *be*, 10–11, 166, 170–171, 188–189
      and information question words, 36
   with *do not*, 47–49
   with *it*, 19–20
   with *let*, 52
Convenience store, 137
Convenient, 75
Corner, 137
Count nouns, 120–121, AP10
   any with, 128–129
   a few with, 130
   how much/how many with, 130–132
   a little with, 130
   a lot of with, 129
   many with, 129
   some with, 128–129
Count on, 259
Counter, 165
Coupon, 127
Co-worker, 221

Create a password, 51
Crib, 187
Crowded, 15
Customer(s), 165

D
Dash(es), 51
Date of birth, 45
Dates, methods of expressing, AP1
Day names, abbreviated form of, AP1
Day off, 67
Decision, 221
Definite article. *See The*
Deli, 75
Deliver, 75
Depends on, 221
Descriptions, *be* with, 18
Desk job, 81
Difference between, 153
Different, 3
Dirty, 9
Do errand(s), 165
Do not/don't, in negative imperatives, 47–49
Do/does
   in information questions, 105–107
   in questions, when not to use, 85
   in *yes/no* questions, 102–104
Don't have to, 117–118
Don't worry, 9
Downstairs, 145
Drive-through, 175
Dryer(s), 9
During, 81

E
Each other, 59
Early, 15
Economical, 221
-ed, in past tense, 242–243. *See also* Simple past tense
   pronunciation of, 242
   spelling of, 243–244, AP5
Educated, 211
Elevator, 145
Employee, 233
Employer, 233
Empty, 9
Enjoy, 59
Enough, 145, 149–151
Enter, 51
Entrance, 175
-er adjective ending, 213–217
-est adjective ending, 224–226

Everything, 3
Excited, 187
Exercise
   as noun, 81
   as verb, 81
Expensive, 51
Expressions
   common, prepositions in, 141–143
   with *it/it's*, 19–20
   of quantity, with noncount nouns, 122–124
   of time. *See* Time expressions
Extras, 221

F
Fast, 25
Fat, 113
Favorite, 119
Fee, 197
F/fe noun ending, 20
Fill out, 45
Financial aid, 51
Fitness instructor, 249
Flight, 269
Fly, 269
For a while, 187
Forget, 45
Free, 15
Frequency words, AP10
   with negative meaning, 63, 68
   position of, 63–65
   with simple present tense, 63–65
From now on, 259
Fuel economy, 221
Furniture, 187
Future tense, AP12
   with *be going to*, 190–191, 261, 270
   information questions in, 273
   time expressions in, 191–195

G
Glossary, AP9–12
Grain(s), 113
Grammatical terms, definitions of, AP9–12
Grill, 59
Guideline(s), 113
Gym, 81

H
Has to. See Have to/has to
Have fun, 59
Have to, 264–265
   yes/no questions with, 271

Have to/has to, 94–99
   information questions with, 105
   pronunciation of, 94
   with question word as subject, 107–108
   uses of, 94
   vs. must, 116–117
   in *yes/no* questions, 102–104
Headache, 137
Health club, 249
Healthy, 81
Helpful, 3
Hire, 197
Holiday, 25
Home supply store, 145
How long questions, 202–203
How much/how many questions
   in future tense, 200–202
   how many as subject, 85–86
How much/many questions, 82–84, 156
   count *vs.* noncount nouns with, 130–132
   with modal verbs, 105
   in present continuous tense, 178–179
How often questions, 82–84. See also Questions
How questions. See also Information questions
   with *be*, 237–238
   in simple present tense, 82–84
   word order in, 36
Hurt, 101

I

Identity document, 45
-ies noun ending, 20
Immigrant, 3
Imperatives, AP10
   affirmative, 46–47
   negative, 47–49
   use of, 46
In a hurry, 91
Income, 113
Indefinite article. See *A/an*
Infant, 101
Infinitives, 263, AP10
   with simple present verbs, 71–73
Information, 127
Information questions, 36–37
   with *be*, 237–238
   with *be going to*, 200–202
   be in, 36–37
   in future tense, 200–202, 273
   intonation of, 37
   with modal verbs, 105–107, 274
   in present continuous tense, 178–179, 273
   review of, 272–278
   in simple past tense, 274
   in simple present tense, 82–84, 272
   statements compared with, 37
   with *there is/there are*, 156–159
   word order in, 36
   and *yes/no* questions compared, 156
-ing, as verb ending, AP10
   spelling of, 167–168, AP4
Instead, 241
Interview
   as noun, 233
   as verb, 233
Intonation
   of information questions, 37
   of *yes/no* questions, 30
Invite/invitation, 59
Irregular plural nouns, 33
Irregular verbs. See also *Be*
   past forms of, 244–245, 253–254, 271, AP6–7
   negative, 245–247
   yes/no questions with, 250–251
   -s forms, AP3
   in simple present tense, 60–61
Is there/are there. See *There is/there are*
It takes time, 91
Item(s), 9
It/it's, expressions with, 19–20

K

Keep, 67
Kids, 25

L

Lamp, 145
Laundromat, 3
Law(s), 91
Less than, 113
Let, 45
Let's, 52
Life, 3
Lightbulb, 145
Look up, 51
Lunch box, 119

M

Make mistakes, 241
Many, 149–151
   count *vs.* noncount nouns with, 129

Map of United States, AP13
Meal(s), 113
Mean, 67
Mechanic, 221
Microphone, 175
Middle initial, 51
Mileage, 221
Modal verbs, AP10
   can, 92–93, 102–104, 105–107, 107–108, 264–265
   have to/has to, 94–99, 102–104, 105–107, 107–108, 264–265
   information questions with, 105–207, 274
   must, 264–265
   question words with, 107–108
   should, 93–94, 102–104, 105–107, 107–108, 264–265
   yes/no questions with, 102–104, 271
Month names, abbreviated form of, AP1
Move, 197
Mover, 197
Much, 124
   count *vs.* noncount nouns with, 129
Mushroom(s), 75
Must, 114–115, 264–265
   vs. have to, 116–117
Must not, 114–115
   vs. don't have to, 117–118

N

Negative imperatives, 46–49
Negative statements
   with *be*
      and affirmative statements compared, 16
      long and short forms, 16–17
   in simple past tense, 234–235
   in simple present tense, 260
   with *be going to*, 189–190
   in simple present tense, 68–69
Neighborhood, 197
Never, 29
Newcomer, 259
Next door, 81
No, 149–151
Nonaction verbs, AP10
Noncount nouns, 120–121, AP10
   any with, 125, 128–129
   a few with, 130
   how much/how many with, 130–132
   a little with, 124–125, 130
   a lot of with, 124–125, 129
   much with, 124–125, 129

quantity expressions with, 122–124
some with, 125, 128–129
Note, 127
Nouns, AP10
adjectives describing, 18–19
comparatives with, 217–219
count. *See* Count nouns
noncount. *See* Noncount nouns
plural. *See* Plural nouns
possessive, 26
singular. *See* Singular nouns
superlatives with, 226–228
Numbers, cardinal and ordinal word forms, AP2
Nutrition, 113

O

Object, AP10
pronouns as, 53–54, AP10
Of course, 35
On (my, your) mind, 29
On sale, 15
On the way, 101
On time, 25
Online, 51
Operation, 269
Opportunity, 259
Order, 75
Ordinal numbers, AP2
Out of, 137
Outdoor concert(s), 59
Outlet mall, 101
Overtime, 67

P

Pack, 197
Package(s), 15
Paragraph, AP10
Park, 81
Participle, present. *See -ing*, as verb ending
Pass a test, 91
Passenger, 101
Past forms, of irregular verbs, AP6–7
Past tense, simple. *See* Simple past tense
Patient, 249
Permit, 91
Pharmacy, 137
Phrase, AP11
Physical therapist (PT), 249
Pick up, 165
PIN, 35
Place, prepositions of, 140–141
Plural nouns, 12, 20, AP11

articles with, 20
and *be* contractions, when not to use, 10
irregular, 33
spelling rules, AP3
pronunciation of, 20, 33
Polite, 29
Position, 233
Positive, 241
Possessive adjectives, 27, AP11
Possessive nouns, 26, AP11
Postage, 165
Postal clerk(s), 165
Pound(s), 15
Prefer, 145
Prepared food, 75
Prepositions, AP11
object pronouns with, 53
of place, 140–141
of time, 138–139
time expressions without, 139–140
Present continuous tense, AP12
affirmative statements in, 166–167, 260
information questions in, 178–179, 273
-ing form in. *See -ing*, as verb ending
negative forms in, 170–171, 260
time expressions in, 171–173
uses of, 168–169
yes/no questions in, 176–177, 270
Present participle. *See -ing*, as verb ending
Present tense, progressive. *See* Present continuous tense
Price, 15
Print, 45
Probably, 175
Product(s), 15
Project, 269
Pronouns, AP11
as object, 53–54, AP10
as subject, 4–5, 27, 53–54, AP11–12
Pronunciation
of *can/can't*, 92
of *-ed* past form, 242
of *have to/has to*, 94
of information questions, 37
of plural nouns, 20, 33
of *-s* form, 20, 33
of *yes/no* questions, 30
Provide, 211
PT (physical therapist), 249
Pump

as noun, 101
as verb, 101
Punctuation, AP11. *See also* Apostrophe ('); Question mark (?)

Q

Quantity expressions, with noncount nouns, 122–124
Quantity words, 149–151
Question mark (?), use of, 30
Question words
with *be*, 237–238
with *be going to*, 204–206
meaning of, 36
as subject, 85–86
with modal verbs, 107–108
as subjects, 180–182, 238–239, 253–254
Questions
with *how*. *See* Information questions
for information, 36–37
short answers to. *See* Short answers
with *wh-*. *See* Information questions
with *what*, 36
yes/no. *See* Yes/no questions

R

Really, 259
Reference, 233
Regular verbs, AP11
simple past tense of
affirmative form, 242–243
negative form, 245–247
yes/no questions with, 250–251, 271
Relative, 187
Relax, 67
Rent, 197
Repair, 221
Resale shop, 187
Résumé, 241
Ride a bicycle, 81
Right, 9
Roll, 175

S

-s noun ending, 12
pronunciation of, 20
spelling rules, 20, 61–62, AP3
-s verb ending, 60–61, AP11
irregular forms, 60
spelling rules, AP3

Salary, 67
Sample(s), 15
Scale, 165
School supplies, 127
Seasons, AP1
Seatbelt, 101
Secret, 35
Security guard, 35
Sentence, AP11
Serious, 29
Serve, 113
Service, 145
Shampoo, 153
Sheet(s), 9
Shelf/shelves, 15
Short answers, *be* in, 30–32. See also *Yes/no* questions
Short forms, of words. See Contractions
Should, 93–94, 264–265
   information questions with, 105–107
   with question word as subject, 107–108
   yes/no questions with, 102, 271
Should not/shouldn't, 93–94
Sign, 45
Simple past tense, AP12
   with affirmative statements, 242–243, 261
   -ed form, spelling of, 243–244, AP5
   in information questions, 252, 274
   with irregular verbs, 244–245, 253–254, 271, AP6–7
   with negative statements, 245–247, 261
   with regular verbs, 242–243, 271
   in subject questions, 253
   in *yes/no* questions, 250–251, 271
Simple present tense, AP12
   with affirmative statements, 37, 60–61, 260
   expressions of time in, 70
   with frequency words, 63–65
   infinitives with, 71–73
   in information questions, 82–84, 272
   with negative statements, 260
   negative statements in, 68–69
   uses of, 62
   yes/no questions in, 76–79, 270
Singular nouns, 12, 20, AP11
   a/an with, 38–40
   articles with, 20

Sneaker(s), 81
Some
   with count nouns, 128–129
   with noncount nouns, 125, 128–129
Spelling
   of comparatives, 213–217, AP6
   -ed form of simple past tense, AP5
   of *-ing* form of verbs, 167–168, AP4
   of *-s* noun endings, 20, AP3
   of *-s* verb endings, 61–62, AP3
   of superlatives, 224–226, AP6
Spend time, 59
Statements, with *be*. See also Affirmative statements; Negative statements
   information questions compared with, 37
   yes/no questions compared with, 30
Stroller, 187
Subject, AP11
   pronouns as, 4–5, 27, 53–54, AP11–12. See also Pronouns
   question words as, 85–86, 180–182, 238–239
   with modal verbs, 107–108
Superlatives, 223, AP12
   with nouns and verbs, 226–228
   spelling of, 224–226
Supermarket, 3
Sure, 15
Surprised, 233
Syllable, AP12

T

Take-out, 75
Team, 59
Tell the truth, 113
Teller, 175
Temperature, 29
Temporary, 249
Tenses, AP12
   affirmative and negative form, review of, 260–262
   future. See Future tense
   present continuous. See Present continuous tense
   simple past. See Simple past tense
   simple present. See Simple present tense
Terrible, 119
Than, with comparatives, 213

That, 12–13
The, AP9
   with superlatives, 223
The same, 15
Then, 91
There is/there are, 146–147
   with *be*, 260–261
   information questions with, 156–159
   negative forms of, 148, 260
   yes/no questions with, 154–155
These, 12–13
This/that/these/those, 12–13
Those, 12–13
Through, 35
Throw away, 119
Time, prepositions of, 138–139
Time expressions
   with *be going to*, 191–195
   in the past, 235–236
   in present continuous tense, 171–173
   review of, 266–267
   in simple present tense, 70
   without prepositions, 139–140
Together, 9
Towel(s), 9
Traffic, 29
Training, 91, 249
Trip, 101
Truck, 197
Tube, 175
Tuition, 211
Turn, 25, 175
24/7, 137

U

Uniform, 127
United States, map of, AP13
Used, 187
Usually, 29

V

Vegetarian, 75
Verbs, AP12
   base form of, AP9
   comparatives with, 217–219
   -ing form of, AP10
      spelling of, 167–168, AP4
   irregular
      past forms of, AP6–7
      simple present tense of, 60
   modal. See Modal verbs
   nonaction, AP10
   question words with, 85–86
   -s ending. See *-s* verb ending
   simple form of, AP11

superlatives with, 226–228
tense of. *See* Tenses
-ves plural noun ending, 20
Village, 269
Vision test, 91
Vocabulary in context. *See also individual vocabulary words and phrases*
  American lifestyles, 59, 67, 75, 81
  choices, 211, 221
  driving, 91, 101
  errands, 165, 175
  filling out forms, 45, 51
  getting a job, 233, 241, 249
  giving back, 259, 269
  making changes, 187, 197
  school, 113, 119, 127
  shopping, 130, 145, 153
  time and money, 25, 29, 35
  welcome to the U.S., 3, 9, 15
Volunteer
  as noun, 259
  as verb, 259
Vowel, AP12

W
Wage, 67
Washing machine(s), 9
Watch, 25
Weigh, 165
What about, 51
What about, 51
What questions, 156. *See also* Information questions
  contraction with, 36
  in future tense, 200–202
  what as subject, 85–86
Wheelchair, 269
When questions. *See also* Information questions
  contraction with, 36
Which, as subject, 85–86
Who questions. *See also* Information questions
  answers to, 85
  contraction with, 36
  who as subject, 85–86
Why questions, 156. *See also* Information questions
  contraction with, 36
Wife, 25

Without, 91
Word lists. *See* Vocabulary in context
Word order
  with frequency words, 63–65
  in information questions, 36
Words, numbers as, AP2
Written test, 91

Y
Yes/no questions
  with *be going to*, 198–200
  be in, 30–32, 236–237
  and information questions compared, 156
  intonation of, 30
  with modal verbs, 102–104, 271
  in present continuous tense, 176–177, 270
  in simple past tense, 250–251, 271
  in simple present tense, 76–79, 270
  with *there is/there are*, 154–155